CLAUDE SIMON AND THE TRANSGRESSIONS OF MODERN ART

Claude Simon and the Transgressions of Modern Art

Michael Evans

MACMILLAN
PRESS

© Michael J. Evans 1988
Softcover reprint of the hardcover 1st edition 1988
All rights reserved. No reproduction, copy or transmission
of this publication may be made without written permission.

No paragraph of this publication may be reproduced, copied
or transmitted save with written permission or in accordance
with the provisions of the Copyright Act 1956 (as amended),
or under the terms of any licence permitting limited copying
issued by the Copyright Licensing Agency, 33 – 4 Alfred Place,
London WC1E 7DP.

Any person who does any unauthorised act in relation to
this publication may be liable to criminal prosecution and
civil claims for damages.

First published 1988

Published by
THE MACMILLAN PRESS LTD
Houndmills, Basingstoke, Hampshire RG21 2XS
and London
Companies and representatives
throughout the world

British Library Cataloguing in Publication Data
Evans, Michael, 1951–
Claude Simon and the transgressions of
modern art.
1. Simon, Claude
I. Title
843'.914   PQ2637.I547Z/
ISBN 978-1-349-19473-5   ISBN 978-1-349-19471-1 (eBook)
DOI 10.1007/978-1-349-19471-1

For Margery, Helen and Laura

Contents

Acknowledgements	x
Introduction	xi

Part One: Frame

1.	What is Frame?	3
2.	The Framework of *La Route des Flandres*	22
	I Narrative frame	22
	II In search of frame	29
	III Intertextual paradigm: Metaphors of the poetic impulse in Apuleius, Nerval, Proust and Simon	37
3.	The Framework of *Le Palace*, *Histoire* and *Les Géorgiques*	47
	I Variations of narrative frame	47
	II Interchangeability	52
	III *Les Géorgiques* and biographical frame	58

Part Two: Intertextuality

1.	What is Intertextuality?	67
	I Global definition	67
	II Intrusion (in praesentia): Borges's *El Inmortal*	74
	III Allusion (in absentia): Proust's *A la recherche du temps perdu*	79

2. *La Bataille de Pharsale* and its Fragments   89
   I   Patterns of textual relation   89
   II Intertextual triptych: reading across *La Bataille de Pharsale*, *La Jalousie* and *A la recherche du temps perdu*   101
   III Intertextual embedding   112

Part Three: Materiality

1. The Materiality of Fiction   121
2. Currents of Description in *Les Corps conducteurs*   134
   I   Fragmentation and articulation   134
   II Jean Ricardou's 'Le Dispositif osiriaque'   148
   III Descriptive fusion and confusion   154

Part Four: Self-Reflexivity

1. The Language of Mirrors   177
   I   Categories of 'mise en abyme'   177
   II That obscure reflection of an image in Sábato's *El Túnel*   185

2. *Triptyque*: Topography or Topology?   191
   I   Generative description   191
   II Metatextual 'mises en abyme'   198
   III Fictional 'mises en abyme'   202
   IV Frame shifts   207

3. Frame Conflict in *Leçon de choses*   217
   I   Interior and exterior   217
   II Intertextual motivation: Impressionist painting and *Madame Bovary*   224
   III Intersequential conflict   234
   IV Fromentin and the view from the light-house   240

Conclusion	247
Notes and References	250
Bibliography	314
Index	323

Acknowledgements

I am indebted to the Editions de Minuit for permission to quote from Claude Simon's novels. Three sub-sections in this book first appeared as articles. 'Intertextual motivation in *Leçon de choses*' first appeared in *Nottingham French Studies* (vol. 19, no. 1, May 1980); 'Intertextual Triptych in *La Bataille de Pharsale*' first appeared in *Modern Language Review* (vol. 76, no. 4, October 1981); and 'Intrusion: Borges's *El Inmortal*' first appeared in *Forum for Modern Language Studies* (vol. xx, no. 3, July 1984). I am grateful to the editors for permission to reprint.

All the translations of quotations which can be found at the end of the book are my own and are unauthorised. The authorised English translations of Simon's novels are available from John Calder (Publishers) Ltd, London, and Riverrun Press Inc., New York.

I am particularly grateful to Malcolm Bowie for his generous help and advice. Thanks must also go to Roger Huss and friends at Warwick University with whom I have had many stimulating discussions over the years. I am indebted to my editor, Frances Arnold, for agreeing to publish this book and to Margaret Leach for her meticulous correction of a rough-hewn typescript. The unfailing support and encouragement of my parents and brother have been invaluable. This book is theirs as well as mine. Finally, my wife, Margery, has been a companion and inspiration throughout.

Introduction

> la transgression
> n'est pas la négation de l'interdit,
> mais elle le dépasse et le complète
>
> Georges Bataille, L'érotisme[1]

A forbidding trail of questions lies in the wake of the storm that has swept the world of fiction since the start of the century. So many of the traditional precepts and assumptions concerning literature, such as the distinctions between prose and poetry, between description and narration, between writing and reading, have been exposed or 'deconstructed' that the modern reader has often felt bewildered and alienated by texts which are not conceived according to the familiar and unambiguous codes of literary convention. It might seem strange that this feeling of alienation should have arisen at a time when the reader has been at the centre of unprecedented attention. For increasingly he has found that he no longer occupies a discrete vantage-point on the side-lines of literature; no longer is he an unobserved eavesdropper on a world which lies on the other side of his own reality. It is as if the curtain has been torn down and the inner light of fiction has flooded over the inquisitive observer peering in. Yet it would be wrong to suggest that there has been a sudden shift of the spotlight on to the reader and away from all other areas of focus: rather the spotlight has, as it were, expanded to absorb the reader within the bounds of the world of fiction. Authors, critics and the novel genre as a whole seem to be increasingly preoccupied with the reader. Even when the latter is not being openly addressed or abused, as in John Barth's *Lost in the Fun-house*, he is very often a subject of interest in the book he reads. Admittedly, overt references to the reader are so common a feature of contemporary fiction that they have become a convention in their own right, and the reader has learnt to dissociate himself from them by treating them as innocuous literary clichés. But in order to appreciate fully the wider significance of this outward gaze of fiction which goes beyond mere playful winks and ironical glances, and in order to respond in a more positive fashion than one might at first be tempted, it is necessary to relate this focus on the reader to some of the central issues of modern art.

If the aim of poetics, as Tzvetan Todorov has declared[2], is to define an abstract structure, 'literarity', common to all literature, a poetics of modern fiction is correspondingly aimed at outlining the abstract notion of 'modernity'. In one of his earliest works, Todorov saw no contradiction between the broad scope of his aims and the fact that his analysis was entirely restricted to one novel; namely, Laclos's *Les Liaisons dangereuses*: 'La poétique ne peut se passer de la littérature pour discuter de son propre discours; et en même temps ce n'est que dans un dépassement de l'oeuvre concrète qu'elle y parvient'.[3]

For the modern critic, theory and analysis are no longer divergent areas of study but mutually dependent activities. The literary abstractions sought by poetics emerge from a close textual analysis of a specific, 'concrete' work. In this way, the tendency, which has often proved irresistible to literary theoreticians, to compress and distort empirically heterogenous works into vacuous categories by means of sweeping generalisations is counterbalanced by a respect for the individuality of a specific work which only textual analysis can display. Conversely, the suggestion of immanence and 'originality' in a notion like 'individuality', which has traditionally been invoked by literary critics in support of the idea that a text is the fruit of a private process of creation stemming from the author's personal experiences and obsessions (a viewpoint which sees language and intertextuality as mere decorative vehicles for the expression of an individual consciousness, rather than as creative factors themselves), is obviated by the fact that poetics aspires, in the final analysis, to re-define its own premises, to derive its theoretical concepts from its textual readings.

In any discussion of modern art, the critical need to connect the two spheres of theory and analysis is undoubtedly aided by the fact that the works themselves are engaged in questioning the aesthetic basis of creativity. This is particularly true of the 'nouveau roman'. Labels such as 'modern' and 'nouveau' are attractive largely because they draw attention to the logical inevitability of artistic incompletion, transience and evolution. Modern works have traditionally been open-ended and polysemic; they are explorations in uncertainty and complexity, not fossilised affirmations of incontrovertible and universal truths. In the context of modern fiction, it is the writer's attitude to language and composition which has served as a catalyst in the transformation of the genre. Relegated in conventional novels to the subordinate role of faithfully conveying the illusion of reality to the point of self-effacement, language and form have themselves become sources of invention and transformation. The ambiguities and discontinuities characteristic of modern prose fiction derive from an emancipation of the vehicle of writing; what has conventionally been viewed as a means of expression has become a source of textual generation. The 'signifiant' of language, the 'sense datum' of meaning, is no longer exclusively an anonymous communicator of messages but a stimulus for plurality. The more plural a text is, as Roland Barthes has said, the more opportunity there is for the reader's active contribution: 'Plus le texte est pluriel et moins il est écrit avant que je le lise'.[4] Apart from providing the reader with more freedom to construct different texts out of the same work, the modern novelist's general interest in the silent interlocutor is a direct result of his new attitude to language. The rejection of the expressive view of language in fiction, in which the reader is little more than a passive receiver of information, in favour of a more plural system of textual associations inevitably entailed granting the reader a more crucial and participatory role.

Of the reader, André Gide has said: 'L'histoire requiert sa collaboration pour se bien dessiner'.[5] Other writers, like Jorge–Luis Borges, have echoed this statement, laying emphasis on a more widespread textual collaboration: 'I feel that every literary work is a collaboration between author and reader; I feel that the piece is fulfilled only at the moment it is read'.[6] For Alain Robbe-Grillet, the reader's new role is elicited by the ambiguity of the modern fictional world: the movement of description dispelling all confidence in the objects described; the blurred identity of the characters; and 'ce présent qui s'invente sans cesse comme au fil de l'écriture, qui se répète, se dédouble, se modifie, se dément, sans jamais s'entasser pour constituer un passé – donc une 'histoire' au sens traditionnel – tout cela ne peut que convier le lecteur (ou le spectateur) à un autre mode de participation que celui dont il avait l'habitude'.[7] Claude Simon has described the relationship between author and reader in phenomenological terms. The act of writing consists in throwing reality into question; the reader's complementary role is to build up associations and draw inferences from that action: 'L'écrivain *dit* le monde et les choses (ou plutôt *un* monde et *des* choses): il ne les explique pas. L'aboutissement de son travail est essentiellement une mise en question. Au lecteur d'effectuer cet autre travail qu'est la lecture. Il est partie prenante dans l'affaire (que serait un livre sans aucun lecteur?) Il n'existe pas d'objet sans sujet'.[8]

Whilst, on the one hand, the reader is allowed to participate more actively in the creative process, the writer, on the other hand, has assumed a more interpretative and self-analytical role. 'Premier lecteur', says Michel Butor, 'l'écrivain commence à propos de son propre travail ce qu'il se sait faire pour celui d'autrui. Son activité va se réfléchir comme dans un miroir'.[9] Running parallel with this view of the writer as reader of his own work is the fact that the author no longer proclaims himself as a fount of wisdom and enlightenment but as a baffled and avid consciousness groping for patterns and meanings in the 'foisonnement désordonné' of experience.[10] The narrators in the novels of Proust, Faulkner and Claude Simon are amongst the most powerful examples of this dramatisation of the affinity between author and reader. In *Le Vent*, the narrator drowns in his efforts to arrest the confusion surrounding Montes's life, just as the reader is swamped by the deluge of the narrator's unharnessed discourse:

> Et puis j'y fus de nouveau, entraîné malgré moi, comme par le noyé [. . .], tiré moi aussi à sa suite, placé dans la perspective de ce temps qui s'allongeait comme un mur gris sans commencement ni fin, décrépi, avec ses vieilles affiches déchirées aux pans soulevés par le vent, leurs caractères délavés, leurs fragments de textes sans commencement ni fin non plus, sans suite, se juxtaposant, se contredisant [.][11]

The convergence between writer and reader, therefore, results from an erosion in both cases of a stable identity whose functions and expectations do not precede the text as object but are defined by the text as event. Indeed, the lines quoted from *Le Vent* provide a vivid complement to Borges's definition of the 'ideal reader' as 'one who would not look for too many intentions in what I have written but would abandon himself to the reading as I have abandoned myself to the writing'.¹² Both writer and reader must abandon themselves to the polysemic digressions of the text, must enter into 'le jeu du signifiant' in order to induce 'le pluriel du texte'.¹³ This abandonment is motivated, in short, by one of the most persistent impulses underlying modern writing: namely, the desire for transgression. The distance which has traditionally separated writer and reader, as opposite poles of an axis of communication, is foreshortened; and the transgression lies in the intertwining of the two functions of reading and writing.

The conventional novel has been dominated by a mimetic perspective in which fiction represents reality, illusion contains truth, and interior mirrors exterior. The structure of discourse accompanying this binary and predicative system of composition has correspondingly been in the form of a speaker addressing a listener. But the modern conception of fictional writing has reacted against this representational aesthetic by seeking to interweave the two sides of the referential equation. Although different authors have focused on different levels of structural transgression, one of the most common and fundamental has been the modern writer's emphasis on the overlapping functions of invention and reflection.

Defending himself against the accusation that his novels are tailored to fit the theoretical writings of Jean Ricardou, Simon has referred to his fictional work as the mainspring of some new critical concepts which have since secured an important place in modern critical discourse:

> C'est par exemple après *La Bataille de Pharsale* qu'il a élaboré sa théorie des générateurs. Pour ma part (et je l'ai dit aussi à Cerisy), je reprends tout à fait à mon compte le schéma par lequel il montre le chevauchement constant, l'engendrement constant et réciproque de la théorie par la pratique et de la pratique par la théorie, avec cette seule différence que je remplacerai ce dernier mot par *réflexion*.¹⁴

The critical framework of the present work, therefore, consists of a dovetailed pattern of considerations. The need to allow for the reciprocal counteraction between theory and analysis in my discussion of Simon's work was reinforced by the author's own recognition of the interdependence between 'practice' and 'reflection' which in turn is symptomatic of the general transgressive tendencies governing modern art as a whole. The main objective of my study is to demonstrate that in addition to the concept of 'générateur' Simon's novels engender and transform four more concepts which are equally vital in a definition of modernity in fiction. Although the four concepts ('frame', 'intertextuality', 'materiality' and 'self-reflexivity') are analysed in separate sections and are applied to different novels in each case, it will be evident that they are closely interrelated. Constantly throwing each other into relief, they offer a mobile critical perspective which modifies according to the particular focus one selects, thereby preserving a little of the fluidity and elusiveness which prevails when one reads a modern text.

Although I have concentrated almost exclusively on Claude Simon's later novels, from *La Route des Flandres* to *Les Géorgiques*, my aim is not to give an exhaustive account of the thematic concerns and formal properties of his 'oeuvre'. Indeed it is hard to see how such an approach could fulfil the objective I have already described of defining the double-edged relationship between the processes of reading and writing, reflection and practice, theory and analysis. There are only fleeting references to the author's earlier novels; and those works which I have dealt with invite further exploration involving different critical approaches. I have not sought to be the bearer of the 'last word' on Claude Simon; my analyses are primarily an expression of intense pleasure and excitement in reading the work of, undoubtedly, one of the leading novelists of the twentieth century.

Part One
Frame

1
What is Frame?

And having been created in this way, the world has been framed in the likeness of that which is apprehended by reason and mind and is unchangeable, and must therefore of necessity, if this is admitted, be a copy of something.

Plato, *Timaeus*

voix derrière la voix, intervalles vides martelant la voix, voix ressemblant des voix dans les accents de leurs traces, table rase et cylindre, roue et infini du volume remis à plat, sortie du cadre, de tous les cadres-séquences, fantasmes cadres, frontalement encadrés pour l'écran d'on ne sait quel cinéma.

Sollers, *Paradis*[1]

The concept of 'frame' as used in art and literary criticism has its roots in the writings of Russian Formalists like Iouri Lotman and Boris Uspensky. Following in the footsteps of these critics, and acknowledging his debt to them, Erving Goffman has applied the concept to analysis of social behaviour.[2] Frame, therefore, is not a concept which is restricted to literature or even to art in general but is an abstract notion which refers to the complex system of operations dictating the relationship between the subject and all forms of 'organization' (to use Goffman's term) or 'composition' (to use Uspensky's). The value of this concept lies in the fact that it embraces both the internal structure of a given work and its reception. It not only presupposes that analysis of the different readings of a text or painting involves analysis of the work's internal composition, but also that a study of the latter remains totally inadequate if it fails to include an account of the different means of approach available to the reader. Goffman's use of the concept with regard to certain categories of events in social life similarly implies a two-way process of analysis:

> definitions are built up in accordance with principles of organization which govern events – at least social ones – and our subjective involvement in them; frame is the word I use to refer to such of these basic elements as I am able to identify.[3]

Whilst the etymology of the French word 'cadre' relates to the static geometrical depiction of the Latin word 'quadrus', meaning 'square', the English 'frame' derives from the more dynamic indication of 'furtherance' and 'advancement' expressed by the Old Norse 'frame' and Old English 'fram'. In the context of this etymological background it is possible to discern two interrelated functions of frame. Lotman defines the frame of a painting as the border-line separating the content of a painting ('texte') from everything surrounding it ('non-texte'),[4] and adds that the spectator is never conscious of the one while contemplating the other. Thus at the same time as creating a sense of interior and exterior, frame denies the spectator a simultaneous view of both. Furthermore, this border-line can still have the same function without physically existing at all. As Lotman points out, in eighteenth-century theatre the most prestigious seats were located on the stage itself, and thus some of the spectators occupied the same physical space as the actors. And yet the remainder of the audience, seated in the auditorium, did not identify the privileged spectators with the play itself since the latter was enacted in an 'artistic space' that was circumscribed by an invisible yet determining frame: 'c'est pourquoi le spectateur voyait des spectateurs sur la scène, mais ne les remarquait pas'.[5] This aspect of frame may be called its 'syntactic function' since, rather like the use of brackets in a sentence, it marks the point of contiguity between a 'text' and its immediate environment.

There is also a 'semantic function' operated by frame. As Lotman says, the content of a work of art is at once specific and universal. *Anna Karenina* describes the life of a particular woman as well as being about all men and women. The first level of the novel may be called 'representational' (Lotman's word is 'fabulous') and the second 'expressive' ('mythological').[6] With reference to visual art, the distinction can be expressed in the following two sentences describing the same painting: 'This is a painting of a nude'; 'This is a painting about jealousy'. The role of frame is to provoke such comments; in other words, it invests a given object with representational and expressive qualities. A poster showing a can of soup beside other posters on the wall of an underground railway station is merely an advertisement for soup, but a 'hyperrealist' painting of a Campbell's soup tin by Andy Warhol hanging amongst other paintings in an art gallery elicits a different type of response from the observer. Firstly, the latter spends more time examining the visual aspect of the painting (the use of colour and line) although this may be exactly the same as in the advertisement hastily glimpsed in the tube station. Secondly, the spectator feels inclined to interpret the painting as a comment on art, or the consumer society, and thus draw inferences which will relate the work with the world beyond its contours. Similarly, a mere collection of bricks in a room full of sculptures becomes a work of art with representational and expressive potential, while the same arrangement of bricks outside the museum is just a collection of bricks. This semantic function of frame is best summed up by the passage in Kafka's *Journal* in which the author remarks that no-one would dream of going on stage before a large audience merely to crack nuts, but that if someone were to do this there would be something behind the action.[7]

The theatre provides perhaps the clearest illustration of the two functions of frame in art. The stage is a constant physical reminder of the spatial and ontological perimeters of what is taking place before the spectators' eyes. Confined within these perimeters, the play reveals a self-enclosed universe, an 'artistic space', inhabited by animated fictional characters who confront and address the audience across the ontological divide which separates them. For this reason works which were conceived at moments when the combined impetus of the expressive and representational aspirations of art reached its apogee are heavily imbued with the influence of drama, as, for instance, in Renaissance painting and in the nineteenth-century novel. One need only think of the title of Balzac's *Comédie Humaine* and the predominantly melodramatic nature of the work, or of Alberti's view of painting as a dramatic representation, full of action and movement, complete even with a chorus figure to direct the spectator's response:

> First, I believe that all bodies should move in relation to one another with a certain harmony in accordance with the action.

Then, I like there to be someone in the 'historia' who tells the spectators what is going on, and either beckons them with his hand to look, or with ferocious expression and forbidding glance challenges them not to come near, as if he wished their business to be secret, or points to some danger or remarkable thing in the picture, or by his gestures invites you to laugh or weep with them.[8]

It is true that, in the twentieth century, theatrical 'happenings' involving audience participation, and the creative work of artists like Jasper Johns and Robert Rauschenberg who incorporate real objects in their constructions, are partly motivated by a desire to cancel out the boundary between art and external reality. However, their inevitable failure to achieve this end, particularly if the cancellation is to be brought about by art crossing over into everyday reality, is eternally ensured in the *a priori* conditions of all art. Whether a construction is physically framed or not, whether it is exhibited in an art gallery or not, it will always be circumscribed by a syntactic and semantic frame simply by virtue of the fact that it is 'put forward', that it draws attention to itself as a work of art.

So far I have only been considering what may be called 'external' or 'outer' frame. Physical manifestations of this phenomenon (picture frame, proscenium stage and curtains and so on) are situated by Lotman and Uspensky in the same spatial context as that of the observer and not in the 'three-dimensional space represented in the painting'. However, the same cannot be said of the three different forms of 'internal frame' which can occur in painting. The first type, particularly widespread in Dutch painting, appears as a literal reproduction of frame within frame and takes the form of the representation of such spatial enclaves as mirrors, windows, doorways, or pictures. When the content of the miniature frame is a replica of the content of the outer frame, as in Van Eyck's 'Portrait of the Arnolfinis' (1434. National Gallery, London), one can speak of 'mise en abyme', a term coined by André Gide and based on the heraldic pattern of embedded escutcheons. More often, however, the content is different, sometimes showing unrelated scenes presented from an alternative angle of perspective. Uspensky outlines a second form of 'internal frame' when he notes that in medieval Russian icons 'frame is created by the shift from the internal point of view, which structures the central part of the representation, to the external point of view, which structures the periphery'.⁹ The centre of the painting is structured from the point of view of an internal viewer, and the periphery of the painting is structured from the point of view of an external viewer:

> This shift may be realised in a picture in the alternation between forms in the central part, represented in inverse perspective, which is manifested by concave forms, and forms on the periphery, represented in 'sharply converging' low eye level perspective, which is manifested by convex forms.¹⁰

As an example of a combination of the two points of view, Uspensky cites the typical representation of a building in medieval painting where the interior is depicted in the centre of the picture and the exterior on the periphery; 'we can simultaneously see both the internal walls of a room, for example (in the main part of the painting), and the roof of the house to which this room belongs (in the upper part of the representation)'.¹¹ Finally, a third type of internal frame in painting, also based on the principle of alternation, is the juxtaposition of different styles:

> For example, in painting, a flat decorative background (represented in linear perspective) contrasting with three-dimensional figures in the central part gives the effect of live actors in front of a painted scenery. Note also the gestures and frontality of representation in the foreground of a painting, and sharp foreshortening and baroque elements in the representation of the background figures, the 'extras'.¹²

The examples chosen by Uspensky, such as Antonello da Messina's 'St Sebastian' (1478. Dresden Gallery), are ones where this type of internal frame is used to create a sense of foreground and background in painting, where a difference in style separates the focal three-dimensional foreground of the painting from its 'purely decorative' background.

To recapitulate, the notion of 'frame' with regard to painting can be divided into two types (external and internal); and the latter, in turn, is composed of at least three variants (frame within frame, frame produced by alternation of perspective, and frame produced by alternation of style). External frame, it was argued, has both a syntactic and a semantic function. Internal frame possesses a syntactic function which in all its variants resembles the one attached to external frame except for the fact that the spatial contiguity is not between text and non-text but between the content of the inner frame (micro-text) and the content of the outer frame (macro-text). However, the semantic function of the variants of internal frame differ, although in each case the function is as active as the one in external frame. An exhaustive account of the semantic function of internal frame lies outside the scope of this chapter. It is sufficient for my purposes to establish that there does exist a semantic function; in other words, that internal frame does contribute to the network of signification in a given painting. To begin with, as well as focusing on the content of the miniature, frame within frame draws one's attention to the presence of frame itself which, as was noted earlier, is not the case with external frame. Now the observer can contemplate the content and its frame simultaneously. One of the consequences of this is to stress the fictionality or artifice of the work, reminding the onlooker that what he is gazing at is a painting which has been fabricated and structured from a particular perspective selected from countless others. Secondly, in the case of frame as alternation of perspective, the semantic function is translated into an alternation of internal and external points of view. Thirdly, frame as alternation of style produces a hierarchical evaluation of the scene depicted by foregrounding and backgrounding the different figures. Thus the wide-ranging manifestations of internal frame in painting are not mere decorative adjuncts to the main representation but play a specific role in influencing the 'reading' of the work as a whole.

What, it remains to be asked, are the literary equivalents of the different variants of frame which I have outlined so far? It should, of course, be remembered that although literature and painting are commonly referred to as 'sister arts', this 'family tie' does not over-rule the fundamental differences between them. One should therefore guard against looking for identical manifestations of frame. Both Lotman and Uspensky have pointed to the beginnings and endings of novels as equivalents of external frame in painting.[13] One could, by extension, cite the example of the seventeenth- and eighteenth-century European novel where prefaces and postscripts were frequently used either as authentification of the new genre or for ironical purposes. Uspensky mentions as a further instance of literary external frame the traditional formula ending the Russian folktale in which an 'I' suddenly appears, 'even though no narrator has taken part in the action until this moment'.[14] A converse example would be the anonymous narrator who disappears after the first few pages of *Madame Bovary*. But are all these, strictly speaking, examples of external frame? The external frame of a painting, as the Russian Formalists themselves emphasise, is located in the external world and not in the three-dimensional world of representation. Yet one cannot say the same about the prologues and epilogues of the early novel, let alone the first person narrator who appears in the main narrative whether at the beginning or at the end. Clearly the editor in *Adolphe*, for example, is a fictional character and the 'Avis de l'éditeur' at the beginning and the 'Lettre à l'éditeur' and 'Réponse' at the end of the novel are intimately linked with the thematic and compositional structure of the central narrative.[15] An equivalent of pictorial external frame would have to be the front cover of a book, an introduction or notes by a 'real' editor. And yet a novel does not have to be bound, typed, introduced or annotated in order to be recognised as a novel. It is here that the compositional features of visual art and literature are at their most irreconcilable. The structural function of external frame in painting is neatly summarised in Magritte's *La Condition humaine I* (1933. Collection Claude Spaak, Choiseul) which shows a canvas representing a scene that seems to exactly match the view it masks. The content of the painting thus occupies two spatial contexts simultaneously: it can either be viewed as a painted representation on the canvas or as part of the landscape perceived through the window. The spectator is able to choose between the two interpretations depending on whether he disregards the easel, the faint line marking the border of the canvas, and the vertical studded right-hand edge which serve as frame, or whether he includes them in his vision of the whole work. Magritte's painting thus pinpoints the syntactic and semantic roles played by external frame in painting. With the novel, however, the question of equivocation or ambiguity of recognition does not arise. The reader could never encounter any given novel without its frame, despite what might be inferred from Stanley Fish's remark that literature is 'language around which we have drawn a frame, a frame that indicates a decision to regard with a particular self-consciousness the resources that language has always possessed'.[16] In contrast with visual art, the frame of a literary work is comprised of the same material as its content: language. Its frame is precisely its inherent qualities, the way in which it stands out from nonfictional discourse. It is true, as Jonathan Culler demonstrates,[17] that a fragment of journalistic prose can be transformed into poetry merely by setting down the same and otherwise unaltered sentence in the conventionally recognisable format of a poem 'surrounded by intimidating margins of silence'; but one needs to stress that it is the visual aspect of the poem which is fulfilling the role of external frame in this case. No such typographical rearrangement is possible or even meaningful in as extensive a literary work as a novel.

Examples of internal frame, on the other hand, proliferate in literature and play a vital part in influencing the interpretation of a given work of fiction. An equivalent of frame within frame is, obviously, the story within a story or, in drama, the play within a play. Examples of 'mises en abyme' (where the micro-text reflects the macro-text) are 'The Murder of Gonzago' in *Hamlet* and the tale of 'Cupid and Psyche' inserted at the centre of Apuleius's *The Golden Ass*. Fictional frames within frame which are not 'mises en abyme' take the form of in-set narratives such as the picaresque and pastoral tales embedded in *Don Quixote*. In fact, works of fiction are capable of more variants of frame within frame than paintings. For instance, many novels project different viewpoints of the same event or series of events: most of the chapters in Faulkner's *The Sound and the Fury* and *As I Lay Dying*, and Claude Simon's *Le Tricheur* and *Le Sacre du printemps* are narrated by a different person in each case. In *As I Lay Dying* the chapters are narrated by different members of the family taking part in the funeral. Robert Browning's *The Ring and the Book*, written in verse form, is composed of a succession of monologues by the different people who, in one way or another, are involved in the Franceschini murder case. A variant of this type of frame within frame, focusing on an alternation not of narrational point of view but of formal genre, is Brasillach's *Les Sept couleurs* where each of the seven chapters, covering different episodes of the same story, is written in one of the following literary forms: 'récit', 'lettre', 'journal', 'réflexions', 'dialogue', 'documents', 'discours'. A more provocative work than Brasillach's novel, which manages to maintain the homogeneity of its narrative intact despite the formal variations, is B. S. Johnson's *Travelling People*. In the prelude to this book, the author explains that he chose the novel genre because it possessed the fewest limitations of all literary forms, and points to the generative process underlying the relationship between form and content in his work:

> I decided that one style for one novel was a convention that I resented most strongly: it was perhaps comparable to eating a meal in which each course had been cooked in the same manner. The style of each chapter should spring naturally from its subject matter.[18]

Uspensky argues that an equivalent of frame as alternation of perspective is the alternation between the descriptions made from the point of view of one of the characters and descriptions made from an external, 'objective' or authorial vantage-point. Flaubert's technique of 'style indirect libre' may be said to have played on this feature of internal frame, often confusing the reader as to whether a particular comment is made by one of the characters or by the 'narrator'. Albert Thibaudet saw Flaubert's stylistic device precisely as a means of establishing a neutral common ground between exterior and interior:

> la force de ces imparfaits de discours indirect consiste à exprimer la liaison entre le dehors et le dedans, à mettre sur le même plan, en usant du même temps, l'extérieur et l'intérieur, la réalité telle quelle se déroule dans les choses.[19]

Finally, frame as alternation of style is manifest, according to Uspensky, in the depiction of the characters. Similar to the figures in the background of a painting, the 'extras' or 'puppets' in a fictional work contrast with the rounded main characters. The critic views the difference between the description of the boarders and the description of the protagonist in Kafka's *The Metamorphosis* (where the former are no more than symbolic cardboard figures) as an example of foregrounding and backgrounding in literature.[20]

The idea of frame carries with it, as do all boundaries, the possibility of transgression, and it is this overlapping movement which constitutes the principal impulse engendering the discontinuities and displacements characteristic of modern art. Yet one must not deny the fact that examples of frame transgression, in the visual arts at least, stretch back as far as history permits. Often the movement is conveyed in the depiction of a figure who appears to be leaning or stepping out of the canvas. A painting attributed to Paolo Ucello, 'The Virgin and Infant' (c.1445. National Gallery of Ireland, Dublin), shows the child on the point of stepping out of the painting with both feet poised on the painted frame at the bottom of the representation. The large repertory of illusionistic devices in art, formally known as 'trompe l'oeil', has been drawn up with the intention of misleading the spectator into viewing part of the represented scene as belonging to the external world. Broken panes of protective glass, shreds of torn paper nailed to the edge of the canvas, the facsimile signature of the painter written on a scrap of paper with curling corners pinned onto the canvas, all give the impression of being real objects because of their meticulous life-like rendering based on a strict observance of the rules of linear perspective and the gradations of light and shadow.[21] The effect of these illusionistic devices can be interpreted in two ways: they can either be seen as creating the illusion that real objects are incorporated in the painting, or that the painted image is protruding into external reality. Formulating his reading of this phenomenon from the second point of view, Uspensky interprets illustrations of frame break as a desire 'to achieve the greatest degree of verisimilitude':

> Efforts to violate the borders of artistic space, generally speaking, seem to be motivated by an understandable desire to bring together, as closely as possible, the represented world and the real world, in order to achieve the greatest degree of verisimilitude – of realism – in the representation. Attempts to break down the frame are many: the removal of the curtain in contemporary theatre; the many cases in pictorial art where the representation extends beyond the frame; and the overcoming of the borders of artistic space and the joining of life and art, as expressed in the motif of the living portrait (a motif which is characteristic of the work of Wilde and Gogol).[22]

It would appear, however, that Uspensky's critical reasoning is here betrayed by a blind adherence to the tenets of art as representation of life. It seems perverse to construe the motif of the living portrait in literature as a sign of the desire for verisimilitude when it is precisely this motif, and others like it, which defines such 'unrealistic' genres as those of the Gothic and the Fantastic. In Walpole's *The House of Otranto*, one of Manfred's forbears descends from his portrait to distract the prince from raping Isabella; in

Gautier's *La Cafetière*, the narrator witnesses a number of ancestral portraits hanging in his bedroom come to life and partake in a night of continuous dancing with music provided by the animated image of an orchestra woven on a tapestry. Is this the stuff of realism? And even with reference to instances of frame break in painting, realist interpretations, however apposite they may be in explaining the semantic function of medieval paintings, are often totally irrelevant, as for instance in one's reading of the pattern of frame break displayed in Cézanne's 'Nature morte avec amour en plâtre' (1895. Courtauld Institute) in which the folds of blue drape spill out of the canvas leaning against the wall in the lower left-hand side of the painting and trespass onto the 'external' space of the apples and cupid standing on the table in the foreground. Cézanne's concern is not one of a search for mimesis but of constructing a spatial balance based on the relationship between several contiguous planes of surface enclosing conflicting perspectives and whose contours are transgressed either literally, as in the case of the drape, or by repetition of motif and colour. What kind of desire for verisimilitude motivates, furthermore, the inverted frame play in Delvaux's 'La Fenêtre' (1936) which shows a window opening internally onto a landscape inside the room, or Magritte's 'L'Eloge de la dialectique' (1937. Musée d'Ixelles, Bruxelles) where a window opens inwards onto the façade of the building inside the room? The inclination to fix on a single all-embracing interpretation of a given artistic phenomenon which has recurred in different works throughout history has all too often proved irresistible for the literary historian. But if his critical apparatus is to be at all relevant to a reading of the specific works of art and literature which it purports to encompass, the critic must resolutely avoid the temptation, latent in the very notion of poetics, of viewing certain textual and pictorial structures as devices whose meaning and function are invariable, regardless of the context in which they appear. Bearing this caution in mind, I must hasten to add that my own reading of the frame breaks in modern art and fiction may well not be pertinent to all instances of the phenomenon in the twentieth century. I am, though, suggesting that my reading of the compositional principle of frame break is related to a certain strain of artistic endeavour found in works which have been defined as 'modern' precisely because they challenge the Aristotelian ideals of unity and mimesis.

In modern fiction, one of the most prominent self-conscious

examples of frame break is to be found in Gide's *Les Faux-Monnayeurs*, a novel which is renowned for the 'mise en abyme' mirror reflection cast by the novel which Edouard, the central character, is in the process of writing and which is also entitled *Les Faux-Monnayeurs*. The delineation of a contour once again gives rise to a desire for violation. Indeed, while expounding his ideas on the novel to Bernard, Laura, and Mme Sophroniska, Edouard declares that the genre has suffered from the following weakness: 'Il n'a jamais connu, le roman, cette "formidable érosion des contours" dont parle Nietzsche'.[23] Towards the end of the novel one comes across an instance of just such an erosion of contours when Edouard asks Georges to read a passage from his novel, the plot of which concerns a series of events similar to the one in which Georges is embroiled. In the passage, Audibert discusses with a friend, Hildebrant, what to say to another character, Eudolphe, who is clearly a mirror image of Georges himself. At the end of the text, Audibert decides, on Hildebrant's advice, to transcribe the conversation they have just had and to offer it to Eudolphe to read. By reading the passage, Georges, Eudolphe's model, is thus engaged in a kind of inter-frame communication with the characters in Edouard's novel, a communication which derives from the erosion of the contour separating two fictional contexts. Unamuno's *Mist* is also a novel which includes an interplay between interior and exterior: the frame break in this case takes the form of a confrontation between fiction and 'reality'. At the end of the novel, the protagonist, Augusto Perez, is so frustrated by the endless run of misfortune in his life that he travels to Salamanca with the intention of confronting his creator, Unamuno, before committing suicide. The frame break is thus brought about by the character's migration from the world of fiction to the world of 'reality'. The model for the structural frame break in Unamuno's story is the ending of the second part of *Don Quixote* where the knight and Sancho Panza comment on the inauthentic version written by the 'impostor' Avellaneda. The discussion is occasioned by the appearance of Don Alvaro Tarfe, a character who features in Avellaneda's book and who now wanders into Cervantes's novel. A similar literary example is Borges's *The Wizard Adjourned*, although the transgression here is not between fiction and 'reality' but between two fictional contexts: one 'realist', the other 'magical' or 'fantastic'. An ambitious dean visits a magician, don Illán, in order to learn the art of magic. While leafing through the books in the magician's cabinet, the dean receives news of the imminent death of his uncle which sets off a series of ecclesiastical promotions for him, culminating in his election as pope. But as the dean continually refuses to repay don Illán for his help, the tale ends with a return to the magician's cabinet and the preceding experience is revealed to have been a magical test of the extent of the dean's loyalty to don Illán. The tale thus contains two frame contexts linked by two hinge-points: the arrival of the two men with the uncle's letter; and don Illán's utterance, 'In that case, I shall have to eat the partridges that I ordered for tonight', which straddles both contexts.[24] The shift of context in both tales is signalled by the motif of travel: Augusto Perez journeys to Salamanca to meet Unamuno; don Illán and the dean travel from Toledo to Rome. Indeed, don Illán's parting words to the dean, on which Borges's story closes, ironically accentuate the latter's disillusionment as he is shown the door by the magician who wishes him 'a safe journey home'.

Reading itself becomes an act of transgression when it is conceived as a process whereby the reader is transported into the world of fiction. Thus, for Butor the motif of travel is a metaphorical expression of 'cette distance entre le lieu de la lecture et celui où nous emmène le récit'.[25] However, the examples from Gide, Unamuno, and Borges are ones where the motif of travel reflects the transgression of the distance between separate fictional contexts. Further examples can be found in most of Butor's work dating as far back as *La Modification*, and in Simon's oeuvre the same reading is suggested by the description of the train journey to Barcelona in *Le Palace*, the trips to Greece in *Histoire* and *La Bataille de Pharsale*, the plane flight in *Les Corps conducteurs* and, as will emerge in the next chapter, the different itineraries, mainly on horseback, in *La Route des Flandres*. As my analysis will indicate, the motif of travel in Simon's work as a whole is framed as a reflection of the poetic impulse, the metaphorical movement of associating heterogenous units through the articulatory process of writing.

Illusion, as the word suggests, is a game with precise rules and objectives which can nevertheless be reviewed and reformulated, as they have been at various stages throughout history. Whilst for the moderns the rules themselves have become the subject of reflection, for the humanists and ancients from whom they draw their inspiration the rules provided the basis of a strategy for deception. Championing the cause of the art of painting, Leonardo da Vinci enumerates a series of 'trompe l'oeil' successes which demonstrate the skilful dupery of art. Curiously enough, the implausibility of his examples paradoxically undercuts his argument on the plausibility of optical illusion:

> I have seen a picture that deceived a dog because of the likeness to its master; likewise I have seen dogs bark and try to bite painted dogs, and a monkey that did an infinite number of foolish things with another painted monkey. I have seen flying swallows light on painted iron bars before the windows of buildings.[26]

The mathematical rules of Renaissance linear perspective are designed to achieve the basic objective of all 'trompe l'oeil' painting: the representation of a three dimensional space on a two dimensional surface. Describing the canvas as a screen, Alberti sees the picture plane as an 'open window' behind which the third spatial dimension is carefully and accurately projected. Relief, 'the soul of painting' according to Leonardo, is to be created by the foregrounding of objects against a coloured background. Furthermore, the creation of a contour separating foreground from background is attained by a sharp contrast of colour and not by the delineation of a dark outline. Despite the shared definition of a boundary as the juxtaposition of contrasting colour forms, what distinguishes Leonardo's approach to composition from Cézanne's is that the former sees the foregrounded figure enclosed by the contours as being detached from the background, whereas the latter focused on the permeability of contours whereby the enclosed space and the bounding space exchange repercussions of colour. Thus, Cézanne enthusiastically endorsed Emile Bernard's comment that 'tout objet participe sur ses bords ombreux de son voisin'.[27] For Leonardo, on the other hand, the isolation and solidity of the represented object is of prime importance. As Liliane Brion-Guerry noted in her outstanding study of the construction of space in Cézanne, nowhere is the imperviousness of the contour more essential than in the Renaissance conception of the nude. The contour surrounding the foregrounded figure detaches it from its spatial context and invests it with an air of autonomy: 'le personnage devient alors semblable à un microcosme qui vit de sa propre vie, qui se pose comme une existence en face de l'existence du monde'.²⁸ The contour of the foregrounded figure, its frame, is thus motivated by the imperative to fulfil a specific semantic function. Cézanne, however, replaced Renaissance linear perspective, where figurative distribution of space was motivated by an expressive objective, with a new conception of artistic space in which the materiality of a painting (colour, light and shade, volume) was freed from the constraints imposed upon it by the delineation of contour:

> L'incertitude volontaire du contour est évocatrice de mobilité: l'objet ne s'emboîte pas rigoureusement dans un cerne limitatif, il se rétracte ou déborde son propre volume suivant que les jeux de la lumière suscitent contraction ou épanouissement, et cette alternance devient une sorte de respiration qui met en mouvement les masses d'air.²⁹

The twin aims of nineteenth-century fiction, expressivity and mimesis, were pursued along lines which ran parallel to those of Renaissance perspective. Henry James's metaphor, 'the house of fiction', the windows of which provided the reader with a view of the clearly defined interior bears a close resemblance to Alberti's earlier formula, the open window in painting. Indeed, in his adulatory lecture 'The Lesson of Balzac', James described the novel as 'being everywhere an effort at *representation* – this is the beginning and end of it', an assertion which tellingly depends on a metaphor of frame as an expression of finitude. The Balzacian novel was above all concerned with establishing a fixed frame, with arranging its component elements in a certain irreversible and hierarchical order of foreground and background. The most important consequence of this was that description, as Robbe-Grillet explains, was relegated to the status of backcloth, subservient to the two decisive compositional elements, character and plot:

> Et il est certain que ces descriptions-là ont pour but de faire voir et qu'elles y réussissent. Il s'agissait alors le plus souvent de planter un décor, de définir le cadre de l'action, de présenter l'apparence physique de ses protagonistes.³⁰

A reader who was anxious to follow the line of the plot, Robbe-Grillet adds, could even miss out the descriptions: 'il ne s'agissait que d'un cadre, qui se trouvait d'ailleurs avoir un sens identique à celui du tableau qu'il allait contenir'.[31] Butor similarly stresses the visual aspect of description as frame in Balzac's novels where the narrator is no more than an eye observing and noting all the objects and details which constitute the décor:

> Plantant son chevalet ou sa caméra dans un des points de l'espace évoqué, le romancier retrouvera tous les problèmes de cadrage, de composition, et de perspective que rencontre le peintre.[32]

The terms 'décor', 'backcloth', 'background', borrowed as they are from the vocabulary of theatrical discourse, postulate a hierarchical division, a scale of values according to which the component parts of a text or painting are modulated. The notion of differentiation sets itself up as a positive value rejecting the indeterminate, and therefore insignificant, spread of uniformity. However, a system of perspective which is wholly concerned with the enhancement of its foreground inevitably relies on the idea of the indeterminate which it evokes as the neutral, monotonous ground from which the figures, the subject matter, are singled out. This, as was seen earlier with reference to Uspensky's discussion of the depiction of minor characters in Kafka's *The Metamorphosis*, is one of the main functions of the structure of frame as alternation of style. Thus although the foregrounded space drawn by linear perspective appears to be the antithesis of undifferentiated sameness by the fact that its immediate effect is to impose its distinctive features on the consciousness of the observer, it nevertheless necessarily entails the visible presence of the indeterminate. A symbiotic interdependence binds the two antithetical yet indissociable values. The 'vraisemblable' critic who protests that, after all, linear perspective is merely obeying the laws of visual perception commits the eternal error of misrepresentation by hasty and inaccurate correspondence. It is true that, in Merleau-Ponty's eyes, 'every perception is the perception of something solely by way of being at the same time the relative imperception of a horizon or background which it implies but does not thematize'.[33] But it is the question of 'relative imperception' which is vital since in this context relativity is determined by the observer's gaze. When the latter focuses on the background it automatically takes on the status of 'foreground' implying its own relatively imperceived horizon. This interchangeability of optical perspective is absent in works which 'thematize' their background by depicting a flat, sketchy landscape peopled, if at all, with 'cardboard' figures. Claude Simon has alluded to the strong tradition in painting of affording thematic prominence to background:

> Dans *la Bataille de Pharsale*, j'ai fait allusion à la critique que formule Elie Faure lorsqu'il parle des peintres allemands de la Renaissance auxquels il reproche justement cette absence de valorisation, c'est-à-dire d'accorder une attention aussi passionnée au dessin d'une herbe, d'un caillou ou d'une hallebarde qu'à celui d'un corps en mouvement ou des figures de la Foi ou de l'Espérance.... Et effectivement cette peinture s'oppose de façon radicale à l'invention italienne du clair-obscur (Rembrandt aussi...) où toute la lumière (et l'attention) sont concentrées sur un ou quelques personnages entourés de grands pans d'ombre [...] Au contraire, dans cette peinture allemande (et Breughel – je pense au 'Portement de la croix' ou au 'Chemin de Damas' où il faut longuement chercher un Christ ou un saint Paul minuscules, perdus au milieu d'une foule d'autres personnages et d'un immense paysage), l'attention est répartie de façon égale sur la totalité de la surface de la toile: ce n'est plus l'homme centre de l'univers mais l'homme faisant partie de [.][34]

In addition to this 'thematization' on the level of 'signifié' of what has been conventionally regarded as background material, one can find a parallel concern among painters, particularly those who have followed on from Cézanne, to achieve an effect of spatial reversibility and alternation, on the level of 'signifiant'. The 'jigsaw effect' in painting, manifest above all in the work of Dubuffet and Escher, derives from the fact, noted by Patrick Heron, that the depiction of a contour, or any line, defines a space on either side of it 'with equal intensity':

> The so-called space between the arm and the hip in a nude by Michelangelo is itself a shape, on the picture-surface, every bit as definite and positive and complete as the shape of the arm or the torso to either side of it. In other words, the outline of that hip is a line which defines with equal intensity in two directions simultaneously. All paintings are thus like a jigsaw:

every area-shape – like the pieces of a jigsaw – must be formally complete in itself and at the same time must be wholly accommodating to all the other contingent pieces surrounding it. All its edges mutually define both the piece itself and one side of an adjacent piece. But when your eye is fixed on one piece, you read that piece's outlines, or frontiers, as defining that piece only. The moment your eye crosses over into the next piece – the frontier line you have just crossed becomes readable in reverse.[35]

A major distinctive feature in the evolution of Claude Simon's 'oeuvre' is the increasing dominance of what may be called the jigsaw principle of composition. Already visible in an early novel like *Le Vent*, it becomes a decisive structural determinant from *La Route des Flandres* onwards, assuming total compositional control in *Triptyque* and *Leçon de choses*. The syntagmatic dimension of Simon's novels thus takes the form of a mosaic of referential units which by their juxtaposition create an endless series of narrative disjunction and interruption. Simon often compares his method of construction with the principle upon which the 'set theory' in mathematics is based. Two groups of figures are initially assimilated through a common denominator or quality possessed by both 'sets':

> For example, consider set A composed of different coloured triangles, one of which is red, and set B composed of different geometric forms (squares, trapezoids, rhombuses, circles, triangles) all of which are red. The two sets intersect at the red triangle. The mathematician then 'merges' the two sets A and B including all the elements common or not common to both.[36]

Viewed in this light, Simon's fictional writing can be seen to depend on a similar double process of association through metaphor and metonymy. The sudden shifts from one narrative sequence, or referential unit, to another, creating the effect of a contour which outlines the boundary between each unit, is achieved through metaphorical association. The internal components of the unit itself, the elements within each boundary, are connected through metonymic association. Finally, the 'trompe l'oeil' effect of harmony and unity cast by the conventional novel thus makes way for a new fictional perspective. The text is no longer an instrument of persuasion wielded in the dual concern for representation and expression, but an infinitely suggestive web of relations generated by the dynamics of language.

2
The Framework of *La Route des Flandres*

> la route torse, la route sur laquelle le pied sent les pierres, la route qui retourne en arrière, c'est cela la route de l'art. Le mot rapproche le mot, le mot ressent le mot, comme la joue fait avec la joue. Les mots se disloquent, et au lieu d'un ensemble unique – mot prononcé automatiquement, jeté comme l'est une tablette de chocolat par un distributeur automatique – naît un mot-son, un mot-mouvement articulatoire.
> V. Chklovski, *Sur la théorie de la prose*[1]

I NARRATIVE FRAME

The dilemma facing the reader of *La Route des Flandres* has been succinctly described by Bernard Pingaud in an article which appeared shortly after the novel's publication:

> Ce récit qui ne distingue pas, ne se distingue pas non plus, si l'on peut dire, de lui-même. Il n'est pas vraiment situé. Il n'a pas un foyer, mais plusieurs, et semble amalgamer au moins trois discours différents: un qui serait tenu pendant l'exode, un qui daterait de la captivité, un troisième qui se déroulerait après la guerre. D'où l'égarement du lecteur; nous échouons à reconstituer l'histoire, non pas seulement parce que les interprétations y occupent plus de place que les faits, mais aussi parce qu'il n'existe pas de point fixe autour duquel ces perspectives diverses puissent s'ordonner.[2]

The apparent chaos and confusion facing the reader of this novel defies reorganisation and recuperation. There is no fixed point for the reader surrounded by the swim of textual multiplicity. Most conventional novels include some sort of interpretative support for the reader, providing a particular angle of approach, a way of making sense out of the material at hand. The most common device is the delineation of point of view either through the authoritative presence of a narrator or, as Uspensky shows with regard to *War and Peace*,[3] through the guiding influence of the narrative framework itself. The reader of *La Route des Flandres*, however, cannot rely on the narrator to help him 'reconstitute' an order out of the multiple interpretative possibilities suggested by the text since the narrator too is constantly, and unsuccessfully, trying to do the same. Acknowledging this 'impasse', Pingaud abandons analysis of the novel's narrative structure and turns to its thematic content for the underlying meaning or 'vérité particulière qu'elle [. . .] doit révéler'.[4] But the conclusion he reaches, namely that the underlying truth is the theme of time, is, to say the least, unsatisfactory. Certainly such a theme does play a part in the novel, but for the reader to be able to detach it as easily as Pingaud does would imply that despite the fact that the novel's narrative structure is indistinct, disordered, and ambiguous, its themes are, on the contrary, distinct, ordered, and unambiguous. Form and content are thus peeled apart and held to be mutually independent. But is it possible to separate narrative and theme in this way? Surely, if the one is riddled with doubt and complexity so too is the other? Furthermore, it seems perverse that the critic should eschew the problems relating to *La Route des Flandres*'s narrative framework when they are so emphatically foregrounded throughout the novel. The reader, in fact, has no choice but to approach the novel by way of its narrative structure, though in order to make any headway he must first shed all pretensions at being detective or excavator digging for truths.

As Pingaud says, there is not one strand of narrative discourse in Simon's novel but three. The reader is made conscious of these three distinct (yet inextricably entangled) discursive strands at their moment of birth: three moments of 'éclat de narration'[5] when the time and place from which the narration seems to be constructed are radically displaced. Thus, the novel begins in the first person narrative:

Il tenait une lettre à la main, il leva les yeux me regarda puis de nouveau la lettre puis de nouveau moi, derrière lui je pouvais

> voir aller et venir passer les taches rouges acajou ocre des chevaux qu'on menait à l'abreuvoir, la boue était si profonde qu'on enfonçait dedans jusqu'aux chevilles mais je me rappelle que pendant la nuit il avait brusquement gelé [.] (p. 9)[6]

The opening sentence refers to two time spans: the imperfect and preterite tenses refer to events in the past, and the present tense ('je me rappelle') refers to the present moment in which the past is recalled. The present tense, therefore, can be said to form a frame for the narrative, outlining a moment of discourse: the present of the moment of writing would appear to be the same as the time in which the words 'je me rappelle' are spoken. Equally, the spatial context may be taken to be the same. A few pages later, however, the first narrative break ('éclat de narration') occurs. The narrative has been unfolding a series of disconnected descriptions of moments from the past relating the experiences of Georges, the narrator, at the disastrous battle of La Meuse in 1940, when suddenly there is a break in the narration:

> Ouais! . . .' fit Blum (maintenant nous étions couchés dans le noir c'est-à-dire imbriqués entassés au point de ne pas pouvoir bouger un bras ou une jambe sans rencontrer ou plutôt sans demander la permission à un autre bras ou à une autre jambe [.] (p. 20)[7]

The displacement affects both the temporal and the spatial narrative framing of the opening pages. The 'je me rappelle' of the first sentence is now seen to have been spoken by Georges in a moment of the past to Blum whilst being shunted to a POW camp, having been captured by the Germans. Moreover, the shift creates a vacancy for a new moment and locus of discourse since the train segment is itself narrated in the imperfect tense. What, the reader now asks, is the narrative frame of the events related which include Georges's discussion with Blum in the train?

The second narrative break, appearing a few pages later, does not provide an answer to the problem posed by the first break, but introduces an additional problem: a shift from first to third person narrative. The break occurs in a passage where Georges is recounting to Blum events which took place before his capture by the Germans and, specifically, his first encounter with the dead horse lying on the road:

et ce dut être par là que je le vis pour la première fois, un peu avant ou après l'endroit où nous nous sommes arrêtés pour boire, le découvrant, le fixant à travers cette sorte de demi-sommeil, cette sorte de vase marron dans laquelle j'étais pour ainsi dire englué et peut-être parce que nous dûmes faire un détour pour l'éviter, et plutôt le devinant que le voyant: c'est-à-dire (comme tout ce qui jalonnait le bord de la route: les camions, les voitures, les valises, les cadavres) quelque chose d'insolite, d'irréel, d'hybride en ce sens que ce qui avait été un cheval (c'est-à-dire ce qu'on savait, ce qu'on pouvait reconnaître, identifier comme ayant été un cheval) n'était plus à présent qu'un vague tas de membres, de cornes, de cuir et de poils collés, aux trois quarts recouvert de boue – Georges se demandant sans exactement se le demander[.] (pp. 26–7)[8]

The shift from first to third person narrative results in a split of identity, or 'dédoublement' of the subject. From this moment onwards the text alternates between the two types of narrative discourse. However, this alternation is unlike the Tolstoyan technique of movement from 'il' to 'je' which, as Uspensky demonstrates, corresponds to the movement of perspective from outside a character's mind to within it. The substitution of narrative frames in *La Route des Flandres* involves more than 'psychological' considerations of individual characters' point of view, it causes an upheaval of the structure and reading of the whole novel.

The third narrative break maintains the third person narrative form but introduces a new spatio-temporal frame. The war is now over and Georges is lying in a hotel bed with Corinne remembering his past experiences:

il ne dormait pas, se tenait parfaitement immobile, et non pas une grange à présent, non pas la lourde et poussiéreuse senteur de foin desséché, de l'été aboli, mais cette impalpable nostalgique et tenace exhalaison du temps lui-même, des années mortes et lui flottant dans les ténèbres, écoutant le silence, la nuit, la paix, l'imperceptible respiration d'une femme à côté de lui et au bout d'un moment il distingua le second rectangle dessiné par la glace de l'armoire reflétant l'obscure lumière de la fenêtre [.] (pp. 42–3)[9]

Again, once a spatio-temporal frame is delineated the problem then arises as to how to define the frame or point of discourse in which that delineation is made. One may argue that the hotel scene is the one fixed point or frame of the whole novel since it reappears towards the end with Corinne leaving Georges, angry with him for his obsession with the past (p. 295). However, such an interpretation is ruled out when the reader discovers that Georges has been meeting Corinne in the hotel for three months before their final rupture. Indeed, is it at all possible to 'explain' the narrative framework of this novel along psychological lines? It is clearly unlikely that such an intricately composed novel is meant to appear as the spontaneous flow of memory emanating from one character's mind. Conventional novels which do have one fixed frame generally avoid drawing the reader's attention to the fact of narrative perspective. But *La Route des Flandres*, with its absence of fixed frame, repeatedly underlines this feature of its composition. The spatio-temporal points of discourse thus fall within the scope of the text's self-reflective gaze. Each of the apparently fixed points of the present is in turn 'narrativised'. In other words, what is at first perceived as a voice speaking, narrating a string of events, later fills out into a picture of the narrator as a character talking in a particular time and place with a particular person (Georges with Blum in the train, or with Corinne in the hotel). Moreover, the scene itself is later put into diachronic perspective: that is, the events leading up to and following these scenes of discourse are elaborated. The successive narrative frames thus are themselves transformed into stories, fictions narrated from a different point of time.

It would, however, be wrong to infer that the narrative structure of *La Route des Flandres* can be analysed as a distinct unit, detached from the other levels of the novel's composition. In fact, the three moments of narrative break are foreshadowed and, to a certain extent, precipitated by the motifs and 'mise en abyme' descriptions in the passages immediately preceding. The long paragraph leading up to the first 'éclat de narration' contains a description of Georges riding with his captain along a 'coupe-gorge'. Various civilians, knowing that the soldiers are heading straight for the Germans, call on de Reixach, from the road-side, to turn back. The speakers of the unreal voices remain unseen, but Georges imagines them carrying their belongings and empty suitcases. De Reixach is un peu interdit, impatient, comme si dans un salon quelqu'un l'avait brusquement abordé sans lui avoir été présenté ou interrompu au milieu d'une phrase [.] (p. 18)[10]

He reacts with cold politeness and disinterest:

pensant sans doute qu'il est inévitable de rencontrer toujours partout et en toutes circonstances – dans les salons ou à la guerre – des gens stupides et sans éducation, et cela fait – c'est-à-dire remémoré – oubliant l'interrupteur, l'effaçant cessant de le voir avant même d'avoir détourné les yeux [.] (pp. 18–9)[11]

Georges proceeds to visualise de Reixach's racing society ('Et il me semblait y être, voir cela des ombrages verts' (p. 19))[12] and the horse-like women. It is at this point that Blum interrupts Georges's monologue and the narrative frame is broken. One can therefore say that the description of the civilians' interruption of de Reixach and his company pre-empts Blum's interruption of George's narration. This parallel between the two scenes is further stressed by the term used to denote de Reixach's mental response, 'remémoré', which echoes Georges's own recollection of the event.

A passage quoted earlier showed that the second narrative frame break ('Georges se demandant sans exactement se le demander') was immediately preceded by the description of the dead horse lying in the centre of the road. Compared with the road-side civilians, the dead horse provokes a more emphatic interruption of the riders' progress. Although the passage echoes the earlier one in the reference to 'tout ce qui jalonnait le bord de la route' and to Georges's difficulty in seeing the horse ('plutôt le devinant que le voyant'), a new perspective of circularity accentuates the motif of interruption. The riders have to make a detour in order to avoid the horse. Once again the soldiers' itinerary mirrors the process of narration. The circular perspective ('il le vit pivoter au-dessous de lui comme s'il avait été posé sur un plateau tournant'[13]) reflects the circular logic of the paradoxical phrase in which the 'éclat' appears ('Georges se demandant sans exactement se le demander'). Furthermore, as Dominique Lanceraux notes,[14] the horses' semi-immersion in the earth is reflected in Georges's semi-immersion in sleep. This motif of burial can itself be seen to predict the eruption of the third person narrative by which Georges is semi-immersed in the text, caught in the subsequent alternation between first and third person narrative.

The third narrative break is immediately preceded by a description of the soldiers' arrival at a village in the middle of the night. The weary men are led to a barn by a farm girl bathed in the pale light of a lamp she is holding up. This passage heralds the eclipse of one narrative frame by another, with the 'paysanne' serving as an intermediary figure in the substitution of interlocutors. George's perception of the girl is set against his description of Blum's physical appearance. The latter's face is like a monotonous, grey mask ('la bouche grise aussi') covered with the same uniform greyness which pervades the surrounding area ('cette matière inconsistante, spongieuse et uniformément grise').[15] In sharp contrast, the 'paysanne' is perceived as a luminescent apparition 'comme si sa peau était elle-même la source de la lumière'. She is also described as 'une taie sur un ôeil aveugle',[16] an image which adds further poignancy to the fact that Blum, blinded by his drowsiness, fails completely to see the woman. Corinne herself, Georges's interlocutor in the third narrative frame, emerges out of the language of the imagery relating to the 'paysanne'. The latter is described as a symbol of femininity:

> sommairement façonnés dans le tendre argile deux cuisses un ventre deux seins la ronde colonne au cou et au creux des replis comme au centre de ces statues primitives au nom de bête, de terme d'histoire naturelle – moule poulpe pulpe vulve – faisant penser à ces organismes marins et carnivores aveugles pourvus de lèvres et de cils [.] (pp. 41–2)[17]

The image leads directly to a break in the narrative frame and a reference to the scene of the hotel room with Georges lying in bed beside Corinne remembering the past. The textual motivation of Corinne's appearance here is later explained when Georges alludes to the paronomastic association between her name and the word 'corail' (p. 235). The structural link between the two women is further emphasised by Georges's description of his first meeting with Corinne after the war, which is couched in the same subaqueous imagery as that evoked with reference to the peasant girl:

> comme si elle était faite d'une matière semblable à celle des

éponges, mais d'un grain invisible, se dilatant et se contractant, semblables à ces fleurs, ces choses marines à mi-chemin entre le végétal et l'animal, ces madrépores [.] (p. 236)[18]

One can, to summarise, read in the opening pages of *La Route des Flandres* a preliminary exposition of its own narrative structure, an outline which is subsequently dilated, blurred, and negated. This self-conscious and, in some ways, prefatory opening also reveals that the text, progressing through a series of narrative frames, is gradually cast in a perspective of femininity and eroticism. But eroticism in Simon's novel is not just fodder to appease the eternal appetite for symbolic readings and interpretations; it forms, as I shall argue in the following section, an integral part of the structural and linguistic relations spanning the work as a whole.

II IN SEARCH OF FRAME

In *Orion aveugle*, a book commissioned by the publisher Albert Skira for the series 'les sentiers de la création' in which authors are invited to chart the creative paths taken by their work in its genesis, Claude Simon states categorically that his novels do not recount the exemplary tales of a hero or heroine 'mais cette tout autre histoire qui est l'aventure singulière du narrateur qui ne cesse de chercher, découvrant à tâtons le monde dans et par l'écriture'.[19] In the case of *La Route des Flandres*, the narrator's search for knowledge is indissociably bound up with a pursuit of his own identity; a pursuit which is not formulated in the conventional ontological question 'who am I?' but one which, since it is carried out 'dans et par l'écriture', 'puts into question', as Stephen Heath argues,[20] 'the fiction of identity' and, correspondingly, the fiction of narration.

Although the discussion of the 'éclats de narration' in the previous section will have provided some support for such a reading of *La Route des Flandres*, to claim at this stage of my analysis that this novel exposes the fiction of identity and narration is to beg a few questions. One which requires immediate clarification is the assumption that identity and narration are intimately connected. Yet if, in a given text, the concept of identity is fractured into a plurality by the work of language and writing, it is difficult to see how the concept of narration, which has traditionally relied on a sense of unity either embodied in the stable 'I' of the narrator or in the consistent presence of that other 'I' shadowing the third 'person' narrative, can remain undisturbed. Loss of narratorial identity in *La Route des Flandres* is principally evident in the oscillation, triggered off by the second narrative frame break, between 'je' and 'il' with reference to Georges. Another equally striking case is the 'depersonalization'[21] of dialogue produced by the arbitrary identification of Georges with Blum: 'Et Blum (ou Georges) [. . .] et Georges (ou Blum)' (p. 188). George's pursuit of knowledge, however futile and derisory, can be read in counterpoint to the unremitting process of disintegration and dissemination operated by the text. This search for knowledge and identity takes the form of attempts to imagine or interpret a number of internal stories set within the novel. Thus Georges and Blum strive to reconstitute de Reixach's past in order to discover the reason for his apparent suicide. This leads to conjectures about the life of one of de Reixach's ancestors whom Georges, basing his argument on the evidence of a portrait and an engraving, also imagines to have committed suicide on account of an unfaithful wife. But the different threads of enquiry and speculation are increasingly interwoven and lead to haphazard invention rather than historical reconstruction; a fact which is explicitly acknowledged when Georges accuses Blum of intermingling elements from the lives of the two de Reixachs. Blum's reply is that the so-called evidence upon which they are building their hypotheses is a total fabrication on the part of Georges's imagination. Indeed the fictionality of all the narratives in the novel is further outlined by the interchangeability of the different discourses in which the narratives are set. Throughout the novel the chaos and uncertainty of the world which Georges perceives and imagines around him is matched by the uncertainty surrounding his own identity. Frame delimiting the field of epistemological enquiry and frame specifying the unity and identity of narrative discourse are thus simultaneously and correlatively displaced, as the following lines expressing the convoluted nature of the novel's narrative structure exemplify:

> et Georges (à moins que ce ne fût toujours Blum, s'interrompant lui-même, bouffonnant, à moins qu'il (Georges) ne fût pas en train de dialoguer sous la froide pluie saxonne avec un petit juif souffreteux – ou l'ombre d'un petit juif, et qui n'allait bientôt

The Framework of La Route des Flandres 31

plus être qu'un cadavre – un de plus – de petit juif – mais avec lui-même, c'est-à-dire son double, tout seul sous la pluie grise, parmi les rails, les wagons de charbon, ou peut-être des années plus tard, toujours seul (quoi-qu'il fût maintenant couché à côté d'une tiède chair de femme), toujours en tête-à-tête avec ce double, ou avec Blum, ou avec personne): 'Nous y voilà: l'Histoire [.]' (p. 187)[22]

The long parenthesis separating the name of the speaker from his speech underlines the overwhelming uncertainty as to who is speaking, from where and when: in other words, the brackets and brackets within brackets draw our attention to the basic absence of a stable narrative frame. Visual symbols of frame abound in the novel. There is the baroque lettering on the cover of an old edition of a Rousseau text:

Hic liber – l'H démésuré, emphatique, en forme de deux parenthèses se tournant le dos et reliées par un trait onduleux, les extrémités des parenthèses s'enroulant en colimaçon comme les motifs de ces grilles rongées de rouille qui gardent encore l'entrée de parcs envahis par les ronces [.] (p. 83)[23]

The 'trait onduleux', linking two adjacent frames, can be read as a sign of the transfer of elements from one narrative context to another. A more complex sign of this compositional feature is the fragment of an Italian manuscript which describes a print representing a female centaur and focuses on the indeterminate point of metamorphosis between woman and horse:

le noeud et la jointure où la partie umaine finit avec la partie cheval est certainement admirable l'ôeil distingue la délicattefse de la blanche carnation dans la femme de la netteté du pelage éclatant dans la bette d'un bay clair mais on confond ensuite en voulant déterminer les Confins [.] (pp. 55–6)[24]

The repetition in 'confond' and 'Confins', marking the absent frame or hinge-point between the human and the equine, reflects the double metamorphosis displayed by the manuscript. Paralleling the dual nature of the centauress, the text is written as an attempted, incomplete translation eliding from French to Italian. Thus on both levels, that of language and that of its referent, of 'signifiant' and 'signifié', the fragment oscillates between two divergent contexts.

Georges's perception of the external world is presented along similar lines in that his visual field, 'cette sorte de frange qui s'étend à droite et à gauche de notre vue', often does not enclose clearly defined, nameable objects but a spattering of sense-data 'sous forme de taches, de vagues contours' (p. 250).[25] In the case of the dead horse encountered on the road by the depleted platoon, perception of its fluctuating contours is due to the fact that the observer, Georges mounted on his own horse, is mobile. Mobility of the subject of perception is thus transposed onto the object of vision:

> les contours se modifiant d'une façon continue, c'est-à-dire cette espèce de destruction et de reconstruction simultanée des lignes et des volumes (les saillies s'affaissant par degrés tandis que d'autres reliefs semblent se soulever, se profilent, puis s'affaissent et disparaissent à leur tour) au fur et à mesure que l'angle de vue se déplace [.] (p. 29)[26]

But the subject need not be in physical motion for the field of vision and the objects it encapsulates to adopt a fluid and equivocal perspective. Georges's mental vision of his past, for instance, which is composed of a stream of conflicting and transmuting scenes is experienced from a point of physical immobility: the hotel bed. By elaborating a kind of Chinese box superimposition of mnemonic frames which allows elements to permeate and overlap from one anecdotal context to another, the process of memory continually distorts and displaces that which it seeks to secure within its grasp. And by a further refraction of the text's self-reflexive gaze, the effect of retroactive interference can be particularly felt at precisely those scenes which include a visual representation of frame. In one particularly vertiginous passage Georges recalls sitting at a bar, hopelessly drunk, examining a mirror which hangs at an angle above him. After dwelling on its highly ornate frame, his eyes turn to the forward inclining perspective formed by the geometrical patterns reflected in the mirror:

> et sans doute à cause de l'ivresse, impossible d'avoir visuelle-ment conscience d'autre chose que cela cette glace et ce qui s'y

reflétait à quoi mon regard se cramponnait pour ainsi dire comme un ivrogne se cramponne à un réverbère comme au seul point fixe dans un univers vague [.] (p. 207)[27]

The mirror, however, performs precisely the opposite function to that of a 'point fixe'. Inverting the relation between screen and frame, the mirror overturns the perspective of the field of vision:

cette fois je pouvais voir grace à la glace dans l'encadrement de la porte le bas de la jupe de la femme ses deux mollets et ses deux pieds chaussés de pantoufles le tout incliné comme si elle tombait en arrière [.] (p. 207)[28]

In addition to evoking the external circumstances of the memory act, namely the lovemaking between Georges and Corinne, the woman standing 'dans l'encadrement de la porte' brings to the reader's mind the description of the engraving in which the 'servante' is standing in the doorway of her bedroom 'n'ayant pas encore, elle, franchi le seuil' (p. 86),[29] and the earlier description of the 'paysanne's' silhouette at the barn entrance:

sa silhouette se découpant un instant en sombre tant qu'elle fut dans le pénombre de la grange, puis, sitôt le seuil franchi, semblant s'évanouir [.] (p. 39)[30]

The repeated visual image of a woman hesitating momentarily on the border-line of frame is related to the web of associations denoting the motif of sexuality and eroticism as one of the main vehicles for Georges's pursuit of identity and knowledge. The description of the soldiers' nocturnal arrival at the village, which, as I argued in the previous section, introduces the motif of femininity as a dominant structural force, is suffused with an atmosphere of womb-like engulfment. The soldiers enter the barn, 'comme s'ils avaient pénétré [. . .] dans une sorte d'espace organique, viscéral' (p. 38) at the centre of which Georges perceives the woman: 'cette sorte de tiédeur pour ainsi dire ventrale au sein de laquelle elle se tenait' (p. 39).[31] The farm woman is defined as a crucible, a source, 'l'orifice de cette matrice le creuset original qu'il lui semblait voir dans les entrailles du monde' from which flows the endless stream of humanity in the shape of armies 'se multipliant grouillant se répandant sur la surface de la terre' (p. 42).³² Crudely parodying the drift of Georges's thoughts, Blum short-circuits the metaphorical digressions of his comrade's narrative and points directly at the transgressive nature of the sexual act:

> elle semble attendre un acte de précision et d'une nudité sinon chirurgicale comme le suggère l'idée de quelque chose qui perce, pénètre, s'enfonce en crissant dans l'étroite chair, du moins presque médical [.] (p. 192)³³

Some of the conclusions drawn by myth-conscious commentators who interpret the erotic motif in *La Route des Flandres* along neo-Freudian obsessional lines are myopic to the extent that they preclude all the other areas of textual signification with which this motif is crucially related. Thus, Georges's penetration of the female body through the sexual act is not pre-eminently a desire to re-experience 'the protected existence of the foetus' in the womb of the 'archetypal Good Mother'³⁴ but a thematic variant among others (some mentioned above) of the general structure of frame transgression which underlies the whole novel. Similarly, and on a more detailed point, the allusion to the milky light glowing from the farm woman's body is not to be read exclusively as a sign of the subliminal lure of the 'primal liquid' flowing from the maternal breast, although this may form part of the clutch of connotations surrounding the reference, but its significance lies no less in a number of other avenues of textual exploration. On an intertextual level, the reference mirrors the milky whiteness of Cupid's neck ('cervices lacteas') revealed to Psyche by the light shed from her candle as she imprudently relents to her indomitable 'curiositas' in the 'mise en abyme' story at the centre of Apuleius's *The Golden Ass*. (The close ties between this novel and *La Route des Flandres* will be discussed in the following section.) Furthermore, the glow of milky light relates to the image of the crucible which dominates the passage describing Georges's vision of the farm woman. 'Creuset' derives from the Old French 'croiseul' and Latin 'crucibolum' meaning 'night lamp'; an etymological association which is not only pertinent to the lamp held by the 'paysanne' as she ushers the soldiers to the barn, but also to Georges's view of her body as source of light. The range of the metaphor of the crucible, the 'space' in question, extends beyond any local reference to the internal life-giving space of the womb: it evokes and, to a certain

The Framework of La Route des Flandres   35

extent, provokes a reaction against the idealist, taxonomic assumptions behind the mimetic view of art. A seminal component of Plato's cosmogony in the *Timaeus* is his conception of an idealised space, a 'mother substance' which is essentially invisible and formless but which takes shape on 'receiving the impressions' of the elements. Pursuing his analogy further, Plato marks out the precise divisions between the natural forces which constitute the mimetic principle of life:

> For the present we have only to conceive of three natures: first, that which is in the process of generation; secondly, that in which the generation takes place; and thirdly, that of which the thing generated is a resemblance. And we may liken the receiving principle to a mother, and the source or spring to a father, and the intermediate nature to a child [.]35

But Plato's notion of 'generation' or 'becoming' (γιγόμενον) is intended to signify a faithful reproduction of an ideal model, for the world is a 'copy', or icon, 'framed in the likeness of that which is apprehended by reason and mind and is unchangeable'.36 Transposing this three-part division of nature onto the domain of art, one may conclude that external reality, the source of art, is the father; the *a priori* conditions of art, that invisible yet formative matrix which moulds the principle of generation and reflection, in a word its frame, is the mother; and the work itself, the product, is the child. By conferring on the woman figure the status of space as origin, the image of the crucible in *La Route des Flandres* blends the ternary structure of idealist perspective into a continuous, self-generating process. The 'paysanne' embodies the generative process of language, her luminescence serving as a visual analogue of 'les images chatoyantes et lumineuses' produced by the incantatory magic of language (p. 184). The artistic text, no longer viewed as a 'receiving vessel', as being enclosed in an external or idealised frame, elaborates its own space, projected from an internal, infinitely elusive source of generation. But Georges, bent on the discovery of an 'absent telos'37 or elusive truth lying behind the screen of the observable world, is anxious to pierce through the veil of language and empirical data. A noteworthy example of this attitude is his interpretation, as a child, of the crack on the surface of the portrait of de Reixach's ancestor as deliberately representing the blood-stained wound sustained on the putative occasion of his suicide. Georges's interest in the truth concerning the man's life, described to him so often by his mother Sabine, prompted him to scour the wall behind the painting for traces of the bullet. The discovery that language and signs are ultimately opaque, that attainment of hidden truths and universal meanings is illusory entails, in Georges's case, disenchantment with the sexual act:

> qu'avais-je cherché en elle espéré poursuivi jusque sur son corps dans son corps des mots des sons aussi fou que lui avec ses illusoires feuilles de papier noircies de pattes de mouches des paroles que prononçaient nos lèvres pour nous abuser nous-mêmes vivre une vie de sons sans plus de réalité sans plus de consistance que ce rideau sur lequel nous croyions voir le paon brodé remuer palpiter respirer [.] (pp. 274–5)[38]

Negation of the 'au-delà' of language ('la disparition de toute idée de tout concept' (p. 299)),[39] of acceding to an ever-receding essence or reality beyond language, is related to a negation of interlocutors and consequently of narration:

> Ce n'était pas à son père qu'il voulait parler. Ce n'était pas à la femme couchée invisible à côté de lui, ce n'était peut-être même pas à Blum qu'il était en train d'expliquer en chuchotant dans le noir [.] (p. 100)[40]

To define this relationship as causal, to view the ambiguity of the narrative frame as being responsible for the indeterminacy of the narrative content would be to give no more than a partial account of the structural relations subtending this novel. Multiplicity of point of view does indeed destabilise and disperse the phenomenal world Georges initially sets out to comprehend and recreate. But narrative multiplicity is not imposed externally on the novel out of an ideological impulse to counter the fixed and single point of view of traditional perspective inherited from the Renaissance. Plurality of perspective is internally, and in its own turn, created by the generative power of language. The dove-tailed relationship between content, perspective and language is subtly, and self-consciously, elaborated in the textual play around the idea of frame. After a final negation of frame, 'Mais l'avais-je vraiment vu ou cru le voir ou tout simplement imaginé après coup ou encore rêvé, peut-être dormais-je n'avais-je jamais cessé de dormir les yeux grands ouverts' (p. 314),[41] the novel ends with a metaphor of the neutrality of fiction and narration in which the 'vie de sons' is the only distinctive feature of an otherwise empty frame:

> le canon sporadique frappant les vergers déserts avec un bruit sourd monumental et creux comme une porte en train de battre agitée par le vent dans une maison vide [.] (p. 314)[42]

III INTERTEXTUAL PARADIGM: METAPHORS OF THE POETIC IMPULSE IN APULEIUS, NERVAL, PROUST, AND SIMON

When Lucien de Rubempré in Balzac's *Illusions perdues* writes to his sister that the illustrious men of an epoch, and by that he means poets like himself, are 'les oiseaux de la forêt' because 'ils chantent, ils charment la nature, et nul ne doit les apercevoir'[43] he provides a classic example of the expressive view of art dominated by the ideal of oneness and homogeneity. The poet qua social individual withdraws from the world only to pervade it more completely through a kind of pantheistic omnipresence. And just as the gap between the poet and nature is eliminated, so too the world's reception of his work is construed as a kind of spontaneous wonderment, an effortless absorption of its charm and beauty which is unbroken by any sense of time or distance. While reserving for the novelist the task of uncovering the 'mécanisme de toutes choses' governing social reality, Balzac sees poetry as a mystical and instantaneous communication of truth and essence through the lyrical medium of music and song:

> Cette cohésion d'âmes manque-t-elle, le poète se trouve alors comme un ange essayant de chanter un hymne céleste au milieu des ricanements de l'enfer.[44]

Prior to Balzac's expressive version of the image of poet as songbird in the forest, Chateaubriand had spoken of the magic sound of a thrush which evoked memories of the same bird in his youth, thereby transporting him into the past:

> Hier au soir je me promenais seul [. . .] je fus tiré de mes réflexions par le gazouillement d'une grive perchée sur la plus

haute branche d'un bouleau. A l'instant, ce son magique fit reparaître à mes yeux le domaine paternel; j'oubliai les catastrophes dont je venais d'être le témoin, et, transporté subitement dans le passé, je revis ces campagnes où j'entendis si souvent siffler la grive.[45]

Whereas for Lucien the bird in the forest is a metaphor of the poet himself, for Chateaubriand the song of the thrush is a metaphor of the transporting powers of memory. And in contrast with the immediate cohesion of souls between poet and audience envisaged by Balzac, Chateaubriand's experience is based on a sense of spatio-temporal breadth; a breadth which is admittedly telescoped by the memory of the thrush's song but which equally depends on an awareness of a distance separating two lived moments of the self. In one case poetry is defined as an act of union or 'redoublement' between subject and audience, in the other the poetic experience is seen as producing a feeling of division or 'dédoublement' within the subject himself. Proust, who quotes the Chateaubriand passage in *Le Temps retrouvé* as an example of a prior work which has been concerned with the same aesthetic impressions as those at the heart of *A la recherche du temps perdu*, was to build upon Chateaubriand's reference to the songbird and to confer on the image a crucial structural significance by inserting it at the start of his novel:

Je me demandais quelle heure il pouvait être; j'entendais le sifflement des trains qui plus ou moins éloigné, comme le chant d'un oiseau dans une forêt relevant les distances, me décrivait l'étendue de la campagne déserte où le voyageur se hâte vers la station prochaine.[46]

The image is now not only a metaphor of the process of memory, but a metaphor of the process of metaphor. Furthermore, Proust's image stresses the fact that the bird's song evokes an expanse of distance and the image of the train or of the voyage is now presented as the movement of association from one point of time to another, from one point of analogy to another. The instantaneous cohesion has been stretched apart and both the poetic experience and the reader's response to the text which is woven by that experience can best be described as an unending and circuitous journey.

The title alone of *La Route des Flandres* will alert the reader to the strong possibility that the road as metaphor is consciously deployed throughout Simon's novel. It is also an image which can be suitably applied both to the narrative progression and, as Stuart Sykes suggests, to the process of reading the novel:

l'errance des cavaliers se double de celle du lecteur, ceux qui se perdent sur la route des Flandres imitent ceux qui risquent de s'égarer dans *La Route des Flandres*, victimes, ensemble, d'une confuse sensation du 'déjà vu/lu'.[47]

However, the notion of 'losing one's way' is misleading here in so far as it presupposes the converse possibility of arriving at a destination, something which neither Proust nor Simon ever imply.

The particular course which my reading will follow in this section will therefore remain open-ended, an intertextual reading which neither claims to be a discovery of sources of influence nor poses as a master-key to the novel's secret mysteries, but it does argue that the 'route torse', to use Chlovsky's phrase, followed by the narrative, the plurality emanating from the circular perspective of 'déjà vu/lu', need not lead to sterile confusion, but to a creative participation in the multiple directions of textual signification.

A network of connections between *La Route des Flandres*, Proust's *A la recherche du temps perdu*, Nerval's *Sylvie* and Apuleius's *The Golden Ass* is woven around the assumption shared by those works that the creative process is primarily a movement towards an unattainable goal. The movement may be external or internal, in space or time, forward or backward, through sensory perception or memory, but it is always one that the different narrators are constrained to make in the dark, groping with little or no sense of direction. It is in the middle of the night that Gérard[48] returns to le Valois, the setting of his youth, via 'la route de Flandre'. Proust's *A la recherche*, echoing the 'demi-somnolence' in which Gérard's youth is reawakened in his mind, begins with a description of the momentary loss of self experienced in the nocturnal half-sleep out of which the whole novel evolves. It is in the dark that Georges, either in bed with Corinne or in the train with Blum, recalls his past. And Lucius's picaresque wanderings in the metaphorical darkness as an ass are set in motion when, at twilight, spurred on by an insatiable desire for knowledge, he rubs himself with the magic ointment which he mistakenly believes will transform him into an owl. Lucius's peregrinations take place, as Robert Graves says, 'from one rose-season to the next'[49], for roses provide the only anti-dote to the magic potion, and remain tantalisingly beyond his reach throughout the novel until the final intervention by the Goddess Isis. There is a direct allusion to the Latin author and his novel at the start of *Sylvie* when Gérard admits to belonging to an age which bears similarities with that of Peregrinus and Apuleius:

> L'homme matériel aspirait au bouquet de roses qui devait le régénérer par les mains de la belle Isis; la déesse éternellement jeune et pure nous apparaissait dans la nuit, et nous faisait honte de nos heures de jour perdues.[50]

The myth of Isis, the Moon-Goddess, is present throughout *Sylvie* but it is particularly apparent in the depiction of Aurélie and Adrienne. Influenced by his uncle's dictum that actresses are not real women since they have no heart, Gérard accounts for his interest in Aurélie with the words: 'c'est une image que je poursuis, rien de plus'.[51] In Gérard's mind, Aurélie is an image of Adrienne, a metaphorical relationship which is based on a close visual resemblance ('Aimer une religieuse sous la forme d'une actrice'[52]). However, Adrienne herself is no more than an evanescent image radiating an aura of infinite reflection which is conveyed by the way her voice imitates 'par un frisson modulé la voix tremblante des aïeules'[53] as well as by her ethereal apparition imbued with the pale moonlight suggestive of Isis in particular and of cultural heritage in general:

> fleur de la nuit éclose à la pâle clarté de la lune, fantôme rose et blond glissant sur l'herbe verte à demi baignée de blanches vapeurs.[54]

Although *A la recherche* makes no mention of *The Golden Ass* or of its author, the novel emulates *Sylvie* in associating moments of creative inspiration with the rose (either as flower, or its concomitant colour in the French language, pink).[55] For Marcel, the irresistible attraction of both Gilberte and Albertine is due to the visual allure of pinkness. The setting of Gilberte's initial apparition is dominated by the pink hawthorns from behind which she appears to emerge;[56] and the sexual feelings which Albertine arouses in the narrator stem from the enchanting pinkness radiating from her body. There is always a promise of an essence lying behind this colour, and Marcel's eager anticipation of the long-awaited secret meeting with Albertine betrays an excitement at the prospect of tasting the forbidden fruit of knowledge: 'j'allais savoir l'odeur, le goût qu'avait ce fruit rose inconnu'.[57] But if, as I have been arguing, the distance between the subject and the inaccessible ideal is often expressed by the metaphor of the road or journey, then this is most evident in the description of Marcel's train journey to Balbec at sunrise in *A l'ombre des jeunes filles en fleur*. Looking out of his carriage window, Marcel becomes engrossed with the view of a pink trace of dawn on the sky which is soon snatched away from him when the train suddenly veers in a different direction. But Marcel is deprived of 'ma bande de ciel rose' only to be presented with a substitute vision. As the train stops at a village station, the narrator is struck by the sight of a milkmaid bathed in the rosy hue of dawn approaching the train: 'Empourpré des reflets du matin, son visage était plus rose que le ciel'.[58] The vision of the milkmaid is more than just a pleasurable sensory or aesthetic experience for Marcel, it awakens in him the desire to accede to a hidden realm:

> cette belle fille que j'apercevais encore, tandis que le train accélérait sa marche, c'était comme une partie d'une vie autre que celle que je connaissais, séparée d'elle par un liséré et où les sensations qu'éveillaient les objets n'étaient plus les mêmes, et d'où sortir maintenant eût été comme mourir à moi-même.[59]

The interrelated imagery I have been describing is recast in *La Route des Flandres*, though the extent to which Simon's novel distorts them can be gauged from the fact that they have escaped the notice of commentators in the twenty years following the novel's publication. Admittedly, the backcloth of war, imprisonment, escape, and the explicitly erotic passages place the novel on a more violent emotional register than the more restrained *Sylvie* and *A la recherche*. But the difference is mainly one of tone and no more fundamental than the shift of emphasis from pink to red, a colour which is associated with Corinne in particular. Despite these variations, one can discern the same pursuit of an unattainable essence in *La Route des Flandres* as in the earlier works. Aside from the title, there are many parallels between *La Route des Flandres* and *Sylvie*. Just as in the latter work Gérard takes the road back (both in time and space) to his vision of Adrienne, the inaccessible ideal, so too Georges sees the peasant woman who prefigures Corinne and is glimpsed briefly at the village as the ultimate objective of his otherwise aimless military meanderings:

> comme si toute cette interminable chevauchée nocturne n'avait eu d'autre raison, d'autre but que la découverte à la fin de cette chair diaphane dans l'épaisseur de la nuit [.] (p. 41)[60]

The Watteau-like setting of the 'fête de l'arc' in the woods of le Valois is also transposed, with certain modifications, to the woods in which Georges finds himself after the destruction of his platoon and prior to his reunion with de Reixach and the death of the latter:

> je me tins debout au milieu de la route dans la sylvestre paix où je pouvais toujours entendre les coucous et de temps en temps le rapide invisible et paresseux saut d'un poisson hors de l'inaltérable miroir de l'eau [.] (p. 164)[61]

The passage depicts a 1940 war-time 'voyage à Cythère' with the same reflexive waters, the sylvan peacefulness (ironically evoking the name Sylvie), and the repeated reference to the song of the cuckoo which, reminiscent of the cuckoo clock belonging to Gérard's concierge, provides an interesting variant of the image of 'l'oiseau dans la forêt'. As well as denoting the passage of time, the cuckoo is also a figure representing death. In his imaginative reconstruction of the events surrounding the ancestor's suicide, Georges suggests that three decapitated ducks rather than three (unmutilated) doves would have made a more fitting emblem of the de Reixach family:

> rien qu'une histoire de cous coupés en somme puisque selon la tradition la version la flatteuse légende familiale c'était pour éviter la guillotine que l'autre l'avait fait [.] (p. 90)[62]

The 'coucou' heard in the forest echoes, through 'cous coupés', Georges's fascination with death which is conceived as a desire to penetrate the 'au-delà', the elusive realm reached through an act of transgression ('comme on passe de l'autre côté d'un miroir' (p. 259)).[63] But the obsession with death is merely a variant of the central poetic motif, for the cuckoo is also a mirror-image of Corinne, and women in general, and therefore leads on to the metaphor of transgression through the sexual act. There is a constant textual association between birds and women which is produced either through metonymic juxtaposition as, for instance, the reference to the woman standing behind the undulating curtain with the peacock design, or through metaphorical assimilation, as in Georges's description of the sensation of touching Corinne:

> je posai la main sur elle juste au milieu c'était comme du duvet de légères plumes d'oiseau un oiseau dans la main mais aussi un buisson proverbe anglais [.] (p. 275)[64]

The same image is used by Georges in his account of the first meeting with Corinne when he describes the sensation of touching her arm as being similar to picking up a bird in his hand. His description also dwells on the perception of a film, a barrier no thicker than a sheet of paper, interposed between himself and Corinne. Like the 'liséré' separating Marcel from the universe of the milkmaid, these symbols of frame stimulate the desire for transgression and it is through the sexual act that this desire is momentarily fulfilled. For a brief instant the transgression is achieved:

> comme si nous avions un instant été vidés tout entiers comme si notre vie toute entière s'était précipitée avec un bruit de cataracte vers et hors de nous s'arrachant s'extirpant hors de nous de moi de ma solitude [.] (p. 265)[65]

The transgression is momentary in so far as the outward flow by which the self is freed, transported through a kind of erotic metempsychosis, promptly turns into a refluent wave which surges back to sweep the self back within the confines of its own identity: 'de nouveau emprisonné, heurtant avec fureur les parois les étroites et indépassables limites'.[66] Indeed it is perhaps misleading to say that any effective transgression ever takes place in the erotic passages since, as the repeated use of 'comme si' suggests, the sexual act is again only a metaphor, a fictional enactment of the underlying creative impulse. Seen in this light, the allusions to Apuleius provide an intertextual confirmation of the desire for 'carnal knowledge' whereby the subject, through striving to break out of himself and into the realm of the unknown, is metamorphosed into the shape of an animal:

> je n'étais plus un homme mais un animal un chien plus qu'un homme une bête si je pouvais y atteindre connaître l'âne d'Apulée [.] (p. 292)[67]

The only effectual transgression in *La Route des Flandres* is of the textual kind: it is by means of the associative play of language and the discontinuous articulation of the narrative that Georges, qua textual construct, straddles two landscapes: Flanders and Corinne's body. Among some of the words which act as hinge-points between the two contexts,[68] the reader will not be surprised to find, given the intertextual background I have been reviewing, the word 'rose' serving as the vehicle of transition. Georges, like his forerunners Lucius, Gérard, and Marcel, is mesmerised by the colour 'pink' on several occasions including his escape from captivity when the first object he sights is a pink rag draped over a hawthorn hedge ('la tache rose luisant faiblement dans la pénombre' (p. 251)),[69] and also during his nocturnal exploration of Corinne's body ('lappant son chose rose' (p. 257)). A few pages later the text operates a double shift between the two contexts by pivoting precisely on the words 'rosée' and 'rose':

> les aubes grises l'herbe aussi était grise couverte de rosée que je buvais la buvant par là toute entière la faisant entrer en moi toute entière [. . .] pressant buvant son ventre les boules de ses seins fuyant sous mes doigts comme de l'eau une goutte cristalline rose tremblant sur un brin incliné sous cette légère et frissonante brise qui précède le lever du soleil reflétant contenant dans sa transparence le ciel teinté par l'aurore [.] (p. 260)[70]

For Claude Simon the metaphor of the road serves above all to describe the process of writing which, to a large extent, has engendered his fictional work. It is a process in which a number of key words, like 'rose' in the passages mentioned above, appear as 'carrefours où plusieurs routes s'entrecroisent'.[71] These verbal crossroads are intersected by several chains of signification which deflect the narrative onto unexpected paths of digression, entice the reader into elaborating his own patterns of association, and delay the ultimate encapsulation of the fluid text within the boundaries of a solid narrative frame. All of which is possible only when author and reader jettison the notion of language as a transparent medium whose purpose is to express and translate a pre-existing nonverbal reality, and instead focus their attention on the 'materiality' of language:

Et si, plutôt que de [. . .] traverser rapidement ces carrefours en ayant déjà décidé du chemin à suivre, on s'arrête et on examine ce qui apparaît à leur lueur ou dans les perspectives ouvertes, des ensembles insoupçonnés de résonances et d'échos se révèlent.[72]

At certain points of the novel, the paronomastic potential of a word is released in the form of a short burst of intense phonetic association, as in 'moule poulpe pulpe vulve' (p. 53), 'la même houri la même haletante hoquetante haquenée' (p. 296), and 'Liessies, comme leisse kermesse Hénin nénnin Hirson hérisson hirsute' (p. 309).[73] Elsewhere the textual ramification of words is more implicit and diffuse, extending over the whole novel by means of amphibological repetition. One example of this is the chain of relations stemming from the word 'sailli' which refers respectively, and at times simultaneously, to horse-riding, sexuality, and formal perspective. Linking up with the pun in 'chevaucher' and the description of Corinne as 'l'alezanne-femme', the word is used to refer to de Reixach's race meetings, 'discutant de saillies (bêtes et humains)' (p. 20) and to his sexual prowess, 'qui avait chevauché, sailli sa femme ni plus ni moins qu'une jument' (p. 283).[74] And as if to highlight self-consciously the contextual transference which can be actuated by its polysemic potential, the word appears in a description of frame instability, when Georges perceives the dead horse as a mass of changing contours: its meaning here is that of 'protrusion', in the sense of formal relief.[75]

In conclusion, the plurality of textual connections cannot, of course, be reduced by any critic to a single, rigid scheme. The novel itself would seem indirectly to disparage any such attempt when it pinpoints the discrepancy between the neat and methodical drawings on the Ordnance Survey map and the real itinerary taken by the soldiers:

> cette représentation schématique des évolutions des différentes unités ne tenant évidemment compte ni des accidents du terrain ni des obstacles imprévus surgis au cours du combat, les trajets réels ayant en réalité la forme de lignes brisées zigzaguant et quelquefois se recoupant s'embrouillant sur elles-mêmes [.] (p. 299)[76]

In *Contre Sainte–Beuve*, Proust observes a similar parallel between two types of journeys in *Sylvie* and remarks on the fact that the intermingling of past and present in Nerval's work forces the reader to turn back the pages in order to determine the temporal frame of the lines he is reading at a particular moment:

> Il [Gérard] arrive après cette nuit d'insomnie ce qu'il voit alors, pour ainsi dire détaché de la réalité par cette nuit d'insomnie, par ce retour dans un pays qui est pour lui un passé qui existe au moins autant dans son coeur que sur la carte, est entremêlé si étroitement aux souvenirs qu'il continue à evoquer, qu'on est obligé à tout moment de tounrer les pages qui précèdent pour voir où on se trouve, si c'est présent ou rappel du passé.[77]

The intriguing question as to how Proust would have responded to *La Route des Flandres* and Simon's opus as a whole, where the intermingling of time spans and the practice of frame transgression in general is developed to a far greater degree, must, unfortunately, remain unanswered.

3
The Framework of *Le Palace*, *Histoire* and *Les Géorgiques*

I VARIATIONS OF NARRATIVE FRAME

More than a synonym for 'narrative structure', the concept of 'narrative frame' which I have been employing so far refers to the system of narrative order emanating from a stable 'point fixe' which in most conventional novels either takes the form of a reliable narrator (as in first person narratives) or a fixed spatio-temporal setting (as in third person narratives). In other words, as Uspensky and Lotman underline in their reference to visual art, the stress is on perspective. Narrative frame is the perspective from which the narration is formulated, as well as the perspective from which the reader can decode this formulation. However, the main characteristic of the 'nouveau roman' is that this frame is fundamentally undermined. As the previous chapter showed, the 'point fixe' of narrative perspective in *La Route des Flandres* is missing. Whilst the narrative perspective in this novel may be described as the self-conscious awareness of an 'absent frame', in *Le Palace* the perspective is one of 'multiple frame', and in *Histoire* it may be termed 'frame shift'. The profound disintegration of narrative perspective which gathers pace in *La Bataille de Pharsale* and culminates in *Les Géorgiques* will be discussed later.

A crude distinction between *La Route des Flandres* and *Le Palace* is that the former novel is written (more or less completely) in the first person narrative while the second is in the third person narrative. But such a distinction is clearly unsatisfactory since neither novel is structured in such an unambiguous way. Although the central character in *Le Palace* appears in the third person, it is nevertheless from his point of view that most of the events in the novel are narrated. However, the actual narration is in the third person and is thus situated outside the consciousness of the main character. The instance of narration is, as Dominique Lanceraux says,[1] 'un présent de l'écriture'. Furthermore, the narrative covers two separate time spans. The novel begins with a description of events taking place in Barcelona (though the city is never named) at the time of the civil war. A few pages later a new time span is introduced:

> Puis il se vit, c'est-à-dire des années plus tard, et lui, ce résidu de lui-même, ou plutôt cette trace, cette salissure (cet excrément en quelque sorte) laissée derrière soi: dérisoire personnage que l'on voit s'agiter, ridicule et présomptueux, là-bas, très loin, comme dans le petit bout de la lorgnette, gesticulant, répétant éternellement à la demande de la mémoire [. . .] répétant indéfiniment la même tranche de vie, importun, odieux, s'imposant s'immisçant de force – pouvant donc se voir avec une sorte d'étonnement un peu agace, d'incrédulité, pensant: 'Ça: moi? Ça . . . ?' regardant le double microscopique et effaré de lui-même: c'était presque quinze ans plus tard [.] (p. 20)[2]

The student has now returned, fifteen years later, to Barcelona and is reconstructing his former visit in his mind. The introduction of a new time span is accompanied by a consciousness of 'dédoublement' on the part of the protagonist. However, unlike *La Route des Flandres* and *Histoire*, the narrative framework of *Le Palace* is not itself seriously damaged by 'dédoublement'. This is partly due to the fact that the novel is in the third person narrative and is consequently less prone to shift of narratorial identity, but also partly because the novel is based on a principle of multiplicity of frame or of narrative 'redoublement'. Thus the student's experiences in Barcelona 1936 are mirrored in his experience in the same city fifteen years later. Furthermore, the narrative of the student's experiences is itself paralleled by the narrative of the Italian anarchist, 'l'homme-récit'. Although the shifts from one narrative to the other often produce ambiguity and although there are many similarities and points of contact between the different layers of discourse, the novel contains no crisis of narratorial identity.

Dominique Lanceraux's analysis of this novel implicitly acknowledges the relative stability of the narrative framework:

Le Palace, Histoire *and* Les Géorgiques 49

L'Italien, l'étudiant, le scripteur: trois voix (rôles, instances) narratives qui se superposent, s'entrecroisent, imprimant son mouvement au texte; celle qui rapporte les conditions de l'écoute et organise sa propre 'entente': L'étudiant 'lit' dans le Récit de l'homme-fusil ce qu'il se rappellera s'être représenté de l'épisode; celle enfin qui réalise l'inscription.[3]

The three 'voices' are separated from one another by their different functions. The Italian is 'l'homme-récit', driven by an indomitable urge to recount, as John Sturrock has noted:

The function of the Italian in the novel is to be the Story-teller with a capital S, and his ultimate suicide is an acknowledgement that the need for him is now past, that the story has now been told.[4]

The student's function is one of reassessment and reconstruction. Thus, there are frequent references to the student visualising the events which the Italian relates to him. The student's function is as futile as the Italian's. The former strives after cognition ('Mais pourquoi raconte-t-il tout ça?' (pp. 58, 76))[5] and the latter struggles to give an accurate description of the past, the futility of which is expressed by the detailed, geometrical sketch which he draws on a piece of paper (pp. 60–3). The 'scripteur', finally, is the anonymous third person narrative which structures the novel's composition placing its various elements, including the characters, in relation with one another.

The compartmental nature of *Le Palace's* narrative structure distinguishes it from the structure of *La Route des Flandres*. In the latter novel the narrator is at once story-teller, interpreter, and, fictively at least, 'scripteur'. In *Le Palace* the three functions are kept apart.[6] However, despite this functional division, a sense of ambiguity and confusion may arise from the continuous flow of the writing, the innumerable shifts from one time span to the next, and from the absence of explicit delineation of narrative frame. For instance, readers have experienced a certain amount of confusion with regard to the suicide at the end of the novel. Dominique Lanceraux identifies the suicide as that of the student, whereas for Anthony Pugh and John Sturrock it is the Italian who commits suicide.[7] The importance, however, lies less in deciding which reading is correct and which false than in the fact that the confusion arises at a moment of double death: the suicide of a character and the end of the novel. It is almost as if the artificial dividing line between the different narrative agents (the student, the Italian, and the anonymous narrator) dissolves and the three separate units merge into the coalescent reality of the text. The principle of 'redoublement' governing the narrative and fictional structure of the novel indirectly determines the fusion of the characters' identities:

> (l'Américain, l'Italien et l'étudiant – ou plutôt ces trois parties, ces trois fragments de lui-même qui étaient un Américain, un homme-fusil et un jeune étourneau) [.] (p. 157)[8]

Since the depiction of birds is directly related to the movement of writing in the novel, the reference to the starling indicates a desire for identification with the 'scripteur'. The desire for fusion of identity is also earlier reformulated in the student's effort to focus on 'cette invisible lamelle de temps qui isolait deux univers' (p. 96).

While *La Route des Flandres* can be described as a novel whose initial narrative frame is gradually fragmented and dispersed, *Le Palace* can be said to reveal an opposite movement of narrative development. Here the initial diversity of narrative frame is to some extent resolved in unity of identity. The narrative perspective of *Histoire* is different again. In this novel, written in the first person, there are, as in *Le Palace*, two major time spans. The main one, which may be called the 'macroscopic frame' since it englobes all the other 'micro time spans', stretches over a day in the life of the narrator who returns to his childhood home to deal with the inheritance of the property. This sequence of events alternates with another which is set in the narrator's childhood when he lived with his grandmother, uncle Charles, and his cousins Corinne and Paulou. A third series of events is also interspersed throughout the novel: the narrator's visit to Greece with his wife, Hélène. The narrator's relationship with Hélène is clouded with obscurity, the only clear facts for the reader being that the couple separated as a result of infidelity on the part of the husband and also that Hélène is now dead. For Anthony Pugh, this narrative sequence is central to the whole novel:

> l'énigme centrale de *Histoire* [. . .], le récit qui ne se laisse pas raconter, toujours brouillé, contourné, censuré. Le lecteur

imagine, construit, et détruit cette chose que l'on ne veut pas, ou ne peut pas nommer.⁹

In addition, the narrator, inspired by his mother's collection of postcards, attempts to recapture his parents' past and, with the help of a photograph, to reconstruct a moment in his uncle's youth. Thus the novel contains several time spans and yet the over-all narrative frame is unaffected. Unlike *La Route des Flandres*, there are no 'éclats de narration' in *Histoire*: all the events and imaginative reconstructions emerge from within the first narrative perspective (that is, the narrator's return to his childhood home). The 'présent d'écriture' remains, however, outside this perspective since the narrative is written in the past tense. But unlike *La Route des Flandres* which persistently focuses on the absence of global frame created by the 'présent d'écriture', the narrative in *Histoire* is distorted in a different manner. Here the subversion is not due to the undermining of the dominant narrative frame, but to a shift of narratorial identity. The shift occurs during a 'reconstruction' of uncle Charles's visit to Van Velden's studio. Paralleling the 'je'/'il' alternation which I have already discussed with respect to *La Route des Flandres*, a similar play with the personal pronoun 'je' can be found in *Histoire*. But while in the former novel the two pronouns refer to the same identity (Georges), in the latter novel it is the pronoun which remains constant while its referent is substituted or, to be more accurate, its narrative frame is substituted. In the course of his description of the painter's studio, the narrator assumes the identity of his uncle and steps into the scene from the past: 'petits gâteaux farineux Me demandais où elle les trouvait . . .' (p. 287).¹⁰ The shift of identity takes place under very Proustian circumstances. Just as the 'madeleine' acted as a vehicle for transference from the present to the past, so too the tea session with the 'petits gâteaux' at the painter's studio provides the setting for a transference, this time of identity. One can speak here of 'frame shift' since by means of the ambiguous play of the shifter 'je'¹¹ the narrator is transported into uncle Charles's past, defying the logic and conventions of narrative.¹²

II INTERCHANGEABILITY

The instance of frame shift which I have been considering is immediately preceded by a striking description of visual superimposition:

> chaque image empiétant sur la précédente ou plutôt semblant dériver d'elle engendrée par elle en quelque sorte se décollant d'elle comme si elles étaient toutes emboîtées les unes dans les autres à la façon de ces tables gigognes [.] (p. 287)[13]

Similarly, earlier in the novel a sense of spatio-temporal overlap is created by a succession of paragraphs describing the numerous postcards which the narrator comes across inadvertently. The passage consists of a succession of different spatio-temporal settings:

> et un peu plus tôt (huit heures ou neuf heures du matin peut-être, à Saigon (p. 255)
> et peut-être une heure dans la matinée à Eberfeld (p. 255)
> et environ midi la fin de la matinée à Tamatave (p. 256)
> et deux heures de l'après-midi (Singapore) (p. 256)
> et trois heures de l'après-midi (Jura) (pp. 259–60)
> et trois heures de l'après-midi (Singapore) (p. 260)
> et cinq heures du soir (Helvétia) (pp. 260–1)
> et onze heures du matin à Zanzibar (p. 261)
> et cinq heures du soir (Hérault) (p. 262)[14]

The stream of postcards and the images of the past which they evoke create a sense of osmosis which finally floods over the barriers of time and space erected by the reasoning consciousness:

> et aucune heure aucun temps mille ans avant
> ou après et avant quoi et après quoi et pas
> de l'eau mais une étendue jaunâtre boueuse qui
> s'écoule glisse dans un clapotis monotone [.] (p. 262)[15]

The description of the postcards leads immediately on to the chapter which is entirely devoted to the Van Velden photograph which in turn acts as the context of the frame shift mentioned above. The shift of identity is therefore preceded by an emphatic reiteration of the motif of osmosis and interchangeability.

The reader can measure the degree of compositional frame play in both *Le Palace* and *Histoire* by tracing the motif of interchangeability on the narrative, thematic, and descriptive levels of the novel. I have already argued that the desire for transference of identity forms the focal point of both these novels. In the former novel the student identifies himself with the other characters to the point of confusing the reader as to who commits suicide at the end. In the latter novel the narrator actuates the shift by assuming the identity of his uncle. But there is also a parallel way in which the narrative structure of these novels is dominated by this motif.

As C.-G. Bjurström has noted,[16] the episode which is recounted by the Italian in *Le Palace* (the assassination) in 'reality' only lasted a few seconds, while its narration and the subsequent 'reconstruction' made by the student extends over thirty pages. The simultaneity of the event cannot be reproduced by the narration which must content itself with a consecutive description. This discrepancy between fiction and reality, or between description and its referent, is even more striking at the start of the novel where the student's perusal of the interior of the building is translated into seven paragraphs each beginning with an enumeration, 'premièrement', 'deuxièmement' and so on. An equivalent example can be found in *Histoire*: namely, the passage where the narrator attempts to reconstitute the setting of the photograph. The task is made even more difficult here by the fact that the reconstruction tries to encompass what happened immediately before and immediately after the picture was taken. Once again the discrepancy between description and its referent is accentuated by expressions such as 'Ainsi tout d'abord . . .'. The inevitable failure of all writing to represent accurately an external referent renders all interpretative variations equally valuable, as in the case of the three versions of the studio scene proposed by the narrator. The different fabrications of the memory or of the imagination which form the content of the narrative in both novels are, therefore, interchangeable.

Interchangeability on the level of theme is a very common feature of the novels. Firstly, the motif of 'sameness' is repeated throughout. For instance, on his return to the city, the main character in *Le Palace* is struck by the faces of the people around him: 'les mêmes regards, les mêmes visages inusables impénétrables, interchangeables et sans âge' (p. 44).[17] Equally the description of Van Velden's painting in *Histoire* stresses its interchangeability with the thousands of other nude paintings. The word 'même' is repeated thirteen times in the space of one paragraph (p. 270). The themes of commerce and revolution also provide both novels with ample opportunity for highlighting the dominant motif of interchangeability. But there is one particular manifestation of this motif which is of special relevance to my analysis since it is bound up with the simultaneity/successivity antithesis mentioned above. In *Le Palace* history is described as being constituted 'au moyen non de simples migrations mais d'une série de mutations internes, de déplacements moléculaires' (p. 12).[18] The 'palace' itself experiences an interchange of occupants: the decadent rich are replaced by the revolutionaries. The building itself remains. Language, too, in the description of the Italian's obsessive narration, is described in similar terms:

> comme s'il essayait d'arracher, de rejeter de lui cette violence, cette chose qui a élu domicile en lui, se sert de lui [. . .] (comme dans ces jeux où le perdant tire une carte, une figure maudite ou maléfique, qu'il lui faut à tout prix refiler à un autre avant qu'elle le condamne définitivement) le possédant, le consumant [.] (pp. 77–8)[19]

The description of the statues in *Histoire* is moulded by the same motif:

> pensant à tous deux dans le noir avec cette obscurité blafarde sur eux une uniforme couche de peinture grise qui ne les distinguait pas des draps, comme si le lit les draps leurs corps étaient faits uniformément de la même matière inanimée demi-nue dénudés ou plutôt dénués de tout dans cette solitude en quelque sorte bicéphale – apparemment intacts – en réalité en train de se décomposer à toute vitesse comme si sous la surface grise et polie semblable à du marbre travaillant s'acharnait un invisible et vorace grouillement [.] (p. 359)[20]

The delineation of internal, molecular transmutation is also present in the description of the photograph which contrasts the sharp contours of the people who remained still while the camera was in operation, with the blurred face of Van Velden who, having set

Le Palace, Histoire and Les Géorgiques 55

the automatic mechanism, did not have time to compose himself before the shot was taken:

> la trace fuligineuse laissée par le visage au cours de ses divers changements de position restituant à l'événement son épaisseur, postulant (à partir de l'unique cliché et collé à lui de part et d'autre, formant une sorte de barre quadrangulaire, de parallélépipède se prolongeant à l'infini) la double suite des instants passés et futurs, la double série, dans le même cadrage et le même décor, des positions respectivement occupées par les divers personnages avant et après [.] (p. 269)[21]

The description of the internal, molecular activity contained in an outer envelope or frame, as in the earlier examples, is here reformulated in terms of temporal depiction. The blurr in the photograph is a mark of movement, both temporal and spatial. The same frame includes the instants immediately before and after the snapshot was taken. The simultaneity/successivity opposition is re-stated in terms of an opposition between movement and immobility. But unlike the evocation of Muybridge-type photographs[22] where movement is represented in a series of snapshots which give the effect of having all been taken by one camera with a fast shutter, the description of the blurr suggests a synthesis between mobility and immobility. Movement is expressed *within* stasis. Clearly the description is heralding the narrative frame shift which is the focal point of the novel: the internal interchange of identity in the 'dédoublement' between the narrator and his uncle.

Finally, one can discern the same principle of interchangeability governing the descriptive framework of *Histoire*. In this case, two distinct descriptive or fictional contexts are related by the writing. On his way to settle the business of the inheritance with Paulou, the narrator sights his cousin's house from a distance:

> Puis plus rien que les vignes les haies de cyprès les plantations d'abricotiers et les collines de loin en loin les toits d'une maison de campagne ou d'une cave dépassant d'un bouquet de pins de platanes et d'eucalyptus et parvenu en haut de la côte je la vis: à peine plus foncée que le ciel parfaitement immobile d'ici immatérielle comme une bande horizontale de peinture soigneusement passée au pinceau au-dessus du vert acide des vignes [.] (p. 299)[23]

The following paragraph shifts to the Van Velden studio scene and begins with these lines:

> parmi les toiles accrochées au mur il y avait un paysage avec des pins et entre les branches on pouvait voir comme des éclats de ciel enchassés faits d'une pâte grasse bleutée comme des fragments d'émail [.] (p. 299)[24]

The pine trees in the landscape described in the first paragraph are repeated in the painting in the second paragraph. Moreover, the figure of speech 'comme une bande horizontale de peinture soigneusement passée au pinceau'[25] is 'materialised' in the painting hanging on the studio wall. Two independent spatio-temporal contexts are thus articulated. There is a definite foretaste here of the transgressive powers of description later to assume a much more dominant role in a work like *Leçon de choses*.

Claude Simon has admitted that it is with *Histoire* that he began to break loose from the expressive tradition of the novel genre:

> Mais c'est seulement en écrivant *Histoire* que j'ai commencé à avoir une conscience plus nette des pouvoirs et de la dynamique interne de l'écriture et à me laisser guider plus par ce que l'écriture disait – ou découvrait – que par ce que je voulais lui faire dire – ou 'recouvrir'.[26]

The descriptive framework in *Histoire* is one of hidden shifts of context beneath an apparent continuity of the flow of writing. The following passage is at first set in the context of the narrator's holiday in Greece with Hélène:

> Dans les parties du bassin où l'eau reflétait les feuillages sombres des lauriers où on voyait d'autres accumulées dans le fond vert-noir brunes visqueuses pourrissant les plus récentes rousses encore sépia collées ensemble par paquets minces pellicules de temps d'été mort invisibles dans la moitié du bac que remplissait le ciel les nuages éclatants mais après la découpe dentelée de la crête du buisson de lierre on pouvait distinguer nos images quelques unes floues comme si nous étions passés devant l'objectif emportés à toute vitesse Tu vas chez le coiffeur? (p. 380)[27]

The reflection of the 'laurier' in the 'bassin' evokes the earlier description (p. 92) of the film developing session where the 'lierre' is reflected in the 'bac'. Apart from the linguistic echo between the two scenes there is also a formal association between the visual 'dédoublement' produced by the reflection of the 'feuillages sombres des lauriers' on the surface of the water and the leaves at the bottom of the 'bassin', and the narrator looking down at 'nos images quelques unes floues' at the bottom of the 'bac'. A few lines later there is an equally hidden transition between two outwardly unrelated descriptions. The paragraph follows a 'flashback' to the narrator's childhood, focusing on the pattern of dried blood colouring the scratch marks on his knee after a fall:

> les feuillages s'agitant de nouveau: en regardant bien on pouvait voir chaque minuscule goutte de sang sèche était reliée à l'autre par des goutelettes encore plus petites microscopiques quelquefois un mince trait rouge: comme un fil de soie sur lequel on aurait fait des noeuds [.] (p. 381)[28]

The ironical 'en regardant bien'[29] denotes a shift of context to the description of the design on the priest's robe near the start of the novel:

> taches de sang éparpillées sur la croix brodée parmi les petites feuilles sombres aigues elles aussi qui s'enroulaient au croisement des bandes formant une sorte de couronne autour du coeur rouge [.] (p. 15)[30]

A common factor shared by all the foregoing examples of shifts of scene brought about by descriptive articulation is that they are precipitated by a reference to a tree or foliage ('laurier', 'lierre', 'feuillages'). Indeed the pronominal ambiguity in the opening words of the whole novel, 'l'une d'elles', contains an oblique reference to the leaves of an acacia tree brushing against the narrator's window. It has the effect of presupposing the continuous presence of nature, of linking the novel to an immeasurable ongoing process, an open frame of time. But foliage here also embodies the evanescent and delicate intermingling of eidetic and visual images induced by the creative power of the text: the 'magie lumineuse' of language.

III LES GÉORGIQUES AND BIOGRAPHICAL FRAME

Claude Simon's most recent novel returns to the mode of writing which is characterised by a prominent and probing narrative consciousness,[31] and to some familiar themes such as the rhythmic predictability of history, and the impulsive and necessarily flawed attempts to reconstitute one's own and other people's past experiences. It also contains snatches of scenes from the narrator's childhood including glimpses of characters who have already appeared in novels predating *Les Corps conducteurs*. But if, as some commentators have hastened to affirm, *Les Géorgiques* is to be grouped with the novels the author published in the sixties, it would be mistaken to infer that this novel constitutes a retrograde step in the development of Simon's 'oeuvre', for the treatment of the themes to which it returns is markedly influenced by the degree of compositional control and formal orchestration which is attained in *Triptyque* and *Leçon de choses*.

Despite the vastness of the themes of death, war, revolution, the 'mountain' of documentary material written by the illustrious Revolutionary ancestor,[32] and the phenomenological and linguistic problems which perennially confront Simon, *Les Géorgiques* is a rigorously balanced work of art. It is long and complex, but never superfluous or incoherent. The internal thread binding its disparate elements is provided by a continual, self-conscious preoccupation with narrative frame.

Rather like 'Générique' in *Leçon de choses*, the prefatory opening in *Les Géorgiques* immediately presents the reader with a bare outline of the central compositional issues at the heart of the novel as a whole. This prologue consists of a detailed description of a painting which is unnamed but bears some resemblance to David's 'Serment du Jeu de Paume'. The painting represents a military officer seated at a desk gazing at a letter which has apparently been handed to him by a subaltern who faces him standing to attention. Both men are completely naked. The reader's attention is drawn to the fact that figurative distribution of the painting is modulated on the hierarchical principle of foregrounding and backgrounding:

> Il semble que l'artiste, suivant une sélection personnelle des valeurs, ait cherché, dans la scène proposée, à nettement différencier les divers éléments selon leur importance croissante dans

son esprit comme en témoignent les factures particulières dans lesquelles il les a traités, soit, premièrement: les objets inanimés [. . .]; deuxièmement: la chair, les corps aux muscles [. . .]; troisièmement enfin: les têtes des deux personnages [.] (p. 14)³³

Whilst the soldiers' heads are given the full 'realist' treatment and are painted in oil-colours, the rest of their bodies are colourless and drawn in black lead with the cold, meticulous precision of an anatomical illustration. Finally, the inanimate objects, of least importance in the painter's apparent scale of values, are sketched in the spare, geometrical manner of an architectural design. Indeed they seem less depictions of pre-existing objects than abstract assemblages born out of the painter's imagination. The 'frontiers' traced between these shadowless forms do not circumscribe solid objects but 'des surfaces blanches qui s'emboîtent selon leurs inflexions ou leurs angles':

Il est évident que la lecture d'un tel dessin n'est possible qu'en fonction d'un code d'écriture admis d'avance par chacune des deux parties, le dessinateur et le spectateur. Ainsi, de même qu'en geometrie descriptive il est convenu que deux droites qui se croisent signifient – et non pas représentent – l'existence d'un plan, l'espace qu'enferment les murs est simplement suggéré par quelques traits indiquant les arêtes des dièdres qu'ils forment entre eux ou avec le plafond, ou encore le carrelage dont le dessin apparaît dans une perspective rigoureusement calculée. (p. 13)³⁴

The text that follows this opening description proposes a system of compositional values which is diametrically opposed to the one governing the 'David painting'. In *Les Géorgiques* it is the 'white surfaces' of the background and their interjacent contours which are thrown into relief. Thematically, this 'background' is embodied in the references to the permanence and seasonal regularity of nature and geography which serves as the main link between different people and events at different periods in history. The title itself announces, amongst other aspects of the novel, the similarity between the spirit of Virgil's poem on husbandry and the cultivation of the land, and that of the constant flow of letters written by L. S. M., the Napoleonic general, addressed to his housekeeper, Batti, containing urgent, detailed instructions on the maintenance of the vineyards, orchards, and of the various crops grown on the farm. But there is also a structural importance deriving from the prominence of background, and, in view of the salient formal considerations expressed in the prologue, it is this which constitutes the central preoccupation of the novel.

Three visual metaphors are inserted at separate intervals in the text and serve as 'mise en abyme' summaries of the compositional structure of the novel. In the final stretch of the book, Batti's attempts to decipher the letters containing L. S. M.'s telegraphic descriptions of the armies and topography surrounding him on his military expeditions are compared with the unfolding movement of Japanese paper flowers which fan out when steeped in water:

> des rectangles de papier couverts de petits signes à partir desquels (à la manière de ces microscopiques fleurs japonaises qui, precipitées dans l'eau, se gonflent, déploient des corolles insoupçonnés) se matérialisaient à nouveau la terre exigeante, les coteaux [. . .], la lente dérive des nuages, la rosée, les orages, les gelées, dans l'immuable alternance des immuables saisons. (p. 462)[35]

As well as echoing the 'surfaces blanches' in the background of the 'David painting', the allusion to the expansive process of reading exemplified by the Japanese flowers (which in Proust's novel reflect the process of involuntary memory such as that induced by the Madeleine tea cakes) sheds light on the compositional structure of *Les Géorgiques*. After the 'prelude', the first chapter of the novel proper is comprised of a rapid, staccato alternation of sentences whose frame of reference switches between an account of the protagonist's participation in the 1939–45 war, a commentary (at some points a summary, at others a re-description) on Orwell's involvement in the Spanish civil war as recounted in *Homage to Catalonia*, and extracts from L. S. M.'s documents and letters. Thus, three lives, or rather three autobiographical narratives, are juxtaposed; not intermingled to the extent of fusion, but interspersed to create an intermittent effect of three-fold counterpoint repeated at an accelerated pace. At a first reading this initial chapter can prove difficult or 'dazzling to the eye', particularly in the case of the first few pages in which a swift succession of short, referentially alternating sentences blinds the reader with a stroboscopic shimmer of information. However, like the Japanese paper flowers, this embryonic and elliptical blur of data gradually unfolds as each of the three narratives fans out into increasingly larger passages, allowing the reader a more sustained view of the fiction, until finally each of the succeeding chapters is, to a greater or lesser extent, taken up with one of the three strands of narrative.[36]

The second visual metaphor of the novel's structure is related to the one I have just described. The narrator compares Orwell's retrospective thoughts at the time of writing his account of the events in Spain with a kaleidoscope which is composed of layers of memory appearing in reverse chronological order:

comme dans ces kaléidoscopes où l'on peut voir les petites images fragmentaires d'un athlète immobilisé selon les attitudes décomposées de la course à pied, avec cette différence que le cylindre tournerait à l'envers, de sorte qu'il semblait pour ainsi dire avancer à reculons [.] (p. 360)[37]

Again, like the Japanese flowers, a kaleidoscope is based on a process of dilation where the disjointed fragments open up into a series of coloured patterns. But the analogy with the novel's structure is even more precise. The chronological regression alluded to in this analogy between memory and the kaleidoscope is paralleled by the fact that each of the ensuing chapters follows in reverse chronological, or biographical, order. Simon's war experiences unfold in the second chapter; his childhood memories in the third; Orwell's involvement in the Spanish civil war extends over the whole of the fourth chapter; and finally the fifth is entirely spanned by a reconstruction of L. S. M.'s life.

A third visual metaphor is less an image of the novel's structure than a reflection of the underlying narrative concern with the generative process of illusion and memory. The passage in question is an account of the young boy's impressions during his visits to the cinema. The exciting lure of the cinema is that it holds the promise of an accession to a hidden world of fiction lying behind the safety screen advertising the names of commercial firms by whose grace the promised spectacle will be magically materialised. Penetrating the auditorium is in itself like entering a self-enclosed, visceral world. The sprawling family groups ('primitives tribus') presided over by a numinous mother still suckling the latest offspring, occupy entire rows of seats in the stalls and exude an overpowering aura of progeniture which seems to invade the very process of filmic projection. The clouds of cigarette smoke which drift in the projection beam are described as 'une sorte de laitance, de placenta, apparaissant et disparaissant dans l'oblique et pyramidale faisceau de lumière' (p. 212).[38] The projection of the visual images onto a screen which has hitherto been 'virginal et impollué' (p. 207) thus becomes a form of endogenous creation, an outflow of ectoplasmic matter which transforms into the Hollywood screen idols who reflect back to the audience the sublimated, glamorous fictions of themselves. However, the metaphor of endogenous creation is nowhere more apposite than in the context of autobiography and genealogical retrospection. The piecemeal survey of L. S. M.'s life, and the autobiographical element in *Les Géorgiques* are thus encapsulated in the description of the womb-like setting and the progenitive process of a film performance. Indeed, the analogy is made explicit: the protagonist, likened to the hunted figure of the screen heroine whose stereotypic, victimised pose is provoked both by the stereotypic villain on the screen and by the aggressive stare of the audience, is himself plunged into 'la face cachée des choses'[39] when later in life he finds himself at the centre of war and cataclysm. He too will be hunted like a wild animal (just as Orwell had been in Barcelona) by an invisible and ubiquitous enemy who pursues him after his escape from a German POW camp. The biographical juxtaposition of these two periods in one life, with the suppression of all intervening time, is described as follows:

> deux scènes, deux tableaux, deux épisodes qui se succédaient immédiatement sur l'écran n'étaient séparés que par la brève apparition d'un placard où scintillaient [. . .] de brèves indications comme: 'Et le lendemain', ou: 'Quinze ans plus tard . . .', ou encore: 'Quelques années plus tôt . . .' (p. 215)[40]

Memory thus functions as a form of articulation and its effect resembles that of a discontinuous and elliptical narrative. It creates 'un temps soumis à de foudroyantes compressions, de foudroyantes annulations ou régressions' (p. 215)[41] wherein present and past are abruptly and incongruously juxtaposed like consecutive scenes in a silent movie tenuously held together by the laconic insert titles indicating chronological order.

Not all autobiographical writing, of course, is characterised by this two-fold discontinuity of memory and narrative. Orwell's *Homage to Catalonia*, as Simon's narrator repeatedly points out, reveals a fundamental discrepancy between the intensity and confusion of the events experienced in Spain on the one hand, and the neutrality of narrative tone and surface continuity of the writing on the other. Orwell's journalistic style is little more than written speech directed at a specific audience: 'Visiblement il écrit (ou plutôt il parle) à l'intention d'un certain public, un public dont il connaît les penchants, les opinions, peut prévoir les réactions' (p. 314).[42] Language here, unlike its use in *Les Géorgiques*, is neither a dynamic force capable of launching a diversity of narrative directions, nor is it at all scarred by the nature of the experiences it relates or by the process of memory involved at the time of writing.

Yet, despite appearances, expressive language is no more a manifestation of a fluent, linear and orderly progression of thought than any other form of writing. Its surface veneer of continuity is achieved at the expense of a conscious and sub-conscious suppression of a vast quantity of data leaving innumerable wide gaps in the narrative. For example, Orwell offers no account of his arrival in Spain, how he had come by the address of the militia headquarters in the first place, why he chose to join the POUM out of the swarm of left-wing political groups, what mental deliberations accompanied this choice, and so on. Orwell the chronicler of these events is emotionally at a far remove from them. He is described in *Les Géorgiques* as a counterpart to the narrator in Agatha Christie's *Murder of Roger Ackroyd* who conceals his identity as murderer until the end of the book. In Orwell's case, the narrator is not the assassin but the dead victim looking back on the past with detachment. It is as if O. the writer were describing an episode in the life of another man, another Orwell who was submerged in the chaos of the Spanish civil war, who was evidently overwhelmed by the sights, smells and sounds of his environment, who on being pierced through the neck by a bullet felt as though he were 'at the centre of an explosion', and for whom the whole experience in the trenches was 'magical' despite the cold, the lice, and the exhaustion that prevailed. It is with this 'other Orwell', as with L. S. M., that Simon feels a deep sympathy. What links the three men is not merely war and revolution, nor even the historical coincidence of their stays in Barcelona, but the fact that throughout their military 'careers' their sensitivity to the phenomenal world, to the barrage of colour, shape, smell, sound was sharpened all the more. In other words, throughout the historically important events in which they were embroiled, and in which their lives were at stake, their attention to the 'background' of life, to 'nature', intensified.

But such are the distorting powers of literary convention that the writing of these events introduces an *a posteriori* and artificial sense of order which erects a barrier between the subject and the field of perception. Both language and memory are seen as purveyors of the cold light of analysis, and not as infinitely changeable forms of perception. Orwell's book is written according to a scale of values which, *mutatis mutandis*, closely resembles the one obtaining in the 'David painting' described at the start of *Les Géorgiques*. The descriptions of the natural surroundings and the sense impressions which are so overwhelming in the lived experience are cursory and relegated to the background. The emphasis is on an attempt to rationalise the events, on conveying a certain message to a certain readership which is familiar with a certain code of writing. Thus the criticism, at times impassioned, which Claude Simon levels at Orwell is that implicit in the Englishman's work is the assumption that language and narration are somehow aloof and independent of the turmoil of experience; that writing, in short, is not itself another form of lived experience.

To protest on Orwell's behalf that *Homage to Catalonia* was not intended as a 'creative' work, and that one ought not to expect 'poetic writing' in a work which claims to be no more than a personal record and historical commentary is to ignore the fundamental implication of Simon's aesthetic, particularly in works like *Les Géorgiques*, *Histoire* and *Le Palace*: namely, that categories of genre and conventions of narrative structure are essentially arbitrary impositions which fail to accommodate the kaleidoscopic 'internal logic' of matter, history and language.

Part Two
Intertextuality

1
What is Intertextuality?

> But the common people I could not number, nor yet name, not even if ten tongues and ten mouths were mine, and a voice invincible, and a heart within me of bronze.
> (Homer, *Iliad*, II 488)

> Not though a hundred tongues and a hundred mouths were mine, and a voice of iron, could I tell of all the shapes of wickedness and rehearse the names of all the punishments.
> (Vergil, *Aeneid*, VI 625)

The importance of intertextuality in a poetics of modern fictional writing is confirmed by the fact that this concept has been evoked by a multitude of writers who have often ascribed different meanings to it. Yet there is still no booklength study which is exclusively devoted to establishing a common ground between the different definitions. There is certainly not enough space for such a synthesis in the present chapter. However, by outlining the general scope of these definitions it will be possible to situate Claude Simon's contribution to the concept within the current theoretical context.

I GLOBAL DEFINITION

Language belongs to everyone and no-one. Not only has each individual word in this book been used an infinite number of times by other writers and speakers but so have most of the phrases and clauses and some whole sentences. To Seneca's claims of ownership over ideas ('The best ideas are common property'; 'any truth is my own property'; 'what is well said is mine') the linguist will retort that all language is common property. The assertion is not earth-shattering when considered with reference to individual words (who would claim ownership of 'who', 'would', 'claim' etc?) but its truth can be easily overlooked when dealing with larger syntagms. An amusing example is Somerset Maugham's anecdote about a pretentious person who once exclaimed to him: 'A thing of beauty is a joy forever', which prompted the ironical rejoinder from the author that, curiously enough, Keats had said the same thing. With cliché, as with all idiomatic language, it is not just the idea expressed by the phrase but the exact words and their syntactical arrangement which are fossilised and used as the currency of verbal exchange. But clichés, proverbs and other such ready-made units of language are only extreme or caricatural manifestations of the universal nature of all language: a factor without which communication would be impossible. As Todorov has pointed out, the universality of language is not exclusively a feature of everyday speech but is equally apparent and pervasive in the work of the most 'original' poets:

> Il est probable que si l'on épluche soigneusement toutes les publications qui ont immédiatement précédé les *Fleurs du Mal*, on trouvera non seulement tous les mots employés par Baudelaire, ce qui va de soi, mais même tous ses syntagmes [.][1]

Indeed, the well-worn references to a writer's 'originality', 'inventiveness', and 'creativity' must always be understood within the context of the inescapably universal and derivative nature of all language. This view of 'creative' writing was anticipated by Merleau-Ponty who saw language as being endowed with a 'sens institué' and noted that a writer handles material which is 'already signifying' because it has already been used ('des instruments déjà signifiants ou des significations déjà parlantes').[2] But this fact per se is of little use in a poetics of fiction since it in no way contributes to an understanding of the distinguishing features of literarity. However, it is of immense critical interest when a work acknowledges the fact that the language of which it is composed bears the imprint of previous usage by preceding writers and speakers, and that consequently the statements it pronounces and the meanings it conveys are set against an infinite background of prior statements and meanings. The implications of this acknowledgement and the consequences arising out of the relations between a text and the discursive contexts it thus inherits are encompassed by the term 'intertextuality'.

The relations between a text and previous instances of language can be broadly grouped under three headings: theme – ideology – language. Thematic intertextuality is most easily discernible in the use of myth in literature. Drama in particular has a time-honoured tradition of dressing up in the myths and legends of antiquity. Examples proliferate from Shakespeare, Racine and Corneille to Giraudoux, Cocteau and Sartre. Mythological elements are also included in the intertextual fabric of some 'nouveaux romans': the Oedipus myth in Robbe-Grillet's *les Gommes*, the Theseus myth in Butor's *L'Emploi du temps*, the Hercules myth in Simon's *La Bataille de Pharsale*, and the Osiris myth in Ricardou's *La Prise de Constantinople*. Stimulating critical studies have dealt with the treatment of the same archetypal myth by a succession of writers through the ages. But critics' failure to relate their studies of a myth in literature within the wider framework of intertextuality generally results in analyses which are notably blinkered by a concentration on one specific myth to the exclusion of all else and gives rise to such reductive conclusions as the one formulated by Denis de Rougemont claiming that the whole of western literature is centred on the 'crise du mariage' crystallised by the Tristan myth.[3]

A work may be infiltrated, in a less conspicuous fashion than thematic intertextuality, by countless ideological and socio-cultural assumptions and cross-references. Indeed, the broadest definition of the term 'intertextuality' is simply the relationship between text and world. 'World' in this case is seen to be itself composed of a multiplicity of texts. As Jean Ricardou says:

> Ce qu'on a tendance à penser sur tel point particulier comme rapport du texte au monde n'est pas autre chose, sur tel point particulier, qu'un rapport de convenance et même de complicité du texte à l'ensemble des textes dominants à une époque dite [. . .] Ce qu'on appelle le monde n'est en effet que l'idée que s'en fait l'idéologie dominante selon la masse des textes officiellement actifs dans une société donnée. Le statut du hors-texte est donc celui d'un fantasme provisoire correspondant à un rapport d'intertextualité contrôlé par l'idéologie dominante.[4]

Thus language does not have a 'natural' plane of reference ('hors texte') but one which is comprised of the multiple texts constituting the dominant ideology. The meaning of 'intertextuality' here resembles that of 'code'. Julia Kristeva defines the concept in a similar way, claiming that the fifteenth century French novel arose as a result of the transformation of several other conventions such as scholastics, courtly poetry, and oral literature. Intertextuality is the juncture of the different codes and conventions within a given text:

> Nous appellerons *intertextualité* cette interaction textuelle qui se produit à l'intérieur d'un seul texte. Pour le sujet connaissant l'intertextualité est une notion qui sera l'indice de la façon dont un texte lit l'histoire et s'insère en elle.[5]

The third way in which intertextuality is manifest in a given work is through the language itself. A text may contain familiar syntagms (or literary clichés) which repeat unusual images found in prior texts, such as the recurrence of 'soleil noir' in the work of Nerval, Baudelaire and Proust.[6] Any intrusion of language, whether through repetition of cliché or change of style, carries, as Michael Riffaterre has shown, traces of the context (either textual or social) from which the intrusive element has originated:

> Alors le fait de style original est un nouveau venu avec son contexte, le cliché est rattaché au macro-contexte où il parut frappant pour la première fois; il fonctionne donc comme une citation, comme une référence à un certain niveau social, à certaines manifestations de culture.[7]

Where the syntagm has been altered but remains identifiable, as in cases of a shuffle of word order, Riffaterre speaks of 'intertextual scrambling'.[8]

The subtlest form of linguistic back-reference occurs when the meaning of a sentence presupposes the existence of a prior statement. 'Logical presupposition' is the linguistic concept which refers to this phenomenon and Jonathan Culler has presented it as a model for his own definition of intertextuality. Citing, among other examples, Baudelaire's

> Quand le ciel bas et lourd pèse comme un couvercle
> Sur l'esprit gémissant en proie aux longs ennuis[9]

the critic notes that the lines presuppose a prior statement such as 'le ciel pèse comme un couvercle'. The image is taken for granted and is phrased in a way which implies that it has already been said and is part of the stock of common knowledge:

Had he begun 'Parfois le ciel bas et lourd pèse comme un couvercle bas et lourd' he would be claiming to have made a discovery about the world and we might expect explanation, justification, a narrative which located this fact in an experiential context. The decision to presuppose undermines referentiality at this level by treating the fact in question as already given. In cases like this, logical presupposition is an intertextual operator which implies a discursive context and which by identifying an intertext, modifies the way in which the poem must be read.[10]

The different definitions of the term 'intertextuality' outlined above oscillate between a transitive and intransitive view of the associations involved. A given text may either be described as being infiltrated by foreign elements and prior statements or it can be said to refer to them. This distinction will be examined in more detail below with reference to Borges and Proust. However, the common factor linking all the different uses of the term is their focus on a web of relations between a given piece of language and prior instances of language. Intertextual relations, therefore, drive a wedge between a text and the external world to which it is ultimately referring:

whenever a work seems to be referring to the world one can argue that this supposed reference is in fact a comment on other texts and postpone the referentiality of the fiction to another moment of another level.[11]

It would consequently seem logical to include literary relations in the catalogue of different types of intertextuality. Some critics, however, have deprecated the idea of intertextuality as the relationship between literary texts both as a critical stance and as a valuable literary phenomenon. Both these objections are understandable to the extent that critics have often been tempted to associate different works on grounds which are no more solid than subjective comparison, and the appearance of some quotations in novels, especially in the form of epigraphs, can be interpreted simply as a writer's method of stamping his work with the hallmark of an established and respectable literary tradition. Such an over-valuation of literary association is often accompanied by a total lack of interest in the non-literary presuppositions and encodings of a given work and ignores its real intertextual sub-strata. In spite of these reservations, it would nevertheless be unjustifiable to deny the intertextual import of all literary relations. It is undeniably true, for instance, that *Don Quixote* forms part of the intertextual backcloth to Fielding's *Joseph Andrews*, as does *Tristram Shandy* with regard to *Jacques le Fataliste*, and the *Odyssey* to Joyce's *Ulysses*. Moreover, the relations need not be merely between two works but between a work and a whole genre, like Pope's *Dunciad* and epic poetry, or a work and several genres, like *Don Quixote* and the picaresque, the pastoral and novels of chivalry.

The scope of literary intertextual association may be summarised in the following way: extended intertextuality ('intertextualité générale') is the relationship between a work and others by different authors; restricted intertextuality ('intertextualité restreinte') is the relationship between a work and others by the same author.[12] Examples of both types abound. Extended intertextuality has been a prominent feature of European literature at almost every stage of its development, reaching a peak of intensity in the works of T. S. Eliot, Ezra Pound, and James Joyce. The 'nouveaux romanciers' have followed in this tradition: there is an intertextual link between Ollier's *Enigma* and Flaubert's *Salammbô*, as well as between *La Mise en scène* and *Bouvard et Pécuchet*; there is also an association between Butor's *6,810,000 litres d'eau par seconde* and Chateaubriand's *Voyage en Amérique*; equally, there is a relationship between Robbe-Grillet's earlier novels and those of Graham Greene. Claude Simon's *La Bataille de Pharsale*, as will be shown in Part 2, Chapter 2, is one of the most intertextually dense 'nouveaux romans'. A striking example of restricted intertextuality can be found in two pages of Robbe–Grillet's *Topologie d'une cité fantôme*. Taken on its own this passage is irrevocably disjointed, being composed of a set of unrelated sentences and paragraphs. However, syntagmatic discontinuity is compensated for by continuity on a different level produced by the intertextual connections. The section, entitled 'Dans la nature pétrifiée' (pp. 136–8), includes an evocation of *La Jalousie* in the reference to the 'bruissement invisible des insectes qui crissent de tous les côtés à la fois',[13] and in

On lit des vieux romans démodés qui se passent au fond de l'Afrique fantôme, pleins de drames incompréhensibles dans la chaleur moite et la stridulation des criquets.[14]

There is also a repetition of the opening line from 'Trois Visions Réfléchies' in *Instantanés*: 'la cafetière est sur la table'. *Le Voyeur* is implicitly evoked in

> On a volé la bicyclette du voyeur. C'est un ancien vélo d'homme abandonné dans la bergerie (on l'a toujours vu là) et qui s'appelle comme ça depuis une histoire horrible qu'on a inventé à son sujet.[15]

Finally *Projet pour une revolution à New York* is indirectly alluded to in the last paragraph of the section: 'il y a ensuite comme d'habitude, un escalier vertigineux et un couloir, avec du sang qui passe sous la porte d'une chambre fermée à clef'.[16]

Aside from the humour and teasing irony in such hidden references to his own work, these allusions indicate, on a more serious level, Robbe-Grillet's project of research, repetition, and transformation of fictional material. For Michel Butor, restricted intertextuality provides the means whereby a writer can treat his own previous writings as part of the general intertextuality contributing to his current work:

> Nous sommes à l'intérieur d'un complexe de cultures en évolution, à l'intérieur duquel se produisent toutes sortes d'illusions et de gâchis. Pour nous en délivrer il est indispensable de mettre au jour et à l'épreuve les références. Travailler sur les citations c'est mettre en évidence le fait qu'on n'est jamais seul auteur d'un texte, que la culture est un tissu; l'autocitation est un moyen de se considérer soi-même comme un autre. Tout cela mine les murs établis par notre société entre auteur et lecteur, singulier et pluriel. C'est éveil et libération.[17]

The conventional view of the unity and individuality of a writer's 'oeuvre' is thus thoroughly undermined.

II INTRUSION (IN PRAESENTIA): BORGES'S *EL INMORTAL*

Literary intertextual association can be detected in two basic forms: quotation (in praesentia) and allusion (in absentia). The most common literal quotations, in prose fiction at least, are those which appear as epigraphs at the head of a book or of each chapter. Less frequent, but more interesting from the point of view of structural involvement, are instances of quotation which occur internally within a given work and thus blend in with or interrupt the narrative, as in Claude Simon's *Histoire* and *La Bataille de Pharsale* and Philippe Sollers's *Nombres*. Bruce Morrissette has shown that Robbe–Grillet's *Topologie d'une cité fantôme* is constructed on the basis of restricted intertextual assemblage. With the exception of four pages, the entire novel is composed of a montage of passages taken from his earlier publications.[18] Extended intertextual reproduction has a long history dating back to the centos of classical literature which were 'patchwork' compositions consisting entirely of borrowings from earlier writers. 'Imitatio' was a widely practised technique in classical literature and was not, on the whole, dismissed as plagiarism until the seventeenth century.[19] Macrobius, for instance, gives a fascinating and detailed exposition of Vergil's debt to Homer and others in his *Saturnalia*. More modern versions of this device are Thomas Gray's *Pindaric Odes* and T. S. Eliot's *The Waste Land* with their multiple interpolations, some of which are identified by the poets in footnotes to the poems. In prose fiction, it is Borges's *El Inmortal* which exploits this technique to its fullest extent. It is worth glancing briefly at this story as it sheds light on some of the thematic implications of intertextuality in general.

The anonymous narrator of *El Inmortal* recounts that a manuscript was found in a volume of Pope's *Iliad* which was presented to the Princess of Lucinge in 1929 by an antique dealer named Joseph Cartaphilus. The text, which is 'written in English and abounds in Latinisms', is narrated by Marcus Flaminius Rufus, a Roman military tribune fighting in the Egyptian wars and stationed at Berenice. Rufus is overcome with the desire to discover the Secret City of the Immortals and its river 'whose waters grant immortality' (p. 136).[20] His wanderings lead him through deserts inhabited by troglodytes, garamants and augyls before finally arriving at his destination. The city is situated in a region inhabited by 'the bestial breed of troglodytes' (p. 138) who are characterised by their inability to speak and their taste for serpents' flesh. Rufus enters the Immortal City through a dark labyrinth of 'sordid galleries' (p. 139) leading to a palace whose structure is 'interminable', 'atrocious', and 'complexly senseless' (p. 141).[21] On leaving the city, the tribune rejoins a troglodyte who has been faithfully accompanying him and whom he names 'Argos' after Ulysses's dog. That night, Rufus dreams of returning a goldfish to a river in Thessaly and is awakened from his sleep by a downpour of rain. On crying out to Argos, he hears his companion reply by quoting a line from the *Odyssey*, 'This dog lying in the manure', revealing that he is in fact Homer and that he is over a thousand years old. Rufus learns from Homer that the 'mad city' was erected as a 'parody or inversion' of the original city which the troglodytes razed. Infinity, the time span of immortal men, is a period in which 'all things happen to all men' and where opposites counter-balance and cancel one another out. By the same token, the notion of personal individuality is made obsolete:

Homer composed the *Odyssey*; if we postulate an infinite period of time, with infinite circumstances and changes, the impossible thing is not to compose the *Odyssey*, at least once. No one is anyone, one single immortal is all men. (p. 145)

Within the context of this notion of interpersonal universality, the identities of Homer and Rufus merge despite the fact that the two men part at Tangiers. Rufus ends his narrative by alluding to some of the landmarks of his immortal life which includes fighting at Stamford Bridge in 1066 and subscribing to Pope's *Iliad* in Aberdeen in 1714. It is clear that Homer, Rufus, and Cartaphilus are all one person. Finally, in 1921, confirming the doctrine that 'there is nothing lacking compensation in something else' (p. 146), he returns to Berenice and drinks from the spring which restores his mortality. The narrative ends with these lines:

When the end draws near, there no longer remain any remembered images; only words remain. It is not strange that time should have confused the words that once represented me with those that were the symbols of the fate of he who accompanied me for so many centuries. I have been Homer; shortly, I shall be No One, like Ulysses; shortly I shall be all men; I shall be dead. (pp. 147-8)

A postscript is attached in which Borges the narrator alludes to an imaginary critic, Doctor Nahum Cordovero, who attacks the manuscript for being apocryphal in the tradition of the centos of classical literature as well as of the writings of Ben Jonson, Seneca, Alexander Ross, George Moore and T. S. Eliot. He also 'denounces brief interpolations' from Pliny, De Quincey, Descartes and Shaw. As Ronald Christ has pointed out,[22] the text here contains an ironical twist in so far as Cordovero's accusation is 'a case of the apocryphal naming the apocryphal'. Not only is the critic himself imaginary and therefore his comments entail their own un-doing but the title of his book 'A Coat of Many Colours' echoes the 'patchwork quilt' etymology of the word 'cento'.[23]

El Inmortal, like most of Borges's stories, is written in a dense, elliptical style which conveys a sense of enigma and suppressed, implicit information. The archaisms or 'Latinisims', whether actual borrowings or imitations ('fever and magic consumed many men who had magnanimously coveted the steel' (p. 135); 'I dreamt of an exiguous and nitid labyrinth' (p. 137) emphatically announce the intertextual background of the story. An aura of strangeness seeps through the language of the text emanating from the presence of foreign or intrusive elements and contexts. Thus, the unexplained and unproblematical way in which mention is made of the fact that some of Rufus's soldiers' faces are burnt as a result of sleeping exposed to the moon ('A few foolhardy men slept with their faces exposed to the moon; they burned with fever' (p. 137)) produces a halting effect on the reading. Why are the men 'foolhardy'? Is it true, let alone common knowledge, that the desert moon burns? The reader clearly does not share the same discursive contexts as the narrative and the enigma will only be resolved when the intertextual source of these lines is located. In this case the context is a passage from De Quincey which relates the account of a traveller recently returned from Upper Egypt who claims that the moon is capable of burning and that sleeping under the light of the moon had the effect of producing 'a severe complaint upon his eyes'.[24] Apart from the De Quincey connection, the reference to the moon can be seen to have further intertextual significance. As it reflects light borrowed from the sun, the moon is traditionally associated with the imitative or intertextual vein in western literature, as K. K. Ruthven has shown in his beautifully orchestrated book *Critical Assumptions*:

> The Modern hates to think of himself as merely pedicuring the past, and thinks it sufficient to discredit false Moderns merely by calling them 'men content with the connotations of their masters', which was William Carlos Williams' jibe at Pound and Eliot. The literary *ancien*, on the other hand, is inclined to see the whole of modern literature as a series of footnotes to Homer. 'Modern writers are the moons of literature', said Johnson; 'they shine with reflected light, with light borrowed from the Ancients'. Traditionalists are willing to accept this and make their own contribution to the poetry of mirrors, as the allusive Vladimir Nabokov does in *Pale fire* (London, 1962), taking his cue from *Timon of Athens*: 'the moon's an arrant thief,/And her pale fire she snatches from the sun.' Schismatic Moderns will have none of this, preferring (in D. H. Lawrence's image) to 'start with the sun'.[25]

It is the moon rather than the sun which blinds Rufus's soldiers, and this textual association between blindness and the moon is what unites Borges and Homer, for whilst both writers are physically blind (the latter reputedly so), Borges also suffers from a fictional blindness through being struck by the reflected light of intertextuality.

It would be misguided, however, to infer from these intertextual relations that Borges's story is concerned with challenging the reader to trace the origin of the various quotations and thereby to indulge in some vast literary jig-saw puzzle. Although a non-intertextual reading of *El Inmortal* would be incomplete and fragmentary, the reader is nevertheless not primarily directed to turn to the works of De Quincey, Pliny, Vergil, Homer and the others. Indeed, the main object of the story (and one which is underscored by the chorus of intertextual intrusions) is to convey a sense of the indeterminate and the infinite. Instead of naming them 'allusions', the postscript more aptly refers to the intertextual elements in *El Inmortal* as 'intrusions', and one can add that as intrusions they invade the text and fracture it into a mosaic of separate but echoing parts. The two most prominent quotations are from the *Iliad*, II 824, ('the rich Trojans from Zelea who drink the black water of the Aisepos' (p. 138) and from the *Odyssey*, xvii

394, ('This dog lying in the manure' (p. 143)). The former quotation is spoken 'inexplicably' and uncontrollably by Rufus whilst living with the troglodytes, and the latter quotation by Argos/Homer as was mentioned earlier. The intrusive nature of the lines is heightened by the fact that they are uttered almost unwittingly by the characters who serve only as vehicles for mouthing the words.

Intertextuality spreads through the chain of narration (Borges the narrator – Cartaphilus/Rufus – Homer) which forms the skeleton of the story's narrative structure. Each of the 'voices' is comprised of a text or tissue of other voices. The narrator's plurality is indicated by the repeated use of the first person plural narrative ('He was, she tells us, a wasted and earthen man'; 'the version we offer is literal' (p. 135). Borges too, like Rufus and Cartaphilus, is Homer and Ulysses: that is, everyone and no-one.[26] Secondly, the apocryphal text of Cartaphilus/Rufus's narrative is, as has been shown, a mosaic of interpolations from the work of a number of different writers. Thirdly, Homer, the 'absent' figure around whom the whole story pivots, is only known of through his work which is as much the property of the rhapsodists as it is of Homer (p. 143). The narrator further stresses the anonymity of the author of the *Iliad* by attaching a footnote to the narrative in which he alludes to Vico's claim that Homer was a 'symbolic character after the manner of Pluto or Achilles' (p. 148). Moreover, in an essay entitled 'Las versiones homéricas' Borges states the impossibility of knowing what in Homer belongs to Homer and what belongs to language, and points to the use of epithets as an example of this ambiguity. It is interesting that the epithet he chooses for his example is 'los ricos varones que beben el agua negra del Esepo',[27] the words from the *Iliad* which are 'inexplicably' spoken by Rufus.

El Inmortal focuses on the identity of Homer not out of any biographical or historical interest but as a reflection of Borges's continued fascination with the notion of infinity:

> Everything among the mortals has the value of the irretrievable and the perilous. Among the Immortals, on the other hand, every act (and every thought) is the echo of others that preceded it in the past, with no visible beginning, or the faithful presage of others that in the future will repeat it to a vertiginous degree. There is nothing that is not as if lost in a maze of indefatigable mirrors. (p. 146)

Homer is perceived in the text 'as if lost in a maze of indefatigable mirrors' and as if each reflected frame enclosed an image of a different member of the endless succession of rhapsodists and writers who have repeated and re-written his work. Homer is the name which stands for the source of all writing: a source which, like the water jar in Rufus's dream, remains eternally out of reach. Indeed, the experience of reading *El Inmortal* may be described as a vertiginous journey through a labyrinthine text following the thread of an elusive and distant narrative. The prevalence of aquatic imagery and the prominence of rivers in the story links the idea of Homer as source or ever-receding origin with the literal meaning of 'source' as 'fountain-head'.[28] In addition to the premonitory dream of returning a goldfish to a river in Thessaly, there is also a reference to 'tiny streams of rusty water' (p. 139) as Rufus makes his way through the labyrinthine corridors leading to the palace. But even this thematic equation is derivative and motivated by an intertextual origin. At the opening of *Homer and the Homeridae*, De Quincey, before tackling the controversy surrounding the existence of Homer, draws a poetic analogy between the Greek poet and the Nile:

> And, again, if you go upwards to the fountains of this ancient Nile, or of this ancient Homer, you would find the same mysterious repulsion. In both cases you find their fountains shyly retreating before you [.][29]

To conclude, the form which intertextuality takes in *El Inmortal* is one of metonymic or contiguous association. The story is patched together by a juxtaposition of disparate literary fragments and 'voices' which do not combine to produce an over-all effect of unity, but rather one of an absence reflected by the labyrinth or 'maze of indefatigable mirrors' contained in the name 'Homer'.

III ALLUSION (IN ABSENTIA): PROUST'S *A LA RECHERCHE DU TEMPS PERDU*

Allusion, the second and more recurrent form of intertextual association, is the process of drawing together two separate texts by means of a common element and for this reason it can be defined as a type of metaphor.[30] While Borges's chief concern in most of his work including *El Inmortal* is with the notion of infinity, Marcel Proust, on the other hand, was absorbed with the idea and practice of correspondence. One should not, therefore, be too surprised by the statistical claim that *A la recherche du temps perdu* contains more literary allusions than the work of any other French writer apart from Montaigne.[31] Margaret Mein has related Proust's delight in discovering literary precursors, 'ramiers fraternels', to his overriding predilection for creating correspondences:

> It is mainly as a result of establishing an analogy between two particular sensations, between two particular authors that he will glean 'l'essence commune' and will be inspired to create in turn.
> Quite independently, however, of the moot question of literary influence, no one more than Proust can have relished the discovery of a precursor attracted as he always was by the study of affinities, regarded as a variation on the theme of analogies.[32]

In *Contre Sainte-Beuve*, Proust admits to possessing a talent for discerning 'entre deux impressions, entre deux idées, une harmonie très fine que d'autres ne sentent pas'[33] and states that this propensity for drawing affinities extends to his appreciation of art. Two similar paintings may not in themselves be of the least attraction to him, but the discovery of their correspondence affords him ineffable pleasure:

> Mais si dans le second tableau ou le second livre, il [Proust's 'bonhomme de l'analogie'] aperçoit quelque chose qui n'est pas dans le premier, mais qui est en quelque sorte entre les deux, dans une sorte de tableau idéal, qu'il voit en matière spirituelle se modeler hors du tableau, il a reçu sa nourriture et recommence à exister et à être heureux.[34]

The neo-Symbolist depiction of a spiritual 'tableau idéal' was to develop in the subsequent evolution of literary theory into the view of intertextuality as the dismantling of barriers separating different works and the identification of a universal 'texte généralisé'. Philippe Sollers, for instance, sees 'le travail intertextuel' as one of revitalising the web of connections which exists between works:

il fait se couper les livres les uns par les autres et les amène à
s'inscrire au-delà de leurs limites dans un texte généralisé.[35]

But the artistic value of Proust's allusions in *A la recherche* is not
due to any mystical overtones nor are they merely symptoms of
literary atavism. In fact, the importance of allusion in Proust's
aesthetic and its close relationship with the other two structural
corner-stones (involuntary memory unleashed by sense
impressions and the associative play of metaphor) is displayed in
the famous passage in *Le Temps retrouvé* describing Marcel's
thoughts while waiting in the prince de Guermantes's library. As
in the postscript to *The Immortal*, Marcel names some of the texts
which echo the same preoccupations that have absorbed him and
acted as a stimulus to his own writings. The affinities he notes
between himself and Chateaubriand, Nerval, and Baudelaire
depend on the fact that the 'impressions vraiment esthétiques'
which have dominated his life can also be found 'à des traits moins
marqués, mais discernables, et au fond assez analogues' (III 919)[36]
in their works. Although Marcel appears to adumbrate the similarities between his own preoccupations and the work of Chateaubriand, Nerval, and Baudelaire merely in order to establish a
'noble' 'filiation' (III 920)[37] for his own projected 'oeuvre', the
relationship between these same works (and others) and *A la
recherche* is much more subtle and significant. In his analysis of
the intertextual relationship between *A la recherche* and *Mémoires
d'outre-tombe*,[38] Jean Ricardou observes that the associations are of
two types, both of which are modelled on the metaphorical
relations organising the internal structure of the novel. 'Métaphore
ordinale' is the assimilation of two separate units through the
medium of a common denominator; 'métaphore configurale' is the
process whereby the structure of one unit influences the structure
of another. The most obvious example of the workings of 'métaphore ordinale' in Proust's novel is the telescoping of two distant
moments in time through the experience of the 'madeleine'. The
intertextual equivalent of this process is the evocation of the
passage in *Mémoires d'outre-tombe* quoted by Marcel in *Le Temps
retrouvé* as an example of an experience which is similar to the
associations triggered off in his memory by certain sense
impressions:

Hier au soir je me promenais seul [. . .] je fus tiré de mes réflexions par le gazouillement d'une grive perchée sur la plus haute branche d'un bouleau. A l'instant, ce son magique fit reparaître à mes yeux le domaine paternel; j'oubliai les catastrophes dont je venais d'être le témoin, et, transporté subitement dans le passé, je revis ces campagnes où j'entendis si souvent siffler la grive. (III 919)[39]

The common element in the intertextual link between the two passages is the very idea of association through involuntary memory. For an example of 'métaphore configurale' in *A la recherche*, Ricardou turns to the opening pages of the novel where the pattern of 'méprise – confirmation – renversement' underlying the description of the narrator's semi-conscious state is reiterated in the ensuing evocation of the traveller waking in an unfamiliar hotel at midnight. In the first case, the narrator's error (he thinks he is awake when he is in fact asleep) is confirmed by his attempts to fall asleep, and is finally dispelled when these attempts result in waking him up. In the second case, the traveller's error (on awakening at midnight he thinks it is morning) is confirmed by his interpretation of the servant's footsteps as a sign that people have already risen, and is finally dispelled when the light in the corridor is extinguished. This kind of structural linkage can extend to intertextual relations and Ricardou notices that Elstir's 'Port de Carquethuit' painting (where the sea is depicted in terms of the land and vice versa) is prefigured by a passage in Chateaubriand's novel outlining the same compositional phenomenon:

Entre la mer et la terre s'étendent des campagnes pélagiennes, frontières indécises des deux éléments: l'alouette de champ y vole avec l'alouette marine; la charrue et la barque à un jet de pierre l'une de l'autre, sillonnent la terre et l'eau. Le navigateur et le berger s'empruntent mutuellement leur langue: le matelot dit LES VAGUES MOUTONNENT, le pâtre dit DES FLOTTES DE MOUTONS.[40]

One can also perceive an intertextual connection between these lines from Chateaubriand and the description of the entrancing effect of the hawthorns on Marcel immediately preceding Gilberte's first appearance in *Du Côté de chez Swann*. The passage is associated, also through a process of metaphorical configuration, with an earlier description of the hawthorns on the church altar, whose swaying white buds Marcel likens to the coquettish movements of 'une blanche jeune fille'. On genuflecting in front of the altar at the end of the mass, Marcel savours the bitter-sweet odour of the flowers from behind which he imagines the aroma to emanate, just as 'sous leurs taches de rousseur, celui des joues de Mlle Vinteuil'.[41] The comparison between the hawthorns and Mlle Vinteuil's cheeks introduces a new colour ('roux') to the passage and this is immediately transposed to the flowers:

> Malgré la silencieuse immobilité des aubépines, cette intermittente odeur était comme le murmure de leur vie intense dont l'autel vibrait ainsi qu'une haie agreste visitée par de vivantes antennes, auxquelles on pensait en voyant certaines étamines presque rousses qui semblaient avoir gardé la virulence printanière, le pouvoir irritant, d'insectes aujourd'hui métamorphosés en fleurs. (I 113–4)[42]

In the Tansonville passage, Marcel consciously compares the white hawthorns with those on the church altar but his efforts to fathom the exact cause of his pleasure prove, as always, unsuccessful. He turns away from the flowers and contemplates the odd poppy and cornflower lingering on the bank behind the hawthorn bushes:

> ils m'annonçaient l'immense étendue où déferlent les blés, où moutonnent les nuages, et la vue d'un seul coquelicot hissant au bout de son cordage et faisant cingler au vent sa flamme rouge, au-dessus de sa bouée graisseuse et noire, me faisait battre le coeur, comme au voyageur qui aperçoit sur une terre basse une première barque échouée que répare un calfat, et s'écrie, avant de l'avoir encore vue: "La Mer!" (I 138–9)[43]

The intertextual link with the Chateaubriand passage is evident in the sea imagery which invades the description of the sky ('où moutonnent les nuages') and the fields ('l'immense étendue où déferlent les blés'). The verbs 'moutonner' and 'déferler', normally used with reference to the action of waves in the sea, here perform (as does the metaphorical fusion of poppy and fishing-boat) precisely the sort of reciprocal contextual overlapping which is described in *Mémoires d'outre-tombe* and later depicted in Elstir's paintings. Once again, intertextuality can be seen to extend the principle of metaphorical configuration governing the internal organisation of the text beyond the bounds of the novel. Marcel returns to the white hawthorns, but still to no avail. However, his grandfather draws his attention to the even more wondrous sight of a pink hawthorn and it is while he is contemplating these flowers that Gilberte appears before him for the first time: 'Une fillette d'un blond roux [. . .] levant son visage semé de taches roses' (I 140).[44] The metaphorical configuration is complete, though in this case, unlike the Ricardou example cited earlier, the association contains an inverted twist. Whereas, in the first hawthorn passage the allusion to Mlle Vinteuil provokes a reference to the russet colour of the flowers, in the second passage the discovery of the pink hawthorns is followed by the appearance of Gilberte.

Intertextual allusion and metaphorical association also converge in passages dealing with the other agents of involuntary memory. For instance, the tiles on the St Hilaire steeple blaze on a hot summer morning 'comme un soleil noir' (a repetition of the famous Romantic image mentioned earlier) reminding the narrator of the dome of the Saint Augustin church in Paris 'd'un noir décanté de cendres'.[45] The image is later prised apart in the celebrated passage where the Martinville steeples are described as breaking open to reveal their inner secret to Marcel who writes that at one instant the steeples are bathed in sunlight and at the next they merge into 'une seule forme noire' (I 182). Finally, the 'madeleine' episode is itself infused with an undercurrent of intertextual association. The passage is immediately preceded by the description of the narrator's mother reading to him from *François le champi* following the 'drame du coucher'. As Margaret Mein points out, George Sand's novel serves as a 'mirror-composition within *A la recherche*' in that the novel is about the love relationship between François and his adoptive mother, Madeleine:

> The kiss which the heroine, Madeleine, gives to François thus marks the sublimation of the mother-son relationship, an outcome poignantly denied to Marcel in all his love-affairs.[46]

The narrative displacements and lacunae produced by Marcel's mother's edited reading (she censors the love scene descriptions) convey 'un profond mystère' on the novel which seems to Marcel to stem from 'ce nom inconnu et si doux de "Champi" ' (I 42).[47] But it is through 'Madeleine', the name of François's mother and of the tea cake (as well as of the church (I 417) and of the character in Fromentin's *Dominique* (III 709)) brought to Marcel by his own mother in the next scene, that *François le champi* is connected with the associative powers of memory in *A la recherche*. Indeed, so complete is the influence that George Sand's book eventually assumes the function of the 'madeleine' and becomes the agent of involuntary memory (III 883–6). Thus, whereas for Marcel it is the name 'Champi' which holds powers of association, for the reader of *A la recherche* it is indubitably 'Madeleine'.

The importance of allusion, and literature in general, for Proust was that they contributed to the memory store or 'livre intérieur' of each individual reader. But the reader's memory is also filled by the influx of data from the long and intricately textured novel he is reading. The mirror repetitions and internal textual relations are only possible if the reader's memory is sufficiently alert to enable the comparison of passages often separated by hundreds of pages to be made. The place of allusion within this schema is in an extension of the scope of memory beyond the bounds of the text. The reader must already be familiar with *Mémoires d'outre-tombe* and the other texts for the intertextual associations to take shape. For unlike the intrusive quotations in Borges's *El Inmortal*, the intertextual connections in *A la recherche* are not, on the whole, to be found in the novel itself but in the mind of the reader. Inspired by the writings of Borges, the following lines by Gérard Genette more appropriately summarise the poetics of the work of Marcel Proust:

> Le temps des oeuvres n'est pas le temps défini de l'écriture, mais le temps indéfini de la lecture et de la mémoire. Le sens des livres est devant eux et non derrière, il est en nous: un livre n'est pas un sens tout fait, une révélation que nous avons à subir, c'est une réserve de formes qui attendent leur sens, c'est 'l'imminence d'une révélation qui ne se produit pas', et que chacun doit produire lui-même.[48]

Semantic function

The foregoing discussion began with the assertion that 'intertextuality' is a global term which refers to a wide range of textual phenomena. But despite the obvious differences, one can also point to fundamental similarities binding the different uses of the word. As was stated at the start of this chapter, all types of intertextuality outline a view of reference as, initially at least, a set of relations between one piece of language and another. The fact that intertextuality thus drives a wedge between language and the 'external world' (is it ever possible, though, to conceive of an a-linguistic world?) may be defined as its 'syntactic function'. An analysis of the different ways in which intertextuality is manifest in a given work would, therefore, constitute an appraisal of the specific syntactic functions of intertextuality in that work. As I have argued, literary intertextuality should not be excluded from such an analysis. After all, just as allusion is a form of metaphor, so too stylistic intrusions, such as the Homeric epithets and 'Latinisms' in *El Inmortal*, imitate the function of ordinary clichés in language; and, finally, a given work can just as easily presuppose literary discursive contexts as non-literary ones.

The semantic function of intertextuality is particularly active in the case of literary relations. Two or more texts may be linked through varying degrees of respect or parody. Philippe Sollers, for instance, stresses that the quotations in *Nombres* are chosen as a mark of respect or homage to the works and writers concerned:

> Cependant, il y a un choix précis: la plupart des textes appartiennent à un espace occulté par notre culture et, en général, matérialiste [. . .] Le point commun de tous ces acteurs est d'avoir été refusés par le système chrétien: ainsi Bruno, Spinoza, Artaud [. . .] C'est un hommage rendu à un certain 'enfer' de notre pensée.[49]

In sharp contrast, the intertextual links between *Don Quixote* and the chivalresque genre, or between Fielding's *Shamela* and Richardson's *Pamela* are trenchantly parodic or satirical. But even parody is not always viewed as being fundamentally subversive or iconoclastic. Quiller Couch, for instance, defines it as 'a holy thing' because it 'plays with the gods'.[50] It thus combines playful imitation with a deep reverence for the original work 'off which the profane and the vulgar should be carefully warned'. Sollers's homage to his precursors (despite being a homage to iconoclasts) and Quiller Couch's insistence on respect towards the works parodied are both ultimately examples of what Laurent Jenny has called the 'emprunt poli' or 'citation de la Grande Bibliothèque' tradition of literary intertextuality which involves no radical upheaval of established codes of literary and social discourse.[51]

However, reverent homage and comic travesty are not the only semantic functions of literary intertextuality. An alternative function can be seen at work in 'The Oxen of the Sun' episode in Joyce's *Ulysses*. As Stuart Gilbert notes,[52] this 'chapter of parodies' is set in a hospital and the central theme of 'embryonic development' is paralleled by a stunning series of stylistic imitations beginning in the Anglo-Saxon language and proceeding through the style of, amongst others, Bunyan, Mandeville, Malory, Sir Thomas Browne, Pepys, Swift, Addison and Steele, Sterne, Lamb, De Quincey, Newman, Pater, Ruskin, and Carlyle, before degenerating into a 'pandemonium of ejaculations in every form of dialect, jargon, slang, ancient and modern'.[53] Gilbert further comments that Joyce's stylistic imitations (there are also countless borrowings) are not always intended to be satirical:

> But if the texture of the prose be carefully examined, it will be seen that, though in some passages the style is probably meant to satirize the original (as where an *Ars Amatoria* is expounded in the manner of a Bunyan parable), the greater part seems to be devoid of satiric intention; that wilful exaggeration of mannerisms which points a parody is absent and the effect is rather of pastiche than of travesty.[54]

While parody rings with the mocking voice of a parodist, pastiche, on the other hand, is a textual phenomenon which either takes the form of stylistic imitation (as in *Ulysses*) or of fictional rewriting (as in the 'nouveau roman'). This is not to deny the iconoclastic impact of pastiche, but the sardonic voice of a narrator or author organising the assault is absent. Pastiche in the 'nouveau roman' may be defined as a process of transformation. In order to stress the non-parodic aspect of this feature of *La Prise de Constantinople*, Jean Ricardou names the process 'antipastiche':

> En outre, il y a dans *La Prise de Constantinople* ce que j'appelle des antipastiches. Des textes d'historiens sont bien injectés mais ils sont transformés par le texte qui les reçoit, tout au niveau du style qu'au niveau des événements eux-mêmes par une manière d'assimilation.[55]

At the 1971 Cerisy conference, Butor's work came under attack from Robbe-Grillet, Ollier, and Ricardou for not being sufficiently iconoclastic. Butor nevertheless echoes the desire for transformation by stressing the inventive aspect of modern writing, although coupling it with its corollary activity of 'restitution':

> Restitution du texte ancien, invention du texte nouveau sont deux actions corrélatives. Plus je restitue, plus je suis forcé d'inventer (et encouragé dans cette aventure); plus j'invente, plus je suis capable de restituer.
> La littérature courante ne mérite donc même pas le nom de parodie. En effet le modèle ancien n'a pas pu être consulté recouvert par ses imitations innombrables, il n'est pas sortie du rayon. Ombres des ombres d'ombres.[56]

Elsewhere, Butor states that Chateaubriand's text did not serve as a quotation in *6,810,000 litres d'eau par seconde* but as a 'matière première'.[57] Finally, Claude Simon has also emphasised the process of transformation underlying the intertextual framework of *La Bataille de Pharsale*. Replying to a question concerning the quotations in his novel, Simon draws a comparison with the collage structure of the work of Robert Rauschenberg:

> FRANÇOISE VAN ROSSUM-GUYON: Et en utilisant ces textes, les transformez-vous?
> CLAUDE SIMON: Bien sur et Rauschenberg aussi en utilisant des reproductions ou des chromos ou des foulards, il les transforme.[58]

Transformation, invention, assimilation: a 'nouveau roman' recasts the specific intertextual stimuli which have engendered it and submits them to the generative powers of the text. 'Hors texte' becomes text. The tension between the two is double-edged, for while the former is subjugated to the latter, it also robs the latter of its pretentions to a self-enclosed universe. For the reader, the implications of intertextuality are of immense consequence as the dismantling of barriers between fiction and reality deprives him of his traditional 'foothold': the external vantage-point from which he has observed the world of fiction. He must rethink his relationship with the text and discover that he too, perhaps, is Ulysses.

2
La Bataille de Pharsale and its Fragments

> Why, again, have all the constellations, save only Orion with his sworded thigh, strayed from their courses to move unseen through the skies; and why does Orion blaze brighter than usual?
>
> Lucan, *Pharsalia*

I PATTERNS OF TEXTUAL RELATION

One of the more popular literary clichés among French Romantic writers, 'soleil noir', recurs in modified form in the stanza from Valéry's 'Le Cimetière Marin' serving as epigraph to the first part of *La Bataille de Pharsale*: 'Ah! le soleil. . . . Quelle ombre de tortue'. The image is accompanied by two other contradictory locutions, 'Qui vibre, vole et qui ne vole pas!' and 'Achille immobile à grands pas!' which echo Zeno's paradoxes depicting immobility through movement.[1] In one argument, Achilles is said to be incapable of overtaking the tortoise who begins the race with a headstart, since in order to catch up with him he must first cross each of the points reached by the tortoise. Although the distance between the two runners contracts, it remains ineradicable. According to the second paradox, an arrow can only occupy one place at any moment during its flight and is therefore motionless. Progression, seen in the light of this 'reductio ad absurdum' process of reasoning, is inhibited by spatio-temporal decomposition and division; movement is stifled in its very attempt. Valéry's metaphor of the sun as the tortoise's shadow blends the Romantic cliché with the narrative of Zeno's conundrum, with the result that the paradoxical image, set within the context of the poem's oscillation between movement and stasis, active life and contemplative death, now reflects the latter, the interstice of timeless immobility. The sun-shadow, 'l'écart entre l'être et le connaître que développe la conscience de la conscience',² is induced by analytical self-consciousness.

The opening words of *La Bataille de Pharsale* offer a new version of the antonymic image of the black sun: 'Jaune et puis noir temps d'un battement de paupières et puis jaune de nouveau'.³ The image is 'narrativised': the oxymoron is acted out in terms of a momentary eclipse of the sun caused by the sudden flight of a pigeon. The temporal dimension shifts the image from a simultaneous to a successive perspective and heightens the sense of self-conscious analysis: the image is repeatedly subjected to the close scrutiny of the narrator and, more profoundly, of the writing. Jean Ricardou's masterly analysis of the start of Claude Simon's novel and its intricate relation with the Valéry stanza has already revealed the way in which Simon's text grows out of the epigraph.⁴ The latter, indeed, provides a number of generative sources for the flow of textual development but it is the paradox of the sun-shadow which serves as the novel's initial point of departure. What motivates the prominent position which this image enjoys in the novel as a whole? Is it that the light/shade paradox is mirrored, as Ricardou points out, in the title, 'Phare'/'sale' and in the fact that the word 'noir' is metathetically inscribed within 'Orion', the name not only of the blind giant walking towards the sun in Poussin's painting but also of a constellation of stars whose 'blazing brightness', in Lucan's epic poem, heralds the imminence of war? I suggest that instead of viewing these onomasiological instances of the paradox as structural motivators or explanations of the role of this image in the novel, one should read them as part of the web of textual, and intertextual, relations which extends to every area of the novel. Furthermore, though the question of 'prominence' may well beg its own question as to the validity of identifying key images in a modern text, I shall proceed to show that the opening image in *La Bataille de Pharsale* is as multiple and diverse as the novel. To begin with, the image is dualistic in so far as it outlines an oscillation between 'jaune' and 'noir'; it also transforms a visual impression which is perceived as a superimposition (the bird eclipsing the sun), into a linear succession of visual and verbal stimuli. The opening description thus implies an intertextual shift from a pattern of simultaneity to one of alternation.⁵

Looking at Simon's novel as a whole one notices, even at a

cursory glance, its fragmented structure, the importance of which can be inferred from the analogy drawn by the author between this work and the collages of contemporary artists:

> You are also familiar with what artists call constructions or collages. Picasso invented the genre, and he has been followed by such outstanding figures as Schwitter and Rauschenberg. Lately, literature has also produced collages, or what we call 'intertextuality'. I experimented with this in *Histoire* and *La Bataille de Pharsale*.[6]

At times, the use of italics highlights the fragmentary nature of the narrative 'screen';[7] the oscillations created by narrative discontinuity are thus frequently corroborated and made visual by an alternation in typography. But not all the fragments, whether italicised or not, in *La Bataille de Pharsale* are intertextual (in other words, not all are quotations): often the displacement is simply intersequential, a spatio-temporal shift instigated by the combinatory powers of memory. The first occurrence of italics in the novel is a case in point. The passage alternates between a rather imprecise 'present' of narration which, it would seem, is cotemporaneous with the jealous narrator's surveillance of his lover's window, and a flash-back to a moment in the narrator's childhood when he was scolded by his uncle Charles for not adequately preparing his Latin homework:

> Eaux mortes. Mort vivant. *Je comprends parfaitement que tu aies décidé de ne rien faire naturellement c'est de ta part purement et simplement une question de paresse* mortellement triste *mais après tout quoique tu ne puisses pas encore le savoir* Je ne savais pas encore *puisque c'est une chose qu'il faut apprendre et qu'apparemment tu as pris la ferme résolution de ne rien faire* bois mort feuille morte *mais peut-être as-tu raison après tout tout savoir ne débouche jamais que sur un autre savoir et les mots sur d'autres mots* la mort dans l'âme la peine de mort [.] (p. 18)[8]

Fiction and writing are, at this stage of the novel, closely allied. The narrator's memory of his past is recalled as he gazes at the flow of pedestrians emerging from the tube station while he waits jealously for signs of life at the window. Shadowing this act of memory, however, is a complex chain of textual associations, for it is the writing which actually intertwines the two narrative sequences. As an anagram of 'morte', the word 'métro' generates a whole series of different avenues of textual development through the motif of death. It is also a pun on 'mettre eau' ('Eaux mortes' links up with 'chasses d'eau' (p. 16) and with stagnation, a variant of the death motif), and a pun on 'mettre O' which, as well as indicating the compositional pattern of circularity and repetition, leads to the introduction of O as the sign of the vacant locus of narratorial identity. The uncle's comment that 'tout savoir ne débouche jamais que sur un autre savoir et les mots sur d'autres mots' may be read as an oblique reference to the novel's own intertextual structure. But, on a more specific note, the remark can be seen to be textually related to other strands of narrative through the word 'débouche' which, as well as relating to the metro exit ('la bouche du métro' (p. 14)) also links back to the motif of death with reference to the mention made by Plutarch that Crastinus, who set the battle of Pharsalus in motion by throwing his javelin at Pompey's army, died when a sword was thrust into his mouth. The compositional structure of the novel as a whole includes the presence of a number of nodal points through which several divergent narrative threads pass and interweave.[9] The motif of the flighted missile is one such point of convergence. This particular network of associations includes the image of the immobile arrow as formulated by Zeno and Valéry, Plutarch's reference to the death of Crastinus, the flight of a bird ('ailes déployées forme d'arbalète'), the upward gaze of the jealous narrator, the reflection of a cloud drifting across the window pane, the seemingly motionless ascent of the metro passengers on an escalator, a catechism illustration ('Ame du Juste s'envolant'), the curved trajectory of a child's bucket thrown in the air, the javelin in mid-flight depicted in Piero della Francesca's 'Défaite de Chosroès', and the ornamental design of a winged helmet printed on a packet of 'Gauloise' cigarettes: 'les ailes évoquant des images d'oiseaux, de plumes, de flèches empennées' (p. 257).[10]

Thus the narrator's intermittent act of remembrance is paralleled on the formal level of the novel by the retroactive and mirroring play of what one might call 'the memory of the text'. The aptness of the analogy between textual association and the memory process is the main reason why the latter was chosen as the narrative framework of all the novels published by Claude Simon in the sixties. As the following passage from *Histoire* shows, the choice depended on the principle of combination and articulation inherent in the acts of remembering and writing:

> l'oeil non pas voit mais bien plutôt se souvient non de la fatidique succession (ou suite, ou énumération) de parties – chevelure, épaules, seins, hanches etc . . . – dans leur ordre monotone, mais d'une combinaison, d'un ombreux et fulgurant enchevêtrement de lumières et de lignes où les éléments éclatés, dissociés se regroupent selon le foisonnant et rigoureux désordre de la mémoire [.][11]

In a more self-conscious manner, *La Bataille de Pharsale* presents the reader with a reference to its own internal structure:

> On doit se figurer l'ensemble du système comme un mobile se déformant sans cesse autour de quelques rares points fixes, par exemple l'intersection de la droite OO' et du trajet suivi par le pigeon dans son vol, ou encore celle des itinéraires de deux voyages, ou encore le nom PHARSALE figurant également dans un recueil scolaire des textes latins et sur un panneau indicateur au bord d'une route de Thessalie [.] (p. 186)[12]

As well as stressing the principle of intersection, this passage also outlines an implicit binary pattern of composition which echoes the one of alternation set at the start of the novel. This binary pattern is particularly noticeable at the end of the novel's first part where an oscillation between two time spans in the narrative is conveyed by a succession of short paragraphs alternating between the present and past tenses:

> maintenant il n'y a plus de pigeons [. . .]
> il n'y avait plus personne non plus dans le champ [. . .]
> la terrasse du café est déserte [. . .]
> la chatte blanche n'était plus perchée [. . .]
> un nuage se reflète de nouveau [. . .]
> toutes les tables peintes en bleu rangées à l'extérieur du café sur l'étroit trottoir étaient maintenant entourées d'hommes [. . .]
> est-ce qu'il y avait vraiment un terrain de football comment aurait-il pu y en avoir [. . .]
> je peux me rappeler [. . .]

Un couple est venu s'asseoir à la terrasse [. . .]
Le couple ne présente rien de particulier [.] (pp. 95–8)[13]

The alternation marks a juxtaposition of two separate narrative sequences: the urban scene of the square with the metro exit and café (narrated in the present tense) juxtaposed by the sequence (narrated in the past tense) of the rural scene set in Greece, with the narrator searching for the field on which the battle of Pharsalus was fought. Once a pattern is established, however, it is transgressed and the two initially distinct fictional units intersect and converge. Thus, the paragraph beginning 'un âne gris' (p. 96) which is narrated in the present tense refers to the sequence of the narrator's drive through the Greek countryside, thereby contradicting the pattern already established.

These last few paragraphs of part one are, furthermore, influenced through their relationship with the novel's opening passage where the metro description first appears. It is through the naming of colours that the association (the two couplings: grey and pink, and grey and blue) is made. The first grouping appears in a description of two pigeons on the pavement, 'gris à pattes roses' (p. 10), and the second describes the reflection of the sky on the fifth floor window, 'les larges mailles du rideau de filet derrière la vitre plus visibles dans la partie gris sombre que dans la bande remplie par le bleu clair' (p. 11).[14] These two couplings repeatedly intermingle in the final pages of part one:

Dans les parties *ombrées* les collines se teintaient de *bleu* (p. 94)
un camion à moitié chargé de blocs *roses* [. . .] recouverts d'une couche de poussière *grisâtre* (p. 95)
l'asphalte mouillé a séché il est d'un *gris* terne (p. 95)
la terrasse du café est déserte le garçon en tablier *bleu* (p. 95)
un âne *gris* (p. 96)
nuage bas s'allonge se teintant de *rose* (p. 96)
je vis une des trois poules au cou décharné *rose* mais pas les deux autres (p. 96)
le ciel reflété est maintenant très foncé le nuage en paraît d'autant plus éclatant (p. 97)
toutes les tables peintes en *bleu* (p. 97)[15]

The pattern is as follows: grey/blue, pink/grey, grey, blue, grey, pink, pink, blue. No hidden symbolic meaning is suggested here, simply a foregrounding of the interweaving thread of the three colours, producing a pattern of signification in which blue tends to be the dominant colour of the urban, metro sequence, and pink the dominant colour in the Greek, rural sequence. Yet again, however, once an outline of a pattern emerges, the reader stumbles across a flagrant contradiction produced by the 'disruptive force of description'.[16] The paragraph beginning 'toutes les tables peintes en bleu' would at first appear to be another description of the café in the urban sequence, as is signalled by the blue tables. A problem arises, however, when reading on one discovers that the passage is being narrated in the past tense, '[les tables] étaient maintenant entourées d'hommes assis je remarquai'.[17] The use of the shifter 'maintenant' coming straight after the shock of the unexpected tense in 'étaient' ironically indicates that the opposition implied in the statement is not a temporal one ('now' as opposed to the last time I saw the tables) but a textual opposition between this sequence in which the narrator drives past a café in Greece, and the description of the café in the square which is set in the urban sequence. In other words, the opposition is between what one might call the 'pink sequence' and the 'blue sequence', with the inadvertent reader being momentarily confused by the former sequence borrowing from the latter. It is by way of recognition of this interchange that the otherwise inexplicable last line of the paragraph makes a seemingly non-sequitur statement: 'Il n'y avait pas de marchand de journaux'.[18] The reference is to the description, two paragraphs back, of the newsvendor by the metro exit in the 'blue sequence'. The irony here reflects the disturbing 'trompe l'oeil' effect caused by a transgression within the binary system of association: the two contexts are intermingled. The last paragraph continues in this ironic tone with the description of a man and a woman who come to sit at a table in the café. There is no mention of colour. Instead the final words of this section of the novel, while overtly denoting the young couple sitting in the café, self-consciously refer to the binary pattern which has formally dominated throughout the chapter: 'le couple ne présente rien de particulier' (p. 98).[19]

The binary structure is developed on a wider scale in part two which is broken up into seven subsections. The segmented format allows for a pattern of alternation between each subsection. In addition to the switch between present and past tenses, there is also an oscillation between first and third person narratives in four consecutive subsections:

César: First person narrative past tense.
'Me rappelant cette arrivée' (p. 122)
Conversation: Third person narrative, past tense.
'Elle dit [. . .] Il dit' (p. 128)
Guerrier: First person narrative, past tense.
'Il faisait tournoyer [. . .] et nous muets' (p. 135)
Machine: Third person narrative, present tense.
'Une chaîne [. . .] se dirige' (p. 147)[20]

Whilst these four subsections contain no instances of intertextual quotations, the two subsections flanking them, 'Bataille' and 'Voyage', both consist of a mosaic of italicised quotations. The narrative surface of these subsections is fragmented by a polyphony of different narrative voices, and by the ceaseless narrative disruption caused by the quotations. The underlying compositional structure of alternation and juxtaposition is sustained and developed throughout the whole of the second part of the novel but one notices a gradual shift of focus onto the pattern of intersection and a growing textual concern with the delineation and identification of the central point of juncture. In so far as the intertextual fragment is manifestly 'foreign', its 'otherness' stands out against the novel's own narrative, thereby creating a forceful effect of narrative alternation. However, in both 'Bataille' and 'Voyage' this fragmentation is counterbalanced by thematic assimilation. The title of both sections names the common 'signifié' or motif which connects the disparate italicised passages. In 'Bataille', it is the motif of war which acts as a common denominator linking the descriptions of the battle of Pharsalus, of combat in the second world war, of the paintings by della Francesca, Ucello, and Poussin, and of a quotation from Elie Faure on art:

> le massacre aussi bien que l'amour est un prétexte à glorifier la forme dont le splendeur calme apparaît seulement à ceux qui ont pénétré l'indifférence de la nature devant le massacre et l'amour. (p. 119)[21]

In 'Voyage' the italicised passages are bound together by the motif of travel which includes the citing of place names, Sarajevo,

La Bataille de Pharsale *and its Fragments* 97

Marrakech, and the distortion of Proust's title, 'Sodome et Gonhorrée', as well as a more extended example of the motif in a passage from *A la recherche du temps perdu*:

> lumière qui éclaire le spectacle de la terre c'était le fragment d'un autre monde d'une planète inconnue une vue de [.] (p. 170)[22]

Another aspect of this motif is the reference to different nationalities: the phrase borrowed from an English art critic defining the baroque as 'movement into space'; the Italian titles FORZA DEL DESTINO and LA POTENZA E LA GLORIA; and Elie Faure's comment on the German Renaissance painters which also bears on the compositional structure of Simon's novel:

> tout pour l'artiste allemand est au même plan dans la nature le détail masque toujours l'ensemble leur univers n'est pas continu mais faits de fragments juxtaposés [.] (p. 174)[23]

The disjunctive effect of alternation in this subsection is not only produced by the interpolation of intertextual or italicised fragments. It also takes the form of a staccato oscillation between descriptions of a painting of a battle and descriptions of a couple making love. The thematic connection between the two contexts derives from the Elie Faure quotation already mentioned in which 'massacre' and 'amour' are presented as a pair. However, unlike the alternation between the 'pink' and 'blue' sequences at the end of part one, the text here is fractured into a larger number of pieces. For instance, the lovemaking sequence is split in two by virtue of the fact that in one case the male partner is not the narrator, 'maintenant elle entoure ses épaules de ses bras' (p. 121), and in the other it is him, 'un de mes bras passé sous ses épaules' (p. 121).[24] Moreover, the interchange between the present and past tenses seen earlier is here replaced by a continuous neutralising present tense which is signalled by the use of the shifter 'maintenant' at the start of almost every sentence:

> maintenant il tombe (p. 118)
> maintenant il gît sur le sol (p. 119)
> maintenant elle peut le voir (p. 119)
> maintenant je pouvais les entendre (p. 119)
> maintenant il s'élance (p. 120)

à présent le court morceau (p. 121)
maintenant elle entoure ses épaules de ses bras (p. 121)
maintenant deux petites filles (p. 121)
maintenant elle ne fait plus que crier (p. 121)[25]

The repetition of 'maintenant', reminiscent of Robbe-Grillet's novels, no longer conveying any sense of time, acts simply like a signal denoting a moment of shift, like the clicking of a slide-projector in a swift showing of a succession of disconnected pictures. With the temporal element completely neutralised by the writing, 'peut-être le temps est-il une notion qui n'a pas sa place ici non plus que celle d'espace',[26] the polyphonic crescendo of voices clamouring through the narrator's consciousness reaches a self-cancelling pitch of intensity in the final paragraph:

Maintenant elle ne fait plus que crier mais je ne l'entends pas crier presque tous ont la bouche ouverte sans doute crient-ils aussi le uns de douleur les autres pour s'exciter au combat le tumulte est à ce point où l'on n'entend plus rien [.] (p. 122)[27]

Unlike Georges in *La Route des Flandres* who attempts, however unsuccessfully, to reconstruct the past, here the narrator is a passive agent, an open sign intersected by different strands of fiction. The motif of centrality and frame is repeated throughout this section, depicting the self at the centre of a 'maelstrom':

et moi non plus étranger, spectateur regardant [. . .] mais maintenant au centre même de ce maelstrom [. . .] tournoyant sans fin entre les solennelles dorures des cadres et moi au centre [.] (pp. 116–17)[28]

The structure of 'Voyage' is similar to that of 'Bataille' in that the innumerable intertextual fragments are subsumed under a dominant motif. The most recurrent narrative sequence in this section is one which depicts the narrator travelling by train through Italy on his way to Greece. This serves as a variant of the movement/immobility paradox which dominates the start of the novel. The 'static movement' of the people on the metro exit escalator is here mirrored by the narrator's immobility as he sits in the train which wends its way past a succession of signboards:

> emporté immobile sur cette banquette de sorte que je pourrais voir mots suite de mots s'étirant s'inscrivant sur les kilomètres de temps d'air je veux dire comme ces annonces ou ces dépêches dont le texte défile en lettres d'or tremblotantes sur ces écrans lumineux chaque lettre apparaissant l'une après l'autre [.] (pp. 163–4)[29]

The train sequence also relates to the light/shade paradox in the Valéry epigraph when, a few pages earlier, the narrator describes the sudden irruption of light breaking in through the compartment window:

> la vitre le rectangle obstrué éclatant tout à coup se fragmentant l'espace l'air lui-même bruyamment fracassés en pans d'ombre de lumière de barres striés pointillés noir et jaune se précipitant à l'intérieur du compartiment fuyant à toute vitesse puis la femme reprit sa position et de nouveau je ne vis plus que l'immobile quadrillage noir et blanc [.] (p. 157)[30]

The momentary burst of light penetrating the compartment is reiterated, *mutatis mutandis*, in the motion of the train itself, 'continuant à parcourir la vaste terre s'enfonçant toujours plus avant pénétrant' (p. 162).[31] And the sexual connotations inherent in this motif are later foregrounded in the erotic sequences, 'quand il s'enfonce de nouveau en elle faisant entendre un bruit' (p. 176).[32] But the stress on the motif of penetration in 'Voyage' needs to be read in the context of the novel's internal dynamics: that is, the twin structures of intersection and binary opposition. The idea of penetration as an abstract relation, stripped of all metaphorical extensions, is emphasised in the lines referring to an anonymous English art critic,

> qui définit le baroque *movement into space* malheureusement intraduisible le mot *into* n'ayant en français que des équivalents faibles comme au dedans de ou à l'intérieur de [.] (p. 160)[33]

Banned from the self-enclosed stage-like perspective of an Ucello painting, the spectator is able to penetrate and engulf himself, 's'enfonçant', in a work such as Poussin's 'Orion aveugle marchant vers la lumière du soleil levant'.[34] The same stress on the motif of 'movement into' is discernible in the narrator's description of the intensity with which the woman sharing the compartment with him is absorbed in a novel. Her absorption in the book is described in literal terms as a physical event, an efflux of 'quelque chose d'immatériel', like the tiny particles on a magnetic field, abandoning the inert shell of her body to melt into the open pages (p. 172). While some of the descriptions moulded by the motif of penetration reflect the way in which the different semantic or textual units are threaded through specific focal points of intersection, others, such as the following description of the train's movement, mirror the alternating process of confluence and bifurcation between separate narrative strands created by the binary structure of the novel:

> les rails se divisant bruyant s'écartant bifurquant se rapprochant divergeant de nouveau se dédoublant encore se multipliant s'étalant sur une grande surface [.] (p. 164)[35]

The motif as a whole, however, can be read as a sign of the impulse of frame transgression which underlies the relationship between the past and the present in Simon's novel and, correspondingly, between the identity of the narrator and his uncle Charles. It is in the final subsection of part two, entitled 'O', that the motif reaches a peak of abstraction and in which it is most clearly related to the narrative framework. The text returns to the opening sequence in which the narrator jealously surveys the fifth floor window:

> Soit alors O la position occupée par l'oeil
> de l'observateur (O.) et d'où part une droite
> invisible OO' rejoignant l'oeil à l'objet sur
> lequel est fixé le regard [.] (p. 181)[36]

The ambivalent identity of O, which later acts as a neutral pronoun substituting for 'je', 'il', and 'elle', is at this point of the novel formulated in terms of visual perception, the literal setting of 'point of view':

imaginer le spectacle que lui-même peut offrir à un regard extérieur que ce soit celui de l'observatrice dissimulée derrière le reflet de la vitre ou celui de toute autre personne qui pourrait l'observer, soit dans le moment présent, soit, par la suite, O. n'étant donc qu'un simple point compris à l'interieur de tout autre cône de vision balayant la place sans plus ni moins d'existence qu'une trace [.] (p. 185)[37]

O as a neutral sign or empty frame capable of housing different referents can be viewed as the narrative embodiment of the focal points of textual intersection. It thus becomes a structural analogue, albeit functioning on a different register, of the motif of penetration whose role of mirroring the compositional principle of textual intersection I have already discussed.

Alternation and intersection, finally, are two patterns of textual association which spread throughout *La Bataille de Pharsale*. The rhythmic counterpoint of alternation, whose regularity and insistence at times produces an almost musical effect, would seem to spring from the binary and irreconcilable nature of the semantic relation contained in the antonymic image of the sun-shadow. The articulatory principle of intersection, on the other hand, stems from the fictional elaboration of that initial point of departure created by the transforming (in the sense of transgression of form or frame) powers of consciousness. Neither pattern exists objectively in Simon's novel like a skeleton upon which the body of the text is hung and whose clear outline appears, uniform and unchanging, in the light of perfunctory critical X-rays, but rather they are themselves generated by the creative act of reading.

II INTERTEXTUAL TRIPTYCH: READING ACROSS *LA BATAILLE DE PHARSALE*, *LA JALOUSIE*, AND *A LA RECHERCHE DU TEMPS PERDU*.

Reading *La Bataille de Pharsale*, and Simon's work in general, often resembles the act of observing watered silk: different patterns of association emerge depending on the particular optic chosen by the reader.[38] The triptych structure of composition is arguably a more ostensible pattern of construction in this novel than the patterns of alternation and intersection discussed in the foregoing pages since the novel is overtly divided into three parts. A more important indication of this formal structure, however, can be found in a 'mise en abyme' description of the cartoon strip fragment:

> Les trois images côte à côte dans leur ordre de lecture (c'est-à-dire, de gauche à droite: premièrement Hercule nonchalamment appuyé au mur à côté de l'automatique, deuxièmement voluptueuse interlocutrice à la fleur, troisièmement masque crispé au gros plan) composant, peut-être à l'insu du dessinateur, une sorte de triptyque où l'on passerait de la première image à la troisième par une rotation (un rabattement) d'un demi-cercle, le centre étant exactement occupé par la bouche sanglante de la femme dont la vision est immédiatement encadrée à droite et à gauche par l'appareil mural dont la place du premier au troisième dessin s'est trouvée inversée [.] (pp. 69–70)[39]

The structure of the triptych, as is underlined in this passage, hinges on the principle of inversion. Indeed the description clearly demonstrates how a triptych structure involves and combines the two patterns of binary opposition and of focal intersection which I have so far been analysing in isolation from one another. The central picture is said to depict the recumbent figure of a woman lying on a divan, holding a telephone conversation with a man who is represented in the two pictures flanking the central one. In both cases he is facing inwards: the perspective is inverted, and the focal point of intersection is the woman's mouth. A second 'mise en abyme' portrayal of a triptych structure can be found in the final subsection of part two which returns to the novel's opening scene. The narrator, 'O', is standing in the street looking up at a window, 'F', of his lover's room; the line of vision between observer and window is designated 'OF':

> il faut considérer la droite OF dans son sens FO: soit alors un autre observateur (ou observatrice) O. se tenant en F, c'est-à-dire dans la chambre qui correspond à la fenêtre du cinquième étage, et observant l'observateur (qui, de sujet, devient aussi objet – la lettre O pouvant donc également, dans cette situation, continuer à le désigner) [.] (p. 184)[40]

Observer and observed have become interchangeable; the 'normal' relationship of subject and object is inverted. As in the cartoon description, the reader's attention is drawn to the triptych pattern of inversion in the text. This pattern is particularly marked a few pages earlier when the line of vision between O (subject) and O (object) is named OO' (p. 181). In part three, perceptual oscillation makes way for narratorial transference: O becomes an open sign referring, at different moments, to the narrator, his uncle Charles, and the narrator's lover. The frequency with which O's identity changes, and the extent of narrative disruption which this entails, can be gleaned from the following summary:

O = uncle Charles (p. 190); O = narrator (p. 203);
O = woman (p. 211); O = narrator (p. 217); O = woman
(p. 224); O = uncle Charles (p. 229); O = narrator (p. 230);
O = uncle Charles (p. 233); O = narrator (p. 238); O = woman
(p. 244); O = narrator (p. 248); O = woman (p. 253); O = narrator (p. 256).

Just as in the cartoon 'mise en abyme' it is the woman's mouth which forms the point of intersection of the triptych structure so too the line of contact between the narrator and his uncle, between the two time spans in the novel, passes through the 'intermediary image' of the woman figure.

The pertinence of the triptych structure, with its component elements of binary opposition and central intersection, is not restricted to the narrative framework of *La Bataille de Pharsale* but also relates to the intertextual fabric of the novel. The fundamental reason for this is that the manifold quotations and implicit allusions in the novel do not amount to superficial embroidery attached, post facto, to the narrative core but are subtly woven into the fictional preoccupations of the main narrative, providing the reader with multiple extensions for exploration and decipherment. *La Bataille de Pharsale* can thus be viewed as a nodal point of convergence enclosing a network of intertextual associations between innumerable fictional works. The first two parts of the novel are spattered with countless quotations and fragments of writing, some in italics some in Roman type, ranging from the classics (Lucan, Caesar, Apuleius) to passages from Elie Faure's *Histoire de l'Art*. Amongst the more recurrent are fragments from Proust's *A la recherche du temps perdu*.[41] The links with this novel are, therefore, direct and overt. However, there are no quotations from Robbe-Grillet's *La Jalousie* in Simon's novel and yet, as will be revealed in the following pages, an implicit, indirect association exists between the two works. Indeed these three novels can be said to be related in a triptych of intertextual association.

Perhaps one of the most obvious ways in which the three novels are connected is through the theme of jealousy. This particular link is suggested in *La Bataille de Pharsale* by the narrator's attempt to find a definition of the word 'jalousie' in the pages of *A la recherche du temps perdu*:

> Disant que la jalousie est comme ... comme ... Me rappelant l'endroit: environ dans le premier tiers en haut d'une page de droite. (p. 20)[42]

Related to this thematic common denominator is the repetition of an image across the three novels. The repeated reference to the 'mille-pattes' in *La Jalousie* is echoed in the description of the scrum formed by the rugby players in *La Bataille de Pharsale*: 'comme une sorte de bête multicolore de mille-pattes' (p. 54).[43] Could it be that the quotation from *A la recherche du temps perdu* which the narrator in Simon's novel is looking for is the following image formulated by Marcel in *Un Amour de Swann*?

> Sa jalousie, comme une pieuvre qui jette une première puis une seconde, puis une troisième amarre, s'attacha solidement à ce moment de cinq heures du soir, puis à une autre encore. (I 283)[44]

The mirroring of the theme of jealousy across the three novels is paralleled on the level of plot by the 'voyeur' or 'spying' scenes. The description of O looking up at his lover's window recalls two similar descriptions in Proust's novel: namely, the famous episode of Swann spying on Odette in *Un Amour de Swann*, and the passage in *La Prisonnière* where Marcel, returning home, gazes up, with misplaced confidence, at Albertine's window:

> Du trottoir je voyais la fenêtre de la chambre d'Albertine, cette fenêtre autrefois toujours noire, le soir, quand elle n'habitait pas la maison, que la lumière électrique de l'intérieur, segmentée par les pleins des volets, striait de haut en bas de barres d'or parallèles. Ce grimoire magique, autant il était clair pour moi et

dessinait devant mon esprit calme des images précises [.] (III 330)⁴⁵

The similarities between this scene and the earlier episode in which Swann taps at the shutters of what he mistakenly believes to be Odette's window create the same effect of textual reiteration which was to become the hallmark of Claude Simon's writing:

Tout était désert et noir dans ce quartier [. . .] Parmi l'obscurité de toutes les fenêtres éteintes depuis longtemps dans la rue, il en vit une seule d'où débordait – entre les volets qui en pressaient la pulpe mystérieuse et dorée – la lumière qui remplissait la chambre [.] (I 272–3)⁴⁶

Olga Bernal, who has compared the latter passage with the sequence in *La Jalousie* where the implicit narrator spies from within the house, through the shutters of a window, at A . . . and Franck sitting on the terrace, has asserted that 'le roman de Proust est tout entier une tension vers l'au-delà de l'immédiat'.⁴⁷ Yet the conscious attempt to attain that essence which lies behind the veil of the immediate remains permanently thwarted. In fact the intertextual associations I am outlining encourage one to read the two episodes in Proust as an allegory of the elusiveness of truth as glimpsed in art. The metaphor of 'grimoire magique' recalls the earlier analogy between Swann's supposed detection of Odette's secret life and the decipherment of manuscripts. If one interprets what lies behind the window in both scenes as 'l'au-delà de l'immédiat', one can view Swann's gross error as an indication that this remains beyond one's grasp. Similarly Marcel soon discovers that the security he feels in having Albertine to himself is built on an illusion. The 'images précises' of the wizard's book turn out to have been much more ambiguous and indeterminate than Marcel initially imagined. However, in the context of artistic creation, this very ambiguity of 'descriptive surface' becomes a source of inspiration for both writer and reader as it allows for the kaleidoscopic and impressionistic play of formal association upon which the whole novel is based.

The opening sequence in *La Bataille de Pharsale*, which I have argued is a fictional enactment of the sun-shadow metaphor, is thus revealed to be intertextually linked with two specific episodes in *A la recherche du temps perdu*. The complexity of this focal scene is further intensified by the fact that the 'jaune'/'noir' alternation, which is the novel's version of the paradoxical image, is also related to the same passages in Proust's novel. Both passages contrast the surrounding black night with the golden light shining deceptively and therefore momentarily at Odette's and Albertine's windows.

Another point of contact between the three novels lies in the connotation of adultery in the words 'mauvais mécanicien' in *La Jalousie* referring not only to Franck's inability to mend the car but also to his sexual skills. The allusion to sex via the motif of mechanics is reiterated several times, as in the following description of the zip fastener of A . . . .'s dress:

> Au-dessous de la chevelure mouvante, la taille très fine est coupée verticalement dans l'axe du dos, par l'étroite fermeture métallique de la robe.[48]

Is there not a relationship here with *La Prisonnière* where Marcel's trust in the chauffeur, or 'mécanicien' (III 134), whom he has hired to keep an eye on Albertine, is shown to have been possibly misguided when Charlus describes Theodore, the 'cocher' from Combray, hired by one of his friends, as a 'retrousseur de jupons' (III 306)? Simon's novel inverts this analogy between sexuality and mechanics. Whereas in Proust's novel and in *La Jalousie* sexuality (the tenor or 'comparé') is evoked in terms of mechanics (the vehicle or 'comparant'), in *La Bataille de Pharsale* there is a description of the 'mécaniques démantibulées' strewn along the Greek countryside in which the machines (the tenor) are described in terms of sexuality (the vehicle). The metaphor is reversed. The analogy hinges on the pun in 'cocotte' meaning 'whore' and 'the base of a brake lever' ('cocotte du frein' (p. 149)):

> Elles laissent peu à peu entrevoir leurs anatomies incompréhensibles, délicates féminines, aux connexions elles aussi délicates et compliquées. Leurs articulations autrefois huilées, aux frottements doux, sont maintenant grippées, raidies. Elles dressent vers le ciel, dans une emphatique et interminable protestation, vaguement ridicules, comme de vieilles cocottes déchues, des membres décharnés: quelques tringles, quelque brancard pourri, un siège où aucun conducteur ne s'assiéra jamais et qui ne sert

plus que du perchoir à quelques poules maigres au cou
déplumé, rose vif. (p. 153)[49]

This form of inversion, or 'reciprocal metaphor',[50] acts as a bridge
between otherwise unrelated descriptions in *La Bataille de Pharsale*'s
main narrative. For example, there is reversal of tenor and vehicle
between the mineral imagery in the description of the body of a
man making love as 'une masse bosselée, rocailleuse' (p. 212) and
the personification in the description of a landscape: 'épaulement
de la colline pierreuse' (p. 220).[51]

The most interesting example of intertextual association between
La Bataille de Pharsale and the novels of Proust and Robbe-Grillet
arises from the first few pages of the third part of Simon's work.
O, now designating the narrator's uncle, is sitting in a café writing
a letter to his lover, Odette Pa . . ., whose name appears for the
first time. In the light of the quotations from *A la recherche du temps
perdu*, and particularly one in which Swann's Odette is named
(p. 155), the reader is alerted to the parallel with Proust's novel.
What follows is an intensification of this relationship which,
though implicit, influences the generative development of the text
in a crucial way. O glances briefly at the view from where he sits:

> Il regarde la place, la fontaine, les statues. Il regarde ensuite les
> gens assis à la terrasse autour de lui. A la fin il baisse la tête et
> regarde le plateau du guéridon devant lequel il est assis. Sur le
> guéridon est posé son verre au fond duquel un glaçon finit de
> fondre dans un reste de liquide d'un brun jaunâtre. (p. 193)[52]

The word 'fontaine' in the first sentence is phonetically echoed by
'fond' and 'fondre' three sentences later. Similarly, there is
repetition of sound in 'place', 'terrasse' and '*glaçon*'. But beneath
this surface of linguistic association lies a web of intertextual
relations. The triple reference to the square, the fountain, and the
statues is motivated by two fragments from *A la recherche du temps
perdu* which appear in the first part of *La Bataille de Pharsale* (pp. 20,
22, 90, 93):

> Et sur les places les divinités des fontaines publiques tenant en
> main un jet de glace entendu dire me demanda-t-il en me
> quittant que ma tante Oriane divorcerait Personnellement je
> Une gradation verticale de bleus glaciers et les tours du Troca-

déro qui semblaient si proches des degrés turquoises [.] (p. 90)[53]

Reference to 'place', 'fontaine' and 'statues' in *La Bataille de Pharsale*'s main narrative sequence can thus be seen as an infiltration of textual elements from the Proust fragments. The influence extends further. There is an echo of 'jet de glace' and 'bleus glaciers' in the reference to the ice cube ('glaçon') melting in the glass:

> Sur le guéridon est posé son verre au fond duquel un glaçon finit de fondre dans un reste de liquide d'un brun orangé. (p. 193)[54]

The punning play between the words 'fond' and 'fondre' on each side of the word 'glaçon' hints at a pattern of inversion which, as will soon emerge, is magnified by intertextual association. The passage continues with a reference to a della Francesca reproduction ('La Défaite de Chosroès') on one of the postcards:

> A l'intérieur du V renversé que dessinent les jambes on peut voir: [. . .] la main d'un homme encore serrée sur la poignée d'un glaive (l'avant-bras, la main et le glaive qui la prolonge coupent le V renversé à peu près à l'horizontale, à la façon de la barre d'un A située un peu plus bas et légèrement de travers. La main tenant le glaive [.] (pp. 194–5)[55]

Apart from the resemblance between 'la main tenant le glaive' and Proust's 'tenant en main un jet de glace', one can identify an implicit but none the less significant influence of Robbe-Grillet's *La Jalousie*. Firstly, the configuration of the letter A reminds the reader of the central character in *La Jalousie*. Secondly, there is an echo of the obsessive focus on hands in that novel, as in the sequence of A . . . brushing her hair, or clutching the table-knife in the 'mille-pattes' episode, or in the following part of a description of a photograph of A . . . sitting at a café table while on holiday in Europe:

> Posée sur la table à proximité d'un second verre, près du bord de l'image, une main d'homme se raccorde seulement d'une manche de veste, qu'interrompt aussitôt la marge blanche verticale.[56]

Moreover, 'main tenant' evokes, through punning association, 'maintenant': a word which appears with unusual frequency in both *La Bataille de Pharsale*, as I have shown, and in *La Jalousie*. 'Maintenant' is of special structural interest by virtue of the fact that, like all 'shifters' including, in the case of Simon's novel, the pronominal use of 'O', one can only know which specific moment in time the word refers to by knowing the context of each utterance.[57] Since both novels consist of a series of unannounced shifts from one time sequence to another, the obsessive recurrence of the word 'maintenant', although redundant in its normal function of referring to a particular moment in time, paradoxically highlights the disruption of narrative chronology by the generative flow of the writing.

To recapitulate, my reading of the café sequence near the start of the third part of Simon's novel has so far shown that the passage is heavily loaded with textual elements from *La Jalousie* and *A la recherche du temps perdu*. Prompted by these manifold indications of links with the two works, one can pursue the ramifications produced by this reading into the novels of Robbe-Grillet and Proust.

The reader who returns to *La Jalousie* after reading the passage under discussion will surely fix on one particular passage near the centre of the novel. Franck is leaving after having returned A . . . to her home following the overnight trip to town:

> Franck se lève de son fauteuil, avec une vigueur soudaine, et pose sur la table basse le verre qu'il vient de finir d'un trait. Il n'y a plus trace du cube de glace dans le fond. Franck s'est avancé, d'un pas raide, jusqu'à la porte du couloir. Il s'y arrête. La tête et le buste pivotent en direction de A . . ., restée assise.
> 'Excusez-moi, encore, d'être un si mauvais mécanicien.'[58]

A few lines later, a new paragraph begins with the following sentence:

> Au fond du verre qu'il a déposé sur la table en partant, achève de fondre un petit morceau de glace, arrondi d'un côté, présentant de l'autre une arête de biseau.[59]

One can easily recognise the similarities with the sentence already mentioned referring to the melting ice cube in *La Bataille de Pharsale*.

Once again inversion is the main structural principle organising the text. The punning association of 'fond' and 'fondre' acts as the point of contact between the two conflicting statements; 'il n'y a plus trace du cube de glace dans le fond' and 'Au fond du verre [. . .] achève de fondre un petit morceau de glace [.]' The contradiction is of fundamental structural significance since by reading on one discovers that the new paragraph is chronologically anterior to the one it follows in textual contiguity: the passage is now referring to a point in time prior to the trip to town.

The connections with *A la recherche du temps perdu* similarly reveal inversion as the dominating structural pattern. This time the threads of intertextual association are more visible to the reader. The two quotations which, as I have shown, motivated the description of the café sequence in Simon's novel are both part of a long sequence in *Le Temps retrouvé* where the narrator is strolling through the streets of Paris during the war. The passage begins with an inversion between town and country. Marcel describes Paris in terms of the countryside:

et même d'autres éléments de nature qui n'existaient pas jusque-là à Paris faisaient croire qu'on venait, descendant du train, d'arriver pour les vacances en pleine campagne [.] (III 736)[60]

The dominant 'signifiant' in the description is 'glace': the moonlight shines on the boulevard Haussmann as if on 'un glacier des Alpes'; the statues holding 'un jet de glace' seem to have been made 'd'une matière double pour l'exécution desquelles l'artiste avait voulu marier exclusivement le bronze au cristal'.[61] When the passage resumes, after an interruption caused by the reminiscence of Saint-Loup's visit, the reader discovers the second of the two quotations which appear in *La Bataille de Pharsale*, containing another instance of the same 'signifiant'. The sky is no longer 'une mer étendue, mais une gradation verticale de bleus glaciers' (III 762).[62]

The passage we have been considering complies with the compositional symmetry which Proust strove to achieve between *Le Temps retrouvé* and *Du côté de chez Swann* by mirroring a passage which appears near the start of *A la recherche du temps perdu*: the description of Marcel's walks by the river Vivonne. The connections between the two passages include repetition of imagery, such as the description of the shadows of trees on the Parisian snow:

> Les silhouettes des arbres se reflétaient nettes et pures sur cette neige d'or bleuté, avec la délicatesse qu'elles ont dans certaines peintures japonaises ou dans certains fonds de Raphael (III 736)[63]

and a similar description of the reflection of trees on the river:

> les grandes ombres des arbres donnaient à l'eau un fond qui était habituellement d'un vert sombre mais que parfois [. . .] j'ai vu d'un bleu clair et cru, tirant sur le violet, d'apparence cloisonnée et de goût japonais. (I 169)[64]

Another common feature shared by the two passages, and one which also ties up with the passages in *La Jalousie* and *La Bataille de Pharsale* I have been discussing, is the use of the word 'fond'. Here it appears in connection with the baroque perspective of reversibility pervading both descriptions. Thus, for example, the Vivonne's colour is designated as 'bleu ciel' (I 166–7) while the sky over Paris is compared with 'une immense mer' (III 762). Indeed the florid surface of the river is described as a 'parterre céleste' mingling, like a kaleidoscope, 'ce qu'il y a de plus profond' with 'ce qu'il y a d'infini' (I 170).[65] But the most vivid example of inversion, or reciprocity, in the Vivonne passage (indeed in the whole novel) occurs during Marcel's comment on the 'carafes' thrown in the river for the purpose of catching fish:

> remplies par la rivière où elles sont à leur tour encloses, à la fois 'contenant' aux flancs transparents, comme une eau durcie et 'contenu' plongé dans un plus grand contenant de cristal liquide et courant [. . .] allitération perpétuelle entre l'eau sans consistance où les mains ne pouvaient le capter et le verre sans fluidité où le palais ne pourrait en jouir. (I 1680)[66]

An interlocking pattern of inclusion is outlined in which the bottles contain water while themselves being contained in the larger vessel which is the river. Furthermore, this motif of reciprocity is matched, as critics like Ullmann and Genette have perceived,[67] by the 'reciprocal metaphor' in which the bottles are described as 'hardened water' and the river as 'liquid crystal'. The intertextual associations I have been tracing indicate that the ripples of this 'allitération perpétuelle' can be felt in *La Jalousie* and *La Bataille de Pharsale*. At each of the points through which the threads of intertextual association pass, linking the café sequence in *La Bataille de Pharsale* with the passages I have pinpointed in the novels written by Proust and Robbe-Grillet, inversion is revealed to be the underlying principle of composition. The relationship can thus be defined as a further example of extended metaphorical configuration, similar to the structural affinities which Jean Ricardou has observed between *A la recherche du temps perdu* and *Mémoires d'outre-tombe*.[68] Claude Simon's text is allusive in so far as it refers the reader to the novels of Proust and Robbe-Grillet, inviting him to re-read these works from a particular perspective. By responding to this invitation the reader creates a text or tissue or, perhaps, 'intertext' of associations which would otherwise not exist. Such an intertextual reading requires of the reader a new and more creative involvement than the passive role which has hitherto been expected of him. Indeed, this form of reading may be described, to borrow from Jean Ricardou, as 'une lecture qui agit, qui écrit'.[69]

III INTERTEXTUAL EMBEDDING

It is better to copy a drawing or painting than to try to be inspired by it, to make something similar.[70]

Picasso's dictum, and its frequent application in his work, brought what had previously been an implicit assumption to the forefront of twentieth-century artistic thinking. In 'Bacchanale' (1944), 'Portrait d'un Peintre' (1950), and 'Demoiselles des Bords de la Seine' (1950), Picasso forged new works of art out of famous paintings by Poussin, El Greco, and Courbet. He later developed this process further in his cycles of variations based on Delacroix's 'Femmes d'Alger', Velazquez's 'Las Meninas', and Manet's 'Déjeuner sur l'Herbe'. Earlier, Max Ernst had painted his own version of Manet's painting and Salvador Dali had inserted miniature distortions of Millet's 'Angélus' in the background of paintings like 'Portrait de Gala' (1935), while more recently Francis Bacon has re-created Velazquez's 'Pope Innocent X' (1960). Instead of painting from life or nature, Picasso, Ernst, Bacon and Dali, in these works, have painted from painting: the view of art as representation is altered to one of art as re-presentation. Whether these transformations were originally intended as parodic interpretations, or as 'distorted records',[71] or whether they resulted from respectful and obsessive explorations of formal properties, the effect on the spectator is that of seeing two paintings in one. The modern painting is recognised as a superimposition on the original picture which nevertheless continues to seep through like the transparent image of a watermark.

The idea of 're-writing' can sometimes be legitimately construed as a parallel concern in literature. Bruce Morrissette, for example, compares the 'roman africain' which acts as 'mise en abyme' in *La Jalousie* with Graham Greene's *The Heart of the Matter* and quotes Robbe-Grillet on the subject: ' "Les romans de Greene" m'a-t-il dit un jour, "m'ont souvent donné l'envie de les récrire" '.[72] Claude Simon's novel may be said to add a third layer to this intertextual superimposition by 're-writing' *La Jalousie* 're-writing' *The Heart of the Matter*. The intertextual relations between *La Bataille de Pharsale* and Robbe-Grillet's novel have already been analysed, but the evocation of Graham Greene's work occurs no less conspicuously in the reference to the book read by the woman in the narrator's train compartment: 'tandis qu'elle était maintenant toute entière sans doute dans ce monde verdâtre que représentait le dessin sur la couverture coloriée [.]' (p. 172).[73] That this 'greenish world' is truly that of Graham Greene is made evident by the quotation of a title 'LA POTENZA E LA GLORIA' and the references to the jungle setting, the whisky priest, and 'quelque chose d'anglo-christiano-saxon'. Although the novels of Graham Greene and Claude Simon are poles apart, and despite the unmistakably mocking tone of the phrase I have just quoted, it would be wrong to interpret this passage, as some critics have done, simply as a 'résumé férocement caricatural' of Greene's writing.[74] Such an interpretation would imply that Simon's work was inspired by an over-riding expressive intent and would thereby have the unfortunate and misleading consequence of equating the two authors' work on the level of their views as to the nature and purpose of fiction. In fact, it is clear that Simon's text, including the intertextual references in this passage, is organised according to a system of composition which is paronomastic rather than exclusively parodic. For the other title mentioned in this passage, 'LA FORZA DEL DESTINO', is the name of one of Verdi's operas. What Verdi, whose solemn bust engraved on Italian bank-notes is described at other points in the novel, and Greene have in common is the 'greenness' of their names.

The two questions of expressivity and inspiration are intimately linked, for both are concerned with the nebulous realm of thought, ideas and conceptions of 'reality' which lies on the obverse side of language as sign. The use of intertextuality in the work of modern fiction writers is best understood in the light of Picasso's crucial distinction between inspiration and re-creation. The latter lays its emphasis on an exploitation of 'signifiants' rather than a re-affirmation or commentary on the themes and ideas of the work serving, in some sense, as 'model':

> Il est clair que *La Bataille de Pharsale* ne s'inspire pas des autres textes mais relit et les réécrit les redistribue dans son propre espace, on découvre les jonctions, les soubassements à la fois formels et idéologiques les faisant servir à son propre texte.[75]

Françoise Van Rossum-Guyon's remark bears witness to the fact that the intertextual quotations and allusions in *La Bataille de Pharsale* are treated as compositional elements which combine with other categories of textual material (fragments of memory, visual descriptions, and imaginative constructions). Sometimes the intertextual fragments are themselves juxtaposed and interlocked like jig-saw pieces with corresponding contours, as in the following lines which stand out in italics: 'non pas la mort qui est le châtiment réservé à tous mais après ton destin fatal le sentiment de ta mort il reçut dans la bouche un si violent coupe de [.] (p. 67).[76]

It is not until near the end of the novel that one realizes, retrospectively, that the latter part of this fragment, unlike the first part which is a quotation from Lucan's *Pharsalia*, is taken from Plutarch's *Caesar*: 'Il reçut dans la bouche un si violent coup de glaive que la pointe en sortit par la nuque'.[77] Despite the clash of syntax, the fragment exudes an air of continuity by the fact that both quotations allude to the death of Crastinus.

At other times a sense of contextual overlap is created by a semblance of syntactic continuity that glosses over the shifts which take place in the referential dimension. For example, the narrator's description of himself falling from a horse while being pursued by the Germans is transformed into a description of a wrestling match which in turn changes into a description of a painting:

Puis je le vis cabré au-dessus de moi [. . .] j'aurais pu compter les clous chacun des quatre trous pour les crampons choses qui s'immobilisent tout à coup et dont on garde l'image précise: ainsi avant que l'arbitre siffle celui au maillot rose renversé sur le dos les quatre fers en l'air [. . .] et l'autre au-dessus de lui en l'air figure volante à peu près dans la même position [. . .] comme un cheval ruant les pieds ayant déjà quitté le sol le glaive étincelant qu'il tient dans une main pointé vers la gorge [.] (pp. 60–1)[78]

The ironic recognition of the displacement, 'l'image précise',[79] and the contradictory use of the colon and the connective 'ainsi', paradoxically draw the reader's attention to the contours separating one description from the next. Yet the three descriptions are connected by a double chain of association. On the one hand, they are linked by the positions of the figures in each sequence: a man (or horse) falling on top of another man. The juxtaposition of the scenes is underpinned by a relation of textual inversion which unites the whole passage. The reference to the horse in the first sequence is transmuted into a 'comparant' or part of a simile in the third sequence, 'comme un cheval'. The transition is instigated by the metaphor in the second sequence, 'les quatre fers en l'air'. Thus compositional overlap is produced by the generative flow of the writing which draws on elements from specific contextual sources (whether intertextual, pictorial, or 'unmotivated' descriptions) and uses them as malleable textual material in the formulation of new descriptive passages.

From a broader point of view, the mosaic quality of *La Bataille de Pharsale* can be seen as inciting the reader to follow closely the multiple trails which lead from one intertextual interpolation to another. The challenge is easily accepted as from a distance the reader's view of the novel is clouded by a blur of confused impressions. One such trail of intertextual articulation is signalled by the word 'trompette'. The allusions to the sound of trumpet playing at dawn are set in an ambiguous time and place, seeming to refer now to the battle of La Meuse (pp. 33–5, 94–5), now to the battle of Pharsalus (p. 112). The allusion also evokes the depiction of 'le page qui souffle de la trompette' in della Francesca's 'Défaite de Chosroès' (p. 153, 268–70) which is reproduced on a postcard lying on O's table at the end of the novel. The connotations of the word 'trompette' thus branch out into disparate spatio-temporal contexts. Its ramifications also extend to the novel's main narrative in the sound of the 'trompe d'auto' (p. 23) heard by the narrator as he witnesses his lover deceiving him ('tromper'). The articulatory bridge formed by this word also reaches out across intertextual boundaries. At the end of Proust's *La Prisonnière* the sound of 'trompes d'automobile' (whose connotations relate to the 'mauvais mécanicien' motif analysed earlier) and the smell of petrol afford Marcel his final moments of illusory happiness and confidence in Albertine before she leaves him. 'Trompette' is thus one of the 'signifiants' in *La Bataille de Pharsale* which perpetuate the theme of deception in the novel. And the relationship with Proust's text is ironically indicated in the following example of what one might call 'fake intertextuality:

> modèle petite garce qui le trompait avec tout le monde Ce pauvre Charles avec les femmes il était d'une naiveté et celle-là pour enlever sa culotte il ne lui fallait [.] (p. 20)[80]

Coming as it does at the end of a succession of discontinuous quotations from *A la recherche du temps perdu*, the fragment gives the impression of being taken from Proust and of referring to Swann and Odette. This impression is misleading, however, as the lines actually refer to the narrator's uncle Charles. Simon's text thus self-consciously, and not without an element of humour, deceives the reader on the theme of deception. And yet a momentary, hazy fusion is created, an indeterminate common ground is etched out between the two novels as the reader dwells on the enigmatic reference.

The play of intertextuality in *La Bataille de Pharsale* can be described as an extension of the compositional principle of frame transgression which I have shown in earlier chapters to be a major structural preoccupation in Simon's work since *La Route des Flandres*. The merging of heterogenous contexts is often brought about by the intervention of Simon's narrative with the result that a given passage which is intertextually motivated by a number of extraneous sources displays a strongly hybrid character. Thus the repeated description of the nude warrior charging into battle is in part a description of a painting (with elements from della Francesca's Arezzo mural) as well as being a fictional embellishment of the death of Crastinus (signalled by the reference to the thrown javelin and the impending death: 'Dans quelques instants le guerrier va recevoir un coup de glaive qui entrera par sa bouche ouverte' (p. 200)).[81] Like the sudden animation of a photograph of uncle Charles in Van Velden's studio, the text here introduces the element of time and action inside the framework of pictorial configuration. In this way, Simon's use of intertextuality may be said to be more far-reaching than Picasso's variations of former masterpieces, for the transformations in *La Bataille de Pharsale* occur not only on the level of style but on the level of medium as well. Nevertheless, the analogy with modern painting is a valuable one since it hinges on the fact that this form of art is perceived by its audience as a layering of figurative or textual strata which defers the final anchorage in the referential dimension, placing the ultimate point of reference at a further remove.

La Bataille de Pharsale, in sum, is composed of a plurality of fragmented intertextual screens which reflect and overlap creating an overall effect of a mosaic of embedded narratives. At the centre of this infinite play of diversity and refraction the novel's main narrative revolves around the historical enigma of the battle of Pharsalus. But the narrator's attempt to disinter this historical event from the depths of time and literature by locating the site on which the battle is reported to have taken place proves unsuccessful. For not only is the truth of this battle dispersed among all the other wars and representations of combat depicted in the text but the event itself recedes behind the plurality of versions and perspectives offered by the accounts of Lucan, Caesar, Plutarch, Livy and others. In short, the remoteness of the battle of Pharsalus and its manifold textual variations provide an appropriate summary of the status of the referential plane in Simon's writing in general. Replying to a question put to him by Anthony Pugh at the 1974 Cerisy colloquium, Claude Simon clearly revealed how crucial the implications of intertextuality are to his view of writing in general:

SIMON: Lorsque donc Ricardou parle, comme l'autre jour et à juste titre, de conflit entre la dimension référentielle et la dimension scripturale, je me demande si l'on ne pourrait pas dire que dans la composition de la 'dimension référentielle' entre déjà, pour une bonne part, une 'dimension scripturale': l'ancienne et une nouvelle . . .

PUGH: Je pensais que la gravure de Picasso reproduite dans *Orion aveugle*, et qui semble décrite dans *La Bataille de Pharsale*, avait peut-être le sens symbolique que j'ai attribué . . .

SIMON: Vous voyez que l'espace 'référentielle' est là encore constitué par un texte: un dessin [.][82]

Part Three
Materiality

1
The Materiality of Fiction

> La littérature ne m'intéresse donc *profondément* que dans la mesure où elle exerce l'esprit à certaines transformations, – celles dans lesquelles les propriétés excitantes du langage jouent un rôle capital.
> Paul Valéry, *Au sujet du 'Cimetière Marin'*[1]

The 'nouveau roman' has often been defined in terms of its place in the historical development of the novel genre which has, over the last two centuries, narrowed down its broad panoramic view of society and nature, as proposed by global visionaries like Balzac, Zola, Galdós, Tolstoy, and Dickens, to a microscopic close-up of the world of objects and sense-impressions. Dubbing the new novelists 'chosistes' and casting them as members of an imaginary 'école du regard' some critics have interpreted this historical development simply as an increasing preference for one type of realism over another. Early critics in particular held that whereas traditional realism, in all its various guises, aimed at representing as much as possible of the universe surrounding man, either collectively or as an individual, the new blinkered realism of modernity was focusing on a tiny portion of that universe: namely, the world of objects.[2] Thus, for R.-M. Albérès the pure 'objectivity' of Robbe-Grillet's novels stands as the determining feature of the 'nouveau roman' as a whole:

> Le fondateur de l'école, Alain Robbe-Grillet, modifie notre vision en donnant plus d'importance aux *objets* qu'aux êtres [. . .] On se trouve alors en face d'un procédé: refuser toute 'psychologie', et évoquer, assez arbitrairement, une aventure humaine, uniquement par le moyen des *objets* qui l'entourent et la cernent [.][3]

The uncompromising denial of psychological considerations

entailed the elimination of all the symbolic meanings and connotations which our culture has invested in the world of objects. 'As a result', says Vivian Mercier, ' "things *are there*" in Simon's novels, often endowed with an intrinsic importance unrelated to their symbolic value for the human mind that perceives them'.[4] The 'nouveau roman' is thus interpreted as the culminating point of a progressive purification of external reality; by which process objects are divested of their metaphysical and anthropomorphic signification and restored to their unmediated presence as neutral sense-data. One is led to infer from this interpretation that reality in the new novel is both narrow, in the sense of being limited almost exclusively to the 'minutiae of life', and flat, in that it is emptied of all ontological depth. It is, however, conceded that whilst this phenomenological perspective is instituted by a systematic bracketing or suspension of all preconceived attitudes towards external reality, the existence of the latter is nevertheless only asserted as evidence of one's consciousness. In other words, 'presence' is not put forward as an independent, existential fact, but as something which is recorded or apprehended by the mind. Materiality is reduced to its empirical status as sense-datum. Consciousness, in the 'nouveau roman', is mainly represented as an act of visual perception; and the central character is usually a spectator or voyeur. Olga Bernal remarks that Robbe-Grillet's novels present 'images immédiates' which are freed from adjectival qualification and presupposition, and which are cinematic in their rendering of an irreducible and undeniable 'hard core' of observable reality:

> Une image ainsi déliée peut et sera la plupart du temps extrêmement précise et matérielle, minutieuse et réaliste, telle l'image cinématographique dont la caractéristique est qu'elle ne peut pas comporter d'adjectif abstrait.[5]

The modern novel, it would seem, has attained a high degree of concreteness, precision, and realism by relying heavily on a visual apprehension of the external world. The psychological introspection of the conventional novel has been supplanted by an all-absorbing visual consciousness of the present, mingling at times, it is conceded, with the mental scenarios of the imagination but the latter itself is said to unfold in purely visual terms as 'un film intérieur qui se déroule continuellement en nous-mêmes' and

The Materiality of Fiction 123

which also takes place in the here and now.⁶ The 'nouveau roman', according to this line of thought, remains concerned with the representation of space (whether real or imaginary) and the materiality of this fiction is said to be purely visual. In sum, the phenomenology of the new novel derives from its unmitigated reliance on visual data.

And yet, despite some early pronouncements on the 'pouvoir laveur du regard',⁷ Robbe-Grillet has always emphasised the indeterminate and ambiguous nature of the referential dimension of his novels, however firmly it may seem to be grounded in a visual representation of surface reality:

> Le souci de précision qui confine parfois au délire (ces notions si peu visuelles de 'droite' et de 'gauche', ces comptages, ces mensurations, ces repères géométriques) ne parvient pas à empêcher le monde d'être mouvant jusque dans ses aspects les plus matériels, et même au sein de son apparente immobilité. Il ne s'agit plus ici de temps qui coule, puisque paradoxalement les gestes ne sont au contraire donnés que figés dans l'instant. C'est la matière elle-même qui est à la fois présente et rêvée, étrangère à l'homme et sans cesse en train de s'inventer dans l'esprit de l'homme. Tout l'intérêt des pages descriptives – c'est-à-dire la place de l'homme dans ces pages – n'est donc pas dans la chose décrite, mais dans le mouvement même de la description.⁸

The profusion of geometrical indications, therefore, only accentuates the imprecision and instability of the space delineated by the new novel. Robbe-Grillet's analysis applies equally well to Simon's work including *Les Corps conducteurs* which the author had originally intended to name 'Propriétés de quelques figures, géométriques ou non'.⁹ In the following lines taken from that novel, the repetition of words referring to the spatial positioning of the metro exit exceeds any serious striving for topographical exactitude and results in parody:

> L'entrée du métro [. . .] s'ouvre *dans* le trottoîr *parallèlement au* sens de la rue, *à côté de* la cafétéria *au coin de* l'avenue [.]
> (My emphasis, p. 160)¹⁰

The punctilious indication of the exact location of the metro exit is rendered meaningless by the absence of any broader frame of reference. For the reader harbouring the same expectations which are invoked, and only partially fulfilled, by realist fiction, the names of the metro station and adjoining streets would have provided ample information for the scene to be 'set'. Yet this hypertrophy of anonymous topographical specification sketches out a caricature of its own terms of reference. The string of prepositions, of 'dans', 'parallèlement au', 'à côté de', and 'au coin de', presents the reader with a disjointed view of the 'scene' in question; a 'scene' which is, in fact, like a sentence in this and all 'nouveaux romans' where connecting words like 'donc' and 'maintenant' are divested of their logical, referential indication and instead mark out the points of transition between disconnected parts: stumbling blocks rather than helpful signposts.

Simon's original title for *Les Corps conducteurs* transfers the reader's attention from the external world of objects to the semantic infrastructure of textual composition. The 'properties' referred to are entirely linguistic although they include the figurative components which comprise the imagery and referential dimension evoked by the words. Like Valéry, Claude Simon is concerned with the transformational qualities of language and his writing opens up avenues of signification by uncovering the myriad lexical and semantic 'properties' which are normally overlooked in a linear, expressive use of language. This 'oversight' is actively elicited by the realist ideal and is the main prerequisite for the conventional view of what constitutes a 'readable' novel: namely, one which permits the reader to embark on a mental tour of the fictional world depicted by the narrative. In an early essay, Michel Butor referred to this convention by way of a reply to André Breton's dismissal of Dostoevsky and the novel genre as a whole: 'il faut, lorsque l'auteur nous dit que le jeune homme entre dans la chambre que nous acceptions, complices, d'y entrer avec lui'.[11] However, if the reader is to 'step into' the fictional world in this way he must also, so to speak, 'step over' the linguistic materiality of the work. Some of the preconditions for this 'voyeuristic' perambulation are a clearly-defined, 'visible' topography in which the reader can pick his way past fixed and recognisable objects; a chronologically consistent narrative, or, at least, in cases where continuity is temporarily lost it should be ultimately recoverable; a system of composition in which metonymic order prevails over metaphorical association, so that the pursuit of homogeneity and uniformity counteracts all trace of confusion, ambiguity, contradiction and multiplicity; and, most important of all, a view of language as no more than a transparent vehicle for the world it conjures up, one in which it is thus, by some magical and paradoxical process, both functional and inconspicuous.

The specular framework of this conception of the act of reading is a symptom of the commonplace naive confusion between reading and vision which has also been responsible for such outmoded clichés as the reader's ability to 'picture' or 'see with the mind's eye' the universe of the novel unfolding before him or her. This confusion is perhaps not unnatural and derives from our early childhood discovery of language. Merleau-Ponty describes an infant's view of language as being like that of 'un spectateur mal placé au théâtre' who hears the words exchanged by the adults around him, witnesses their reactions, but is frustrated because 'il n'y a rien au bout de ces gestes, derrière ces mots, rien n'*arrive* pour lui'.[12] Merleau-Ponty also alludes to a children's story which tells of a young boy's disappointment when he dons his grandmother's spectacles and stares at the book she has been reading to him, and exclaims: 'Mais bernique! Où donc est l'histoire? Je ne vois rien que noir et blanc'.[13] In the context of literary theory, this pseudo-Cartesian 'ghost-in-the-machine' conception of reading has a close parallel in the illusionistic perspective of 'trompe l'oeil' paintings. The 'hallucinatory' evocation of a fictional world existing intact 'behind' language amounts to a calculated effect induced by what Ricardou calls the 'trompe-lecteur' perspective of writing:

> l'illusion représentative suscite un evident effet connexe: le trompe l'oeil d'une certaine peinture, le trompe-lecteur d'une certaine litterature. Donner au lecteur l'impression d'un contact avec les choses et actions mêmes, c'est en même temps lui faire oublier qu'il est en contact avec un texte. Tout fasciné par l'hallucination des actes et choses, le lecteur ne se rend plus compte qu'il tourne les pages d'un livre [.][14]

Even on its own purely mimetic terms, the 'trompe-lecteur' effect of realist representation is unsatisfactory. With the advent of modern science which dispensed with the Aristotelian notions of unity, order and causality upon which scientific thinking had previously been based;[15] with the formulation of Planck's

Quantum Theory which related the properties of atomic particles with the properties of radiant energy, and of Einstein's Theory of Relativity which proved that all motion is relative and no observer is ever absolutely at rest; and with the writings of phenomenologists and Gestalt psychologists who were influenced by these scientific discoveries and situated them, in particular the idea of the 'relativity of movement', in the context of the individual's consciousness of the external world;[16] in short, with the whole emphasis of modern theory and research on the discontinuities and contradictions of the physical world and our perception of it, the homogenous and immutable 'tableau' of 'realist' mimetic art, and the aesthetic and ideological premises upon which it was built, could no longer be said to fulfil its own declared aim of mirroring empirical reality. Whether consciously, as demonstrated by the following pronouncement made by Salvador Dali in 1956, or subconsciously, the discovery of the intrinsic discontinuity and mobility of the physical world has moulded most of the major works of twentieth century art:

> La découverte la plus transcendentale de notre époque est celle de la physique nucléaire sur la constitution de la matière. La matière est discontinue et toute expérience valable dans la peinture moderne ne peut et ne doit partir que d'une seule idée aussi concrète que significative: *la discontinuité de la matière.*[17]

Responding to the same epistemological stimulus, Michel Butor finally abandoned the novel form altogether in favour of the 'mobile' method of composition which was 'sufficiently flexible to translate the complication of the modern world-in-flux'.[18] Yet resorting to such measures, the most extreme examples of which being the random loose-leaf packages of William Burroughs and B. S. Johnson, is not the only recourse open to the writer who is disenchanted with the stultifying restrictions imposed by the 'trompe-lecteur' novel. Indeed they may even be said to evade the issue of multiplicity rather than accommodate it, for it is the materiality of language, not merely of construction or the 'livre comme objet', which is the empirical medium confronting the reader. Thus the question of complicity between author and reader, referred to by Butor in the quotation given earlier, is reformulated along 'materialist' lines by Morelli in Julio Cortázar's *Hopscotch*: 'All artistic tricks are of no use in obtaining it: the only thing worth anything is the material in gestation, the experiential immediacy'.[19]

Reading the novels of Claude Simon, particularly from *La Route des Flandres* onwards, one is inescapably conscious of the materiality of fiction. Far from effacing the linguistic material by which it is constituted, the referential dimension of these novels is constantly disrupted and re-created by the former: 'il faut *toujours* sacrifier le signifié aux nécessités plastiques'.[20] Often this compositional principle is mirrored in the narrative by descriptions of paintings or photographs where the materiality of the picture impinges upon the representational content. Thus, for example, the description of a poster in *Les Corps conducteurs* alludes to the affinity between the physical quality of the picture and its visual content: 'La mauvaise qualité du cliché, l'encre de l'imprimerie du journal elle-même de mauvaise qualité, grasse et grise, accentuant l'aspect poisseux, suintant et humide de la scène' (p. 149).[21] The relationship between form and content here extends beyond the functional relationship between the materiality of the poster and the scene depicted. This revitalisation of the 'signifiant' is, as Simon has frequently emphasised, a basic feature of the linguistic constitution of his novels:

> Très souvent mon travail rappelle une expression couramment employée dans la géométrie euclidienne: c'est 'considérons telle ou telle figure (triangle, cercle, carré etc.) et cherchons quelles en sont les *propriétés.*'
> Eh bien, il me semble que mon travail c'est exactement cela: prendre une 'figure' (n'importe laquelle: exemple le 'générique' – la description de la pièce en ruines – de *Leçon de choses* et examiner, explorer toutes ses 'propriétés', c'est-à-dire quelles autres images, formes, cette 'figure' initiale a, dans et par la langue, la propriété de susciter, de faire surgir, de s'assembler.[22]

The 'properties' which the novelist analyses and explores are, therefore, not merely the linguistic components of the words on the page but the wide array of extraneous words and images evoked by the initial textual data. The fundamental compositional impulse is, then, a metaphorical one, based on mnemonic, figurative and verbal associations, though once the new material is induced it is elaborated and incorporated into the metonymic chain of the text. But the metaphorical liberty enjoyed by this system of textual production entails a rejection of at least one major aspect of the conventional use and conception of language. As Jean Dubuffet, echoing Proust before him, has stated, a prerequisite for the textual montages and transgressions of modern works of art is the dismantling of the conceptual barriers set up by the taxonomic function of language:

> Mon dispositif fonctionne comme une machine à abolir les noms des choses, à faire tomber les cloisons que l'esprit dresse entre les divers objets, entre les divers systèmes d'objets, entre les différents registres de faits et de choses et les différents plans de la pensée [.][23]

The way in which a writer like Claude Simon subverts the classificatory tendency of names is by focusing on their materiality. An interesting verbal parallel of the description of the poster in *Les Corps conducteurs*, mentioned above, is Simon's exposition, at the 1971 Cerisy conference, of the way in which the transporting powers of Proust's 'madeleine' are present in the word itself:

> La saveur d'une madeleine (c'est-à-dire la qualité d'une certaine sensation – inséparable, doit-on le dire, de la saveur du mot *madeleine*: sa matière, sa morphologie molle, détrempée (ma . . . eleine) dans laquelle s'enfonce, dure, la dent du d), transporte Proust, à travers le temps et l'espace, d'un lieu à un autre.[24]

The sound and texture of the word 'madeleine' impinges upon its meaning and related connotations, just as the physical qualities of the poster in *Les Corps conducteurs* influence the scene represented in the picture. In both cases the 'signifiant' contributes, over and above its normal function in the signifying process, to the elaboration of the 'signifié'. But although in the two examples I have cited this supplementary action on the part of the 'signifiant' is in harmony with the semantic context of the referent, in other cases it is not so. In common usage, a name refers to a specified, predetermined designatum, rather like a magic spell which opens the door onto a clearly delimited field of reference. However, by dwelling on the 'properties' of names, an author can stimulate certain tangential 'signifiés' which detract from the original point of reference. Names of characters are often 'evocative' in this way. For the narrator of *A la recherche du temps perdu*, the name

'Guermantes' embraces 'sept ou huit figures différentes'.[25] Such polysemic variety can produce sudden deviations in the narrative chain, as in Faulkner's *The Sound and the Fury* where narrative oscillation between present and past time spans is triggered off by the recognition of the fact that the word 'Caddy' is both the name of Benjy's sister and the common appellation of a golf attendant. In *La Route des Flandres* the same factor is responsible for the creative invention of the text: thus, the detailed specification of the colour of Corinne's dress 'cette robe rouge couleur de bonbon anglais' is primarily due to the connotations suggested by her name, 'parce que "Corinne" faisait penser à "corail"' (pp. 234–5).[26]

The same structural factors as those I have been discussing recur when one attempts to outline the process of reading. Confronted with the profusion and diversity of data contained in a novel, the reader must select, organise and classify the material at hand. The act of interpretation involves not only the attribution of hermeneutic labels (for example, 'this novel is about *jealousy*') but also the implicit hyponymic processes which are at work in the selection of categories. In semantic theory, 'hyponymy' is said to involve 'the logical relationship of entailment'.[27] A 'superordinate' or 'upper term' subsumes, by way of a hierarchical collocation, several 'hyponyms' or 'lower terms'. Thus 'dog' is a hyponym of 'animal', and it is also a 'superordinate' of 'labrador', 'poodle', 'alsation' and the names of all the other breeds. In this way the nominal aspect of language is built on a hierarchy of interrelated terms. Now although it may be argued that the process of reading is much more intuitive than this semantic model suggests, nevertheless when called on to substantiate the conclusions of his reading a reader will ultimately organise his evidence along similar lines.

Semioticians like Greimas and Rastier have sought to formalise this analogy and to establish the 'scientific laws' which govern the act of reading. Their principle contention is that the 'isotopies' produced by one's reading can be logically deduced from the repetition of classemes in a text. Moreover, by discerning these isotopies or semantic contexts, the reader succeeds in ordering the heterogenous material before him: 'Du point de vue de l'énonciataire, l'isotopie constitue une grille de lecture qui rend homogène la surface du texte, puisqu'elle permet de lever les ambiguités'.[28] Unfortunately, the teleological manner in which both Greimas and

130   *Materiality*

Rastier present the examples which illustrate their argument only reveals the conceptual scaffolding that supports their reading of a text: it by no means proves the validity of that reading. In each case the critics begin by announcing the dominant isotopies of the text in question before proceeding to find textual justification for them. Yet no justification of the 'dominance' of the particular isotopies they select is given, no explanation of how these isotopies over-rule others.

Jonathan Culler has rejected the idea that these 'levels of coherence' can be logically deduced from the repetition of classemes on the grounds that this excludes the subjective contribution of the reader:

> The difficulty is [. . .] that the context which determines the meaning of a sentence is more than the other sentences of the text; it is a complex of knowledge and expectations of varying degrees of specificity, a kind of interpretative competence which could in principle be described but which in practice proves exceedingly refractory.[29]

It may well be that an 'objective' account of the semantic structure of an 'expressive' novel such as Bernanos's *Journal d'un curé de campagne* is invalidated by virtue of its inability to embrace the personal 'literary competence' of each reader.[30] But this need not be the case with disjunctive narrative texts whose intrinsic heterogeneity allows the reader to extrapolate 'levels of coherence' which do not serve the ultimate 'intent at totality of the interpretative process'.[31] The organisational process governing the act of reading a novel like *Les Corps conducteurs* depends on the semantic and textual constituents to a far greater extent than in an interpretative reading of a conventional, homogenous text.[32] Partly as a result of this heterogeneity and discontinuity, the anonymity of much of the referential data counterbalances the reader's instinct to draw from his own extratextual store of knowledge. Thus the anonymity of what is being described often underlines the eponymity of the language in use.

The crucial, 'eponymic' rôle of the 'signifiants' in informing one's reading of Simon's novel can be seen in the following example. The sick protagonist of one of the narrative sequences is, at one point of the novel, convulsed by the urge to vomit: 'Mais il ne vient qu'un peu de salive qu'il crache, se tenant là épuisé, sans pouvoir bouger, incapable même de couper le fil brillant qui pend de ses lèvres et les relie au fond de la cuvette' (p. 112).[33] The reader's reception and interpretative treatment of this sentence is heavily influenced by previous textual data. For instance, the reference to the 'fil brillant' of saliva recalls two preceding, and otherwise unconnected, descriptions of the 'traînée rouge' of the squashed mosquito staining the palm of a soldier's hand, and the 'traînée blanche' trailing the aeroplane in the sky. It also connects with the reference near the start of the novel to the boy pulling ('qui traîne') a string ('ficelle') tied to a toy rabbit with big white ears (p. 20). The correspondence between physical sickness and the shape of billowing clouds is not one which is promoted by subjective 'extratextual' considerations; it is induced retrospectively through the accumulation of previous textual associations, such as the description of clouds in Poussin's painting ('circonvolutions intestinales et cartonneuses' (p. 78)) which in turn is foreshadowed by the description of anatomical organs 'comme du carton bouilli ou du celluloid' (p. 74).[34]

The web of associations linking the different textual data is woven, in this case, around the motifs of 'linearity' (string, vapour trail, saliva) and 'convolution' (clouds, intestines, rabbit).[35] Such a reading thus superimposes a network of interrelations onto the existing narrative order, so that one can identify two sets of isotopies. On the one hand, narrative isotopies distinguish the different fictional contexts, such as the jungle setting and the lavatory scene; and on the other hand, taxematic isotopies can be produced by a reader who groups together textual segments belonging to different narrative isotopies. There is clearly scope for a considerable amount of tension between the two kinds of isotopies, as will emerge in my discussion of Ricardou's 'Le Dispositif osiriaque' which is included in the following chapter.

The term 'isotopy' is borrowed from nuclear physics (another example of its pervasive influence in the domain of twentieth century art and criticism). An 'isotope' is the combination of two or more atomic species (protons and electrons) of the same chemical element having different atomic masses (neutrons). Etymologically, the word is comprised of the Greek 'isos' meaning 'equal' and 'topos' meaning 'place'. The type of relation which the term has been used to outline in physics bears a close resemblance to that of metaphor in language. Indeed, Rastier has defined metaphor as 'toute isotopie élémentaire ou tout faisceau isotopique élémentaire établi entre deux sémèmes appartenant à deux champs distincts'.[36] These metaphorical relations, therefore, consist of semantic units which have been extrapolated from their original, separate sources and combined to form a new context. This, of course, is the main feature of all metaphor, as Victor Chklovski has pointed out:

> Chez les poètes, les objets s'insurgent, rejetant leurs anciens noms et se chargent d'un sens supplémentaire avec le nom nouveau. Le poète se sert des images, des tropes pour faire des comparaisons; il appèlle par exemple le feu une fleur rouge, ou il applique une nouvelle épithète à l'ancien mot, ou bien il dit comme Baudelaire que la charogne avait ses jambes en l'air comme une femme lubrique. Ainsi le poète accomplit un déplacement sémantique; nous sentons ainsi la nouveauté, la mise de l'objet dans une nouvelle série. Le nouveau mot est mis sur l'objet comme un nouveau vêtement. L'enseigne est enlevée.[37]

However, in Simon's text, semantic displacement is brought about not only by way of an insurrection of objects against their 'oppressive' names, but also by the kind of taxematic reading I sketched earlier and which will be analysed more thoroughly in the next chapter. As I have already shown, the reader is able to provoke textual displacements by, for instance, assembling the references to the protagonist's saliva and the plane's vapour trail in the same isotopy. The reader's activity thus complements the tropological constructions elaborated by the writing. Both 'levels of coherence' are metaphorical in structure.

In conclusion, the 'materiality of fiction' can be defined as the point of convergence between the movements of writing and of reading, providing the common, shifting, ground for the complicity between author and reader. It is the ultimate paradox between the solidity and mobility of matter and language, as the following lines from Sollers's *H* affirm:

> je vois un soleil noir d'où rayonne la nuit un peu trop préparé peut-être fluctuat nec mergitur c'est normal que les profs soient intrigués par le langage et pas nous c'est logique que les physiciens soient snobés par la matière et nous plutôt par le mouve-

ment la matière veut du mouvement le mouvement veut du langage le langage nous veut [.][38]

2
Currents of Description in *Les Corps conducteurs*

> Poets are both insulators and conductors of the poetic current.
>
> Novalis, *Fragments*

> Et même une syllabe commune à deux noms différents suffisait à ma mémoire – comme à un électricien qui se contente du moindre corps bon conducteur – pour rétablir le contact entre Albertine et mon coeur.[1]
>
> Proust, *La Fugitive*

I FRAGMENTATION AND ARTICULATION

The predominating view of *Les Corps conducteurs* amongst current French critics of Simon's work is that this novel fails to achieve the level of irrecuperable discontinuity which it nevertheless seems to set as its target. The fractured surface of textual fragmentation is, in the final analysis, reassembled and blended into a homogenous entity by the lingering influence of the Aristotelian ideal of unity. Yet the evidence which is advanced in support of this reading is not always the same and often in conflict.

In their respective articles on *Les Corps conducteurs*, Claud Duverlie, Jean–Claude Raillon and Jean Ricardou have each focused on a particular pattern of association and presented it as the fundamental, underlying structure of the novel. For Duverlie the Orion myth is the unifying element in the novel;[2] for Raillon the 'scène générante de copulation' is the common ground, the point of articulation between the disparate fictional groupings;[3] for Ricardou the novel is a 'fiction où la sexualité "ne marche pas", roman en somme, "de la jambe coupée" '.[4] One's immediate response to this disagreement is to note that, on their own didactic terms, at least two of the analyses must be incorrect, thus indicating that perception of the 'basic structure' is not very straightforward and that the element of continuity or unification is not as strong as all three critics suggest.

Often the unificatory tendency of this novel is outlined in the light of a contrast with another work by Simon. Thus, Duverlie interprets the continuity of *Les Corps conducteurs* as a mark of its 'intentions humanistes' and consequently as a weakness which he contrasts with the 'super-formalisme' of the 'discontinuous' *Orion aveugle* which, in his view, hinges on a disjunctive 'jeu de rapports' between the illustrations and the written text.[5] However, the relationship between text and visual image is not as interesting in *Orion aveugle* as it is in, for example, Robbe-Grillet's *La Belle captive* where the interest lies in the deviations produced by the text which initially emerges as a faithful description of the Magritte reproductions. Apart from the first sentence, the written text of *Orion aveugle* is a word for word replica of the first part of *Les Corps conducteurs*. It is true that *Orion aveugle* contains many, if not all, of the pictures which served as 'stimuli' for the writing. But since this contiguity does not affect the writing, it is of no more than anecdotal interest to the reader. Simon himself has said that the presentation of *Orion aveugle* was less his choice than a compliance with the wishes of the editor of the 'Sentiers de la création' series, all the texts of which are accompanied by illustrations:

> *Orion aveugle* est le résultat d'une commande de Skira. J'ai placé ces stimulants pour montrer comment le texte avait fonctionné puisque le titre de la collection est 'Les Sentiers de la création'. Mais ils ne doivent pas être tenus en compte dans un livre final. Si *Les Corps conducteurs* devaient être accompagné de l'image des stimulants extratextuels, alors ce serait un échec pour moi.[6]

Elsewhere, *Les Corps conducteurs* has been compared with *Triptyque*, the novel which immediately followed it. Ricardou has argued that the fact that one can discern a dominant unifying narrative sequence as well as a dominant theme is proof that the novel is unlike *Triptyque* which he describes as 'pur roman de la discohérence enfin conquise, parfait exemple de très vive modernité'.[7]

The antithetical notions of 'association' and 'fragmentation' have, therefore, featured prominently in existing assessments of this novel, providing a double-edged yardstick by which the work is either applauded or dismissed. However, my argument throughout this chapter will be that these notions are not necessarily mutually incompatible in the context of modern fiction and, furthermore, that they should not be divorced from a meticulous account of the process of reading. Indeed, the pertinence of these two notions will only emerge in an analysis which takes the form of what one might call 'textual semantics', focusing not so much on the meanings thrown up by the patterns and associations woven by the text as on the language of textual signification.

The most rigorous critical work on *Les Corps conducteurs* (just as with *La Route des Flandres* and *La Bataille de Pharsale*) has been undertaken by Jean Ricardou in two separate instances: the first, entitled ' "Claude Simon", textuellement', was a paper delivered at the 1974 Cerisy colloquium on Claude Simon: the second, an expansion of the argument which was sketched at Cerisy, is a chapter entitled 'le dispositif osiriaque' in his remarkable book, *Nouveaux problèmes du roman*.[8] In ' "Claude Simon", textuellement' Ricardou notes that *Les Corps conducteurs* can be summed up as 'l'effet de deux fonctionnements contradictoires: d'une part, la fragmentation, d'autre part l'articulation'.[9] Fragmentation can either be present as 'coupures intra-séquentielles' (which are instances of digression within a particular narrative sequence and are provoked by traditional metaphor, comparison or alternative),[10] and 'ruptures interséquentielles' (which are instances of interruption of one narrative sequence by another and are provoked by productive metaphor acting on the level of 'signifiants'). The opening sentence of *Les Corps conducteurs* contains two 'coupures intra-séquentielles': the dummies' legs in the shop window are likened to the legs of a team of dancers, 'comme si on les avait empruntées à un de ces bataillons de danseuses', and to an advertisement for women's stockings, 'ou encore [. . .] à l'un de ces dessins de publicité'.[11] The extent to which 'coupures intra-séquentielles' disturb the narrative structure is measured by the length of the digression. The first 'rupture inter-séquentielle' is produced by the arrival, in the third sentence, of the second narrative sequence: 'L'infirmier (ou le jeune interne) tient sous son bras, comme un paquet, une jambe coupée'.[12] Both types of fragmentation are produced, as Ricardou says, by 'l'irruption du similaire'. One of the many common denominators of the first two narrative sequences is the word 'jambe'.[13] Equally, there are two types of articulation: metonymic articulation, which is the unification of two or more initially separate narrative sequences; and thematic articulation, which is the unification of two or more seemingly unrelated motifs and themes. An example of metonymic articulation is the 'framing' of the second narrative sequence within the third narrative sequence: that is, the description of the 'jeunes internes' and the bearded surgeon on the point of operating on a laughing young woman is eventually contextualised as a cartoon picture hanging on the wall of the doctor's consulting room which is described in the third narrative segment:

Sur l'un des murs du cabinet de consultation est accroché un dessin sous verre représentant une théorie de jeunes carabins hilares armés de divers instruments chirurgicaux et s'avançant à la suite d'un patron barbu vers une table d'opération où est étendue une jeune femme nue qui rit de tous ses dents. (p. 10)[14]

It is less easy to summarise the specific activity of thematic articulation, but in a general sense, according to Ricardou, the theme of illness forms the 'obsessional pivot' of the novel. Ricardou supports his argument in a more concrete way in 'Le dispositif osiriaque' by charting the 'arborescence' or hierarchical interdependence of the novel's themes and motifs. This will be discussed in the following sub-section of the present chapter.

' "Claude Simon", textuellement' ends with the conclusion that although the process of articulation can be used to produce a more fruitful effect than that of unification (as it is in *La Jalousie* and *La Prise de Constantinople*), in *Les Corps conducteurs* it tends towards a unitary method of composition:

Dans *Les Corps conducteurs*, ainsi qu'il arrive souvent chez Simon, les divers secteurs conduits à s'articuler métonymiquement appartiennent aussi à des unités spatiales très différentes: disons, pour être bref, une marche dans une ville nord-américaine et un congrès dans une ville sud-américaine, seulement il n'est pas impossible de reconnaître un secteur dominant avec cette marche de l'homme malade dans la ville, par laquelle s'ouvre et se clôt le livre et à laquelle les autres secteurs parviennent assez bien à s'articuler.[15]

In sum, the dominance of metonymic and thematic articulation turns the novel into a type of jigsaw puzzle where the reader is initially confronted with a mass of disconnected fragments but which he can ultimately piece together in order to reconstruct a linear and hierarchical order.

There are three main problems arising out of Ricardou's argument. Firstly, it is not entirely satisfactory to describe articulation and fragmentation as two contradictory textual functions: by pinpointing precisely what is being articulated and precisely what is being fragmented it will emerge that their relationship is causal. Moreover, it would be more precise to define articulation as an activity and fragmentation as a state of being or 'disposition' in the French sense of the word. Therefore, instead of saying that there are two sorts of fragmentation and two sorts of articulation one should rather enumerate four types of articulation: fictional articulation is the 'framing' (or association by contiguity) of different narrative sequences together; thematic articulation is the hierarchical association of different motifs and themes; metaphorical articulation is the association of similar 'signifiés'; paronomastic articulation is the association of similar 'signifiants'. The four categories do, however, split up into two groups. The first two form what one might call 'referential articulation' and the second two constitute what one might call 'literal articulation'. The first two create a homogeneity or unification of narrative by associating different sequences and themes; and the second two create a fragmentation of narrative by associating similar 'signifiés' and 'signifiants'. It seems logical to re-name Ricardou's 'fragmentation métaphorique' and 'fragmentation paronomastique' as I have done, by substituting 'articulation' for 'fragmentation', since in the critic's own words, the one 'met en jeu des similitudes des signifiés' and the other 'met en jeu des similitudes des signifiants'.[16] I have also re-named 'metonymic articulation' as 'fictional articulation' in order to avoid any confusion which might arise from this use of the word 'metonymic'. Whereas with metaphorical and paronomastic articulation the associations are linguistic and are produced by, among others, actual metaphors, in the case of metonymic articulation, on the other hand, the associations of contiguity are not linguistic, they do not employ the use of actual metonyms. It is the segments of narrative which are placed in contiguous relation with one another. In other words, the articulation is here based on the level of the writing. The relationship between referential and literal articulation is one of inverse proportion: when fictional and thematic articulation predominate (as in the traditional novel) metaphorical and paronomastic articulation are subdued; when metaphorical and paronomastic articulation predominate (as in Simon's text) fictional and thematic articulation are subdued.

The second problem which arises from Ricardou's argument is clearly related to the definition of the terms 'articulation' and 'fragmentation' which I have been considering. 'Coupures intraséquentielles' and 'ruptures inter-séquentielles' are two forms of fragmentation: they differ only by degree, the second being more fundamental than the first. Both are produced by 'la loi métaphorique' (in other words by literal articulation) but, as already stated, 'coupures' are produced by traditional metaphor, comparison, or alternative and 'ruptures' are produced by structural metaphor and paronomasia.[17] Thus the metaphorical associations producing 'coupures' are effectuated by the writing (as in the first example, 'comme si on les avait empruntées à un de ces bataillons de danseuses'),[18] and the metaphorical associations producing 'ruptures' are made by the reader (as in the number of common denominators linking the first and second narrative sequences). However, Ricardou fails to note in ' "Claude Simon", textuellement' that one can draw a parallel between these two forms of fragmentation and two forms of articulation: intra-sequential connections or 'fusions' and inter-sequential connections or 'confusions'. 'Fusions' are what Ricardou calls 'metonymic articulation' or the 'rencontre de deux séquences'.[19] Consequently, the 'framing' of the second narrative sequence (the description of the surgical operation) within the third narrative sequence (the visit to the doctor's) by situating the former as a description of a cartoon hanging on the doctor's wall, may, by my definition, be called an instance of narrative 'fusion'. An example of 'descriptive confusion' is the 'contamination' of the description of the sexual scene by the description of the anatomical diagram. The man, sitting on the bed where they have just made love, looks at the woman who stands in front of him wrapped in a towel and holding a bowl of coffee:

Le bol s'abaisse et il peut voir alors le visage tout entier. Son regard toujours fixé sur lui, elle dit doucement Non. Non ce n'est pas possible. Sur le mur de la salle de bains le rectangle de soleil vire lentement de l'orange au jaune. Barrant la poitrine d'une droite horizontale à hauteur des aisselles la serviette ne permet de voir que l'extrémité supérieure de l'ouverture en forme de caisse de violoncelle protégée par la plaque de plexiglas derrière laquelle on distingue de gros tubes bleus et rouges dont les branches se divisent et s'entrecroisent. (p. 161)[20]

Without examining the phenomenon too closely for the time being, a summary glance is enough for the reader to detect the interpolation of the two descriptions. The phenomenon differs from an instance of 'fusion' since it is not a question of 'framing' one of the sequences within the other. Neither is it an instance of 'coupure' since the relationship between the two descriptions is not metaphorical. The man is not looking at the woman's body as if he were looking at an anatomical drawing. No analogy or comparison is being made. While articulation in instances of narrative 'fusion' occurs only on the referential level, in instances of descriptive 'confusion' articulation occurs only on the literal level. In other words, unlike the case of 'fusion' where the sequences are 'framed' within one another, 'confusion' is comprised of the interpolation of one description within another. In sum, 'fusion' is the relation of contiguity between specific narrative sequences produced by the unifying narrative macro-structure; 'confusion' is the dislocation of narrative produced by the contiguity, or literal articulation, between parts of different units of description.

The third problem arising out of Ricardou's argument is the most fundamental: his analysis is reductive in so far as it makes no qualitative distinction between what I have named 'narrative sequences' and 'blocks of description'. Ricardou has produced the neatest definition of the former: 'séries d'éléments fictionnels référentiellement cohérents'.[21] The element of referential cohesion is crucial. A narrative sequence is a strand or unit of narrative which is held together by a logic of time or setting, or by a single narrative framework such as memory. The segments within a particular sequence need not follow one another chronologically but the possibility of piecing them together must always exist. The contradictions created by the interplay of sequences may be called, to borrow from Ricardou, narrative 'discoherence'.[22] Examples of narrative discoherence taken from *Triptyque* will be discussed in Part Four, Chapter 2. A narrative sequence, therefore, is basic to all fiction. All novels have narrative sequences, although most

Currents of Description in Les Corps conducteurs 141

conventional novels have only one. On the other hand, blocks of description are a product of reading. Conventional novels, where all description is subservient to the logic of narrative, have no place for description blocks. But the most important distinction between narrative sequences and description blocks is that whereas it is possible to say that the former can be found 'within' a novel, it is not so with the latter. A description block is constructed by the reader who assembles different descriptive units, or 'referents', into different categories. These referents enjoy a certain freedom from the constraints of the narrative structure since they do not 'belong' to any particular narrative sequence. Often they have several contradictory frames; sometimes they are totally unframed, floating in a narrative void. Instances of description blocks are always referentially static, with no development internally or from one repetition to the next, which is why the referents are often in the form of paintings or photographs.

In short, narrative sequences denote progress through spatio-temporal change, while description blocks provide information through accumulation of data. Just as instances of sequences do not always follow one another in chronological order, so too instances of description blocks either provide additional data or variants. The relations between instances of sequences (or narrative segments) are metonymic (connected on an axis of referential contiguity): in other words, the different instances can be assembled into a coherent narrative sequence. The relations between instances of description blocks are synecdochic (connected on an axis of literal contiguity): in other words, each specific instance (part) stands for the block (whole) to which it belongs. The distinction between the relations of metonymy and synecdoche is based on the one made by Gérard Genette in *Figures III* where synecdoche is defined as involving the aspect of 'inclusion', which need not be spatial but is always a logical relationship between part and whole, and metonymy is defined as a relationship of contiguity between different parts of the same whole:[23]

De même pourra-t-on lire *ad libitum*, dans la figure par l'attribut (soit 'couronne' pour *monarque*), une métonymie ou une synecdoque, selon que l'on considère, par exemple, la couronne comme simplement liée au monarque, ou comme faisant partie de lui, en vertu de l'axiome implicite: pas de monarque sans couronne. On voit alors qu'à la limite toute métonymie est convertible en synecdoque par appel à l'ensemble supérieur, et toute synecdoque en métonymie par recours aux relations entre parties constituantes.[24]

The following passage from *Les Corps conducteurs* provides a good example of the difference between the metonymic interaction of instances of narrative sequences and the synecdochic interaction of instances of description blocks:

Le portier, maintenant revenu vers le tambour dont il maintient d'une main l'un des panneaux, sa casquette tenue par son autre main devant sa poitrine, observe la difficile progression de la dame sur l'immensité rouge du tapis. A l'autre bout du fil la voix claire et joyeuse de l'enfant répète Allo? Allo? Au-dessus du plateau de nuages on peut voir la lune dans le ciel vide, comme une pastille blanche pas tout à fait ronde. Entre le lapin couché sur le flanc et la main de l'enfant la ficelle détendue serpente sur le trottoir en courbes molles. Le Serpent est une constellation équatoriale dont le tracé est dessiné par de belles étoiles distribuées sur une large étendue du ciel. Surgissant tout à coup des nuages, l'arête enneigé d'une montagne s'élève au-dessous de l'avion, d'une incroyable minceur, aigue avec ses vertigineux dévers de glace étincelant dans le soleil, presque verticaux, inviolés, et son échine de rochers déchiquetés. Elle ondule et se tord comme la nageoire dorsale d'un congre ou d'une murène émergeant un instant, luisante, dans des remous d'écume. Les nuages fouettés avec violence s'écartent, s'effilochent en écharpes grisâtres accrochées aux parois éblouissantes, les roches en dents de scie semblables aux vertèbres de quelque monstre, quelque furieux et gigantesque saurien au nom fabuleux de titan, de société minière ou de constellation (Aconcagua, Anaconda, Andromeda) se convulsant, écrasant sous son ventre de terre, ses millions de tonnes, la fange verdâtre et puante des marécages et des forêts invisibles, tout en bas, sous l'étouffante couvercle de nuages. (pp. 29–30)[25]

The passage moves from one narrative sequence, describing the progression of a man walking in what seems to be a North American city, to another narrative sequence, describing a journey by aeroplane, to a descriptive fragment (with information on astronomy) and again to the narrative sequence of the airflight. The shifts are produced along an axis of literal contiguity (that is, by metaphorical articulation). The associative image which acts as common denominator is the 'signifié' 'snake' which appears in the first sequence ('la ficelle détendue *serpente*'), in the description block ('Le *Serpent* est une constellation') and in the second narrative sequence ('Elle *ondule* et se tord comme la nageoire dorsale d'un congre ou d'une murène'). There is a stark contrast between the action depicted in the two narrative sequences (the old woman's painful shuffle, the vertical climb of the plane) and the discursive tone of the instances of the description block. While each segment of any one narrative sequence depicts an element of spatio-temporal progression, no such development occurs from one instance of a description to another of the same block. In the passage under analysis the sentence referring to the Serpens Caput constellation evokes the earlier instances of the description block, the context from which it has been taken. This recall also has a generative function since the second appearance in this passage of the airflight sequence is influenced by the astronomical description block. The mountains below are like 'quelque monstre [. . .] au nom fabuleux [. . .] de constellation (Aconcagua, Anaconda, Andromeda)'. The influence is clearly metonymic stemming from the first instance of the description block where the anaconda is first mentioned (p. 19). Moreover, the metaphorical articulation of the whole passage produced by the 'signifié' 'serpent' can be shown to have its metonymic origin in this description block since it is here that the associative image 'serpent' first appears.

Thus the differences between narrative sequences and description blocks are easily detected by an attentive reader. But before proceeding with a closer examination of the particular directions pursued by the currents of description in this novel, it will be useful to enumerate the different narrative sequences encountered by the reader and some of the description blocks evoked by the text. For the sake of brevity the sequences will be named by alphabetical letters, and the description blocks by Roman numerals.

Sequence A is the painful progress of a man walking along the streets of, possibly, New York. The walk is interrupted by several 'episodes' such as the telephone booth conversation, and the drink at the bar. The novel begins with this sequence (the description of the dummies' legs in the shop window) and ends with it (the man reaches his hotel room and collapses on the carpet).

Sequence B relates a man's visit to the doctor. One may infer from the fact that the doctor speaks French that the visit takes place in France before or after the trip to the Americas. The first instance of this sequence occurs on page 8: 'Le docteur lui dit de baisser son pantalon'.[26]

Sequence C describes part of a plane trip somewhere over the Caribbean. The exact itinerary of the flight is unclear. The first instance of this sequence is on page 15: 'L'ombre cruciforme de l'avion se déplace [.]'[27]

Sequence D is comprised of the attendance of a man at a writer's conference somewhere in Latin America. The first instance of this sequence is on page 33: 'En dépit de son attention, il ne parvient à saisir [.]'[28]

Sequence E centres on a scene of sexual intercourse between a man and a woman. No mention is made of where this takes place. This sequence first appears on page 56: 'Dans la lumière laiteuse qui entre par la fenêtre [.]'[29]

As Ricardou says, 'it is not impossible' to see sequence A as englobing all the others. Indeed it may be said to contain the seeds from which the other sequences grow. The surgical element in sequence B may be seen to have developed from the description of the 'jambes coupées' in the shop window. Sequence C has its parallel in the aeroplane advertisement posted in the travel agent's (p. 217). Sequence D develops from the shreds of Spanish political slogans covering a palisade on the street (p. 33). Sequence E is mirrored by the magazine covers in the porn shop (p. 146). One can also justifiably identify the man as being the same in all five sequences, although it is equally 'not impossible' for them to be different. In sequences A, B, D the man is suffering from a pain in his stomach. Sequence C links up with sequence A by the fact that the destination of the flight is somewhere in America (north or south), and sequence E links up with sequence A through the possibility of identifying the woman as the one in the telephone conversation in sequence A. These intersections, being on the level of fiction or plot, tend towards a unifying interpretation of the narrative. Other, more detailed associations can be found in numerous quantity, but they belong to the level of composition, of description, and often contradict the logic of the narrative and undermine its unificatory tendencies.

As I have outlined below, there are four main description blocks in the novel. This should not, however, be taken as an exhaustive list.[30] Although, as already stated, it is relatively easy to distinguish description blocks since their synecdochic character sets them apart from narrative sequences, naming each block does pose a serious problem partly because the choice reveals a particular commitment by the reader on the interpretation of the novel. Further, the generative power of the detail of Simon's novels, and in particular *Les Corps conducteurs*, deliberately obstructs any attempt to discern an order in the novel's macro-structure. On the other hand, there is a critical need to decide on a name since it provides the basis for the assemblage of the disparate elements within each block. These titles should therefore have as general a frame of reference as possible.

Broadly speaking, the four description blocks fall under two categories. Descriptive units in blocks I and III are 'pseudo-sequential' in that they give the brief and confused impression of being narrative sequences, while those in blocks II and IV may be said to act as 'appendices' to the former. The first block, which Ricardou has treated as a sequence, is the most cohesive since it is mainly comprised of the description of a surgical operation. This description cannot by my definition be called a narrative sequence since it is explicitly 'framed' as the description of a picture hanging on the wall of the doctor's consulting room in sequence B. The first instance of this block appears on page 7: 'L'infirmier (ou le jeune interne) tient sous son bras, comme un paquet, une jambe coupée'.[31]

Description block II, which I shall call 'anatomical', is less cohesive in that there are several objects or referents of description and their corresponding frames; the main one being the anatomical drawing which is also framed in sequence B. The other referents and frames are the magazine article on the human anatomy in sequence C, a poster in an optician's in sequence A. The first appearance of a unit from block II is on page 9: 'La planche représente un torse d'homme'.[32]

The second psuedo-sequence, description block III, can be called the 'military' description. It is less textually cohesive than the preceding descriptions since, on the one hand, some of its referents (especially the central one, the description of the soldiers marching through the forest, which is presented as a stamp (p. 39), a print (p. 85), or a photograph (pp. 108–9)) are totally unframed and belong to no narrative sequence. On the other hand, the block covers a larger span of referents: the print or stamp or photograph (unframed), the mural of the cavalry charge in the conference hall in sequence D, the magazine story read by the man travelling by air in sequence C, the cinema advertisement in the newspaper being read by the 'proconsul' in sequence D, the toy soldiers in the shop window in sequence A, and the tourist information on South American forests given by the airline brochure in sequence C. The first instance of description block III is on page 14:

> Un personnage au crâne chauve, à la longue barbe, le buste revêtu d'une cuirasse qui fait place, à partir de la taille, à une courte jupe, se tient debout sur une plage.[33]

Description block IV is the most decomposed of all four blocks. None of its referents are framed in a narrative sequence and therefore it has the most disruptive influence on the novel as a whole.[34] Its central referent forms what one might call a microcosmic block (or block within a block) since it encompasses several motifs: information on snakes, stars, birds, butterflies. All these different referents are juxtaposed in a kind of textual constellation whose overall outline remains fluid and ambiguous. Description block IV thus acts as a 'meeting-place' for several distinct elements, including Orion, Poussin's giant:

> Parmi le scintillement des étoiles de différentes grandeurs qui dessinent les constellations, les centaures, les paons aux plumes couvertes d'yeux, les chèvres à queue de dragons, les loups et les aigles, la silhouette du géant se découpe en noir [.] (p. 112)[35]

The passage is clearly another example of descriptive confusion. In this case, however, the two originally separate referents (Poussin's painting and the anonymous map or drawing) both belong to the same compositional unit: block IV. The appearance of the giant within this passage is instigated by the word 'constellation' which in an earlier instance of this block was associated with the name 'Orion': 'La constellation d'Orion est une des plus belles de la zone équatoriale' (p. 57).[36] Once again one finds that the composition of the novel is dictated by the generative potential of the 'signifiants' which constitute the literal dimension of the text. The effect of this paronomastic control of the referential dimension is not only one of disconcerting interference and disjunction, but of prompting the reader to explore the different permutations of textual relation. What do the multiple facets of what I have called 'description block IV' add up to? What exactly is the mosaic from which all the pieces have been scattered? Is it a reproduction of the painted ceiling of some monument like the Sixtine or the Pantheon (p. 56) or an antique parchment on display in a natural history museum (p. 216) or the product of the imagination of a traveller, the screen for his projected thoughts being the window of an aeroplane (p. 219)? The fact that these questions cannot be answered with any degree of certainty is proof alone that *Les Corps conducteurs* is not dominated by a movement of articulation which binds the different narrative fragments into a unified whole and invites a unitary interpretation from the reader. It may be hypothetically possible to integrate the five narrative sequences by identifying the same man in all five cases and to situate the sequences in a chronological order, but no such spatio-temporal identification is possible involving the anonymous referents of description blocks. Moreover, since all the narrative sequences are intertwined with these referents, making it impossible to separate the one from the other, it is 'in practice' impossible to fuse all the sequences together in a unitary whole. The vital function of the description block, therefore, is to contradict or sabotage the reductive tendencies in any account of the novel's 'macro-structure'. An integrative account of the novel is only possible in a reading which is riddled with gaps of inattention coinciding, in particular, with all the instances of the description blocks.

To summarise, the three main problems in Ricardou's argument are what enable him to discard *Les Corps conducteurs* as a modern text. Conversely, the three points (the interplay between narrative sequences and description blocks, between instances of fusion and confusion, and between fragmentation and articulation) are what define the novel as a modern text. However, the concern of this chapter is not with the defence of *Les Corps conducteurs*'s modernity; such a task would not warrant the space of a chapter and it is hoped that the preceding pages are sufficient to make that point. What remains to be done is to map out some of the patterns of association which structure the work and to assess the participatory role which is assigned to the reader. But before proceeding with my analysis, it is necessary to glance briefly at

148   *Materiality*

Ricardou's second, and most impressive, study of Claude Simon's novel.

II JEAN RICARDOU'S 'LE DISPOSITIF OSIRIAQUE'

This is not the place for a detailed summary or assessment of 'Le Dispositif osiriaque'. Suffice it to say that the lengthy study constitutes one of the first and most thorough works of materialist criticism.[37] It is also a brilliant theoretical study of the structure of the conventional novel and the extent to which *Les Corps conducteurs* conforms to it. Claude Simon has himself expressed wholehearted admiration for the work.[38] The following discussion, and the criticism it proposes, are made in full acknowledgement of the originality and importance of Ricardou's work.

The most important aspect of Ricardou's analysis is the implicit assumption of the need to take theoretical account of the oscillating relationship in a work of fiction between the writing on the page and what is produced by the process of reading. Thus, 'métaphore structurelle' can either be 'actuelle (rupture accomplie nécessairement par l'écriture)' or 'virtuelle (rupture accomplie éventuellement par la lecture)'.[39] In the first case the two component elements in the comparison are adjacent to one another, or in 'immediate correspondence', as in the example of the eight correspondences at the start of the novel between the instances of sequence A and the description of the surgical operation (block I).[40] In the second case the two component elements are at a substantial distance from one another, the correspondence is 'deferred', as in the 'métaphore structurelle virtuelle' that one can discern in the word 'ocre' which is the colour of the plastic legs in sequence A and recurs in the description of the anatomical poster 'rose ocrée' in description block II and thus gestures towards an assimilation of two divergent narrative contexts. The 'actuality' of the structural metaphor is determined, therefore, by the extent to which there is 'brisure' or digressive interruption of the linear chain of the text. Moreover, a metaphor or paronomasia can either be 'structurelle' if 'on insiste sur l'organisation des séquences' or it can be 'transitaire' if 'on insiste sur le passage d'une séquence à l'autre', or it can be 'ruptrice' if 'on insiste sur la fracture d'une séquence par une autre'.[41] The same word can thus be read in three different ways. The distinction between

Currents of Description in Les Corps conducteurs 149

reading and writing enables Ricardou to stress the complementarity of the relationship between articulation and fragmentation, 'similitude' and 'brisure':

> dans la mesure où la règle de brisure suppose au moins une similitude, les ressemblances, dans une fiction aussi morcelée, sont conduites à pléthore. Tout texte soumis à la segmentation analogique tend au camaieu.[42]

Ricardou thus reformulates the opposition between articulation and fragmentation into one between 'le dispositif dimensionnel' and 'le dispositif classificatoire':

> La similitude provoque une brisure dans les seuls textes où l'assemblage est obtenu par la domination d'un fonctionnement qui lui est antithétique. Or, ici, les opérations d'assemblage (jonction, prolongation, continuation, segmentation) tendent clairement, toutes, à réunir les éléments référentielles selon les catégories de l'espace et du temps. Bref, l'assemblage se fait ici à partir de la prépondérance d'un dispostif dimensionnel.[43]

The 'dimensionnel' organises the narrative according to the demands of spatio-temporal considerations, whilst its antithesis, 'le classificatoire', organises 'les éléments à partir de leurs traits commons'.[44] It should be added that these notions correspond exactly with the notions of 'fictional (or metonymic) articulation' and 'metaphorical articulation' described earlier. One must also bear in mind that Ricardou here uses the term 'articulation' in a strictly limited sense referring only to metonymic articulation, or what can very loosely be called 'the development of the plot'. The conflict between the 'dimensionnel' and the 'classificatoire' involves the use of metonymy by the former and metaphor by the latter:

> Briser un assemblage spatio-temporel référentiel, soit selon les ruptures linéaires obtenues par correspondances immédiates (métaphores ordinales actuelles), soit selon les coupures obtenues par comparaisons, (comparaisons, alternatives, et métaphores expressives), soit selon les ruptures translinéaires obtenues par correspondances différées (métaphores ordinales

virtuelles), c'est toujours, à partir de leurs traits similaires, classer ensemble deux segments spatio-temporels distincts.[45]

By focusing on the classificatory aspect of metaphor, Ricardou seems to lodge the responsibility entirely with the reader since it is he who operates the classification. Even in the case of 'immediate correspondences' brought about by 'métaphores structurelles actuelles' such as 'cuisse sectionnée' and 'jambe coupée' where the two separate narrative segments are adjacent to one another, the act of selecting a common denominator (in this case the 'signifié' 'coupure') is left entirely to the reader. In other words, 'classes', or classificatory titles, are always 'virtuelles'. It is with this in mind that one can fully appreciate the following terms which Ricardou has coined and which are valuable in any rigorous attempt to examine the dialectical relationship between articulation and fragmentation which forms the basis of the relationship between reader and text. In the critic's terminology, a 'taxeme' is another term for 'class' or 'common denominator', and an 'arthreme' is another word for 'narrative segment':

> dans le domaine articulatoire, le segment (fragment, séquence, sur-séquence) tire son existence de ce que l'ensemble des éléments qu'il agence peut être subsumé par l'unité d'un titre, ou, si l'on préfère, d'un *arthrème*. De même, la correspondance (immédiate, différée, axiale, radiante) tire son existence de ce que l'ensemble des éléments qu'elle assemble peut être subsumé par l'unité d'un titre ou, si l'on préfère, d'un taxème.[46]

The conflict between articulation and fragmentation thus takes the form of a bid for supremacy made by taxemes and arthremes. Arthremes are agents of articulation in that they assemble referential or fictional elements within a single narrative unit; and taxemes are classificatory and consequently dislocate arthremes. Arthremes are agents of narrative conjunction and taxemes are agents of narrative disjunction. But, as Ricardou remarks, taxemes can themselves be articulated within a new order, can be reassembled under a new title or 'taxo-arthrème'. Taxo-arthremes control taxemes either by fictional articulation, as in the explicit articulation of the taxemes of 'médecine' and 'coupure' within the taxo-arthreme of 'surgery' (it is made explicit by the description of the doctor (médecine) *holding* a scalpel (cutting); or by assimilation, which can either be based on the similarity of 'signifiés' (as in the assimilation of the taxemes 'section', 'coupure' and 'sub-division militaire' where a polysemic relationship is exploited) or on a paronymic relationship of 'signifiants' (as in the assimilation of 'bataillon' and 'section' by means of 'bas/*taillons*' and 'sec/*scions*'; or by incorporation, which is a result of the interaction between contiguity on the level of 'signifiés' and contiguity on the level of 'signifiants', as in the association of the sky-scrapers and the taxoarthreme of 'cancer' by virtue of their colour, 'ocre', which is repeatedly linked with the taxemes of 'coupure' ('jambes de [. . .] couleur ocrée' (p. 7)), 'maladie' ('feuilles [. . .] d'un vert tirant sur l'ocre [. . .] et maladives' (p. 9)), and 'médecine' ('Les chairs sont d'un rose ocré')[47] which are all encompassed by the taxoarthreme of 'cancer':

> Certes, la prise de contrôle classo-articulatoire est d'une fermeté inégale. Avec l'articulation, elle est directe (elle repose sur une immédiate affinité sémantique). Avec l'assimilation, elle est soit indirecte (elle recourt à des sens lointains du champ sémantique) soit décalée (elle passe par l'intermédiaire d'un jeu de mots). Avec l'incorporation, elle est reportée: elle provient d'un montage à partir de plusieurs occurrences. Cependant il arrive aussi qu'elle soit affermie par des effets de 'sur-contrôle': tel élément, c'est de plusieurs manières qu'il est maîtrisé par tel taxo-arthrème dominant. Ainsi 'section': dans l'état actuel de l'analyse, il appartient évidemment au taxème de la coupure et il s'y trouve lié une seconde fois en ce que son analyse phonético-sémantique 'sec/scions' fait apparaître le verbe 'scier'. Ainsi 'bataillon': il appartient au taxème de la coupure en ce qu'il est une section et il s'y trouve lié une seconde fois en ce que son analyse phonético-sémantique 'bas/taillons' fait apparaître le verbe 'tailler'. Mais de plus, dans la mesure où il marque l'idée de multitude, il relève du taxème de la prolifération. C'est donc par plusieurs itinéraires que le taxo-arthrème du cancer tend à en prendre le contrôle.[48]

One can break down Ricardou's analysis of the conflict between the movements of articulation and fragmentation into four axiological components:

A. Arthremes (narrative segments) are disrupted by taxemes

(dominant 'signifiés'), resulting in a break in the writing ('brisure actuelle'), as when the segment containing 'cuisse sectionnée' is interrupted by the segment containing 'jambe coupée'.

B. Taxemes are in turn subsumed under a taxo-arthreme, as in the example of the taxeme of 'médecine' and 'coupure' being contained within the taxo-arthreme of 'chirurgie':

Dès lors, il est clair, d'une part, que le classificatoire contredit au premier degré l'articulatoire en dissociant certains de ses articles au profit de l'association d'un taxème à un autre et d'autre part que l'articulatoire contredit en retour le classificatoire en intégrant au second degré les taxèmes selon l'articulation d'un taxo-arthrème.[49]

C. Separate narrative sequences (arthremes) are subsumed under a dominating, unifying arthreme ('sur-séquence'), as in the example of the integration of the sequence of the soldiers in the forest (in description block III) and the sequence of the journey by plane (sequence C) within the 'sur-séquence' in which the soldiers in the forest are framed as part of a magazine story being read by a traveller on the plane.

D. Identical parts of different 'sur-séquences' ('iso-arthrèmes') are re-assembled within an arthro-taxeme, as in the example of the arthro-taxeme of 'franchissement difficile' which embraces several separate 'sur-séquences' such as the progress of the man walking in the city, the 'conquistadores' and guerrillas in the forest, and the sick man in the aeroplane:

Dès lors, il est clair, d'une part, que l'articulatoire contredit au premier degré le classificatoire en dissociant certains de ses éléments au profit de l'agencement d'un arthrème et d'autre part que le classificatoire contredit en retour l'articulatoire en assemblant au second degré les arthrèmes selon la classification d'un arthro-taxème.[50]

The conclusion which Ricardou fails to draw regarding the degree of importance attached to the reader's contribution to this hierarchy of textual relations is summarised in the table here below, in which the plus signs indicate 'present in the writing' and the minus signs 'absent from the writing, dependent on the reading'.

	A	B	C	D
Association	'brisure' +	−	+	−
Motivation of Association	(?) −	−	+	−

Thus in A the break in the text is actually confirmed in the writing but the motivation of the break is weak, or only partly in the writing, since although the words which actuate the metaphorical association (for example, 'jambes coupées') are clearly in the text, it is nevertheless up to the reader to make the metaphorical association himself: it is up to him to see the words as 'métaphores structurelles'. In B, the association and its motivation are 'virtuelles', depending on the reader to place the dominant 'signifiés' in a hierarchical relationship. In C, both the association and its motivation are 'actuelles', affecting the literal dimension of the text. In D, the association and its motivation are 'virtuelles' relying on the interpretative inclinations of the reader. The table also demonstrates that it would be mistaken to identify articulation with writing and fragmentation with reading, or vice versa, since clearly their relationship is mixed.

The conclusion which Ricardou does draw is the same as the one he made in ' "Claude Simon", textuellement': namely, that the fragments of Les Corps conducteurs are ultimately assimilated within a unifying 'sur-séquence' (voyage to the Americas) which is not seriously undermined by any arthro-taxeme. Indeed the arthro-taxemes mostly serve to reinforce the dominant narrative sequence (such as the cluster of relations which evoke the ability or inability to arrive at a destination):

> Si la dislocation classificatoire est intense dans Les Corps conducteurs, elle reste cependant dominée par l'arborisation dominante: c'est même cette domination qui définit, si contestée soit-elle, l'appartenance au domaine dimensionnel.[51]

We can now follow more clearly the thinking which has led Ricardou to this conclusion, stated so emphatically on two occasions. The reason why the 'dislocation classificatoire' can be ultimately recuperated within a unificatory whole is that the disjunctive nature of the novel is produced by taxemes which are by definition weak, in terms of the conflict between articulation and fragmentation, since they depend too much on the reader. This is why, in Ricardou's opinion, *Triptyque* is more fundamentally dislocated than *Les Corps conducteurs*: the former does not rely on taxemes as agents of disjunction but on the narrative itself whose scattered segments, as will be shown in Part IV, interact within a framework of irreconcilable aggression. One cannot dispute this argument; the classificatory or taxematic interrelations in *Les Corps conducteurs* are ultimately recuperable. But why restrict oneself to a taxematic analysis of this novel? Is there not some other force of dislocation in *Les Corps conducteurs*, just as in *La Bataille de Pharsale* the prime agents of disruption are not the motifs but the intertextual fragments? I shall, for the remainder of this chapter, be arguing that the unruly and anonymous textual components of description blocks form just such a force.

III DESCRIPTIVE FUSION AND CONFUSION

One must point out in defence of Ricardou's analysis, that a taxeme is not a synonym for a motif. It would be more accurate to call it a common denominator. A taxeme is the name of a dominant 'signifié', one which encompasses at least two different fictional elements in a text. However, this titular quality of the 'domaine classificatoire' provides the means by which a reductive reading is made possible. If the reader can name the motivation of each group of associations in the novel then he will be able to collocate them within a global narrative framework. For Ricardou the syntactic level of *Les Corps conducteurs* is dominated by the semantic level. But, as my exposition of the nature of description blocks has suggested, the overwhelming uncertainty on the reader's part in naming each individual block is one of the main distinctive features of these phenomena. This uncertainty is sometimes due to a plurality of contradictory possibilities and sometimes due to a total absence of frame. 'L'enseigne est enlevée',[52] to quote Victor Chklovski. The synecdochic relations between instances of a block only stress this absence further. These 'floating' textual fragments accumulate as the novel progresses; their very anonymity and apparent autonomy challenges the reader to solve the mystery of their contextual provenance. No classificatory solution is possible, however, and the fragments remain both a disruptive and a creative force in the novel.

The central referent of description block I is, as already stated, the cartoon picture of a surgeon and a group of interns on the point of or just after operating on a naked and smiling woman. However, the first instance of the description appears at the start of the novel and is preceded only by the opening instance of sequence A. The 'framing' of the description as a picture (in other words the denial of the segment's status as narrative action) does not come until the following page. Thus, for a short space of time the reader is misled into believing that it is a separate narrative sequence. The framing of the description, however, is accompanied by the emergence of a new narrative sequence: sequence B. It is the special relationship between description block I and sequence B which I shall now consider.

The opening passage is segmented in the following way: sequence A – block I (unframed) – sequence A – sequence B – sequence A – block II – sequence A or B ('zone amphibologique')/ block II/ sequence B/ block I (framed). The 'rupture' between the first and second segments is, as Ricardou says, produced by the structural metaphor linking 'cuisse sectionnée' of the dummies' legs and 'jambe coupée' in the cartoon. The break is signalled by the comparison, 'faisant penser à quelque appareil'.[53] The 'rupture' between the second and third segments is produced by repetition: the nipples of the woman on the operating table are 'd'un rose vif' and 'dressés' which evokes, elliptically, the description of a dog in the first segment who is 'dressé joyeusement sur ses pattes de derrière, aboyant, sortant une langue rose'[54] and brings about a return to sequence A. The 'rupture' between the third and fourth segments is produced by the metonymic association between 'jambe' and 'pantalon'. The short sentence which comprises the fourth segment is the first instance of sequence B: 'Le docteur lui dit de baisser son pantalon' (p. 8). One can say that, in many ways, sequence B grows out of description block I. The doctor and the surgeon are obviously related by profession; and, as Jean-Claude Raillon has pointed out,[55] there is a structural paronomasia linking the passages: 'Bébé Cadum' and 'baisser' are linked by the letters B and C which are in capitals in the former and constitute the phonetic component of the latter. From the point of view of the narrative, it is the appearance of 'lui' which is significant, since there is no-one yet to whom it can refer. The sentence thus stands as an enigma. The 'rupture' between the fifth and sixth segments is signalled by the comparison, 'comme des orgues'. The shift hinges on a correspondence in the descriptive language of the two segments: 'orgue' creates a link with the sixth segment (block II) firstly by paronomastic association with 'organe', and secondly by metaphorical association with 'guitare', (Ricardou would say that the two elements are classified by the taxeme 'musical instrument'); the final sentence of the fifth segment, after repeating 'côté and 'côte, culminates with 'paroi molle' which, with its counterpart 'paroi abdominale', form the transitional pivot. The 'rupture' between the sixth and seventh segments relies on a continuation of the dominance of the taxeme 'musical instrument' with which 'accordéon' is metaphorically associated. There is also a correspondence, between 'Sur le petit dôme formé par la poche verte le dessinateur a posé un reflet jaune pour obtenir un effet de brillant'[56] in segment 6 and 'Le docteur lui demande si cela ressemble à un pincement, une pression ou une brûlure'[57] based on the taxeme of 'resemblance'. Segment 7 may be termed, to borrow from Ricardou, a 'zone amphibologique' since it can either be identified as part of sequence A or as part of sequence B.[58] The unsuspecting reader will first identify it with sequence A as there is a description a few lines beforehand of the man by the shop windows pressing his fingers into his side. But when the reader alights on the description, a few lines later, of the man in sequence B being prodded by the doctor, he is now justified in identifying segment 7 as an instance of sequence B. An indisputable fact about this textual fragment is that it is an instance of descriptive confusion:

> Là où appuient ses doigts se trouve une masse aux contours mous, d'un rouge brique, comme un sac. A peu près en son milieu il y a une poche vert clair, collée à la paroi [.] (p. 9)[59]

There is clearly here a superimposition of two distinct referential contexts. The man's stomach (either sequence A or B) is identified, through the description, as part of an anatomical drawing. The encounter of the two planes of reference certainly upsets the logic of the narrative, but it also serves as an agent of continuity since it authorises the shift from segment 7 to segment 8 (one can assume that the 'planche anatomique' is hanging in the doctor's room). Thus, semantic incompatibility allows for syntactic compatibility. Moreover, description block II plays a vital role as intermediary in the textual process of embedding description block I within sequence B. The descriptions of the cartoon and the anatomical drawing are related not only by the same medical frame of reference but also by the structural metaphor of 'poche': the 'poche ventrale' on the interns' aprons is reiterated by the 'poche vert olive' in the anatomical drawing. The repetition is doubly significant in that the interns' pockets contain surgical instruments (forceps and scissors), whilst in segments 6 and 7 musical instruments are metaphorically and paronomastically related to the anatomy ('orgue'/'organe', and the opening left by the absence of the 'paroi abdominale' which takes the shape of a 'caisse d'une guitare'). As Ricardou would say, the taxemes of 'musical instrument' and 'surgical instrument' are subsumed under the taxoarthreme of 'surgery'. The description of the anatomical drawing (block II) thus intervenes in the metonymic articulation between the cartoon description (block I) and the narration of the visit to the doctor (sequence B). Although the description of the operation has been 'tamed', so to speak, and re-defined as a cartoon description within the broader frame of sequence B, the relationship between these two compositional units is in no way one-sided. On the contrary, the reader cannot fail to observe the decisive influence of the former on the latter, as in the following passage:

> De la cavité à l'ouverture en forme de guitare le docteur retire l'un après l'autre les organes (ou lorsque ceux-ci sont trop gros, des morceaux d'organes) coloriés. Ceux-ci sont faits d'une matière légère, comme du carton bouilli ou du celluloïd. Ils s'emboîtent les uns dans les autres par un ingénieux système d'ergots qui permet de les détacher – ou de les replacer – sur une simple traction ou pression. Le docteur les range avec soin sur une tablette au plateau recouvert d'une serviette blanche disposée à côté de la table d'examen. (p. 74)[60]

The influence of the cartoon on this passage can be inferred from the fact that the doctor is behaving, albeit in an unusual or 'fantastic' fashion, as a surgeon, as well as from the fact that the anatomical parts which he is removing are made of 'une matière légère, comme du carton bouilli ou du celluloïd' which is an echo of the plastic legs at the start of the novel, a recall which seems to have been anticipated by the earlier comparison, 'faisant penser à quelque appareil de prothèse légère',[61] and, by extension, to the 'jambe coupée' held by the intern in the cartoon. Finally the reader is being urged by the text to note that 'carton' is an amphibological word which can also mean 'cartoon'.

Throughout the succeeding occurrences of sequence B the influence of the cartoon description is shaped in the form of a cancerous growth which invades the doctor's premises. This strange element of the fantastic has its origin in the description of a clock in the doctor's waiting-room:

> Accoudée au cadran, une marquise à la robe de métal, à l'étroit corset, penche gracieusement la tête, un vague sourire aux lèvres, vers un jeune homme au tricorne assis à ses pieds et qui gratte une mandoline. Quoique les aiguilles soient immobilisées, il semble que l'on puisse entendre comme un fracas silencieux, comme l'avalanche d'un glacier invisible: quelque chose de grisâtre, immatériel et formidablement lourd qui avancerait sans répit, une avalanche au ralenti, rabotant le plancher, les murs, en marche depuis des milliards d'années, patiente et insidieuse. (p. 88)[62]

The vehicle of the metaphor 'the avalanche of time' takes on a 'reality' and an independence of its own as the sequence develops. It is noticeable that the next few instances of sequence B (pp. 90, 91, 92, 95, 100–3, 106, 111, 127) in which there is no explicit mention of the cartoon, all contain a reference to the 'masse grisâtre' of the cancer. In so far as it connects with the motif of 'surgical operation' and amplifies the idea of growth which was introduced in the text by the reference to the foetus in the cartoon, the cancerous growth can be read as a sign of the generative influence of description block I. This conflict of frames between the two compositional units is reflected in the description of the painting of a boxer which hangs in the doctor's waiting-room:

> Le visage du boxeur n'est qu'une tache ensanglantée et informe où sur un fond rouge sombre le peintre a posé quelques accents vermillon. La tête pendant vers le sol, muet, enfermé dans sa cloche de silence contre laquelle viennent battre les applaudissements et les huées du public invisible dans l'ombre qui entourent le ring, il semble concentrer toutes ses forces et sa volonté dans la poussée de ses bras pour se dégager de la chose

grisâtre où il est maintenant enfoui presque jusqu' aux coudes. (p. 106)[63]

The allusion to sound and immobility clearly denotes a transgression of the conventional laws of description: the picture 'literally' comes to life and is no longer viewed as a representation. The boxer struggles to repulse the greyish matter from the scene of the boxing ring, for the amorphous mass has not only invaded the doctor's waiting-room but has also penetrated the referential confines of the painting. For the reader, this dramatised 'frame break' reflects the underlying textual convergence between two distinct narrative contexts. The description of the events in the doctor's waiting-room (sequence B) is mirrored, and to a certain extent dictated, by the episode which takes place in a bar (sequence A). To begin with, the idea of frame transgression is itself first postulated in the form of a simile: on entering the dimly-lit premises of the bar, the protagonist feels 'comme s'il pénétrait dans une de ces vieilles photographies' (p. 86).[64] Indeed, on the wall behind the counter there hangs an old photograph of a boxer whom the narrator deduces to be the bartender as a young man. In addition to prefiguring the picture in the doctor's waiting-room, the description focuses on the bartender's peculiar ability to switch, 'sans transition',[65] from immobility to rapid movement, like a reptile which suddenly springs into action after hours of frozen immobility: a perspective which is later repeated in the sudden animation of the painting in sequence B. There are also a number of textual correspondences between the two sequences, such as the froth spilling over the rim of the beer glass, 'fragmentant en paquets de bulles agglutinées', and the crumbling avalanche of the greyish magma whose 'parcelles plus ou moins grosses'[66] roll down to the floor of the waiting-room.

One can interpret the growing mound of matter as an image of the relentless advance of time or of intensifying physical pain and debility. But it can also be read as an image of the generative production of the text. The detachment of small particles of matter, and the overflowing bubbles of froth, reflect the way in which the text proliferates by developing contingent descriptions which mutate and finally detach themselves from their original contextual source, rather like a protoplasmic organism which reproduces by shedding parts of its own body. For instance, the attentive reader will find that the cartoon description resembles the description of a postage stamp by virtue of the correspondence between the group of interns led by a bearded surgeon in the former and a group of soldiers led by a bearded man in the latter. Furthermore, the cartoon description is made pregnant with military connotations by the metaphorical extension of the words 'de jeunes *carabins* hilares *armés* de divers instruments chirurgicaux' which later stray from this point of origin and recur in a number of divergent fragments.[67] Some are framed as a postage stamp (pp. 14, 39–41, 85), some are framed as a photograph (pp. 108–9, 194–5). Elsewhere their identity remains ambivalent, such as the description of the 'conquistadores' in Indian territory which the reader is unable to 'situate'. The text thus proceeds with a multiplicity of arthremes which are disseminated in different areas of narrative while remaining connected in a constellation of textual association. The variety of referents which constitute this particular cluster of descriptive association includes the newspaper advertisement of the film 'El Indomable' in sequence D (pp. 148, 157); the magazine photograph in sequence C (pp. 121–4); the story narrated in the first person by Orlando in the same magazine in sequence C (pp. 137, 165); the description of the soldiers at the aeroport in sequence C (p. 187); and the description of the toy soldiers in the shop window in sequence A: 'des colonnes de petits soldats en tenue de camouflage progressaient dans un jungle miniature' (p. 155).[68]

This scattering of half-developed, military descriptions can be mentally collated by the reader to form what I have called 'description block III'. Like description block I, these fragments are 'pseudo-sequential' in that they tend to oscillate between their status as visual representations and a desire for narrative action. Although the first instance of the block (the 'conquistadores' fragment (p. 14)) is clearly framed as a pictorial representation, at the second appearance of the same description one feels a tension in the writing brought about by the verbs of action which set the scene in motion:

> Ainsi le général y fait embarquer tout ce qu'il y a de gens de guerre, laissant à l'ancre les deux autres vaisseaux avec une partie des matelots. Comme les soldats commencent avec beaucoup de peine à surmonter la force du courant d'eau ils aperçoivent un nombre considérable de canots pleins d'Indiens armés outre ceux que l'on voit à terre en diverses troupes, et

qui par leur mouvement semblent dénoncer la guerre et vouloir défendre l'entrée de la rivière par des cris et par ces postures que la crainte fait faire à ceux qui souhaiteraient éloigner le péril à force des menaces [. . .] Sautant hors des embarcations des soldats aux lourdes armures courent dans l'eau qui rejaillit en éclaboussures. (p. 40)[69]

But the animation of the scene is entirely belied when, a few lines later, the identity of the description is re-affirmed as a postage-stamp by alluding to its value imprinted on the sky: 'Le chiffre 35 suivi du mot CENTAVOS est gravé en taille-douce dans le ciel teinté sans doute par la lueur du couchant' (p. 41).[70] One could claim that there is no contradiction here, that the references to movement do not have to be understood literally. The present tense could be read as being used in its 'eternal aspect',[71] conveying a general, 'historical' timelessness appropriate to the style of the commentary on the European invasion of the Americas at the start of the passage. The use of the present tense might therefore be said to be 'a-temporal' or 'descriptive' in these lines. No such interpretation, however, is possible later on in the novel where the references to movement and time in fragments from description block III become more insistent and direct. This element of spatio-temporal progression, which is in total contradiction to the original framing of the description as a postage-stamp, is the means by which the description block strives to transform itself into a narrative sequence:

> Quoique depuis tout à l'heure elle ait certainement progressé, rien apparemment n'a changé dans le décor qui entoure de toutes parts la colonne d'hommes en arms [.] (p. 107)[72]

The depiction of movement in these lines is further stressed by the reference to the flight of a butterfly, 'une tache d'un jaune vif, voletant d'une façon incohérente, s'élevant, s'abaissant, glissant sur le côté, s'élevant de nouveau, comme un morceau de papier ballotté par les courants d'un air mou'.[73] But it is also this same butterfly which undoes the transformation, reminding us that what we are reading is not a narrative sequence but an instance of a description block:

> A l'approche du chef de la colonne le papillon prend de nouveau

son essor, volette un moment, indécis, comme un ivre, puis disparaît sur la droite hors du rectangle de la photographie. (p. 109)[74]

The reference to the 'frame break' in this instance (the butterfly flying out of the photograph) is not unlike the example given earlier of the boxer in the painting pushing out the 'matière grisâtre'. The difference lies in the direction of the movement. Whereas in the earlier example an external element was breaking into the painting, in this instance an internal element (the butterfly) is breaking out of the photograph. The similarity between the two examples goes further. The butterfly, as I shall demonstrate shortly, is an element of description block IV, just as the 'matière grisâtre' in the earlier example was an element of description block I. The reader is therefore confronted with another instance of descriptive confusion, this time between referents of description blocks III and IV. The special ability of elements of description blocks to 'spill over' into a different unit of fiction (whether a narrative sequence or another description block) acts, paradoxically, as a reminder of the description blocks' resistance to articulation. Nevertheless, the main characteristic of a description block is that its elements are constantly prone to 'break frame' and it is this activity, so frequent in Les Corps conducteurs, which should have led Ricardou to classify this novel as well as Triptyque as a 'discoherent' text.

By drawing the reader's attention to pictures, picture frames, the examples present a symbolic depiction, or 'dramatisation', of the ordered world of narrative logic and perception which they subsequently transgress: the butterfly and the 'masse grisâtre' both 'break frame'. This referential focus is paralleled, in other instances of descriptive confusion, by another type of focus, involving this time the writing as 'signifiant'. There are several 'styles' in Les Corps conducteurs: the political style of the conference speeches in sequence D; the racy, journalese style of the magazine story written in the first person narrative in sequence C;[75] the fact-studded, encyclopaedic style of the information on the anatomy in block II and on 'fauna and flora' in block IV. 'Style emphatique' can be described as a caricature of language since, like a cartoon, its exaggerated tenor draws attention to its status as symbol, in other words to the 'expressive function' of frame.[76] If blocks I and III are notable for the profusion of pictorial descriptions (photos, prints, drawings and so on) sketched in their component fragments, blocks II and IV could be said to be essentially 'discursive' in nature. I have already said that blocks I and III are 'pseudo-sequential' and that the other two blocks act as 'appendices' to them. These two characteristics of blocks II and IV (their style and their function as 'appendices') should be considered in the same light.

My analysis of description block I revealed its close relationship with block II. In fact the central referent of block II, the anatomical drawing, is a visual description and is implicitly framed, like the cartoon in block I (except that with the latter the framing is explicit) within sequence B. The reader can assume, although he is never told, that the anatomical diagram is hanging in the doctor's waiting-room. Yet the description is not without its ambiguities. Firstly, a sense of dispersion is created by its variants which are framed in different sequences. The description of the anatomical drawing in block II, 'A partir du diaphragme et jusqu'au ras du pubis la paroi abdominale a été découpée, comme un couvercle que l'on aurait retiré. L'ouverture ménagée affecte à peu près la forme de la caisse d'un guitare' (p. 9),[77] is echoed in the description of the optician's 'planche anatomique' in sequence A:

> Au-dessous et à la même échelle figure une coupe schématique du même oeil montrant la cornée bombée, la chambre antérieure, la pupille, l'iris, le corps vitré, la rétine et le nerf optique. La cornée et la sclérotique qui entoure le globe sont colorées de bleu lavande, la chambre antérieure derrière la partie bombée de la cornée est couleur chair, l'iris rouge orangé, le cristallin est strié de fines lignes bleues, comme un oignon aplati coupé en deux, la masse du corps vitré est d'un gris bleuté, la rétine et le nerf optique sont vert Nil. (p. 154)[78]

A further echo can be read in the description of the anatomical drawing of a brain which the traveller gazes at on the aeroplane in sequence C:

> En haut d'une colonne se trouve un encadré dans la partie supérieure duquel on voit une tache grise affectant vaguement la forme d'un rognon ou d'un haricot et dont le sommet convexe est coupé de petits créneaux. Sur la droite est imprimé le mot CERVEAU. Une flèche, dirigé vers le bas, part d'une pastille

rouge, au centre de la masse, et aboutit à un cercle où est représentée une coupe agrandie de l'hypophyse. De là une seconde flèche décrivant une courbe conduit le regard à une sorte de cornue qui occupe le bas tableau, son bec dirigé vers la droite. Suivant le tracé de la flèche courbe on peut lire: ACTION DES GONADOTROPHINES. Dans la partie ventrue de la cornue se trouve un petit ovale, légèrement oblique, d'où s'échappe un mince serpentin qui après avoir suivi un trajet méandreux redescend finalement selon l'axe centrale du bec de la cornue. (pp. 164–5)[79]

Apart from the taxemes 'coupure' and 'anatomie' which link the three passages, one can also note that certain 'signifiants' in the latter two passages echo one another: 'cornée'/'cornue', 'oignon'/ 'rognon', 'haricot'.

There is, however, another way in which block II trespasses onto different areas of the text. A striking feature of all three passages quoted above is that they contain an unusual amount of technical names ('diaphragme', 'cornée', 'cristallin', 'pubis', 'sclérotique', 'hypophyse', GONADOTROPHINES'). The phenomenon may not seem strange in those particular passages since it is conceivable that the words 'are being read from the anatomical drawing in the magazine in the third passage, and, less conceivably, the words are read from the 'planche anatomique' in the first and second passages. However, this phenomenon is less amenable to the logic of the narrative at other moments of the text, as in the following example:

Bien après que le docteur a retiré ses mains la sensation de pression persiste, ou plutôt d'un corps étranger, énorme, resté fiché comme un coin. Les états inflammatoires aigus du foie, ou hépatites, relèvent de causes infectieuses (virus, spirochètes) ou chimiques (phosphore, alcool, etc.). Certaines inflammations localisées (amibes) peuvent aboutir à l'abcés du foie. (p. 47)[80]

Although the second two sentences follow on from the reference to the medical examination in the first sentence, the passage is clearly divided into two separate fictional isotopies. The first part of the passage is an instance of sequence B and the second part is an instance of description block II. The one links up in a chain of events (the visit to the doctor) and the other acts as an index evoking the textual constellation with which it is related (block II). What distinguishes one isotopy from the other is the introduction of a new discourse which seems to derive from an external and unidentified medical text. But there is no answer to questions like 'Who is reading the medical text? Is it part of a book, an encyclopaedia, or a magazine? Where is it being read and at what point of time?' The reader is instead compelled to take full account of the descriptive confusion which has been created by the juxtaposition of two distinct fictional units (sequence B and description block II).

Instances of descriptive confusion are even more intense at moments when two separate isotopies are not juxtaposed, as in the above example, but superimposed as a result of syntactic integration. The following example is taken from the start of a long instance of descriptive confusion between sequence E and block II:

Sur le lit défait les deux corps nus étendus ont maintenant retrouvé les couleurs de la chair dans la lumière: ocrée, rosée ou laiteuse selon les parties habituellement au soleil et à l'air. Comme ces statues de saints en bois peint que l'on promène dans les processions, vacillantes sur les épaules des porteurs, et où une petite fenêtre vitrée, ménagée sur la poitrine, un membre, permet de voir à l'intérieur quelque fragment d'os, la peau, sur le devant des torses, a été découpée et retirée à partir des seins – des pectoraux – jusqu'un peu au-dessus du pubis. Sur l'ouverture en forme de guitare, légèrement étranglée en son milieu à hauteur de la taille, a été posé un couvercle de plexiglas moulé, reproduisant les reliefs des corps, le sillon entre les abdominaux chez l'homme, le renflement bombé du ventre de la femme au-dessous du pli du nombril. A travers la paroi transparente on peut voir les organes internes [.] (pp. 67–8)[81]

Besides the reference to the internal organs, several elements are repeated from other instances of block II, such as 'Sur l'ouverture en forme de guitare légèrement étranglée en son milieu à hauteur de la taille' and 'tuyaux qui se divisent en branches' which are almost word for word repetitions of parts of the description of the anatomical drawing at the start of the novel.[82] The confusion of the passage thus hinges on the metaphorical elements in the description. This observation is supported by the fact that the transition from the 'straightforward' description of the lovers lying together to one which is confused with elements of the description of an anatomical drawing in block II is brought about through a metaphorical comparison, or what Ricardou would call a 'coupure': 'Comme ces statues de saints'. Thus although the passage is full of references to visual perception ('fenêtre vitrée [. . .] qui permet de voir', 'A travers la paroi transparente on peut voir')[83] the articulation of the two fictional units (sequence E and block II) is textual and not visual. This apparent contradiction is repeated at other instances of descriptive confusion involving description block II:

> Les haillons déchirés découvrent les peaux brulées, d'une couleur terreuse, sous lesquelles saille chaque tendon, chaque muscle et chacun des os du squelette comme ces écorchés des planches d'anatomie. De dos on peut ainsi voir: A: le releveur propre. B: l'omoplate dépouillée de ses muscles, excepté l'Abaisseur propre. C: l'Abaisseur propre [.] (pp. 183–4)[84]

In this case the metaphorical comparison which sparks off the descriptive confusion ('comme ces écorchés des planches d'anatomie') self-consciously refers to the agent of the confusion, description block II, which is here distorting an instance of description block III. Thus the visual aspect of the passage ('on peut ainsi voir') is implicitly offset by the transposition of style. In both the above examples the subject of the perception, the person who is looking, is not only ambiguous but logically impossible. The irrecuperability of the passage is thereby ironically asserted.

Description block IV is the most fragmentary of all the description blocks. The main reason for this is that its central referent is both unframed and ambiguous. Is it a photograph in a magazine or encyclopaedia, being read perhaps by the man travelling by plane in sequence C?

> La page est divisée en trois colonnes verticales. L'accumulation des caractères serrés leur donne une teinte grisâtre. La photo en couleur du boa occupe le haut de la colonne de gauche. L'article Serpent commence à la page précédente [.] (pp. 22–3)[85]

Is it an ancient parchment on exhibition in a museum: (Vélin du Museum national d'Histoire naturelle peint par de Vailly, 80, 54)

Currents of Description in Les Corps conducteurs   167

(pp. 215-17)? And if so, to which narrative segment does the description belong? Or, alternatively, is it a map of the American continent seen through the window of a travel agency in sequence A?

> Au-dessus de l'avion et occupant le milieu de la vitrine se trouve un panneau vertical, un peu plus haut que l'hôtesse de contre-plaqué, sur lequel se trouve la reproduction d'un portulan où est représenté le continent américain [. . .] Toute indication cesse à peu de distance de la côte en même temps que s'estompe la bande verte qui la borde, laissant place à la teinte jaunâtre du parchemin sur lequel sont peints des bouquets de palmiers, d'arbres touffus, des perroquets rouges, des singes, des dragons ailés, des oiseaux bleus ou bruns, des marais [.] (pp. 217-18)[86]

This central and recurrent description contains several 'motifs conducteurs'. Snakes, birds, butterflies, stars are assimilated on the one hand because they are in contiguous juxtaposition on the map, photo or parchment, and on the other hand because fragments of encyclopaedic information are given on all four subjects. Their textual relationship is therefore based on the fact that they are framed by the same though unfixed and unidentifiable visual referent, and also because they are described in the same distinctive style of discourse. To the extent that it assembles several textual elements, without it ever being certain what the framework of the assemblage is, block IV serves as a 'mise en abyme' of the compositional nature of all the description blocks. Its most significant component in this respect is the reference to the constellation of stars. This image is a constellation within a larger constellation, that of the whole description block which is in turn placed within the wider constellation of the novel as a whole. The pointlessness of attempting to read a meaning into the constellation is comically suggested in an instance of descriptive confusion between block IV and sequence E:

> Dans deux groupes d'étoiles rapprochées dessinant deux triangles de grandeur à peu près égale où l'on peut lire schématiquement un visage, certains peuples de l'Antiquité croyaient pouvoir situer les positions successives occupées par la tête de la femme lorsque dans un spasme elle la rejette en arrière, se cambrant, abandonnant le gland qu'elle pressait entre les lèvres,

sa main toutefois toujours crispée sur la verge tendue. (pp. 57-8)[87]

The comic effect is based on a caricature of the interpretative impulse behind the 'reading' of the Orion constellation:

Les différentes étoiles n'indiquent qu'approximativement la position des corps et des membres. La chevelure de Bérénice est dessinée par une vingtaine d'étoiles, de magnitude 4 à 6. (p. 57)[88]

Similar doubts in the process of attaching meanings to or 'making sense of' empirical data prevail throughout the novel, as, for instance, in the failure of the interpreter in sequence D to keep up with the chaotic proceedings at the conference (p. 158), or in the interpretation of the dance of the cocks in block IV: 'la signification de cette pantomime n'est pas claire' (p. 216).[89]

With the absence of an overall meaning, like a key for unlocking the self-enclosed network of coded signs, one is obliged to focus on the patterns of association which are woven into this particular constellation of text. Once again, it is in instances of descriptive confusion that this textual activity is most apparent as it radically disturbs the referential dimension of the novel. I have already shown that instances of descriptive confusion combine two separate and incompatible fictional isotopies. The combination, though often produced by harmonious associations of language, remains dissonant because no unification or integration is achieved on the level of the narrative. It is the style of the fragments involved in descriptive confusion which most compellingly draws the reader's attention to this dissonance, or clash of frames. The most extreme examples of this can be found in instances of descriptive confusion produced by elements from block IV:

Seuls deux ou trois des hommes de la colonne relèvent la tête. Les Aras ont des moeurs sociables: ils forment des bandes comptant quelques dizaines d'individus. L'Ara militaire ou Ara macao est, avec le Cacatoès, le plus grand des perroquets [. . .] Leur plumage est d'un beau rouge vif. Leurs ailes sont jaune et bleu. Quelle fête de couleur lorsque les Aras, ailes déployées, s'envolent dans les rayons de soleil! [. . .] les quelques soldats

Currents of Description in Les Corps conducteurs 169

qui s'étaient laissés distraire baissent à nouveau leur tête et reprennent leur marche. (p. 174)[90]

This passage, triggered off by the description of the pigeons in sequence A, is an instance of descriptive confusion between blocks IV and III. The description of the soldiers' march in the forest is interrupted by the encyclopaedic information on parrots. Despite certain correspondences between the two fictional units, such as 'Ara militaire' mirroring the taxeme of 'militarism' in block III,[91] the incompatibility of the two isotopies is unmistakable. The clichéd, 'emphatic' style of 'Quelle fête de couleur lorsque les Aras, ailes déployées, s'envolent dans les rayons du soleil!' underlines the fact that there is a shift in discourse between the two passages. The speaker in both cases is not the same. The reader is thus confronted with, in Ricardou's words, a case of pure 'dis-articulation' or 'discoherence'. A more insidious instance of descriptive confusion produced by block IV can be found later in the text:

Quelque part l'oiseau rieur, toujours le même semble-t-il, continue de loin en loin à faire entendre son cri. Leur volonté toute entière rassemblée pour faire mouvoir leur jambes, les marcheurs épuisés ne tressaillent même plus lorsque parfois un serpent ou quelque bête détale sous leur pas, ne prêtent plus attention, sauf si leur taille en fait un gibier possible, aux animaux qui peuplent la forêt. Souvent parmi les taches éclatantes qui dansent devant leurs yeux envahis de pus ou troublés par le manque de sommeil, ils ne sont plus capables de distinguer entre les papillons géants et certains oiseaux. Les uns comme les autres ont des couleurs incroyables, des dimensions incroyables [. . .] D'autres à peine plus gros, ont un poitrail bleu ardoise, un ventre olive, des ailes couleur noisette, une longue queue bifide d'un gris d'acier. Acrobates aériens, crochets, piqués, vol au point fixe sont leur exploits de tous les instants [. . .] De même que le Cacatoès huppé, ils semblent être le fruit de l'imagination aberrante d'un peintre. A leur vue, comme à celle des végétaux monstrueux ou des serpents géants, certains des marcheurs se croient dans leur épuisement, la proie d'hallucinations et délirent à voix haute. (p. 212–13)[92]

The passage, an instance of block II describing the soldiers' march in the forest, is thoroughly pervaded with elements from block

IV: the birds, snakes, butterflies and the taxeme of 'gigantism' linking up with Orion ('papillons géants', 'végétaux monstrueux ou des serpents géants'). Of course the reference to sound (the 'oiseau rieur' often denotes a frame break in the forest march description) is itself in total contradiction with the description's visual identity (whether as photo, print, or stamp engraving). However, the most fundamentally disjunctive aspect of this passage, as far as the reader is concerned, is the presence of two separate discourses beneath the apparent surface homogeneity. Some of the sentences, especially the one beginning 'Acrobates aériens . . .') are clearly part of some unspecified natural history text on butterflies. In other words they belong to description block IV. The scientific naming and informative style of the sentence jar with the narrative of the soldiers' march. Other parts of the passage are less clearly identifiable in terms of determining their contextual provenance.

In short, one may define an instance of descriptive confusion as a clash of isotopies. Identification of each isotopy entails noting the way in which the fugitive instances of a description block evoke their generative origin. Thus the sentence beginning 'Acrobates aériens . . .' and the sentence about the 'Ara militaire' in the earlier passage are, despite their appearance 'within' the forest march description, in fact out of context and refer indexically to their original context, that is to block IV. One cannot define this reference as a metonymic association since the concept of metonymy involves the activity of naming; the word has its etymological roots in the Greek word 'metonymia' which means change ('meta') of name ('onoma'). But the reader of *Les Corps conducteurs* who finds himself collaborating in the articulation of disparate textual fragments will also find that the description blocks gathered by his reading resist nomenclature by virtue of the plurality and diversity of the textual elements they englobe. What name, for example, can one assign to description block IV? It includes a number of disaparate elements which are linked in different ways: either visually framed in the same referent, like the map or photograph which places the stars, snakes, birds, and butterflies in contiguous relation with one another; or linguistically linking up through, for example, the word 'serpent'. The existence of a system of association is undeniable, but what is missing is its name, a dominating seme which would refer simultaneously to all the component elements. One reason for this absence, as already stated, is that each component element does not refer to or connect with all the others. Thus, the description of Poussin's painting 'belongs with' block IV only in so far as it links up, through Orion, with the motif of 'constellation' and not with any of the other components of the block. The elusiveness of these textual fragments is one of the most disruptive and disconcerting forces in the novel since it denies the reader any firm basis upon which he can build a hierarchical and interpretative reading. Consequently the act of literary analysis in this case ceases to be a matter of reduction, of sifting the central semantic structure of the text, and becomes a matter of charting a moving pattern. Paradoxically, it is often the exaggerated presence of unusual names (a characteristic of block IV) which spotlights these moments of shift and textual movement. The ironic implications of the exploitation of the linguistic materiality of names in general become clear when one remembers that despite the profusion of exotic and technical names, the 'characters' themselves remain anonymous as does the geographical setting for the action.

The use of proper nouns in descriptive writing bears directly on the broader subject of a writer's basic conception of art and composition. For this reason, Stephen Heath's reply to the common early characterisation of the 'nouveaux romanciers' as 'chosistes' draws attention, by way of contrast, to the use of names in the Goncourt journal:

Here the writing is deliberately absent, the purpose of the passage is confined entirely to notation of the real 'out there'. Its space is that of name and position or distance, and language is reduced to the zero degree of indication, literally a pointing: 'Au fond, le comptoir', 'Derrière le comptoir, porte et fenêtres'. The verb as point of relation and human action has disappeared and the verb *être* has been rendered redundant by the solid presence of the scene out there to which the names point: 'Chez Milan, au coin de la rue de Beaujolais. Petite boutique.' The scene of the writing is expelled as far as possible from the writing and the minimalization of syntax (organization) is the movement of this exteriorization. The writing is no more than a mirror: the organization of the passage is outside itself in the seen and its status is thus strictly taxonomic, it lists, it literally takes stock of the shop. Effectively, the writing here operates to the maximum a kind of repression of the 'signifié', confounding meaning and thing in an extended process of ostensive definition.[93]

Naming is thus central to the taxonomic function of language; in the context of conventional writing, it is synonymous with listing. The countless inventories which have appeared in modern fiction since Joyce's *Ulysses* should, therefore, be seen as a reaction against this didactic use of language. With the 'nouveau roman' too, enumeration becomes an obsolete concept, as in the following lines from *Les Corps conducteurs* which are reminiscent of the obsessive and parodic enumeration of trees in the banana plantation passages in *La Jalousie*:

> On compte environ deux cents espèces à l'hectare: côte à côte des arbres aussi différents que l'hévéa, le palmier, le noyer, le manguier, le bananier, le calebassier [. . .] Tout de suite l'énumération se décourage car elle ne signifie plus rien [.] (p. 131)[94]

This obsolescence is due to the fact that naming is closely related, as Heath says, to the most primitive form of language, that of 'object words' which have 'ostensive definition'. This naïve view of language is founded on the erroneous belief that the relationship between word and object is direct: 'An ostensive definition is one which defines an object by "pointing" to it'.[95] However, linguistics has shown that the relationship is more complicated. The 'semiotic triangle' defines the relationship between 'word' and 'world' as: symbol (or 'signifiant') – concept (or 'signifie°') – referent (or object).[96] There are no objects in *Les Corps conducteurs*, or any other novel for that matter, only 'signifiés'. The crucial difference, of course, is that whereas most fictional works are written in 'trompe lecteur' perspective and disguise this reality, Simon's novel is self-consciously aware of its own representational and ostensive inadequacies. Direct mental contact with external reality is hindered by a screen of 'signifiés' which, as the protagonist in sequence A fully recognises, obey their own linguistic laws of articulation:

> Il avance à la fois assez lentement pour que quelques unes de cette série d'images [. . .] aient le temps de s'inscrire avec précision sur sa rétine, et suffisamment vite [. . .] pour qu'elles

ne fassent qu'apparaître [. . .] dans un vague brouillard de formes non identifiées – ou peut-être reconnus mais oubliées en même temps que perçues, les concepts (passage, souliers, verdure) s'interposant entre le regard et les objects, substituant à ceux-ci une série d'images préfabriquées et sans présence. (p. 76)[97]

It would be absurd to suggest that the language of Simon's text is totally opaque and does not refer to anything outside itself. Such an interpretation would involve an utter denial of the referential dimension of language. All words, by definition, in the semiotic triangle refer to the world of objects and external reality. But it is the complexity of this reference which undermines the idea of division between 'word' and 'world'. Reading Les Corps conducteurs does not consist in piecing together scattered items of descriptive information so as to reconstitute the original field of reference alluded to by the novelist. The quest for unity is thwarted above all, as my analysis has shown, by the recurrent fragments of description blocks whose disruptive influence throughout the novel demands recognition and invites exploration by the reader. It is these descriptive fragments which, like conducting bodies, carry the infinite currents of textual association generated by the creative interaction between reader and text.

It might be argued by some that the approach I have sketched in this chapter is claustrophobic; that I am enjoining readers of Simon's novel to press their nose too close to the page. In a way this objection is ironically countered by the novel itself which ends with the description of the sick man in sequence A finally reaching his hotel room and collapsing onto the floor. His close-up view of the decorative patterns on the carpet can be taken as mirroring the reader's perspective on the novel as a whole: 'Vus ainsi, de tout près, les contours des fleurs, des feuilles, les nervures, obéissant à la trame, se découpent en escaliers' (p. 226).[98] Unlike the Jamesian 'figure in the carpet' viewpoint which seeks after global patterns and cryptic meanings, Simon's writing draws one's attention to the materiality of fiction, to the seams and sutures of textual association.[99] Admittedly, however, my analysis has been deliberately confined to one area of the novel and has not attempted to take account of all the thematic implications which undoubtedly arise from the narrative content. But it would be wrong to label the 'materialist' approach as a microscopic one, with all that that implies of aridity and 'scientific' restriction. Standing back, as far back as Proust's novel, one discovers that the same conclusions regarding the dynamics of the novel still hold. The metamorphoses and transgressions of perspective in Elstir's painting of the port of Carquethuit are achieved, the narrator of *A l'ombre des jeunes filles en fleurs* tells us, by the painter's ability to release objects, or visual impressions, from the intellectual grip exerted by the names with which they are normally designated:

> si Dieu le Père avait créé les choses en les nommant c'est en leur ôtant leur nom, ou en leur donnant un autre, qu'Elstir les récréait. Les noms qui désignent les choses répondent toujours à une notion de l'intelligence, étrangère à nos impressions véritables, et qui nous force à éliminer d'elles tout ce qui ne se rapporte pas à cette notion.[100]

The anonymity of much of the textual material in *Les Corps conducteurs* stems from the same desire to create a new world of metaphorical articulation. Yet the reader's inability to name and define the results of his exploration of the text is not caused, of course, by an absence of names in the novel but by the associative play centring on the materiality of names and of language in general. And this again is a theme and an artistic vision inherited from Proust:

> Et même une syllabe commune à deux noms différents suffisait à ma mémoire – comme à un électricien qui se contente du moindre corps bon conducteur – pour rétablir le contact entre Albertine et mon coeur.[101]

Part Four
Self-Reflexivity

1
The Language of Mirrors

> je veux lui faire voir
> là-dedans un abîme nouveau
> Pascal, *Pensées*[1]

I CATEGORIES OF 'MISE EN ABYME'

At one point in *Frame Analysis* Erving Goffman refers to Susan Sontag's comments on the devices of self-reflection (such as intermittent shots of the cameraman) which Jean-Luc Godard employs in a film like 'La Chinoise'. Sontag remarks that these devices can never fully satisfy the criterion of reflexivity since the spectator would also have to see the cameraman filming the cameraman filming the film and so on *ad infinitum*. Goffman generalises from this observation, adding:

> Sontag only fails to note that this evidence of bad faith holds not only for Godard and not merely for tricky filmmakers but for anyone in any frame who tries to convey something about the character of the frame he is employing; the posture he thereby assumes inevitably denies awareness of the frame in which that posture is struck.[2]

However, this sweeping denial of the 'good faith' of self-reflection in all forms of discourse is founded on doubtful premises. The cinematic example, to begin with, fails to take account of the fact that one is not forced into the infinite regress perspective of an endless chain of cameramen filming one another in order to achieve self-reflexivity in film. All that is required is a mirror reflecting the cameraman filming the film. No hidden trickery would be involved here. But why should deception in any case be regarded as a denial of self-reflexivity? Arguably, all language, whether self-reflexive or not, is deceptive in so far as it takes its own process of production for granted. Any utterance leaves unspoken the conditions and basis, in other words the 'frame', of its articulation. This final, all-inclusive self-designation is always deferred. Yet an utterance which purports to be self-reflexive can in fact be so to a significant degree. It can refer to its functional external frame at the same time as it induces a new frame which remains implicit and beyond the bounds of its reference. Thus self-reflexive language continues to be no more and no less deceptive than ordinary language. The degree of elusiveness, or 'différance' in Derrida's terminology, remains constant. But what does distinguish self-reflexive from ordinary language, of course, is the reference to *an* external frame; to the one, in fact, which is in immediate syntactic contiguity.

As language is primarily a mode of reference and not of representation, 'self-reflexivity' can be construed as a metaphor of 'self-reference': the appearance of the Godard cameraman is not intended as a straightforward inclusion of the film's external frame but as a reference to it. Seen in this light, the failure that Sontag and Goffman evince in this example is not one of self-reflection but of the attempt to fuse the ontologically separate spheres of interior and exterior. In other words, this failure does not relate to the self-reflexive structure of the film in question but to the attitude of the spectator. The infinite sets of cameramen filming each other come into existence only so long as we pursue this particular train of thought. The external frame thus becomes identified with the infinite levels of abstraction constructed in the reader's or spectator's mind. Similarly, the traditional emblem of the 'mise en abyme' alludes to the idea of infinite self-reflection; it does not reproduce it. The idea of infinite repetition is to be pursued by the observer who is, of course, located 'beyond' the external frame of the work. Given this centripetal perspective in which infinite self-reflexivity stems, paradoxically, from the standpoint of the spectator situated outside the work, one can see why the traditional literary conception of the infinite 'mise en abyme' should have been presented as an endless, *inward* projection.[3] Infinity, as described in Aldous Huxley's *Point Counter Point* for instance, is hermetically sealed, self-enclosed yet endlessly multiplying its inner recesses:

> Put a novelist into the novel. He justifies aesthetic generaliz-

ations, which may be interesting – at least to me. He also justifies experiment. Specimens of his work may illustrate other possible or impossible ways of telling a story. And if you have him telling parts of the same story as you are, you can make a variation on the theme. But why draw the line at one novelist inside your novel? Why not a second inside his? And a third inside the novel of the second? And so on to infinity, like those advertisements of Quaker Oats where there's a quaker holding a box of oats, on which is a picture of another quaker holding another box of oats, on which etc., etc. At about the tenth remove you might have a novelist telling your story in algebraic symbols or in terms of variations in blood-pressure, pulse, secretion of ductless glands and reaction times.[4]

The Chinese box stereotype has long been an emblem of self-reflexivity in art and as such has embraced a wide variety of 'mises en abyme' which until recently were largely confused in a haze of ill-defined categories. However, Lucien Dällenbach's penetrating analysis in *Le Récit spéculaire*, written in the aftermath of the explorations in self-reflexivity undertaken by the 'nouveaux romanciers', has provided a firm basis for a systematic study of the phenomenon in the context of narrative fiction. Dällenbach's exposition of the wide variety of literary forms of 'mise en abyme' argues against the tendency towards reductive generalisation to which poetics is notoriously susceptible; namely, that the existence of 'mises en abyme' in almost every period of literature, regardless of the prevailing aesthetic, proves that the 'device' is 'very closely bound up with the representational function which has traditionally been associated with the novel'.[5] A 'mise en abyme' is not an invariable stylistic device or technique but more properly the textual manifestation of a concept which, like 'intertextuality' and 'frame', embraces a number of different functions which can differ radically according to each writer, whether he or she is working in a mimetic or transgressive tradition. Dällenbach's starting definition of 'mise en abyme' is the following: 'est mise en abyme toute enclave entretenant une relation de similitude avec l'oeuvre qui la contient'[6]. The basic requirement, therefore, is a metaphorical relationship between container and content. But of the five categories which the critic outlines it will be noted that not all can be said to conform strictly to this definition.

Fictional 'mises en abyme' (or 'mises en abyme de l'énoncé') reflect the referential dimension of the narrative. Often in the form of a story within a story, this type of self-reflexivity can focus on certain primary features of the macro-text (or outer narrative) and highlights their thematic significance. Thus the in-set narrative of 'Cupid and Psyche' in Apuleius's *The Golden Ass*, according to Dällenbach, acts as a 'mise en abyme' by reflecting the outer story which relates the vicissitudes of Lucius and thus guiding the reader's interpretation of it.[7] Fictional 'mises en abyme' invariably take the form of a single reflection, modelled on the play within a play stereotype, such as the play within a narrative (like the performance of *As You Like It* in *Mademoiselle de Maupin*[8] or *Lucie de Lammermoor* in *Madame Bovary*[9]) or narrative within a narrative (like the *Mad Trist* of Sir Launcelot Canning in *The Fall of the House of Usher*[10]) or a pictorial representation within a narrative (like the 'Vitrail de Cain' in *L'Emploi du Temps*[11]). Acting either prophetically, through anticipation of the ultimate turn of events in the plot, or else retrospectively, by shedding light on the past, fictional 'mises en abyme' reveal to the reader, and often to the characters as well, a hidden message which bears upon the thematic content of the narrative. The unitary form of introspection, whereby an embedded mirror reflection calls out momentarily for special attention, is thus not incompatible with the more traditional and 'representational' aims of narrative fiction. (Though, of course, it would be foolish to underestimate the extent of ironical play with the notion of art as 'representation' or 'revelation' in the works of Gautier, Flaubert, Poe or Butor.) The archetype for this use of the 'mise en abyme' as bearer of truth, is Freud's interpretation of the dream within a dream as the insertion of reality within wish-fulfilment:

> It is safe to suppose, therefore, that what has been 'dreamt' in the dream is a representation of the reality, the true recollection, while the continuation of the dream, on the contrary, merely represents what the dreamer wishes. To include something in a 'dream within a dream' is thus equivalent to wishing that the thing described as a dream had never happened. In other words, if a particular event is inserted into a dream as a dream by the dream-work itself, this implies the most decided confirmation of the reality of the event – the strongest *affirmation* of it. The dream-work makes use of dreaming as a form of repudiation,

and so confirms the discovery that dreams are wish-fulfilments.[12]

Even here one notices that the relationship between inner and outer dreams is not characterised by straightforward, mimetic reflection but by conflict and mutual denunciation. It is this area of conflict surrounding fictional 'mises en abyme' which is explored by writers like Robbe-Grillet and Claude Simon.

Narrational 'mises en abyme' (or 'mises en abyme de l'énonciation') may be said to reflect the agent, process and reception of a narrative text. In other words, they can reflect the writer, the act of communication, or the reader. Clearly both the Huxley and Godard examples (the latter forming a cinematic counterpart) fall under this category in that they reflect the agent and process of production respectively. But in both cases, and particulary in that of *Point Counter Point*, the object of reflection is external to the work itself. The author cannot be defined as the 'container' of the in-set narrative, nor, *a fortiori*, would a reader figure satisfy that criterion. The process involved in these instances is not one of self-reflection (at least, not literally so) but, as emerged in my earlier allusion to Erving Goffman, of frame transgression, of bridging the gap between exterior and interior. In consequence, Huxley's comparison between a novel containing a novelist whose novel contains a novelist and so on and the infinitely self-reflexive picture of a Quaker Oats advertisement is not, strictly speaking, accurate since whilst the visual example consists of a perfectly self-enclosed system of internal repetition, the literary one has as its ultimate object of reflection a figure situated outside it; namely, the *deus ex machina*, the 'real novelist'.[13]

Unlike fictional 'mises en abyme' which reflect the referential dimension of the outer narrative, textual 'mises en abyme' reflect the latter 'sous son aspect littéral d'organisation signifiante'.[14] Dällenbach adds that a textual 'mise en abyme' can reflect the literal dimension of the macro-text either referentially or literally; that is, either by figurative allusion or by textual repetition. An example of the former are the references to the textile craft in Raymond Roussel's *Impressions d'Afrique* which reflect metaphorically the textuality of the work in which they appear. Jean Ricardou has focused mainly on the second definition of this category of 'mise en abyme', seeing it as a reflection of the material properties of the book in question. For instance, the title of his novel *La Prise de Constantinople* is reiterated on the back cover with the minimal yet decisive substitution of one letter, 'La Prose de Constantinople'. Similarly, the two dedications written by Tristram in volumes I and IX of Sterne's *Tristram Shandy* reflect the two 'real' dedications heading volumes I and V. The consequences of this type of 'mise en abyme' are that it creates an ironical interplay between the notions of the 'authentic' and the 'apocryphal'. A third variant of textual 'mises en abyme' consists of a textual segment which encloses a number of motifs, key words or 'signifiants' which recur in the rest of the novel. One such example would be the Valéry stanza serving as epigraph to Simon's *La Bataille de Pharsale*, containing several elements which are subsequently expanded and transformed in the novel.[15]

Metatextual 'mises en abyme' ('mises en abyme du code') reflect the working principle of the novel in question or, as Dällenbach says, its 'mode de fonctionnement'.[16] The description of Elstir's 'Port de Carquethuit' may thus be defined as a metatextual 'mise en abyme' in that it reflects the metaphorical process governing Proust's novel. As I have already demonstrated, the cartoon strip in *La Bataille de Pharsale* also serves this function by delineating the triptych structure and binary pattern of association in the novel. Similarly, the dead horse, 'animal héraldique', in *La Route des Flandres* is described in terms which echo the compositional structure of the whole novel. The fluidity of the horse's contours and the oscillating perspective of its features reflect the blurring of temporal distinctions, the restless mobility of narrative frame, and the alternating substitution of foreground and background. The metatextual 'mise en abyme', and this explains its widespread use in the 'nouveau roman' generally, provides the novel with the means by which it can, in Claude Simon's words, 'denounce itself as text and fiction in process'.[17] Although this may, on the surface, resemble Freud's view of the 'dream within a dream' as reality denouncing wish-fulfilment, its implications are, in fact, in sharp contrast. For with the 'nouveau roman' the 'mise en abyme' questions the appearance of verisimilitude at all levels of the text.

Finally, Dällenbach's fifth category, transcendental 'mise en abyme' is a 'métaphore d'origine'.[18] Its object of reflection is 'ce qui tout à la fois, le finalise, le fonde, l'unifie et en fixe les conditions *a priori* de possibilité'.[19] However, by mirroring the philosophical preconditions which, by definition, transcend the text, the transcendental 'mise en abyme' would seem to overlook the criterion of self-reflexivity or internal reflection. The principle example put forward by Dällenbach is a passage from Beckett's *Watt* which refers to a picture hanging in Erskine's room. The picture consists solely of a circle and a point, but the infinite permutation of relations between the two geometrical figures causes Watt much emotional agitation:

> and at the thought that it was this, a circle and a centre not its centre in search of a centre and its circle respectively, in boundless space in endless time, then Watt's eyes filled with tears that he could not stem, and they flowed down his fluted cheeks unchecked, in a steady flow, refreshing him greatly.[20]

The universe reflected in Erskine's painting seems to derive to some extent from the one described by Pascal as 'une sphère infinie dont le centre est partout, la circonférence nulle part'.[21] One of the authors who has most meditated on the notion of the infinite is, of course, Borges. In 'El Aleph', the narrator gazes into a 'small iridescent sphere of almost unbearable brilliance', a boundless 'mise en abyme' containing everything in the universe including the narrator himself, the reader, and the Aleph itself. As with Watt, Borges's narrator responds to this vision by breaking into tears:

> I saw the Aleph from every point and angle, and in the Aleph I saw the earth and in the earth the Aleph and in the Aleph the earth; I saw my own face and my own bowels; I saw your face; and I felt dizzy and wept, for my eyes had seen that secret and conjectured object whose name is common to all men but which no man has looked upon – the unimaginable universe.[22]

Here again a precedent for this transcendental metaphor of the infinite may be found in Pascal's *Pensées*, XV:

> Je veux lui faire voir là-dedans un abîme nouveau, je lui veux peindre non seulement l'univers visible, mais l'immensité qu'on peut concevoir de la nature dans l'enceinte de ce raccourci d'atome. Qu'il y voie une infinité d'univers, dont chacun a son firmament, ses planètes, sa terre, en la même proportion que le monde visible dans cette terre des animaux, et enfin des cirons, dans lesquelles il retrouvera ce que les premiers ont donné, et

trouvant encore dans les autres la même chose sans fin et sans repos, qu'il se perde dans ces merveilles aussi étonnantes dans leur petitesse, que les autres dans leur étendue![23]

Whilst it is true that the scientific discoveries of the twentieth century have once more turned the attention of writers like Beckett, Borges, Joyce, Robbe-Grillet and Claude Simon to the vertiginous notions of 'l'infiniment grand' and 'l'infiniment petit' it would be manifestly wrong to interpret this attitude as a return to the metaphysical meditations which preceded the scientific positivism of the nineteenth century. Modern art has more in common with the 'univers réversible' of baroque art than with the asceticism of Pascal.[24] The baroque aesthetic does not seek to submit the infinite to the grip of rationalist thought but rather to merge with it in a continuum of metamorphosis and multiple reflection. It creates a perspective in which, as Jean Rousset has stressed, the reader or spectator is ineluctably absorbed: 'la collaboration demandée au spectateur qu'on invite à être en quelque mesure acteur, et qu'on introduit dans le mouvement d'une ouevre qui paraît se faire en même temps qu'il la connaît'.[25] And yet it would also be a distortion to identify the modern too closely with the baroque of the early seventeenth century, for what is missing in the former is the tumultuous clamour of the latter and in its place one can discern an echo of Pascal's whispered admission that 'le silence éternel de ces espaces infinis m'effraie'.[26] The silence of modern fiction is a stereophonic silence, a repercussion of absent sound. Similarly, to return to the specular analogy of the 'mise en abyme', it is evident that modern art rejects the deceptive effects of 'trompe l'oeil' on which baroque art relied so heavily. Indeed, the self-reflexivity of modern fiction, as my ensuing analyses of *Triptyque* and *Leçon de choses* illustrate, does not offer a revelation of any absolute or transcendental truth other than that of its own inherently discontinuous, polysemic and contingent nature.

But before looking in detail at these novels, it is worth glancing briefly at the use made of reflexivity by a much earlier 'modern' novel which focuses on the chasm separating exterior and interior and which hints at the kind of creative transgressions which can be found in the work of Claude Simon and others.

II THAT OBSCURE REFLECTION OF AN IMAGE IN SÁBATO'S *EL TÚNEL*

Published in Buenos Aires in 1948, *El Túnel* is a novel which draws its inspiration from many sources in European literature and thought, including Sartrean existentialism, Freudian psychoanalysis and nineteenth-century Romanticism. But whilst Sábato has since shown an awareness of the 'nouveau roman', albeit mostly through disparaging remarks about the 'objectivist' pretensions of Robbe-Grillet's work, *El Túnel* was conceived prior to the impact of the French new novel and therefore its modernity (the highly self-reflexive pattern of composition) should not be seen as in any way copying a fashion set in France but, in a sense, foreshadowing it.

As the novel is written entirely in the first person narrative, the 'tunnel' of the title can be read as a metaphor for, amongst other things, the exclusive and narrow perspective in which the narrative is enclosed. The book opens with the narrator, Juan Pablo Castel, admitting outright that he has murdered María Iribarne and that the object of his narrative is to set down in plain terms the reasons which led him to commit the murder. Castel proceeds to expatiate at length on the failings and hypocrisy of contemporary Argentinian society and human nature in general; and it soon becomes clear that the narrator is a pathological, self-destructive figure isolated from the world and suffering from a restless, suspicious and tortuous mind which manically analyses, interprets and questions the surrounding world. Castel is conscious of his mental state, offering several metaphorical analogies: his brain is like 'a dark labyrinth', 'a calculator', 'a boiling spring'. His rejection of society, of all collective groupings (particularly intellectual ones) is accompanied by an overpowering need to communicate with one individual. This forms the framework for the narration; it is its underlying 'raison d'être':

and although I do not have many illusions about humanity in general and about the readers of these pages in particular, I am spurred on by the feeble hope that someone may succeed in understanding me. EVEN IF IT IS ONLY ONE PERSON.

Castel is a famous painter and it is at an exhibition of his work that he first discovers María whom he notices is absorbed by one of his paintings, entitled 'Maternidad'. The foreground of the painting shows a maternal figure watching a little boy playing and in an in-set scene depicted through a window in the top left-hand corner one can see a woman standing on a solitary beach looking out to sea, as if waiting for something: 'The scene suggested, in my opinion, my anguished and absolute solitude'. It is María alone, amongst all the spectators, who is drawn to this embedded scene, finding in it, as she later admits, an expression of her loneliness and her 'blind search for a silent interlocutor'. But the painting as a whole, including the interior scene in the foreground, is also important as it is the first 'mise en abyme' to appear in the novel. The three figures in the painting pre-empt the triangular relationship which the text outlines between Castel, his mother and María. On several occasions Castel consciously thinks of María in general terms of motherhood, but, as the novel progresses, one can also detect an implied specific identification between María and Castel's mother. Indeed one of the factors behind the intrinsic hopelessness of his relationship with María is that he sees her with the distorting eyes of a child. María has to conform to an ideal, an absolute which is pure and unblemished, similar to the one which he believed, until maturity showed him otherwise, was embodied by his mother.

After much agonised deliberation and calculation as to the most effective way of striking up a conversation with her, Castel finally meets María and is confirmed in his belief that they share a common understanding, primarily through the medium of his painting, based on intuition and emotional empathy as opposed to rational thought.[27] Again, Castel describes the scene in the painting in similar terms. He was entranced like a sleepwalker when he painted it, and its meaning remains obscure to him as it is for María and it is this very obscurity or ambiguity which serves as the hermeneutic ground for their communion:

> It would be more accurate to say that you *feel* like I do. You were looking at that scene as I would have done in your place. I do not know what you were thinking and neither do I know what I was thinking, but I know that you were thinking as I did.

María later reiterates the same idea when in a final, rare moment of peaceful communion she describes to him the significance of the scene in the painting for her:

> At times it seems as if we have lived this scene always together. When I saw that solitary woman in your window, I felt that you were like me and that you were searching blindly for someone, a kind of silent interlocutor.

As a 'mise en abyme' of the narration, the allusion to the silent interlocutor implied by the painting is also an allusion to the reader, that absent, speechless partner so coveted by Castel's narrative. Interior and exterior are thus brought together. The reader, of course, belongs in that hypothetical, other world which is inaccessible to characters in fiction and so the 'mise en abyme' here suggests a transgression of the laws separating fiction and reality.

The transgressive implications of Castel's painting are evoked most poignantly in María's letter which the painter receives after days spent in great agitation, desperately trying to understand the reasons for her sudden departure to Hunter's ranch. Castel describes the letter in the following way:

> But this sun was a black sun, a nocturnal sun. I do not know if one can say that, but although I am not a writer and although I am not sure how precise I am, I will not withdraw the word 'nocturnal'; this word was, perhaps, the most apt with reference to María of all the words which constitute our imperfect language.

Castel insists on the Romantic image of 'sol negro', which as I have mentioned earlier was a topos employed by Baudelaire, Nerval, Proust and others, to refer to absolute beauty, poetry, truth or creativity, depending on the language of each author's particular aesthetics. The appeal of the image is that it conveys a sense of the ineffable, of a purity which is inaccessible, which can be perceived only indirectly, 'nocturnally', through the medium of paradox. And in the context of *El Túnel*, the contradiction inherent in the image serves as a symbol of boundaries transgressed, of *a priori* incompatibilities reconciled. The transgressive quality of María's letter, the aptness of the 'sol negro' image in qualifying it, lies in the suggestion of a re-shuffle of time past, present and future:

> I have spent three strange days here: the sea, the beach, the roads which have been evoking memories of other times. Not only visual images but also voices, cries, long silences of days gone by. It is strange, but living consists of constructing future memories; at this very moment, facing the sea, I know that I am preparing detailed memories, that sometime in the future will evoke melancholy and despair. [. . .] Have you imagined and painted this memory of mine or have you painted the memory of many people like you and me?

Past and future have become interchangeable and the status of the present, María's solitude on the beach, is moulded out of the fiction of Castel's painting. In a sense, María is here consciously acting out the window scene in 'Maternidad', and by so doing she creates a transference between different planes of reality.

María's elusiveness and her ability to partake in a multiplicity of relationships, a source of all-consuming jealousy and agony for Castel, is precisely a kind of personified display of the associative and multiple nature of metaphor. Her blind husband, Allende,[28] clear-sightedly encapsulates this essential quality of María in a self-reflexive metaphor:

> She is like someone who had stopped in a desert and then suddenly changed place at great speed. Do you see? Speed is unimportant, she always remains in the same landscape.

The landscape is always the same because metaphor is ultimately reductive in that it links two remote contexts by establishing a common ground. To this extent, therefore, metaphor consists of a paradoxical combination of movement and stasis. In *Uno y el universo*, Sábato makes this point clearly:

> Metaphor is, perhaps, one aspect of the tendency towards unity underlying diversity and it consequently tends towards indifference and absolute immobility, since time is revealed through change.[29]

In a discreet twist of dramatic irony which reaches us over the head of the blinkered Castel, Allende modestly plays down the penetratingly accurate metaphor of metaphor which he has just formulated by adding: 'No, I don't know if that's it exactly. I don't have much of a talent for metaphors.'

Although the 'ontological value of metaphor', to borrow Sábato's phrase, has the effect of creating unity and immobility, its textual role, on the other hand, is to induce movement and transgression. The image of this movement in *El Túnel* is that of a frame which fails to retain and immobilise the fleeting images reflected within its confines. In an echo of the 'ventanita' scene in 'Maternidad', there is a passage following Castel's visit to the ranch in which he speaks of the acute sense of the transitoriness of life he felt as he sat in a train bound for Buenos Aires. This feeling was elicited by the appearance of a woman whom he saw through the window ('ventanilla') of his compartment:

We were passing by a ranch; a woman standing under the eaves, looked at the train. A stupid thought occurred to me: 'I am seeing this woman for the first and last time. I shall not see her again in my life.' My thought floated like a cork in a river. [. . .] But I could not help thinking that she had existed for a moment for me and that she would no longer exist; from my point of view it was as if she were already dead [. . .] Everything seemed fleeting, transitory, useless, imprecise.

The passage is reminiscent of the one in Proust's *A la recherche* where Marcel describes the milkmaid glimpsed through the window of a train.[30] Whilst the frame of the window remains fixed, both its content and its external context, the train, are caught up in a Heraclitean flow of time. The anonymous woman seen here by Castel is also, of course, a reflection of María, the exclusive and elusive object of his desire, of his urge for sexual and psychological possession.

The recurrence of frames in this novel can be interpreted as a sign of Castel's mental operations; they are variants of the distant and hallucinatory opening at the end of his tunnel. The instrument of Castel's framing procedures, his inquisitorial pursuit of truth, is language and the concomitant mechanism of reason or, more precisely, ratiocination. However, language too refuses to be subjected to the strictures of Castel's willpower and his attempts to make scientific sense of the world around him are doomed to fail. Castel's failure to govern events and to fathom the enigma of María's hidden side is thus also due to the fact that he too is overshadowed by the paradoxical light of the black sun. For Castel is divided by two antithetical selves representing light and darkness: a duality which he acknowledges openly in his narrative, which he fictionalises visually in his dreams, and which is reflected implicitly in a 'mise en abyme' formulated by Hunter, his arch rival. The 'mise en abyme' takes the form of a hypothetical book within a book. Hunter outlines the plot of a detective novel he once imagined but never wrote, in which a man's mother, wife and son are respectively murdered. As the police fail to solve the crime, the protagonist decides to assume the investigations himself. Applying a series of 'inductive, deductive, analytical and synthetical methods' he arrives at the conclusion that the murderer will appear at a certain time and place. However, as he waits fruitlessly at the inevitable hour, the realisation dawns upon him that he himself had committed the murders in a subconscious state: 'The detective and the assassin are the same person.' The logical conclusion of the story is that the protagonist commits suicide but whether it is 'out of remorse or whether the assassin self kills the detective self' remains a mystery.

In conclusion, it is clear that self-reflexivity in *El Túnel* is a trangressive force. It provokes an erosion of barriers by creating a pattern of introspective mirrors (dream sequences, 'mises en abymes') which threaten to break down the limits of the central narrative. Indeed, the outer frame of this fiction, Castel's narration, is itself both an act of introspection and the ultimate source of ambiguity casting the entire novel in a perspective which is fundamentally unreliable. The reader cannot take Castel at his word and consequently everything which he relates in his narrative is permeated with doubt. The subject in *El Túnel* is a neutralising force and it in turn is neutralised. 'Insensato', the word hurled at him by Allende when he learns of Castel's act, and which Castel ponders over within the confines of the four walls of his prison cell, tells us that Castel's madness is profoundly sense-less, for he has turned language inside out and emptied it and himself of meaning. With *Triptyque* and *Leçon de choses*, as we shall now see, fiction takes a new turn. The oppressive shadow of narratorial perspective is supplanted by the generative articulation of language and text.

2
Triptyque: Topography or Topology?

> Long before there were people on the earth, crystals
> were already growing in the earth's crust. On one day
> or another, a human being first came across such a
> sparkling morsel of regularity lying on the ground or
> hit one with his tool and it broke off and fell at his feet,
> and he picked it up and regarded it in his open hand,
> and he was amazed.
>
> M. C. Escher, 'Approaches to Infinity'

I GENERATIVE DESCRIPTION

Triptyque is arguably Claude Simon's most accomplished work; the product of the author's masterly sense of formal control and literary innovation. Its crystalline structure, a source of infinite pleasure for the reader who pursues its internal echoes and vibrations, will surely earn *Triptyque* recognition as a landmark in the evolution of the modern novel. Yet to call it a 'landmark' is already to adopt a critical terminology which has the unfortunate effect of implying that a work of language is a topographical object.

Partly because of its title and partly because of the critical convenience of treating the text as a spatial object, most textual analyses of this novel have been dominated by the topographical metaphor. In consequence, it has been described in inert visual terms either as a triptych composed of three panels, or a jig-saw puzzle with interlocking pieces. The generative movement which underlies the complementary acts of writing and reading is thus frozen into a montage of different parts. To this extent, despite the theoretical differences between Sylvère Lotringer's 'Cryptique' and François Jost's 'Claude Simon: topographie de la description et du texte', both analyses are stamped with the same conception of the compositional nature of Simon's novel.[1] The spatial perspective which they both postulate distinguishes between the 'mise en abyme' descriptions in the novel and the metonymic chain of the text. Lotringer and Jost differ, however, in their evaluation of the importance of these two compositional elements. Lotringer dismisses the unifying tendencies of the novel's macro-structure in favour of the 'migration de sèmes similaires'[2] which constitutes its micro-structure. For Jost, a 'generative analysis' of Simon's novel is no longer adequate, while the structural, topographical analysis offers the reader 'des plaisirs plus raffinés'.[3] Both arguments are distorted by the conceptual assumptions implicit in the language employed to formulate them.

Lotringer deprecates the function of the descriptions of the jigsaw puzzle, the film posters and the film strips as being the agents of unification in the text: '(les unités moléculaires postulent par définition et finissent toujours par imposer, une homogénéisation au niveau molaire)'.[4] Although the analogy with biology is intended to clarify Lotringer's argument it in fact gives rise to a number of highly questionable assumptions about the nature of Simon's text. It is curious that while openly doubting the role of science in relation to a modern text, the critic should nevertheless couch his argument in scientific terms. The reference to the notions of 'molecular' and 'molar' units, reminiscent of the writings of Gestalt psychologists,[5] is itself presented as an ipso facto justification for dividing the text in the same way. But is it true that there are some elements which can be called 'integrateurs romanesques' (fictional unifiers) and others 'désintégrateurs textuels' (textual dividers) and that the former dominate over the latter in *Triptyque*? And is it also true that the sequence of the 'noce' is positioned at the head of this hierarchical structure, thus forming 'le pivot du roman'? Lotringer claims that the reason for the privileged position of this sequence is that it has only one 'mise en abyme':

Il n'est par contre pas d'autre mise en abyme de l'histoire de la noce que celle de l'affiche même [. . .] C'est en fait l'absence d'un simulacre propre qui fait de l'histoire de la noce le pivot du roman.[6]

However, this confident claim is in fact based on false premises

Triptyque: *Topography or Topology?* 193

since, as I shall soon demonstrate, the wedding sequence is reflected in a second 'mise en abyme': namely, the book being read by the woman in the beach resort sequence. This 'mise en abyme' is also visual in that the book cover depicts three separate scenes from the narrative. It is consequently inaccurate, in the critic's own terms, to single out the wedding sequence as the 'volet "central", sur lequel semblent pivoter et se surimposer les deux autres compartiments'.[7]

The spatial framework in which François Jost's critical approach is set is even more prominent. The text as topography means that there is spatial order: a 'map'. The jig-saw puzzle, therefore, is for Jost the most apt image of the novel's composition:

> Tout segment numéroté s'enchaîne avec le suivant par une transition associative. Toutefois, certains mots auraient pu aiguiller la narration dans d'autres directions que celle qu'elle prend effectivement. De ce fait c'est avant tout la topographie globale du texte qu'il faut tenter de comprendre pour expliquer le choix d'une orientation.[8]

Jost sets out to show the extent to which the 'mise en abyme' descriptions determine the particular directions followed by the narrative sequences. Some of the detail of his readings pose no problem. It is true, for instance, that the lines describing a couple struggling in an alley-way (in the urban sequence) which interrupt the description of a clown's circus act, are 'motivated' by the reference to the tear at the centre of the circus poster (in the countryside sequence) which reveals another poster beneath it showing the two lovers in the alley. But does this discovery of textual self-reflection justify the assertion that the lines of the urban sequence occur *at the centre of* the circus description? Surely the reader does not gaze down at the whole text from an overhanging vantage-point, but his reading proceeds as the consecutive chain of the text unfolds? Neither can the anaphoric nature of the textual associations, which prompts the reader to turn back and forth from passage to passage, be put forward as evidence of a global topography. Moreover, is not the concept of 'motivation' misleading in its implication that the motivating elements are at a remove from the remainder of the text, treating them as points of origin which are not themselves produced or transformed by the generation of the text? Are not the 'mise en abyme' descriptions, in Jost's words, both 'structurés' and 'structurants' at the same time? Clearly a number of important questions are inevitably begged by the spatial analogy in textual analysis.

The main problem in Jost's 'microscopic' and 'macroscopic' viewpoints and in Lotringer's 'molar' and 'molecular' units is that they both impose an artificial division of Simon's text. On the other hand, one can, without distorting the novel, distinguish between two separate but interdependent levels of isotopic organisation: namely, 'descriptions' and 'narrative sequences'. There are three main narrative sequences in *Triptyque*: the rural sequence which culminates in the drowning of the little girl (sequence A); the urban sequence in which an adulterous bridegroom returns to his bride after being assaulted in an alley on his wedding night (sequence B); the beach resort sequence which involves unclarified references to corruption, drugs, and juvenile delinquency (sequence C).

An analysis of the specific function of the 'mises en abyme' in *Triptyque* should not isolate the latter from the background of generative description in the novel as a whole; for they do not constitute the sole productive or 'motivating' force. Description here and in *Leçon de choses* is best defined as a process of articulation in which the narrative evocation of people, objects and setting cannot be dissociated from the internal propagation of the text. Each 'scene' or descriptive fragment both 'feeds off' an earlier description and serves as a source of development for ensuing textual units. Thus an assessment of description in *Triptyque* cannot be limited to a survey of the 'micro units' which are placed in association, but must include the process by which the associations are produced.

As the following examples will now demonstrate, this process is primarily one of binary interrelation. The novel opens with a description of a postcard lying on a kitchen table. The photograph on the card is of a beach esplanade along which holiday-makers are seen to be strolling, shaded by their 'ombrelles'. Two pages later the description of the countryside, contained in a totally separate narrative isotopy, dwells momentarily on the shape of some flowers:

> Les tiges des ombelles sont recouvertes d'un fin duvet blanc qui, dans le contre-jour, les cerne d'un halo lumineux. Sur les minces pédoncules s'évasant comme les baleines d'un parapluie

et qui supportent le plateau des fleurs, les poils duveteux
s'allongent, se rejoignent et s'entre-mêlent, formant comme un
brouillard neigeux. (p. 9)[9]

The explicit comparison between the flowers and the umbrellas
points to the linguistic association between 'ombrelle' and
'ombelle'. The reader is being shown that the 'ombelles' emerge
textually from the 'ombrelles' through a binary process of descriptive generation.

The relationship already mentioned between the clown act and
the erotic description in sequence B is another case in point. For
Jost this relationship is restricted to two passages: the lines from
sequence B which suddenly appear 'at the centre of' the circus
description and the ones set in sequence A which describe the
superimposition of posters. However, as I have already suggested,
Jost's 'topographical' approach is inappropriate since the reader
does not sweep his gaze across the whole novel as he would over
a painting, but reads it as a text. Moreover, the spatial perspective
does not account for the relationship between the two descriptions
at other moments in the novel. To a large extent the clown description 'feeds off' the sexual description. Thus the 'pantomime' action
of the clown (p. 117) echoes the 'pantomime' movement of the
lovers (p. 104); the description of the spotlights in the circus, 'un
poudroiement argenté par le faisceau de lumière' (p. 116) corresponds with that of a car's headlights in sequence B, 'le poudroiement argenté de la pluie dans le pinceau des phares d'une auto'
(p. 115).[10] Equally, the influence is inverted: thus, the clown's cry,
'Vous êtes pas marteau!' (p. 107) is repeated by the girl in sequence
B, 'T'es pas un peu marteau' (p. 112);[11] and the reference to the
'sciure' on the café floor (p. 132) echoes the reference to the 'sciure'
on the floor of the circus arena (p. 23). In fact, the passage quoted
by Jost (and dismissed by him for not explaining why the lines
appear at the centre of the circus description) contains a self-
conscious indication of the process of inter-penetration binding
the two descriptions: 'La sciure mouillée est de la même couleur
que les bras noisette et la chevelure de la fille' (p. 23).[12] A second
self-mirroring allusion highlights the way in which, as in the
'ombrelle'/'ombelle' association, the description embraces its
generative origin in the form of a simile. The man and woman,
their lovemaking at an end, trip along the alley-way,

comme ces morceaux exécutés pianissimo dans les cirques, conduits par la baguette distraite du chef à demi tourné vers la piste, servant de décor sonore et facétieux aux acrobaties ratées des clowns que ponctuent les sauvages éclats de rire du public invisible' [.] (p. 61)[13]

Overt metaphorical comparison is once more used not for an expressive purpose but as a means of stressing the binary, contrapuntal structure of the process of generative description.

This auto-generative process of description is by no means restricted to these two episodes in the novel. Elsewhere, the description of the skinned rabbit lying on a 'plat de faïence *blanche*' (p. 84) in the kitchen in sequence A grows out of the description of the woman in sequence C lying on the 'draps *blancs*' of her bed (p. 81). In both descriptions there is a reference to the 'cage thoracique'. The anatomical comparison in the description of the rabbit is an unmistakable echo of the anatomical comparison in the description of the woman:

> sur les membres et les différentes parties du corps dépouillé on peut voir comme sur une planche d'anatomie les muscles allongés, renflés en forme de fuseaux, qui s'entrecroisent, se tressent, s'étirent parallèlement ou s'imbriquent les uns dans les autres. (p. 84)[14]

> Selon une technique classique, l'artiste à l'aide d'un rouge de Venise qui s'éclaircit jusqu'au rose sur les reliefs, a d'abord modelé le corps en camaïeu, en détaillant avec soin l'anatomie comme sur ces planches des anciens traités de peinture, modelant des muscles en forme de fuseaux ou de lanières qui s'entrelacent, se croisent et s'imbriquent les uns dans les autres. (p. 81)[15]

The 'cameo' effect of the pink and red light in which the rabbit is bathed mirrors the pink and red cameo in the painting of the woman. The 'reflets *nacrés*' (pp. 84–5) glinting on the rabbit's body reiterate the 'couleur chair ou *nacrées*' (p. 82)[16] of the light in the painting. The rabbit's head, 'ensanglantée' (p. 85), refers back to the 'préparation sanglante'[17] in the earlier description. Furthermore, the reference to the swaying movement of the light-bulb in the kitchen description (sequence A) grows out of a similar description in sequence C:

sans doute la femme [. . .] a-t-elle heurté avant de sortir le
ruban [. . .] car celui-ci, l'abat-jour et l'ampoule se balancent
légèrement. (p. 85)[18]

unique ampoule qui était probablement heurté par quelque
échelle ou quelque partant, se balance au-dessus du lit [.]
(p. 82).[19]

In both cases the words employed to indicate the movement of
the shadows cast by a swinging light bulb in the two passages are
identical: 'les ombres [. . .] s'étendent et se rétractent' (pp. 85
and 81).[20]
Thus the terms of the language used to describe the rabbit in
sequence A are taken from the description of the woman in
sequence C. It is also evident that there is no 'topographical'
motivation behind the connection between the two descriptions.
Moreover, the causal influence (sequence A description deriving
from sequence C description) is itself inverted at a later point
in the novel (sequence C description deriving from sequence A
description (pp. 150–1)).
The binary character of this descriptive process is echoed in
the dual associations on the level of the narrative. There are, for
example, two erotic scenes: one which takes place in a barn in
sequence A (seen through a hole in the wall (p. 14)), and the other
in an alley-way in sequence B (first glimpsed through the hole in
the circus poster (p. 20)). Similarly, there are two cinemas: the
barn in sequence A, and the cinema flanking the alley-way in
sequence B. The self-conscious reference (p. 96) to the fact that
the same actor appears in the film posters of sequences B and C
can be read as an indication of the binary structure of composition
and as an oblique reference to the process of frame transgression.
It might also be argued that the depiction of the 'impasse' in
sequence B separating the 'cinéma' from the 'estaminet' (p. 63)
can be read as a second metatextual reference to the underlying
binary structure. In this case the allusion is textual and a counterpart of the narrative indication. The ironic punning in the word
'impasse' might evoke in the reader's mind a linguistic variant
of the central triptych panel serving as hinge-point between the
anagrammatical correspondence of 'cinéma' and 'estaminet'.

II METATEXTUAL 'MISES EN ABYME'

Claude Simon has often remarked on the influential rôle played by Francis Bacon's paintings in the conception of *Triptyque*. Not only was the title and structure of this novel suggested by Bacon's triptychs which Simon first saw at the Paris exhibition in 1971, but the author has admitted that narrative sequence C is inspired by Bacon's work,[21] the other two being inspired by the paintings of Delvaux (sequence B) and of Dubuffet (sequence A). This inspiration is primarily on the level of narrative figuration. But the structure of descriptive imbrication, or overlapping, which is fundamental to *Triptyque* can also be observed in the work of Francis Bacon.

A painting entitled 'Three Studies of Isabel Rawsthorne' (1967. Nationalgalerie Staatliche Museen Preussischer Kulturbesitz, Berlin) contains three depictions of the same person who appears simultaneously inside a room, closing the door behind her with one hand on the door key, outside the room, visible in the narrow opening of the door, and in a portrait which hangs on the wall. Each depiction is thus installed within its own frame. However, Bacon's portraits are, in his own words, 'distorted images' whose autonomous flow is checked by the different motifs of fixity which the artist inserts into his paintings like the Nazi armband or the hypodermic needle: 'I've used the figures lying on beds with a hypodermic syringe as a form of nailing the image more strongly into reality or appearance'.[22] Similar use is made of the rectangular frames inserted in so many of his paintings:

> I use that frame to see the image – for no other reason [. . .] I cut down the scale of the canvas by drawing in these rectangles which concentrate the image down. Just to see it better.[23]

In 'Three Studies of Isabel Rawsthorne' the distorted image of the portrait hanging on the wall spills out of the canvas and onto the white frame surrounding it where it is impaled with a nail. One may here immediately think of the contrary description in *Les Corps conducteurs* of the 'masse grisâtre' being pushed out by the boxer in the painting. This image of inter-frame transgression is clearly also relevant to *Triptyque* and its overlapping descriptions.[24] However, it is the motif of fixity, the vain attempt to control the distorting flow of the images, to 'nail them down', which is

Triptyque: *Topography or Topology?* 199

reflected in the description of the clown act at the centre of the novel.

Standing at 'le centre de la piste', the clown asks for a hammer to nail down the vamp of his shoe which is 'garnie de clous' and periodically flies open emitting a series of loud barks. He is given a hammer but, on the point of striking his shoe, 'son bras à mi-course',[25] he realises that it is tiny and absurdly disproportionate to his enormous shoe. The clown is indignant and responds with a caustic 'jeu de mots':

> Il y a maintenant trois ombres sur la piste: les deux ombres divergentes du clown et celle de l'homme en habit éclairé par un seul projecteur qui découpe sur son visage des ombres dures. Doublant le dialogue parlé, les trois silhouettes plates et télescopées s'agitent sur le tapis aux couleurs fanées avec des mouvements à l'amplitude déformée. Le clown crie Je vous ai demandé un marteau mais maintenant je vous demande si vous êtes pas marteau! (pp. 108–9)[26]

He continues to hurl abuse at his partner while 'vrillant son index ganté contre sa tempe et le faisant tourner plusieurs fois en même temps qu'il roule les yeux' (p. 109).[27] The metatextual significance of this passage emanates from at least three of its features. Firstly, the reference to the clown standing at the centre of the 'piste' reflects its position at the centre of the novel. Secondly, the distorted movement of the three shadows on the ground reflect the shifting movement of the three narrative sequences in the novel. Thirdly, the clown, around whom the swivelling shadows are cast, may be interpreted as a fictional variant of the nail as image of fixity in Bacon's paintings.[28] The pun on 'marteau', the metaphor in 'vrillant' and the business of nailing down the vamp urge the reader to note that the word 'clou' is phonetically embedded in the word 'clown'. The motif of fixity is thus not to be taken at all seriously. The clown is a figure of ridicule and, as his tail which curls up into the shape of a question mark indicates (p. 198), of uncertainty. This paradoxical aspect of the references to nails as symbols of fixity recurs in another metatextual 'mise en abyme', the description of the doors on the rabbit cages in narrative sequence A:

> Les portes se ferment au moyen d'un loquet rudimentaire, un

simple morceau de bois qui pivote autour d'une vis et vient se coincer dans une gâche constituée d'un gros clou recourbé au marteau et rouillé. (p. 160)[29]

The nail, therefore, is the hinge-point between the different 'panels' of the triptych, the point of connection between the shifting descriptions. The fact that it is rusty should guard the reader against the temptation to look for a point of fixity or centrality which is too firm and secure.

A second pervasive 'mise en abyme' in the novel is the motif of the camera. It recurs throughout the novel either in references to static pictures, to films shown in the cinema, or in references to shooting in a production studio. Its metatextual function lies in the fact that the camera motif reflects the descriptive flow of the text.

The novel opens with a description of a postcard next to the skinned rabbit on the kitchen table. The kitchen door opens onto a courtyard which gives onto a plum orchard which stretches out to a river which runs under a bridge close to which stands the church which is separated from the road by a 'terre-plein planté de quatre vieux noyers'.[30] The river runs to a hamlet out of which a road, leading to the saw-mill at the foot of the water-fall, forks and, passing by a barn, climbs up the valley. The description thus 'pans' through the landscape like a mobile film camera moving from one object to the next. The overall effect is one of an attempt at exhaustivity. This reading of the movement of description is explicitly corroborated much later in the novel when the same sequence is framed as a film: 'Un long travelling suit la course des deux garçons derrière lesquels, de droite à gauche, glisse le fond de feuillages' (p. 148).[31] The impossibility of achieving 'linear exhaustivity' is symbolised by the point at which the road forks and the writing has to choose between the two routes ahead. A fundamental discrepancy is revealed between the linearity of description and the infinite profusion of the field of reference. The description thus reaches a point of 'enlisement', as Ricardou would say,[32] where it gets bogged down by its inability to cope with this unmanageable diversity.

The linear flow of the description being thwarted in this way, the text adopts an alternative strategy and immediately the second aspect of the camera motif as metatextual 'mise en abyme' is introduced. Now the panning movement of the description is substituted by three static or 'photographic' descriptions:

> De la grange on peut voir le clocher. Du pied de la cascade on peut aussi voir le clocher mais pas la grange. Du haut de la cascade on peut voir à la fois le clocher et le toit de la grange. (p. 9)[33]

Unlike the 'horizontal' movement of the first perspective of description the attempt at total inclusion is now made from a static, dominating position. The top of the waterfall provides a vantage-point from which both the steeple and the roof of the barn can be seen. From this moment onwards the novel contains a series of descriptions framed from an overhanging viewpoint. Each narrative sequence is framed by at least one such description: sequence C by the picture postcard; sequence A by the jig-saw puzzle; and sequence B, slightly different in that it is a mixture of the two perspectives, filmed from above by a movie camera:

> Sans doute la caméra a-t-elle été hissée au sommet, soit d'un clocher, soit encore de l'un de ces échafaudages de poutrelles métalliques qui s'élèvent au-dessus du puits d'une mine et qui dominent l'agglomération, mais en tout cas dans l'axe de la longue artère car l'on découvre celle-ci en vue plongeante, faiblement éclairée de loin en loin par les réverbères. (p. 126)[34]

The aerial framing of each of the three narrative sequences can be construed as an image of the search for total inclusion. However, if the first perspective fails on account of its linearity (as well as by the very fact of its movement), the second fails through its inability to provide a diameter wide enough to encompass the entire referential plane. Thus the 'pullback dolly shot' of the boys peeping at the lovers through a hole in the barn wall, can be interpreted as the movement of the description towards total inclusion:

> tandis que le mouvement de la caméra se poursuivant les deux s'éloignent, comme aspirés en arrière et rapetissant, aspirant avec eux la piste du cirque, le dompteur aux bottes et à la chevelure cosmétiquées . . . (p. 90)[35]

The description continues with a list of the people and objects drawn into the ever-expanding 'scope' of description. But, as if to break away from this endless involuted, all engulfing swirl, the novel 'cuts' to a description of a notice on the wall of a church, one of the objects sucked onto the screen:

> A l'intérieur du cadre se trouvent punaisés le recto et le verso d'un bulletin paroissal dont le premier est ornée dans sa partie supérieure d'une croix entourée de rayons, un horaire des offices en caractères de ronde appliquée où alternent les pleins et les déliés, et une image imprimée, sommairement coloriée, représentant de jeunes garçons coiffés de bérets sur lesquels est épinglée une petite croix de métal [.] (p. 91)[36]

The two metatextual 'mises en abyme' under analysis (the clown description and the movie/snapshot perspective) throw light on the same compositional factor underlying the structure of *Triptyque*. If the one highlights the unsteadiness of the points of fixity and centrality, the other emphasises the absence of global frame. In both cases, it is the analogy between text and space which breaks down.

III FICTIONAL 'MISES EN ABYME'

The absence of an effective global 'mise en abyme' in a novel like *Triptyque* which is founded on the principle of self-reflexivity means that it is extremely difficult to apply an interpretative reading which would single out any one fictional element or theme without distorting the work as a whole. Although the 'mise en abyme' of the picture on the biscuit tin in *L'Herbe* may well lend support, as John Sturrock claims, to a 'selective reading' and be seen as reflecting Louise's predicament in the novel, such foregrounding is impossible, however, in a work like *Triptyque*.[37]

In this novel the main principle at work is one of partial 'fictional mises en abyme' which, as Dällenbach says, 'ne représentant chacune qu'un des trois lieux, elles ne sauraient mettre la fiction en abyme dans son intégralité'.[38] Instead of a global perspective ordering the different parts of the novel into a continuous hierarchy, the use of partial fictional 'mises en abyme' ensures a hierarchical deadlock between the different parts of the narrative:

Triptyque: *Topography or Topology?* 203

Au niveau des macro-structures, tout l'intérêt de *Triptyque* tient en effet à l'équilibrage qu'il réalise entre trois séries dont chacune exerce sa suprématie sur les deux autres en les contenant sous forme de représentation.[39]

An uncompromising pattern of discoherence thus results from the relentless conflict between the three narrative sequences each of which dominates and is dominated by another through the multiple use of 'captures' or 'framings'.[40] For example, sequences A and C are both framed as film posters outside the cinema in sequence B (pp. 64–5). The latter, on the other hand, is itself framed as a film poster on the barn wall in sequence A (pp. 14, 44, 94–5, 145) and as a novel being read by the actress in sequence C (pp. 126, 216–7). In fact, the three descriptions are closely related in the play of repetition illustrated in the following summary:

	Pages 64–5	Pages 94–5	Pages 216–17
Frame:	2 posters in sequence B	2 posters in sequence A	Book cover in sequence C
Content:	Description of sequence C	Description of sequence C	———
	Description of sequence A	Description of sequence B	Description of sequence B

The same play of descriptive repetition as the one I analysed at the start of this chapter is again at work in this particular group of association. Despite appearing in two referentially independent narrative sequences, the film posters of sequence C are described in almost identical terms:

La première des deux bandes tranche sur un fond bleu nuit où s'égrènent comme un chapelet de perles les globes de lampadaires à la lueur desquels on entrevoit vaguement un alignement de palmiers et des architectures pompeuses . . . (p. 64)[41]

Sur l'une des bandes on peut lire le mot PROCHAINEMENT et sur l'autre la mention CETTE SEMAINE qui se détache sur un fond bleu nuit où s'égrènent comme un chapelet de perles les globes de lampadaires à la lueur desquels on entrevoit un alignement de palmiers et des architectures pompeuses . . . (p. 94)[42]

The two passages go on to mirror each other almost word for word. The only difference between them is an inversion in the use of the words 'éploré' and 'angoisse'. In the first passage the woman's face is 'encore belle à l'expression angoissée' and her hand is held against her mouth 'd'un geste éploré'.[43] In the second passage her face is 'encore belle à l'expression éplorée' and her hand is held against her mouth 'd'un geste d'angoisse'. This detail of inversion in an otherwise straightforward reiteration can be construed as a pointer to the contrary pattern of association between the two posters in the same passages. Here one can discern a common denominator between the two otherwise totally unrelated descriptions. The description of the film poster of sequence A in the first passage and that of sequence B in the second are thus linked by the repetition of one 'signifié'. The 'visage éploré' (p. 66) of the mother in the first description is echoed in the 'yeux noyés' (p. 95) of the bride in the second description. The structural significance of this repetition lies in the fact that the mother in the first passage is crying at the drowning of her little girl. Thus, the 'yeux noyés' in sequence B reflect the 'noyade' in sequence A.

The overall pattern of association binding the three narrative threads together can be accurately compared to the 'strange loops' and Escher-like conceptions of space described by modern mathematics: 'Agencement comparable à une bouteille de Klein où l'intérieur parvient à englober son extérieur; paradoxes topographiques par lesquels s'efface, nous le savons, toute prétention à la hiérarchie'.[44] The following summary may serve as a skeleton of the topological structure which accounts for the 'topographical paradoxes' of *Triptyque*:

Narrative sequence A = countryside, 'noyade' sequence.
Narrative sequence B = urban, 'noce' sequence.
Narrative sequence C = beach resort, 'Nice' sequence.[45]
        ? = unframed description.

Triptyque: *Topography or Topology?*

Sequence A	Sequence B	Sequence C
	A p. 14 (film poster)	A p. 7 (postcard)
		A p. 27 (negatives)
		B p. 33 (film)
C p. 42 (engraving)	A p. 44 (film poster)	B p. 52 (film)
B p. 64 (film poster)		B p. 64 (film poster)
		A p. 80 (negatives)
		A p. 84 (postcard)
B p. 90 (film)		A p. 94 (film poster)
	A p. 95 (film poster)	A p. 96 (negatives)
		A p. 103 (film)
		B p. 104 (film poster)
	C p. 126 (book)	? p. 127 (painting)
		? p. 130 (film studio)
		B p. 137 (picture on juke-box)
		A p. 137 (film)
	A p. 145 (film poster)	A p. 147 (film)
? p. 148 (film)		
? p. 160 (film)		A p. 171 (negatives)
B pp. 195–7 (erotic film)		
C p. 196 (engraving)		A p. 200 (postcard)
		A p. 215 (film)
	C pp. 216–7 (book cover)	B p. 219 (negative)
C pp. 220–4 (jig-saw puzzle)		

The traditional principle upon which the 'mise en abyme' is commonly said to be based,[46] namely that of internal microcosm reflecting global macrocosm, is thus overturned by the interlocking system of reflections and framings, in which the three narrative sequences repeatedly exchange roles as microcosm or macrocosm, container or content.

It should be noted, however, that framings or 'captures' do not only consist of visual descriptions. Once more the snare of spatial perspective must be diligently avoided. Although specular descriptions are by far the most prevalent fictional 'mise en abyme' in *Triptyque*, framings do not necessarily have to be visual. The framing of sequence B as a book being read by the actress in sequence C (p. 126) is thus a case in point.

The irresolute pattern of 'discoherence' establishes *Triptyque* as 'un espace impensable',[47] a truth which is self-consciously inferred by the text: 'Il est malaisé de se faire une idée de la disposition des lieux' (p. 62).[48] On the other hand, by shifting emphasis away from the spatial content of the 'mise en abyme' and its macrocosm, Simon's writing focuses on the hinge of association or 'frame space' between them. The novel thus frequently lingers on the moments of 'captures' (or 'ateliers' in Ricardou's terminology[49]). The most striking 'atelier' is the description of the studio set which forms one of the framings of sequence C:

> l'espace trop vaste du studio dont les limites (les murs sales, le toit au-dessus des passerelles) se perdent dans des ténèbres creuses où résonnent, répercutés en échos, des bruits de marteaux, des grincements, et des voix multipliées. (p. 131)[50]

This 'atelier' has a double role as 'mise en abyme'. It is a fictional 'mise en abyme' in so far as it reflects the framing of narrative sequence C as a film being shot in a studio. It is also a metatextual 'mise en abyme' in that the limitless space of the studio mirrors the descriptive search for a global frame which was examined earlier. Furthermore, the focus on the 'cadre provisoire' in the following lines taken from the same 'setting' draws the reader's attention even more impellingly to the subversion of the spatial perspective and to the instability of the narrative framework:

> Il se dégage de l'ensemble une sensation de vacuité, d'anonymat et de désolation, comme si les protagonistes n'étaient là que de passage, dans un cadre provisoire et factice auquel ils n'ont aucune part, disposé la veille par des machinistes prêts à le démonter et isolé par des projecteurs comme une minuscule et

éphémère îlot de lumière dans l'immensité du cosmos ou, plus simplement, d'un vaste hangar de studio, tout aussi noir et tout aussi vide. (p. 172)[51]

IV FRAME SHIFTS

The retreating, all-absorbing movement of the description referred to in the second section of this chapter was seen to be an image of the search for an all-inclusive outer frame. The way out of this perspective, it was shown, was through a sudden 'zoom' on the content of an internal frame within the global frame: namely, the parish bulletin pinned on the church wall. One can infer from this example that the institution of a fixed, hierarchical narrative structure is resisted primarily by an internal play of inclusion and exclusion, or 'frame shift'.

The pattern of association produced by the shifts between the three narrative frames closely resembles the involuted structure of a Moebius strip whose contour twists inwards and is engulfed by the space it encloses. This contradictory chain of association is visible in the way in which the narrative sequences are embedded in one another and in the location of their initial textual provenance. Thus, at the start of the novel sequence B develops out of the description of a film poster in sequence A attached to the barn wall and through which two boys peep at a couple in the act of making love. Sequence C develops out of a film being shown in the cinema in sequence B flanking the 'impasse' which appears in the film poster. The setting of sequence C is a luxury hotel room on the wall of which hangs a copper-plate engraving showing a 'valet' and 'servante' making love in a barn. The print encloses an internal frame out of which two boys can be seen watching the lovers: 'Dans l'encadrement d'une lucarne, au-dessus du couple, on peut voir les têtes de deux gamins rieurs qui contemplent le spectacle' (pp. 42–3).[52] The narrative has thus drawn a full circle, or rather a strange and paradoxical loop.

If one turns to the central description of each of the novel's three chapters one will find a similar metatextual 'mise en abyme' in each case reflecting this aspect of the novel's structure. At the centre of the first chapter one finds a description of an instance of sequence A in which the boy, distracted from his geometry homework, holds a magnifying-glass in the sunlight over a sheet of paper:

> Au centre du disque grisâtre projeté par l'ombre de la loupe sur la feuille de papier de soie que la garçon a sortie de son tiroir et posée sur la table après en avoir lissé les plis, apparaît un rond minuscule où se concentrent les rayons de soleil qui frappent la surface de la lentille. En dépit de l'attention du garçon, la main qui tient la loupe est agitée de légers mouvements auxquels correspondent sur le papier d'infimes déplacements du foyer lumineux que le garçon s'efforce de maintenir au même endroit. Au bout d'un moment, le papier commence à roussir, puis, tandis que s'élève une légère fumée, un trou se forme, aux bords noircis qui vont s'élargissant. (pp. 39–40)[53]

Half-way through the second chapter one finds a description, also set in sequence A, of a little girl on the point of swimming naked in a river and being spied upon by the same two boys mentioned earlier:

> Une tache rousse flamboyant au soleil s'insère dans l'un des fragments. Agités par la brise les rameaux qui se croisent sont animés de faibles mouvements, montant et descendant, masquant et démasquant tour à tour la chevelure, le visage, les épaules et les bras d'une fillette debout derrière un buisson. La peau très blanche, laiteuse, semble concentrer sur elle la lumière ou plutôt, comme dans ces films surexposés, scintiller faiblement, comme si elle était elle-même une source de lumière. Le visage auréolé par la flamme orangée est parsemé de taches de son. (pp. 118–19)[54]

At the centre of the third chapter there is a description of the erotic scene in sequence A, framed as a film in sequence B. The film suddenly jams at the precise moment when the camera focuses on the man's dark red tongue licking the woman's 'peau laiteuse' (a repetition of the image evoked with reference to the naked girl earlier). The vision thus captured and immobilised on the screen acquires a prominence and solemn importance incommensurate with its 'normal' status as a fleeting, barely perceived moment in the constant flow of time and action. But the spectacle is eventually devoured by the dilating reflection of the film burning in the projector:

> jusqu'à ce que, comme pour confirmer l'impression de catastrophe, apparaisse une tache blanche, aveuglante, dont le pourtour roussi s'agrandit avec rapidité, dévorant sans faire distinction les deux corps enlacés, les outils et les murs de la grange, les lumières se rallumant alors, l'écran vide maintenant, terne et uniment grisâtre. (pp. 194-5)[55]

The three passages echo one another as 'mises en abymes' of the structure of narrative shift as produced by internal embedding. More specifically, they contain the same dual reference to the colours 'white' and 'red', and elicit the same symbolic interpretation from the reader. Thus, the boy's sheet of paper in the first passage, the girl's flesh in the second, and the screen in the third are related by their 'whiteness'. Equally, the colour 'red', with its concomitant notion of 'fire', forms another bridge across the three passages. The magnified sunlight first reddens the page ('le papier commence à roussir') and then burns a hole in it; the girl's face is 'auréolé par la flamme orangée' and her skin 'très blanche, laiteuse, semble concentrer sur elle la lumière'; the 'tache blanche' which grows out of the film in the third passage devouring the figures on the screen is encircled by a 'pourtour roussi'.

In as far as these 'mises en abyme' descriptions symbolise the intense concentration of the novel's self-reflexive gaze, they might be said to form part of a text which, as Stephen Heath has said of Sollers's *Drame* and *Nombres*, 'burns in the reading of its own production.[56] But, as I have argued with reference to *La Route des Flandres*, the special connotations of red, russet, and pink in Simon's work corresponds to another literary topos which has evolved with writers like Proust, Nerval and Apuleius who have treated this colour as a symbol of poetic inspiration. In Simon's novels the influence of Apuleius is particularly marked and the idea of poetic inspiration is translated into one of 'creative metamorphosis'. The juxtaposition of references to red and white in the three passages quoted elicits a reading in which white is the virgin, blank space that is consumed, inscribed and transgressed by the piercing light generated by the text. Moreover, the repeated configuration of a white space circumscribed by a red border can be construed as a visual image of the novel's focus on the transgressive movement of frame shift.

This reading of the three passages can be further corroborated by turning to the first appearances of sequences B and C. Here red is associated with black. The central passages I have been examining and these initial moments of narrative generation are closely linked. The first appearance of sequence B includes a description of the lovers in the alley-way. It must be stressed that although a description of the poster showing the same scene has already appeared a few pages earlier, this is the first time there is any reference to movement. Ricardou would describe this as an instance of the process of 'libération': 'Au bout d'un moment on s'aperçoit cependant que le bras de l'homme qui maintient sa campagne le dos au mur est agité de faibles mouvements de va-et-vient' (p. 19).[57] This, therefore, is the moment at which narrative sequence B is set in motion. The reference to the man's bow-tie 'noeud de papillon noir' reverts the reader's attention back to the description in sequence A of a butterfly alighting on a flower. The association hinges on the word 'papillon': 'Le papillon va finalement se poser sur une ombelle' (p. 18). The distinctive features of this butterfly are its 'ailes rouges et noires'.[58]

The first instance of sequence C occurs shortly afterwards with the description of an enigmatic man standing in the corridor of a hotel hesitating in front of a closed door. Once again, although sequence C may already be said to have appeared in the description of the postcard at the start of the novel, this is the first time that the sequence 'comes to life': 'Au bout d'un moment, [note the identical phrase to the one in sequence B] soit indécision, soit que la porte se trouve fermée à clef de l'autre côté, la main lâche la poignée et retombe le long du corps' (p. 23).[59] The man's bird-like appearance, 'une de ces silhouettes d'oiseaux immobiles' recalls the description immediately preceding in which a lady-bird, having explored the white flowers of an umbel, finally flies away:

Une coccinelle à la carapace rouge semée de points noirs disposés symétriquement progresse avec lenteur sur le plateau rond, à la surface inégale, que forme la réunion des petits fleurs blanches de l'ombelle [. . .] Brusquement elle soulève les élytres, laissant apparaître ses fines ailes noires et transparentes qu'elle déplie, puis prend son vol. (p. 22)[60]

Triptyque: *Topography or Topology?* 211

The similarities between this passage and the one describing the butterfly are evident. Structurally, the fact that both the butterfly and the lady-bird are coloured red and black tempts the reader into interpreting this colour combination as a sign of the creative and disruptive impulse of the text. A further common point is that in both passages the surface traversed by the insects is the white disc formed by the bunching of the umbel's white flowers. One might feel inclined to draw an analogy between the umbel with its white 'plateau rond' and the central passages of the novel's three chapters, in which the motifs of whiteness and circularity are heavily underlined. Such an interpretation would be further supported by a retrospective glance at the first reference to the 'ombelles' near the start of the novel.

I have already analysed this passage and noted its metatextual reflection of the binary nature of the process of generative description. It was argued, firstly, that the alternation between focus on the flowers and focus on the steeple indicates the spatial problem facing any attempt at establishing a global frame; and secondly, that the play on 'ombelles' and 'ombrelles' introduces an overlapping between descriptions which, in a sense, answers the problem posed by the search for spatial exhaustivity by stressing that the space of a written text is totally linguistic and that language can never reproduce reality (though it may refer to it) but must always produce fiction. The only space which one can speak of in this respect is, therefore, that produced by the interrelations of different areas of the novel both on the level of 'signifiés' and 'signifiants'. It is this textual space which is mirrored in the description of the 'ombelles':

> Les tiges des ombelles sont recouvertes d'un fin duvet blanc qui, dans le contre-jour, les cerne d'un halo lumineux. Sur les minces pédoncules s'évasant comme les baleines d'un parapluie et qui supportent le plateau des fleurs, les poils duveteux s'allogent, se rejoignent et s'entre-mêlent, formant comme un brouillard neigeux. (p. 9)[61]

The criss-cross network of the down surrounding the stems provides a vivid 'mise en abyme' of the textual associations in Simon's novel. Moreover, this description is itself indirectly related to the central section of each chapter through the mesh of associations I have been outlining. For instance, in the central passage of the central chapter, the 'visage auréolé' of the little girl mirrors the 'halo lumineux' around the umbels. In this way, the reader is persuaded by the accumulation of textual connections to view the motif of the white surface encircled by a red contour as a reflection of the underlying structure of frame shift.

An example of a particularly extended sequence of frame shifts occurs near the centre of the novel. The passage develops in the following way: (p. 126) the alley-way episode in sequence B is framed as a film being shot (references to 'caméra' and 'écran'); (p. 126) the same incident is framed, a few lines later, as a novel being read by the woman in a hotel room in sequence C ('Arrivée à ce point du récit qui, d'ailleurs, clôt un chapitre, la femme interrompt sa lecture');[62] (p. 127) the hotel episode in sequence C is itself framed as a painting ('Il semble que l'artiste . . .'); (p. 130) the same description is framed a few lines later as the shooting of a film in a studio (references to 'la voix du metteur en scène', 'techniciens', 'acteur', 'actrice'); (p. 131) the actress in sequence C picks up the book she was reading earlier and 'feuillète en arrière'. At this point an ambiguous sentence opens onto a long, unbroken passage of sequence B in which the events (hitherto withheld) leading up to the alley-way incident are related:

La sonnette annonçant le début imminent de la séance s'est tue depuis quelques instants quand parvient du dehors le tapage de deux voitures qui semblent se poursuivre . . . (pp. 131–2)[63]

The reader's initial reaction is to identify the 'sonnette' and the 'séance' as the bell announcing the next 'take' in the film studio since the sentence follows on immediately from a reference to the lights being switched on again and the actress taking up her position. However, such an identification would involve a self-contradiction since the sentence refers to an episode in sequence B and not one in sequence C. If on the other hand the 'sonnette' and the 'séance' refer to the warning bell in the cinema showing the film of sequence B, there would still be a clash. To begin with, sequence B has just been framed as a book. But even allowing for a substitution of frame and accepting that the events are now part of a film, a further question arises concerning the spatial context designated by the word 'dehors'. It cannot, without defying the laws of narrative order, refer to the street outside the cinema since the events are taking place inside on the screen. The lines remain in a topologically undefined context where, none the less, sequence B and sequence C briefly converge.

In sharp contrast to the smooth 'panning' movement of the description at the start of the novel, the text now reveals itself as a 'montage' of disconnected parts. The passage under analysis moves from one scene to the next through a system of frame shifts culminating in a sentence the referential context of which is constituted by what Dällenbach would call 'l'espace impensable', a textual 'no-man's-land' where separate narrative sequences meet contrary to the laws of narrative discourse.

The junctures between separate narrative isotopies are reflected in, for instance, the 'zones floues' separating the three representations on the film poster (p. 96). Once again the self-reflexive gaze of the writing turns the reader's attention to frame. Similarly the landscape description at the start of the novel highlights the same phenomenon:

> Les bois qui couvrent les flancs de la vallée sont bordés de taillis de noisetiers, et de charmes. Leur lisière serpente le long des prés en pente, dessinant des courbes, des golfes et des caps dont l'un atteint presque l'arrière de la grange.
> (p. 11)[64]

A few lines later the same metaphors are used but this time with reference to the clouds in the sky:

> De l'endroit où se trouve la grange on entend distinctement le bruit puissant et continu de la cascade répercuté par les falaises de roches grises apparaissant çà et là entre les feuillages touffus des bois sur les pentes abruptes de la vallée qu'elles couronnent parfois, couronnées elles-mêmes par des bouquets d'arbrisseaux dont les racines s'enfoncent dans leurs interstices et dont les troncs malingres se tordent devant le ciel où les nuages glissent calmement, leurs contours sinueux ou dentelés se déformant sans cesse, dessinant des boursoufflures, des golfes et des caps qui saillent, se creusent et se déchirent. (pp. 11–12)[65]

The reflection of the earth in the sky, textually rendered by the transgressive use of metaphor, recalls the baroque perspective of a reversible universe which also plays a dominant role in *A la recherche du temps perdu*. It is perception of the outline of the clouds'

Protean contours which gives rise to the comparison with the edge of a coastline. Thus metaphorical osmosis, in Simon's writing, is constantly accompanied by a designation of the frame break involved. The same metaphor recurs throughout the novel, each time in a different descriptive context. Indeed each of the three narrative sequences includes a reference to the same depiction of contour.

Sequence A is framed at the end of the novel as the composite picture of a jig-saw puzzle in sequence C. The latter also serves as a mirror-image of the whole novel not because of the reader's ability to reassemble all the parts into a unified whole but because each of its parts is insulated by a clearly-defined, meandering contour:

> Leurs découpures méandreuses ont été calculées de façon qu'aucune d'entre elles, prise isolément, n'offre l'image entière d'un personnage, d'un animal, d'un visage même. A part de très rares exceptions [. . .] leur ensemble présente toute la gamme variée des verts [. . .] et elles forment un archipel de petites îles creusées de baies, de golfes, hérissées de caps, sur le fond rouge de la moquette. (p. 224)[66]

A similar allusion to contours is inserted, with the same purpose of delineating the referential divisions necessary for textual osmosis, in a passage describing the alley-way episode in sequence B:

> Les formes agrandies et emmêlées des feuilles ovales balaient indifféremment les visages douloureux de la femme aux doigts endiamantés, celui de la jeune mariée, le chapelet de perles des globes lumineux qui s'étire le long du golfe et l'impasse obscure où les deux silhouettes, obscures elles aussi, au contour cerné d'une auréole par la lumière qui vient de la rue, exécutent au ralenti une sorte de pantomime qui tantôt rapproche les deux corps, les confondant, tantôt les sépare. (p. 104)[67]

I have already suggested that the pantomimic behaviour of the couple echoes the clown's performance. Equally, the swaying movement of the 'feuilles ovales' and the reference to the 'auréole' of light foreshadow the central description (p. 119) in which the little girl whose face is 'auréolée par la flamme orangée' is spied upon by the two boys peering in between the swaying movement of the branches of an oak tree.[68]

Furthermore, the indifferent sweep of the leaves' shadows across the two film posters, one of which represents sequence B and the other sequence C, has the textual effect, a few pages later, of intermingling elements from the two scenes: the alley-way is said to be covered 'de petits îlots de lumière qui révélent les façades rougeâtres et violacés et vont décroissant. Entre les réverbères s'étendent de larges zones d'ombre' (p. 114).[69] The reference to 'îlots de lumières' is an echo of the 'globes lumineux' bordering the 'golfe' in the poster of sequence C and recurring later in a filmed version of the same scene:[70]

> un commentaire [. . .] accompagnant le lent déplacement, sur le fond noir, d'un chapelet ininterrompu de lumières dessinant les formes de golfes, de péninsules, de caps et jetées qui glissent de droite à gauche. Sur la plage de ténèbres, rien, de part et d'autre des festons lumineux, ne permet de distinguer la mer de la terre [.] (p . 138)[71]

The recurrence of the word 'golfe' and the accompanying idea of topographical osmosis in these passages is manifestly inspired by the description of Elstir's paintings in Proust's *A la recherche du temps perdu* where the sea appears to merge with the coast-line, 's'enfonçant en golfe dans les terres', making it impossible for the observer to distinguish 'de frontière fixe, de démarcation absolue, entre la terre et l'océan'.[72] Once again Claude Simon has drawn from Proust only to transform this influence to his own ends. Whilst the Elstirian perspective is one of metaphorical assimilation, a harmonic fusion of land and sea, in *Triptyque* the line of demarcation is constantly thrown into relief. Thus in the passage I have just quoted it is only the demarcation-line, the 'chapelet ininterrompu de lumières' which is visible and not the sea or land on either side.

Finally, the luminous globes of the street lamps lining the beach esplanade reflect the referential contours transgressed in the novel, and the role played by the 'mise en abyme' descriptions whose inter-reflections are the primary cause of this transgression of frame. Moreover this motif can also be read as a visual analogue of the novel as a whole which resembles a crystal ball engendering a sparkling succession of textual predictions and retrospections.

This crystalline brilliance was enthusiastically recognised by Jean Dubuffet in a letter to Simon shortly after the novel's publication:

> C'est un livre à utiliser comme un tapis de Perse. Ou encore comme un talisman, une boule de cristal.[73]

3
Frame Conflict in *Leçon de choses*

> Grand délice que celui de noyer son regard dans l'immensité du ciel et de la mer! Solitude, silence, incomparable chasteté de l'azur! une petite voile frissonante à l'horizon, et qui par sa petitesse et son isolement imite mon irrémédiable existence, mélodie monotone de la houle, toutes ces choses pensent par moi, ou je pense par elles (car dans la grandeur de la rêverie, le *moi* se perd vite!); elles pensent, dis-je, mais musicalement et pittoresquement, sans arguties, sans syllogismes, sans déductions.
>
> Baudelaire, 'Le *Confiteor* de l'artiste'[1]

I INTERIOR AND EXTERIOR

The musicality of *Leçon de choses* derives not merely from 'le son de choses' but also from the novel's rhythms, refrains, variations of motif, the musical interludes ('Divertissements' I and II), and the fugue-like three-part structure of the main text ('Expansion' – 'Leçon de choses' – 'La Charge de Reichschoffen'). But the title of the novel's prelude, 'Générique', invites comparison with the cinema. This short opening piece presents a few seminal starting-points which later expand and engender the whole novel. However, unlike the opening credits of a film, 'Générique' does not divulge the names of individuals or circumstances which have contributed to the production of the novel. Instead it acknowledges that language and the internal dynamics of writing are the vital source of the novel's creation.

'Générique' is brief and prefatory, yet pregnant with anticipation of what is to follow. It is composed of three paragraphs: the first begins with a description of the torn, faded wall-paper on the walls of a dilapidated room; the second focuses on the débris of plaster lying on the floor; and the third reflects on the hypothetical elaboration of the scene:

> La description (la composition) peut se continuer (ou être complétée) à peu près indéfiniment selon la minutie apportée à son exécution, l'entraînement des métaphores proposées, l'addition d'autres objets visibles dans leur entier ou fragmentés par l'usure, le temps, un choc (soit encore qu'ils n'apparaissent qu'en partie dans le cadre du tableau), sans compter les diverses hypothèses que peut susciter le spectacle. (pp. 10–11)[2]

The parentheses in this sentence deserve special attention. In one, the word 'composition' is presented as a synonym of 'description', thereby implying that the latter is not seen as a process which reproduces a pre-existing reality but one which creates what it describes. In another, almost cursory 'aside', the whole passage is framed as a painting. The reader is told that some of the objects in the room are fragmented by virtue of the fact that they are only partially enclosed within the borders of the 'painting'. However, this pictorial status of the dilapidated room is immediately transformed. The scene is 'dramatised' by the introduction of movement and characters. The elliptical reference to the external space excluded from the 'painting' is also 'dramatised' by the designation of an adjoining room which casts dark shadows into the immediate scene. Moreover, the allusion to 'le *cadre* du tableau', mirrored by 'l'*encadrement* de la porte', and the enigmatic reference to a mysterious figure in the doorway (a builder, a soldier, one of the 'promeneuses', or the anonymous narrator?) adumbrate the compositional principle which governs the ensuing pages.

This principle may be described as the topological rivalry between two distinct narrative isotopies, or, in short, 'frame conflict'. Before proceeding with a close analysis of the way in which this conflict determines the interaction between the narrative sequences throughout the novel it will be useful to consider the specific friction and rivalry between two pictorial contexts.

'Expansion', the novel's first main chapter, opens with a description of a seascape painting which hangs on the wall of the dilapidated room described in 'Générique' and which remains anonymous until the close of the chapter when it is identified as Monet's 'Effet du soir'. The reproduction, 'l'image de l'immobile tempête' is glued to a sheet of fluffy grey-green paper. Beside the picture, a window 'encadre un paysage champêtre'. This second visual space at first offers a view of three women wearing old-fashioned dresses and carrying parasols, preceded by a little girl wearing a boater hat, walking down a sloping field of poppies or umbels. The view is subsequently erased and the landscape becomes empty save for the amorphous debris of war as seen by a soldier scanning the area through the sights of his rifle.

The soldier then turns his attention to a calendar pinned on the wall: its picture, surrounded by columns of saints' names, is that of the same group of 'promeneuses'. In other words, this descriptive segment has abandoned its initial framing as an external scene viewed through the window and assumed a new location and identity as a reproduction decorating a calendar inside the room. Claude Simon has indicated that this scene stems from Renoir's 'Chemin montant dans les herbes'.[3] At the end of 'Expansion', the Monet reproduction is named, the word 'L'ILLUSTRATION' written on the 'papier pelucheux et grisâtre'[4] suggests that the picture has been pulled out of an art magazine.

At the close of the third main chapter, 'La Charge de Reichschoffen',[5] it is the Monet seascape, now entitled 'Les Tas de Pois (Finistère)' which is said to lie on the floor and which the builder picks up to admire before letting fall to the ground again. No mention is made of the 'promeneuses' picture, but clearly the impending substitution is foreshadowed in these lines. Finally, it is in 'Courts-Circuits', the final section of the novel, that the crossover takes place. The reader is informed, with rather more outward display of precision than has hitherto been manifest, that there are two pictures hanging on the wall. One of them adorns the Post Office almanac surrounded by the habitual lists of saints' names and religious festivities. The other adheres to a 'papier grisvert, grenu, formant encadrement'[6] and droops diagonally from one of its corners. However, much to the reader's surprise, it is the calendar picture which now represents 'dans une harmonie verdâtre et violacée une côte rocheuse qui plonge dans la mer',[7] and the reproduction glued to the grey-green back-sheet which depicts the three women. Monet and Renoir have changed places.

What inferences can one draw from this measured convergence

and reciprocal displacement of two pictorial isotopies? Firstly, set against the background of the narrative conflict which the reader will have encountered throughout the novel before reaching 'Courts-Circuits', this localised rivalry between the Monet and Renoir reproductions illustrates the pivotal movement of 'frame conflict' which determines the relations between the three narrative sequences. This reading is further supported by the reference to the green line bordering the Renoir picture, now transplanted onto its new screen. The line curls into three loops at each of the corners of the picture:

> Un filet d'un vert plus foncé court dans les marges à chaque coin desquelles il dessine un motif décoratif composé de trois boucles (une grande encadrée de deux petites) comme des pétales en fer de lance. (p. 179)[8]

Seen from a broader point of view, the relationship between the Monet and Renoir settings is a symptom of the interaction between exterior and interior which prevails throughout the novel. The 'promeneuses' scene, it was shown, first takes place outside the house before trespassing inside in the guise of a calendar reproduction, and finally usurping the place of the Monet seascape. This topological accommodation of the outside within the boundaries of the space it englobes is dramatically thrown into relief at the end of the novel by the 'illogical' entry of the women and their escort into the room which has been occupied by the builders and soldiers. Narrative preoccupation with an intrusive exterior is paralleled, on the level of sentence structure, by the use of preterition.

Unflinching in his critical distinction between the 'telestructural composition' of a text and its 'literal consecution', François Jost has claimed that *Leçon de choses* is not built on a system of 'transits' but of preterition:

> C'est à partir de ce qu'il ne dit pas (cf. 'Ainsi il n'a pas été dit . . .' 'Il n'a pas fait mention . . .') que le roman va se développer. Le schéma simple présentation du matériel à travailler ('générateurs') – disposition de ce matériel (récit éclaté) n'est plus un modèle d'explication suffisante.[9]

However, the opposition between the function of transition and of preterition is a false one. Preterition is precisely one form of transition. The definition of this figure of speech is that it is a statement in which the negative form is inverted: that is, a statement which does refer to what it says it will not refer to. As the following example will illustrate, the use of preterition is one of the means by which a remote textual context exerts an influence on a particular setting from which it is absent:

> Quand elle voit tout près dans l'obscurité la pastille incandescente du cigare elle a comme un haut-le-corps, un recul, comme quelqu'un abusé par quelque illusion d'optique et se heurtant tout à coup à un obstacle prévu mais dont il a mal apprécié la distance comme de ces bateaux au loin sur la mer et soudain (parce qu'on a cessé de les suivre des yeux et quoique l'on sache que leur immobilité n'est qu'apparente) tout proches. La barque de pêche est maintenant au-dessous d'eux et longe le pied de la falaise. [. . .] Loin devant la robe claire de la petite fille court sur le chemin en haut de la falaise qui s'abaisse dans une déclivité, précédant les deux ombrelles qui oscillent en sens contraires comme des fleurs. Sur la falaise il n'y a pas de coquelicots. Elle entend sa voix. Il se détache de la barrière, et s'avance vers elle, noir dans le noir, précédé de la tache rouge du cigare qui semble suspendue dans la nuit. (pp. 51–2)[10]

The passage oscillates between two sequences, or rather, as will become clear later on, between two time spans of the same narrative sequence. Sequence A1 is the description of a group of women walking along a cliff-top (already the sequence has veered away from the original rural setting of the Renoir painting). During the walk, the man escorting the group extracts a promise from one of the 'promeneuses' (the mother of the little girl) to meet him alone that evening. Sequence A2 takes place at nightfall when the woman, having put her daughter to bed, steals away to the 'rendez-vous' at the gate by the edge of the wood where her lover awaits. The intersequential movement in the passage quoted above, therefore, is: A2 – A1 – A2. The first shift, from A2 to A1, is produced by the reference made to boats in the explicit comparison 'comme de ces bateaux' which immediately evokes the movement of the boats off the coast in A1. The second shift is produced by the reference to poppies in the preterition 'Sur la falaise il n'y a pas de coquelicots', which immediately evokes the 'taches *rouges* du cigare' in A2. For an explanation of this shift one needs to place the passage within the context of the entire chapter which revolves around the production of the whole of narrative sequence A. The first instance of this sequence, the view seen through the window, reveals the textual play surrounding the word 'coquelicots':

> A gauche du bois, le terrain se relève en pente sur le versant d'un coteau planté d'arbres fruitiers clairsemés, comme un verger à l'abandon ou mal entretenu au sol couvert de longues herbes et constellés de pastilles (ombelles, coquelicots?) blanches ou rouges. Trois femmes au teint sans doute fragiles qu'elles protègent du soleil par des ombrelles descendent la pente du verger. (p. 16)[11]

The transition here is triggered off by the link, already exploited in *Triptyque*, between 'ombelles' and 'ombrelles'. But the focus on 'rouge' and 'coquelicot' is also significant in that it is repeated at several instances of sequence A: as, for example, in the allusion to the 'pavots d'un rouge passé' in the calendar picture (p. 17). The textual explanation or motivation of this recurrence is that sequence A1 is to some extent born out of the description of the Monet painting at the start of the chapter: 'coquelicots' stems from 'bataille de *coqs*' and from 'coups de *pinceau*' by way of 'ponceau' which can either mean 'culvert' ('pour diriger le canon de l'arme sur le ponceau où sont entassés et enchevêtrés . . .' (p. 21)[12] or 'corn-poppy'. The shift from 'coquelicots' to 'tache rouge du cigare' in the passage under analysis is based on the association between poppies and the colour 'red'. The transition, however, also depends on a metonymic, 'telestructural', system of textual organisation. An earlier reference to poppies, this time on the wallpaper in the builders' sequence (narrative sequence C), 'Sur le papier sont représentés de grands coquelicots (pavots?)' (p. 33),[13] immediately follows the description of a cigar-box which, as Jost observes, acts as 'mise en abyme' and agent of transformation in the production of sequence A2. The generative role played by the cigar-box description with regard to sequence A2 is reflected by the fact that it is only after this description that there is any mention of the man in sequence A smoking a cigar. Thus whilst the preterition, 'Sur la falaise il n'y a pas de coquelicots', expresses an absence on the level of representation, this same negative expression introduces an element which has decisive textual consequence.

A second example of the use of preterition in the production of shift from one sequence to another can be found in the second main chapter of the novel:

> Elle suit des yeux le vol affairé d'un frelon. A ras de terre se trouvent de petites fleurs jaunes. Il y a, là aussi, quelques scabieuses. [. . .] Dans sa position (seulement appuyée sur un coude), la jeune femme voit se balancer mollement les hautes ombelles au-dessous de la chaîne des nuages boursouflés qui se confondent presque avec le ciel. Le frelon va de l'une à l'autre où il ne se pose qu'un instant. Il parcourt plusieurs fois aller et retour l'intervalle qui les sépare, croisant ou dépassant le petit voilier qui se hâte dans l'encadrement des tiges légèrement inclinées. Son corps velu et trapu est d'un brun orangé, strié de noir. La vache ne figure pas dans le tableau. [. . .] Le chargeur lit lentement le titre de la reproduction punaisée sur le mur parmi les coquelicots géants: sur la falaise. (pp. 91–3)[14]

The preterition, 'La vache ne figure pas dans le tableau' pinpoints the motivating factors behind the shift in the passage which begins as an instance of sequence A1 (the 'promeneuses' on the coast) and ends as a description of a painting in sequence B (a reproduction attributed to Boudin, entitled 'Sur la falaise', hanging on the wall of the farm-house occupied by the soldiers). Apart from noticing that the Renoir reproduction has made way for a Boudin, the reader may observe that the reference to the cow marks a contextual association with an earlier passage in the novel describing an instance of sequence B. This is the first reference to a cow in the novel, occurring in the description of the war-torn landscape viewed through the window:

> Les rayons du soleil commencent à décliner. Ils frappent maintenant sous un angle différent les quatre piquets qui sortent de l'herbe du pré, encadrant la masse gonflée où l'on peut à présent reconnaître le ventre ballonné, blanc et rose, d'une vache couchée sur le dos et figée dans une complète immobilité. (p. 22)[15]

A comparison of the two passages reveals that the instance of sequence A1 in the first passage is deeply impregnated with elements from sequence B in the second passage. The 'encadrement des tiges' is an echo of the 'quatre piquets [. . .] encadrant la masse gonflée'; the impression of the yacht's sudden displacement, 'comme si quelque main géante l'avait soulevé et reposé' (p. 92),[16] mirrors the impression produced by the position of the cow: 'comme si on l'avait prise et retournée telle quelle, tout d'une pièce, à la façon d'un jouet' (p. 22).[17] The infiltration of sequence B within an instance of sequence A1 leads inevitably to the complete domination of the latter by the former: A1 is framed as a painting set in B.

The use of preterition in *Leçon de choses* can therefore be construed as a sign of a more general preoccupation with the interplay between interior and exterior, between presence and absence, between identity and difference. It is here again that the reader can explore the unbounded regions of intertextuality.

II INTERTEXTUAL MOTIVATION: IMPRESSIONIST PAINTING AND *MADAME BOVARY*

Critics have often been tempted to equate Simon's novels with specific schools of painting and in particular with Impressionism. André Rousseaux, for instance, speaks of *La Route des Flandres* as an example of an 'art impressioniste, dont le chatoiement verbal est comparable à la peinture du même nom'.[18] Similarly, Maria Elisabeth Kronegger describes Simon's novels as 'Impressionist', noting that the 'rhythmic phrase form, the dynamics, the articulation and the tone colour are basic in his work, as in impressionist creation'.[19] The analogy with painting is natural given the author's undeniable preoccupation with and profound discernment of works of visual art. Nevertheless, he is also quick to spell out the fundamental differences separating literature from painting:

> l'écriture n'est pas la peinture, le pouvoir évocateur de la figuration picturale d'un corps est tout autre que celui de la description scripturale d'un corps, la peinture est surface, simultanéité, l'écriture est linéarité, durée, etc.[20]

Like Lessing, Valéry and Borges before him, Claude Simon warns against excesses in the comparative, interdisciplinary approach adopted by writers who have interpreted Horace's maxim 'ut pictura poesis' as a declaration of an equivalence between the two art forms. It is the substance of both forms of art which predetermines their incompatibility: spatial simultaneity on the one hand, and linguistic consecution on the other.[21] Nevertheless, Simon has referred to the 'bricolage' nature of his writings as the means by which the constraints imposed by linguistic successivity are overcome. The textual associations produced by a system of verbal correspondences disturb the linear flow characteristic of ordinary prose writing. By assimilating passages which are several pages apart and which are unrelated by narrative ordering, the reader participates in giving rise to an effect which, to some limited degree, is analogous with the visual simultaneity of painting. The limits of this analogy are defined by the fact that the materiality of such an associative reading is not visual or spatial, but linguistic:

> Comme le peintre, et en dépit du fait qu'il n'a à sa disposition, au lieu d'une surface, qu'une durée, l'écrivain peut cependant parvenir à 'abstraire de différentes séries' des éléments qu'il assemble en une sorte de mécanique ou de système non pas, bien sûr, optique mais scriptural.[22]

In order to be fully appreciated, the references to Impressionist painting in *Leçon de choses* need to be seen in the light of this formal tension.

The intertextual associations between *Leçon de choses* and Impressionist painting and between Simon's novel and *Madame Bovary* are located in the figurative content of sequence A. The characters and setting are reminiscent of the depictions of sea and cliffs in Monet's 'Etretat' (1886) and 'Etretat, mer agitée' (1883), of the women and poppy-field in 'Les Coquelicots' (1873) and 'La Promenade sur la Falaise, Pourville' (1882), and the numerous paintings by Boudin of the Etretat cliffs such as his 'Etretat, la Falaise d'Aval' (1889), and his series of cow paintings including, for example, 'Vache sur la Falaise' (1885–90).[23] Of course, it would be false to suggest that the novel is a mirror reflection or literary translation of visual motifs found in Impressionist paintings. The extent to which the descriptive aspect of the intertextual relationship is in this case 'anti-representational' can be gauged by analysing the passages dealing with the two paintings openly attributed to Monet and Boudin in the novel.

The most striking feature of the description of 'Effet du Soir' at the start of 'Expansion' is the focus on the material quality of the painting (the thickness and angles of the brush-strokes) and the sparseness of its account of the scene depicted.[24] The overwhelming impression of opacity is due to the fact that the passage, indeed the whole novel, is governed not by a desire to reproduce an external reality but by the urge to re-employ certain external or intertextual motifs, based in Impressionist paintings, which are incorporated and projected across the span of textual relations in the novel. A close look at the three sentences which comprise the description of the turbulent seascape reveals that the passage serves as a base from which several textual elements are subsequently disseminated throughout the novel, echoing across the three narrative sequences. The first sentence describes the short, curved brush-strokes on the canvas:

Les flots verdâtres, les roches violets, l'écume, le ciel bas, sont figurés indifféremment au moyen de petits coups de pinceau en forme de virgules ou de minuscules croissants. (p. 15)[25]

The typographical imagery ('virgules' and 'croissants') is later repeated in the description of the little girl's eyelashes, 'deux minces croissants comme des parenthèses horizontales' (p. 32);[26] and the description of her hair, 'comme de larges coups de pinceau sur un fond d'aquarelle où leurs contours se dissolvent' (p. 32),[27] matches the reference to the 'petits coups de pinceau' in the painting. (The allusion to the ill-defined contours also echoes the 'contours estompés' in the second sentence of the Monet passage.) The same imagery reappears in the description of the picture ('figure no. 120') inserted in the 'leçons de choses' textbook (a standard general knowledge textbook which was formerly on the syllabus in all French schools) read by the soldier in sequence B: 'Les vagues sont figurées au moyen de traits en formes de larges accents circonflexes très aplatis, et ressemblent aux rangées de tentes alignées et basses d'un camp militaire' (p. 75),[28] which in turn is echoed in the description of the tattoo on the builder's arm in sequence C:

Deux parenthèses couchées, comme deux cupules, soulignant chacune un point, figurent les seins. Au-dessous de la sirène clapotent trois courtes rangées d'accents circonflexes alignés comme des tentes d'un camp militaire ou les crêtes d'une eau agitée. (p. 156)[29]

The second sentence in the seascape passage describes the visual impression of the painting viewed from a distance:

De loin, dans l'ensemble papillotant se dessinent des masses aux contours estompées cependant que les milliers de touches semblent voltiger, comme ces tempêtes chatoyantes mêlées de duvet en suspension dans un poulailler après une bataille de coqs, s'élevant, tournoyant, et retombant en se balançant. (p. 15)[30]

Once again, some of the elements are later repeated and transformed. The simile in this sentence is recalled in the description of the chicken whose feathers are plucked by one of the soldiers in sequence B: 'Il souffle à plusieurs reprises entre ses lèvres serrées pour décoller les fins duvets' (p. 19).[31] It is again echoed in the description of the cloud of feathers which rises into the air as the enemy shells strike the farm-house: 'Un épais nuage de poussière fuse de sous les décombres, d'abord à ras du sol, puis s'élève en tournoyant, emportant les plumes des deux poules qui tourbillonnent comme des flammèches' (p. 44),[32] and in the description of the dust cloud hanging in the room in sequence C: 'Une impalpable poussière d'un blanc jaunâtre stagne en permanence dans le local, impondérable, suspendue en l'air' (p. 27).[33] The motif of the 'immobile tempête' as expressed in the description of a cloud (whether of dust, feathers or vapour) suspended in mid-air is also repeated in at least two other passages: the description of the cargo-boat ('vapeur') in sequence A which, through distorted perspective, appears to float above a group of clouds and which seems 'à la fois doué d'immobilité et de mouvement' (p. 89);[34] the second description is that of the fire guard ('plaque de fonte') in sequence B whose ornamental design shows a figure resembling 'ces personnages impondérables représentées sur les fresques ou les plafonds, flottant dans les airs' (p. 161)[35] and whose feet seem to be standing on a cloud. Furthermore, the reference to 'bataille de coqs' in the description of the Monet painting is paronomastically echoed in the allusion to the 'coque' of the cargo-boat and the *impondérable* (pun on 'pondre' meaning 'to lay eggs') appearance of the woman on the fire guard.

The third sentence describing the Monet reproduction outlines what can be seen from a close inspection:

De tout près on peut distinguer la matière de chacune des touches dirigées de droite à gauche, d'abord empâtée, puis s'élargissant, dérapant en même temps qu'elle se relève comme une queue. (p. 15)[36]

The paste-like texture of the paint is later brought to mind by the extract from the 'leçons de choses' book in which the mortar required for the construction of walls is described as a 'pâte molle' (p. 91) and also by the description of the Boudin painting which immediately follows:

les deux bateaux [. . .] semblent baigner dans une même épaisseur de pâte gris-bleu nacrée et transparente, que le peintre aurait étalée sur toute la surface de la toile [.] (p. 92)[37]

The reference to the tail-end of the brush-strokes reverberates in the recurrence of the word 'queue' at later points in the novel, such as the 'longues queues velues' of the poppies on the wallpaper in sequence C which 'ondulent au-dessous d'eux comme s'ils flottaient sans poids dans une eau rosâtre' (p. 34),[38] and in the description of the little girl's hat in sequence A: 'Le vent tend presque à l'horizontale les queues de son ruban collées maintenant l'une à l'autre et parcourues de rapides ondulations' (p. 44).[39]

The description of 'Sur la Falaise' is even more overtly 'anti-representational' than that of 'Effet du Soir'. Claude Simon has confirmed to me that whilst the Monet description is more or less modelled on an existing work, the Boudin is a complete fabrication. Both content and title are the invention of the author, or, more precisely, of the text, since the passage is an instance of 'capture' in which the cliff-top promenade sequence is framed as a reproduction by Boudin eyed by one of the soldiers in sequence B. Thus the references to sound (the intermittent exchange of words between the women) and to movement (the flight of the wasp, and the progression of the boats) clash with the gradual identification of the passage as a painting. The 'capture' begins with a reference to the figurative space of the painting ('La vache ne figure pas dans le tableau' (p. 92) which is followed by an

Frame Conflict in Leçon de choses 229

allusion to the painter's techniques (the thickness of paint and use of colour) and culminates in the naming of the painting and artist.

Just as with 'Effet du Soir', the text is not here concerned with shedding light on an external referent but with re-employing certain external 'stimuli' for its own ends. The verbal (as opposed to pictorial) interest in the description of this 'painting' is explicitly indicated by the pun on 'Boudin' made by the 'chargeur':

> Il se relève et dit Boudin tu parles d'un nom y en a mince on se demande où i vont les chercher mince à part ça je m'en taperais bien un morceau. Le tireur tourne la tête sur le côté, le regarde sans comprendre et dit un morceau de quoi? De boudin hé saucisse, dit le chargeur. (p. 93)[40]

The loader's pun is also a signal to the reader of the implicit ways in which the word 'boudin' pervades the text. For instance, one can argue that the identification of 'Sur la Falaise' as a painting by Boudin is to some extent motivated by an earlier description of the boat on the horizon 'comme ces insectes dont le thorax n'est relié à l'abdomen que par un corselet aussi mince qu'un fil' (p. 88).[41] By retroactive association one can observe that the image of the corset has foreshadowed this reference to Boudin through the unwritten presence of the word 'boudiné' which means 'wearing a tightly fitting garment'. The repetition of the word 'mince' in both passages serves as an added thread of association. Two further segments, occurring several lines after the depiction of 'Sur la Falaise', are similarly linked by the word 'boudin'. The first is a description of the fishermen washing their nets on the beach in sequence A: 'Penché sur la lisse, l'un d'eux les secoue dans l'eau, rassemblés en boudins, et ils ondulent comme de gros serpents bruns' (p. 94).[42] The explicit use of 'boudin' (meaning, this time, 'rolls') is echoed in the narrative segment immediately following which describes the scene of adultery:

> La ligne onduleuse des collines avec les bourrelets d'arbres et de haies se découpe en noir sur le ciel couleur puce où ne luisent que quelques étoiles. (p. 94)[43]

'Boudin', synonymous with 'bourrelet' when referring to the pad or fender of a boat, is silently present in the text. The marine connotations of 'bourrelets d'arbres' are emphasised by the reference to the 'ligne onduleuse', echoing the undulating motion of the fishing-nets in the description mentioned above. An earlier passage also contains an association between two consecutive narrative segments revolving around different meanings of the word 'boudin'. One of the builders in sequence C accidentally hammers his thumb in the course of work. At first there is no sign of blood: 'on ne distingue sous la couche de poussière qu'un bourrelet de peau' (p. 34).[44] Thus, another meaning of 'boudin', this time as 'fat finger', is implicitly evoked by the reference to the swollen thumb. The passage then switches to a description of narrative sequence A in which the woman is peeling an orange for her daughter: 'A la fin, la lourde spirale étirée, à la fois rugueuse et vernie d'un côté, pelucheuse de l'autre, tombe dans l'herbe' (p. 36).[45] Here, 'boudin' is evoked by 'spirale'. The connection is reinforced by mirror repetitions such as the focus on the woman's thumbs ('Elle sépare les côtes des deux pouces'[46]) and the recurrence of the adjective 'pelucheuse' with reference both to the skin on the builder's thumb (p. 35) and the inner surface of the orange peel (p. 36).

The intertextual relationship between *Leçon de choses* and Impressionist painting takes the form of a process of verbal incorporation, whereby Simon's novel transforms and manipulates 'stimuli' based in the work of Renoir, Monet and Boudin for its own purposes of textual production and signification. The relationship with *Madame Bovary*, however, differs radically. As well as being 'stimulated' by Flaubert's novel (in other words, expanding and transforming some of its elements), Simon's novel invites the reader to apply the same kind of textual reading to *Madame Bovary* as the one it elicits for itself. To begin with there are several points of comparison linking the two novels. The names 'Saint Charles' and 'Sainte Emma' appear in the list of saints on the calendar in sequence B (p. 108); 'Charles' is also the name of the absent cuckolded husband. The similarities between the two 'heroines'; between Rodolphe and the lover in Simon's work; and between Emma's daughter, Berthe, and Evelyne, the daughter in *Leçon de choses*, remain implicit but no less striking. Apart from the characters, there are other common points between the two novels. The description of the cliff-top sequence with the view below of the fishermen washing their nets on the beach recalls the idyllic setting in Emma's dream: 'un village de pêcheurs, où des filets bruns séchaient au vent, le long de la falaise et des cabanes'.[47] However, it is sequence A2, consisting of the lovers' nocturnal rendez-vous, which is the most reminiscent of the Rodolphe/Emma episodes in *Madame Bovary*. The repeated reference to the frogs' cries in the wood is an echo of the reference to the 'grenouilles' around the pond when Rodolphe and Emma go riding together.[48] The dominating presence of the cows which frighten the adulteress in *Leçon de choses* (p. 102) mirrors the reference to Emma's fear of cows as she makes her way to the rendez-vous at la Huchette.[49] Further connections between the two novels come to light on re-reading the following extract from the account of Rodolphe and Emma's first horse-ride together:

> Les ombres du soir descendaient: le soleil horizontal passant entre les branches, lui éblouissait les yeux. Çà et là, tout autour d'elle, dans les feuilles ou par terre, des taches lumineuses tremblaient comme si des colibris, en volant, eussent éparpillé leurs plumes. Le silence était partout; quelque chose de doux semblait sortir des arbres; elle sentait son coeur, dont les battements recommençaient, et le sang circuler dans sa chair comme une fleuve de lait. Alors, elle entendait tout au loin, au-delà du bois, sur les autres collines, un cri vague et prolongé. Une voix qui se traînait, et elle l'écoutait silencieusement, se mêlant comme une musique aux dernières vibrations de ses nerfs émus. Rodolphe, le cigare aux dents, raccommodait avec son canif une des deux brides cassées.[50]

The loud heartbeats and the image of the stream of milk are reiterated in Simon's novel ('Son coeur bat violemment dans sa poitrine' (p. 53) and 'il regarde la coulée de chair laiteuse' (p. 101).[51] Equally the 'cri vague et prolongé' is echoed in the cries of the frogs and crickets in sequence A2; and Rodolphe's cigar, with its sinister overtones, is matched by the focus on the lover's cigar in *Leçon de choses*. In consequence, whilst sequence A1 can be described as in some ways a fictional animation of 'stimuli' drawn from Impressionist painting, sequence A2 can be interpreted as a modern version and transfiguration of 'stimuli' from *Madame Bovary*. In this way, *Leçon de choses* may be said to absorb, transform and regenerate the sources from which it has evolved.

Although the associations with *Madame Bovary* are not explicitly acknowledged by the text and may be situated on a more subconscious level of writing than those with Impressionist painting, the intertextual overlap which they outline is for the reader a source of creative pursuit. The elements from *Madame Bovary* which are transformed and expanded in *Leçon de choses* also play a structural role in Flaubert's novel. One such example is the metaphorical play surrounding the word 'voile'. In sequence A1 the two prospective lovers look out to sea and to the fishing-boat at the foot of the cliff. Immediately, the description focuses on the woman's hat: 'Le vent iodé joue avec le long voile vert qui entoure son canotier et le lui plaque sur le visage' (p. 52).[52] The double polysemic play in 'voile' meaning 'veil' and 'sail', or by synecdochic extension 'sailing-boat', and in 'canotier' meaning 'boater' (hat) and 'oarsman' exerts a determining influence on the text at two subsequent moments. The first occurs in the description of the same scene with the sole difference in the description being that the lovers are no longer looking at the fishing-boat beneath them but at a sailing-boat in the distance ('le voilier à la mâture inclinée?' (p. 76)).[53] The substitution of boats is produced by the shift from veil to sailing-boat in the 'voile'/'voilier' association. The second passage which is influenced by the description of the woman's hat alludes to an illustration in the textbook being read by the gunner in sequence B:

> Sur la mer calme, représentée à l'aide de fines lignes parallèles, à peine ondulées, on aperçoit deux voiles claires, triangulaires, l'une dans le lointain, et au premier plan, une barque vue de face (ou de l'arrière, le mauvais encrage ou le demi-jour ne permettant pas de distinguer) de chaque côté de laquelle dépassent de longs avirons, l'un presque à l'horizontale, l'autre légèrement incliné vers le haut. Des franges de goutelettes lumineuses, diamantines, pendent aux extremités des rames d'où elles retombent dans la mer. On distingue sur le flanc bombé du canot des lignes qui suivent la courbe du bordage et se détache dans le reflet doré du soleil sur la peinture noire. (pp. 99–100)[54]

The scene is clearly a re-presentation of the view from the clifftop in sequence A1. Moreover, the veil and hat in the earlier description are recalled here in the references to the sails ('voiles') and to the rowing-boat ('canot'). The rounded hull streaked with horizontal lines, the brilliant spray falling from the oars suggest the shape and surface of the woman's veil. As with the extensions of the word 'boudin', Simon's novel is here governed by an undercurrent of textual relations which emanate from a cluster of associations surrounding one or two kernel words, or, to borrow from Ricardou, 'vocables producteurs'.[55]

It is, once again, *Madame Bovary* which provides the external motivation for this associative play rotating around the word 'voile'. Spurred on by the correspondences between the two novels, the reader is encouraged to return to Flaubert's novel, approaching it from a perspective prepared by his reading of *Leçon de choses*. The following is a description of the hat worn by Emma on her first outing with Rodolphe:

A travers son voile, qui de son chapeau d'homme descendait obliquement sur ses hanches, on distinguait son visage dans une transparence bleuâtre, comme si elle eût nagé sous des flots d'azur.[56]

Influenced by *Leçon de choses*, the reader is alerted to the linguistic play in these lines. Beneath the denotative level of the sentence in which 'voile' refers to the veil on Emma's hat, the connotations of the sea in 'transparence bleuâtre' and 'flots d'azur' are aroused by the simultaneous reference in 'voile' to sailing-boats.

Another such reading of *Madame Bovary* centres on the word 'boudin' whose multiple meanings I have already shown to be textually exploited in *Leçon de choses*. Here again, 'intertextual motivation' may be defined as a 'reading' of one novel by another. When Emma returns one morning from a night spent with Rodolphe at la Huchette, she is startled by Binet who is illegally out duck shooting. Binet springs out of his hide-out, a barrel, 'comme ces diables à boudin qui se dressent du fond des boîtes'.[57] Through repetition, the words 'boudin' and 'tonneau' create a link between Charles and Binet: thus, 'boudin' appears in the description of Charles's hat ('Ovoïde et renflée de baleines, elle commençait par trois boudins circulaires')[58] and the 'tonneau' out of which Binet leaps reappears in the description of Charles's imagination which 'assaillie par une multitude d'hypothèses, ballotait au milieu d'elles comme un tonneau vide emporté à la mer et qui roule sur les flots'.[59] Hence the suggestion of circularity and repetition contained in the word 'boudin' can be seen to reflect the circularity and repetition underlying the textual composition of Flaubert's novel.

In *Leçon de choses* the Flaubertian pattern of circularity is distorted into an equally vertiginous but more transgressive spiral of associations whose every twist and turn, as I shall now proceed to show, short-circuits the conventional laws of narrative order.

III INTERSEQUENTIAL CONFLICT

Fictional and textual 'mises en abyme' play a crucial role in establishing a 'discoherent', spiralling pattern of relations between the three main narrative sequences in *Leçon de choses*. The clearest example of this triadic paradox of narrative is the contradictory chain of inclusion whereby sequence A appears as a newspaper item in sequence C (p. 167) which appears as a newspaper item in sequence B (p. 145) which in turn appears as a newspaper item in sequence A (p. 181). The main effect of this intertwining series of fictional 'mises en abymes' is to foreground the absence of an overall narrative hierarchy in the novel. However, far from being a sign of creative deadlock, this hierarchical stalemate is responsible for a complex system of intersequential conflict.

On one important level, the dramatic focus of *Leçon de choses* centres on the development of narrative sequence A, the object of contention between the other two sequences. As I have already pointed out, the 'promeneuses' sequence, viewed through a window of the dilapidated farm-house, is initially set in an ambiguous narrative context. The same scene is then transposed onto a calendar hanging inside the room occupied by the soldiers, and thus becomes embedded in narrative sequence B. The influence of sequence B over sequence A in this first main chapter, 'Expansion', is such that it induces a rift in the latter. At the end of their afternoon excursion, the women choose between two alternative routes for their return home: 'Les femmes discutent entre elles sur le chemin que l'on suivra au retour en se demandant si on prendra par la ferme ou par la falaise' (p. 31).[60] Their decision to take the cliff-top path has the profound textual effect of bifurcating the narrative sequence into two separate strands.[61]

The off-shoot narrative, which I have already referred to as 'sequence A2', is inaugurated by a passage in which the mother embraces her sleeping daughter before embarking on her promiscuous adventure. This description is separated from the foregoing reference to the 'promeneuses's' choice of routes only by an extract from the 'leçons de choses' textbook read by the soldier in sequence B. The extract, entitled 'Ouvriers collant du papier sur les murs d'une chambre', is a 'mise en abyme' framing of sequence C. Set against this passage, which stresses the whiteness of the walls and paper, the trace of scratch marks on the plaster and the design of the wallpaper, the description of the little girl's hair, couched in terms of painting, takes on a contrasting significance:

Les cheveux, les plis du drap, le rebord du lit dessinent des ombres noires, estompées, comme de larges coups de pinceau sur un fond d'aquarelle où leurs contours se dissolvent. (p. 32)[62]

The same imagery is repeated in a description of the cigar box which immediately follows this opening instance of A2: 'Le mot CLARO est peint au pochoir, de biais et à l'encre *noire* sur la planchette qui forme le fond de la boîte, *striée de veines fines comme des cheveux*' (my italics, p. 33).[63] The cigar box, one of the few objects discovered in the house and pilfered by the soldiers in sequence B, is decorated with a picture of a procession led by a horseman. The piecemeal, hesitant description of the box contains several elements which contribute to the narrative of the adulterous encounter. Thus, the 'cavalier' figure himself foreshadows, as François Jost has argued, the style and behaviour of the adulterer.[64] The influence takes the form of metonymic transference at the end of the chapter when the woman first sees her lover by the light of the burning tip of the cigar he is smoking.

In the central chapter, 'Leçons de choses', sequence A2 is dominated by the builders' sequence. Correspondingly, the motif of blackness is substituted by one of whiteness. The chapter opens with a meticulous description of one of the builders eating a hard-boiled egg during a lunch-break:

Tandis qu'il mastique sa main repose le pain puis saisit une petite salière avec laquelle il saupoudre la partie restante de l'oeuf. Le jaune forme un disque parfait, légèrement verdâtre sur les bords. Il s'effrite chaque fois sous l'action des dents, présentant une surface irrégulière, alors qu'elles coupent de façon nette l'anneau blanc à consistance élastique qui l'entoure. (p. 73)[65]

At the centre of the chapter the reader discovers an instance of sequence A2 which is perceptibly influenced by the above description:

> Sans cesser de fouiller de sa langue la bouche mouillée de nouveau collée à la sienne, l'homme pétrit la boule tiède et gonflée. Il serre et desserre sa main ou frôle de la paume le mamelon élastique. Il s'écarte. Elle enfouit de nouveau sa tête dans son épaule. Sans cesser de la caresser, il regarde la coulée de chair laiteuse aux contours imprécis dans l'obscurité, marquée d'une lune sombre par la large aréole. Il se penche brusquement et l'engloutit de sa bouche. (p. 101)[66]

The description of the woman's uncovered breast is clearly modelled on that of the builder's egg. The association is based on similarity of texture ('mamelon élastique', 'consistance élastique'), of shape (the breast is described as a 'boule tiède et gonflée'), of colour ('chair laiteuse'), and on the fact that the lover devours the woman's breast ('l'engloutit de sa bouche').

In the first half of the novel, therefore, narrative sequence A2 is coloured and shaped by sequences B and C respectively. Although this alternating ascendancy continues throughout the latter half as well, there is also evidence here, albeit sketchy and liable to being overlooked at a first reading, of a retaliatory influence of A2 over the other two sequences. Thus, the structural dominance of C over A2 in 'Leçons de choses' is inverted at the end of the chapter. Now it is sequence C which is momentarily divided in two, and the motivating influence in this case is sequence A2:

> Le verger, le pont avec son amoncellement hérissé ainsi que le chemin se fondent dans l'ombre. Cependant le tracé de celui-ci se divine encore aux taches blanches (journaux, linges?) que l'on distingue dans le crépuscule, éparpillé sur ses bords. Cette fois le sourd fracas de l'éboulement secoue la maison toute entière. Il est encore suivi pendant quelques instants par les bruits des chutes de quelques pierres ou de quelques briques, puis le silence se fait. Les coups de masses ont cessé de retentir. Pendant un moment le silence est complet jusqu'à ce que la voix du jeune maçon se fasse entendre, appelant à l'aide, à l'intérieur de la maison d'abord, puis dehors. (p. 114)[67]

Frame Conflict in Leçon de choses 237

The first two sentences belong to sequence B since they describe the view out of the window of the room occupied by the soldiers. The reference to 'taches blanches', however, heralds the transformation which will take place in sequence C: the collapse of the roof over the builders' heads. One can discern the influence of the two passages I have just quoted in these lines. Apart from the focal delineation of the white patches, the word 'éboulement' echoes the previous use of the word 'boule' to denote the woman's bare breast. It is the articulatory force of language which unites, on a textual basis, the collapse of the house with the moral fall of the adulteress.[68]

The third sentence in this passage switches to sequence C and introduces a new development in the plot. However, this new turn of events remains abortive since the catastrophe is subsequently negated by the description of the builders leaving the house without mishap at the end of a normal day's work. The account of the disintegration of the house can therefore be defined as an off-shoot of sequence C and thus bears some resemblance to sequence A2. Structurally, the impact between the episodes is as follows: sequence C (builder eating egg); sequence A2 (lovers embracing); sequence C2 (house collapsing). This network of relations is strikingly re-affirmed in the 'mise en abyme' description of the boiled egg at the start of the third main chapter, 'La Charge de Reichschoffen':

Le jeune maçon frappe à petits coups la coquille d'un oeuf dur contre un angle de la plus haute des briques qu'il a empilées en guise de table. Ses mouvements s'accompagnent d'un faible bruit de calcaire écrasé. (p. 135)[69]

Already one can see that the writing associates the eating of the egg with the crumbling of the house. Apart from the suggestion of structural disintegration evoked by the cracking of the eggshell, the passage also makes an oblique allusion to the erotic scene through the sexual metaphor in the reference to the global surface of the egg as a 'microcosme ovulaire'. On a different, yet concurrent level of significance, the description of the egg, whose convex screen reflects in miniature the surrounding universe, serves as a metatextual 'mise en abyme' of the novel's macrocosmic structure. When the shiny dome of the egg is bitten off, the opaque substance of the halved yolk appears to consist of the dense compression of all the images penetrating through the external surface, 'comme si la totalité des images attirées et pénétrant par la surface luisante venaient pour ainsi dire se précipiter, se concasser dans un noyau serré, à la fois commencement et fin' (pp. 136–7).[70] In terms of the fiction as a whole, the dilapidated house itself is the 'microcosme ovulaire', the central forum where the different strands of narrative converge. Moreover, the description of the egg is immediately followed by a striking example of frame transgression in which the two lovers are no longer making love by the edge of the wood, but in the same room which the builders have been decorating: 'Il cherche à la renverser sur le côté. Les tréteaux de l'échaffaudage grincent à chacun de leurs mouvements' (p. 137).[71]

In 'La Charge de Reichschoffen', sequence A2 now retaliates against sequence B and induces an embryonic variant which I shall name sequence B2. It consists of a re-description of the first instance of sequence B1, narrating the fall of bombshells over the soldiers' heads. It might be argued that B2 provides a retrospective explanation of the 'original version' of the war sequence since it is the gunner's impulsive action of firing at the German 'side-car' which provokes the retaliatory shelling. But the main difference between the two narrative segments is that in B1 it is the sergeant who enters the room to castigate the soldier while in B2 it is the lieutenant who enters. Moreover, while sequence B1 exerts a textual influence over A2, it is the latter which, as is revealed in the following passage, dominates sequence B2. Their lovemaking at an end, the adulteress is horrified at the thought of becoming pregnant:

> Les sanglots l'étouffent. Il lui tapote gauchement l'épaule, porte à sa bouche le mince cigare qu'il tient entre deux doigts, se ravise et l'éloigne de ses lèvres sans l'allumer [. . .] Elle dit vous m'aviez promis vous m'aviez promis que vous feriez attention. Il dit allons. Elle laisse retomber sa jupe. Elle tient le morceau de tissu trempé et gluant roulé en boule de sa main. Elle a une geste comme pour le jeter puis se ravise [. . .] On n'entend que les faibles bruits de sanglots qui s'échappent de la gorge du pourvoyeur, comme des cris de souris ou un rat qui couine. Le tireur continue à aspirer de lentes bouffées de son cigare dont chaque fois la faible lueur croissant et décroissant extrait de l'ombre son visage qui se fond de nouveau dans l'obscurité. Brusquement, sans qu'aucun bruit ni aucun mouvement visible l'ait annoncé, le chuintement rapide d'une fusée tirée de derrière

Frame Conflict in Leçon de choses 239

ou de l'intérieur du petit bois déchire le silence. Le bruit soyeux de l'air froissé s'intensifie et décroit rapidement tandis que le sillage d'étincelles s'élève en ondulant dans le ciel noir. Arrivée très haut, en bout de course, la tête de la fusée éclate, éparpillant autour d'elle une pluie de brandons. (p. 169)[72]

The description of the war episode is here textually overshadowed by the description of the scene of coition. To begin with, the crash of shell-fire hitting the soldiers' refuge is textually precipitated by the connotations of architectural disintegration in the word 'boule' (linking back to the 'éboulement' in sequence C) which refers to the piece of linen rolled into a ball by the adulteress. Furthermore, the loader's sobs echo those of the woman; the gunner's cigar recalls that of the adulterer; the sound of the airborne shells tearing the silence, 'le bruit soyeux de l'air froissé', is overlaid by the earlier reference to the 'bruit de soie déchirée' in A2 (p. 140); the word 'chuintement' has also already been used to denote the woman's gasps of pleasure while making love; and finally, the description of the explosion in the last sentence strongly resembles that of an amplified ejaculation.

However, the embryonic variant of the war sequence is short-lived. Indeed both B2 and C2 are no more than faint sketches to be filled out by the reader himself. They bear witness to the text's intrinsic incompleteness and are palpable proof of the process of infinite generation announced in 'Générique': 'La description (la composition) peut se continuer (ou être complétée) à peu près indéfiniment . . .' (p. 10)[73]

In brief, it is the elaboration of sequence A2 which occupies the centre stage of the drama of narrative conflict in *Leçon de choses*. As I have shown, this three-sided duel is acted out on two simultaneous levels: that of narrative encapsulation and that of descriptive infiltration. The parallelism and interchange between these two methods of textual control are most evident in the compositional variations surrounding the 'plaque de fonte'. The fire-guard is first described in a segment of sequence B: the 'pourvoyeur' examines it for a moment and asks the 'tireur' the meaning of the word 'FRÜ-LING' which is inscribed on it. In contrast, the narrative segment is immediately preceded and followed by segments of sequence C. Furthermore, the reference to the 'caisse de la dernière couvée éclose dont les poussins échappés s'égaillent sur le carrelage' (p. 87)[74] in the scene engraved on the fire-guard recalls the earlier reference to the egg which the builder eats for his lunch. At its second appearance, near the end of the novel, the fireguard's contextual framing and descriptive influence are reversed. The description is now set in sequence C (pp. 160–2); it is flanked by segments of sequence B; and through an emphasis on blackness and a pun in 'pétales *bombés*', it is overshadowed by the war sequence. Moreover, some of the figurative components of the engraving are drawn from the cigar box description (for instance, the repetition of 'balustrade', 'terrasse', 'baldaquin'). In mirroring the cigar box it inherits the association already established between the 'cavalier' on the cigar box and the unscrupulous lover. The dazzling effect of multiple refraction can be observed by comparing the following two sentences:

> Son *bassin* avance et recule en même temps qu'il est animé d'un mouvement de bas en haut, à la façon d'un *cavalier* se laissant aller souplement sur sa selle pour accompagner la houle d'un cheval au galop. (p. 155) [my emphasis][75]
>
> A gauche, la balustrade s'interrompt et on peut voir à l'arrière-plan les côtés d'un rectangle en perspective *cavalière*, un *bassin* sans doute dans le parc qui s'étend au-delà. (p. 161) [my emphasis][76]

The overlap is produced through an interplay of two 'mises en abyme'. The description of the fire-guard connects with the narrative of the adulterous lovers through the intermediary evocation of the cigar box description ('cavalière', 'balustrade'). What lies beyond the bounds of this self-enclosed space is the isometric projection of the text's continuation in the unwritten pages of the reader's mind.

IV FROMENTIN AND THE VIEW FROM THE LIGHT-HOUSE

In a sense, too, part of what lies beyond or behind *Leçon de choses* is the intertextual background against which it is set and against which it is opposed. As I have continually argued, much can be gained by reading Simon's 'oeuvre' in the light of earlier literature and this is equally true in the case of *Leçon de choses*.

Eugène Fromentin's *Dominique* is a work which is heavily

Frame Conflict in Leçon de choses   241

imbued with the cult of the land; both in the sense of land ownership, proprietorial security and feudal dominance, and in the sense of a spiritual attachment to nature in its most permanent and quiescent shape. 'J'ai le goût et la science de la terre', the novel's eponymous hero informs the anonymous narrator.[77] At the same time, however, the depiction of nature in this novel is essentially subjective and takes the form of an outward projection of the individual's inner self. Early in the novel, the narrator's account of the countryside surrounding Dominique's home, Trembles, draws a close analogy between geographical and human features: 'Et puis dans ce contraste du mouvement des vagues de bateaux qui passent et de maisons qui demeurent, de la vie aventureuse et de la vie fixée, il y avait une intime analogie dont il devait être frappé plus que tout autre'.[78] Despite the suggestion of 'une intime analogie' what distinguishes this perspective from the Elstirian one in Proust's *A la recherche du temps perdu* is that the divisions between land and sea, immobility and movement are not transgressed by metaphor nor indeed by specular interpenetration. The sharply defined frontier in Fromentin's topography contrasts with the absence of a 'ligne de démarcation' in Elstir's paintings, and with the metaphorical transgressions created by the depiction of the sea in terms of the land and vice versa. Moreover, Elstir's work is composed in a perspective which is imposingly discontinuous and where, in one painting, the intermittent appearance of a road which, despite being truncated by the interposition of land and sea constitutes the only source of appeasement for the spectator's culturally induced need for continuity.

While influenced by *Dominique* (particularly as regards the thematic association between memory and physical data), Proust draws an implicit analogy between his view of Fromentin and the decline of Bergotte. The latter is overtaken by the irrepressible arrival of new writers on the literary scene, writers who are like 'oculists' adjusting the reader's eye to a new perspective of the external world. Bergotte is outdated mainly on account of the limpidity of his depiction of objects: 'Toutes choses s'y voyaient aisément, sinon telles qu'on les avait toujours vues, du moins telles qu'on avait l'habitude de les voir maintenant'.[79] So too with Fromentin: 'Il y eut un temps où on reconnaissait bien les choses quand c'était Fromentin qui les peignait et où on ne les reconnaissait plus quand c'était Renoir'.[80] But now, the narrator continues, people are forever encountering Renoir women, Renoir carriages,

Renoir waters and so on. Art, therefore, plays a crucial role in dictating our perception of the physical world which in turn divests obsolete forms of art of their vividness and representational value.[81]

If Fromentin the painter is superseded by Renoir, then Fromentin the author is also outstripped by Proust and, at a later stage, by Claude Simon. Not that the latter would wholeheartedly approve of the Proustian metaphor of scientific progress in art, which can all too easily lead one to envisage it as a kind of literary relay race. However, the weakness in *Dominique* lies primarily in the fact that the limpidity of its depiction of the natural world is an idealist, mimetic limpidity which mirrors the 'psychological' make-up of the self-analytical hero. It is a mirror with a message, or as Barthes said, 'une leçon morale, "leçon de sagesse": le repos est l'un des rares bonheurs possibles'.[82] The dichotomy between the terrestrial calm of spiritual retreat and the turbulent sea of passion is embodied in the symbolic and complementary personalities of Augustin and Olivier; the one preaching the virtues of social and material success, the other stating that to kill 'l'ennui' would constitute the epitome of heroism. Although the reclusive, spectator-like attitude to life is condemned by Augustin as dangerously flirting with a suicidal form of narcissism, Dominique admits that his final decision to lead a life of retreat and tranquil seclusion is in key with the teachings of his former tutor:

> j'ai suivi très tard, avec moins de mérite, moins de courage, avec autant de bonheur, l'exemple que ce coeur solide m'avait donné presque au début de sa vie. Il avait commencé par le repos dans des affections sans trouble, et j'ai fini par là.[83]

As Barthes says, this novel is founded on the bourgeois ideology of conformism, an ideology which is conveyed not only as a thematic constant but also by the structural inviolability of its narrative discourse. The perceiving subject remains firmly intact, protected from the swell of visual and mental impressions beating against its shore. In 'Le *Confiteor* de l'artiste' Baudelaire who, like Proust and Barthes, had mixed feelings about Fromentin's confessional novel admits to a dispersal of the subject in the contemplation of the azure mirror of the infinite: 'toutes ces choses pensent par moi, ou je pense par elles (car dans la grandeur de la rêverie, le *moi* se perd vite!)'.[84] Memory too leaves Dominique undisturbed by any sense of involuntary and unexpected association, unlike its effect on the narrator of *A la recherche du temps perdu*. The past is held in check; buried under the cyclical regularity and predictability of seasonal changes and of 'cette bonne prose de l'agriculture'.[85] All signs of seismic eruption are reassuringly confined to the tame flutterings of birds (Dominique's predilection for game shooting can be read in the context of his description of Olivier as a caged bird which had learnt to fly about in its prison as if it were in the open air), and also to 'Trembles', the muted, dormant tremors in a name.

But it is the climactic scene of the view from the light-house which best illustrates the self-conscious depiction of a 'psychological' frame, and the need to resist transgression. Having scaled the spiral staircase to the top of the light-house, Dominique, Madeleine, Olivier and Julie lean against the perilously fragile balustrade protecting them from the abyss below, from the stormy fusion of sea and sky:

> Il fallait y regarder attentivement pour comprendre où se terminait la mer, où le ciel commençait, tant la limite était douteuse, tant l'un et l'autre avaient la même paleur incertaine, la même palpitation orageuse et le même infini. Je ne puis vous dire à quel point ce spectacle de l'immensité répétée deux fois, et par conséquent double d'étendue, aussi haute qu'elle était profonde, devenait extraordinaire, vu de la plate-forme du phare, et de quelle émotion commune il nous saisit.[86]

Dominique and his friends stand at the edge of their world, on the brink of submitting to the chaos of transgression and osmosis. They are overwhelmed at the sight of this cataclysmic vision of the infinite, of a region where language takes off, leaving behind the 'terra firma' of reason, restraint and order. But the moment passes; it is blotted out, stored away in the obscure and silent graveyard of oblivion.

The broad aim of this book has been to situate Claude Simon's 'oeuvre' on the other side of this artistic and ideological barrier. Simon's narrators are plunged into the chaos of the 'foisonnement désordonné' of experience, of which war is but one highly dramatised manifestation. The perceiving subject is placed at the centre of the storm. George Orwell's description in *Homage to Catalonia* of his sensations on being struck in the neck by a bullet is that of being 'at the centre of an explosion'. The same is true of Simon's narrators around whom the scattered fragments of the phenomenal world fly in all directions. In *Leçon de choses*, where narratorial identity and continuity are irrevocably banished, the repercussions of this explosion are still felt in the compositional implications of the collapse of the farmhouse, the central locus of narrative convergence.

The aesthetic worlds of Claude Simon and Eugène Fromentin are direct antipodes of one another. In *Leçon de choses*, the dichotomy between movement and stasis portrayed in *Dominique* is from the very start reconciled in the description of the Monet seascape. This 'image de l'immobile tempête' is situated at the very heart of the novel: fictionally located in the *interior* of the house; and serving, as I have shown, as a textual matrix from which the multiple chains of association evolve. Similarly the sexual reticence between Dominique and Madeleine is swept aside in the unabashed vividness of the turbulent scene of coition in sequence A2. But the polar opposition between these two novels emerges most clearly if one compares the light-house scene in *Dominique* with the final pages of *Leçon de choses*. With Simon's novel the metaphor of the light-house as a platform affording momentary glimpses of the infinite is modified by the reference to a beacon located on the horizon transmitting its light from the very eye of the 'storm': 'Soudain, au fond de l'horizon où le ciel ne se sépare plus maintenant de la mer, scintille sur la gauche la brève lueur d'un phare' whose rhythmic flash seems to mark 'l'instant, la seconde précise de la séparation du jour et de la nuit' (p. 171).[87]

The focus on the division between day and night mirrors the recurrent motif in the novel of the opposition and conjunction between black and white; a motif which is embodied in the sexual intercourse described in sequence A2 and summarised by the 'plaques blanches et noires aux contours sinueux et imbriqués'[88] of the cow which looms over the scene like an impassive spectator. In contrast with the connotations of whiteness connected with the adulteress ('cou blanc', 'chair laiteuse'), the dominant visual feature in the appearance of her lover and their nocturnal meeting place is one of blackness:

Les voix noires des petites grenouilles se font assourdissantes [. . .] Tout est noir. Au-dessus d'elle elle ne voit plus que son visage sans forme, noir. L'odeur noire du cigare est plus forte que celle des prés humides. (p. 100)[89]

The synaesthesia in 'voix noires' and 'odeur noire' is symptomatic of a general fusion of opposites throughout the novel, including the earlier suggestion of synthesis between light and darkness in a reference to the visual paradox printed on the lid of the cigar box: 'Le mot CLARO est peint au pochoir, de biais et à l'encre noire' (p. 33).[90] As the frequent allusions to typography indicate throughout the course of the novel, it is writing which articulates the different sets of fictional and semantic opposites. In this light the erotic episode as a whole can be read as an allegory of the transient combination of black and white, writing and page: 'à l'intérieur de la chair obscure le long membre raidi se tend encore lâchant de longues giclées de sperme noir' (p. 163).[91]

The chiaroscuro motif also gives rise to a further twist of meaning through the spiral of textual association. Light, is personified by the adulteress whose name, 'Estelle', is revealed, along with several alternatives, after the reference to the light blinking on the horizon like 'quelque signal venu d'étoiles, d'astres lointains'[92] marking the imperceptible interstice between day and night. In consequence, Estelle might be seen to represent the evanescent illumination of fiction and the imagination which is aroused by the 'magie lumineuse' of language and which briefly inhabits the black expanse of nullity and extinction. In this optic too the callous adulterer might be interpreted as an impersonal, ironic version of Simon's earlier narrators for whom sexual intercourse seemed to offer a means of penetrating an elusive realm, and thereby provides a sensual analogue, or simulation, of the transgressive impulse of creation.[93]

Conclusion

Modern writing focuses on the seams and sutures of literary invention. It recognises that fiction is not a house with open windows but a linguistic fabrication conforming to a given set of literary and ideological conventions. The bricks and mortar of all narrative fiction are language and perspective. Reading the 'nouveau roman' one is made aware of the fact that 'realism', at least the traditional brand of 'realism' which, in literature, has produced novels 'containing' rounded characters, a continuous plot and psychological insight, is in essence a figurative embodiment of the Aristotelian ideal of unity. By seeking roundedness, continuity and insight, realism relies heavily on the formal restrictions imposed by the laws of unity and homogeneity in art. 'L'effet de réel', to quote Barthes, is doubly deceitful since it glosses over both the polysemic 'realities' of the language and formal properties upon which it is built and, by overlooking the infinite, the incomplete, the equivocal, it misrepresents that very 'reality' which it claims to reproduce.

However, the poetics of modernity ought to be viewed less as an alternative to the realist ideal of unity than as an exploration of the limitations and lacunae present in that code. Claude Simon's work, in this respect, is not governed simply by an eclectic preference for the discontinuous over the uniform; the writer has not chosen between what one critic calls 'une copie vériste de la réalité' and the sculptural transformation of the real as 'un objet brut'.[1] It is the very notion of verisimilitude in fiction which is challenged. Cataloguing the discrepancies which separate a 'real' event from a written text, Simon points to the pluralities and discontinuities stemming from the subjective processes of consciousness, of composition and of language which obtain at every moment of writing:

1. des imperfections de nos facultés de perception; 2. des imper-

fections de notre mémoire; 3. du choix, volontaire ou non de certaines de ses caractéristiques au dépens d'autres qui sont rejetées ou passées sous silence; 4. de la nature même de l'écriture qui se déroule dans une durée, est donc obligée de dire successivement ce qui, bien souvent, est perçu simultanément (d'où l'obligation encore de choisir un certain ordre, lui aussi fatalement arbitraire et subjectif); 5. des nécessités et contraintes formelles de l'écriture (syntaxe, composition, rythme, sons); 6. de la dynamique de celle-ci (nous sommes pour le moins autant conduits par notre langage que nous le conduisons) . . .[2]

The pattern of frame transgression which I have traced in this book must consequently be understood primarily as a creative exploration of those areas of composition which are passed over in silence by mimesis. The commingling of spatio-temporal units in *La Route des Flandres* and *Les Géorgiques*, the fusion of identity in *Le Palace* and *Histoire*, the descriptive confusion in *Les Corps conducteurs*, and the reciprocal interaction between separate narrative sequences in *Triptyque* and *Leçon de choses* are first and foremost signs of the transgressive impulse of modern art and should be recognised as such before one attempts to interpret them in terms of memory or psychology. In addition the critical concept of 'frame' and its cognates provide the reader with the means by which he can relate to the text in question since of all the contours which have lined and divided the fictional world it is the one separating reader from text which is most immediate to him. A similar pattern of transgression, less conspicuous but no less crucial than the dramatic overlaps which occur in the narrative structure of these novels, is repeated by the metaphorical and paronomastic associations which comprise the 'materiality' of the text, or what Ricardou has termed 'le grain du texte'.[3] Here it is linguistic, semantic and contextual contours which are intermittently violated. Moreover, both textuality and intertextuality, whether intrusive or allusive, emerge in these works as primary forces of transgressive articulation. On each of these different levels of structural organisation, Claude Simon's writing probes the limits of creativity to the point of transgression. In doing so the author reveals the intrinsic arbitrariness of all literary convention and explores the largely unmapped territories that lie beyond these formal limits. So it is in this sense that the experience of reading Simon's novels is a profoundly educative one; for the immensely enriching creative opportunities it offers the reader necessarily entail a re-appraisal of the main compositional principles which have governed the production and reception of prose fiction. Indeed, it is by maintaining a constant self-reflexive gaze, by exposing the skeletal joints and articulations underlying its narrative that, as Simon has declared, the modern text reveals to the reader some of the hidden truths concerning fiction:

> Maintenant, si vous me demander de préciser ce qui distingue plus exactement notre modernité [as opposed to that of preceding generations], je hasarderai peut-être, qu'en gros, elle me paraît dominée par deux caractéristiques principales (chacune à y bien réfléchir, découlant d'ailleurs de l'autre) qui sont, d'une part, la fragmentation, l'éclatement des formes; d'autre part, l'abandon du 'trompe-l'oeil', du 'faire-semblant', en profit de la mise en évidence du médium ou, si l'on préfère, du 'matériau', je veux dire le tableau s'offrant comme peinture, le roman se donnant et se dénonçant comme texte et *fiction en procès*.[4]

Notes and References

INTRODUCTION

1. 'transgression does not negate prohibition, but it goes beyond it and completes it.' Bataille, *L'érotisme*.
2. Tzvetan Todorov, *Poétique* (Paris, 1973), p. 25.
3. 'Poetics cannot do without literature in order to discuss its own discourse; and yet it is only by going beyond the specific work that it succeeds in doing so'. Todorov, *Littérature et signification* (Paris, 1967), p. 8.
4. 'The more plural a text is, the less it is written before I read it.' Roland Barthes, *S/Z* (Paris, 1970), p. 16.
5. 'the story requires my collaboration for it to unfold well.' André Gide, *Journal des Faux-Monnayeurs* (Paris, 1927), pp. 30–1.
6. Quoted by Ana María Barrenechea in *Borges the Labyrinth Maker*, edited and translated by Robert Lima (New York, 1965), p. 150.
7. 'and this present which endlessly invents itself with the flow of the writing, which repeats, splits, changes, contradicts, without ever piling up to constitute a past – so a story in the traditional sense of the word – all this can only encourage the reader (or the spectator) to participate in a different way to that which he was accustomed to.' Alain Robbe-Grillet, *Pour un nouveau roman* (Paris, 1963) pp. 133–4.
8. 'The writer *says* the word and objects (or rather *a* world and *some* objects): he does not explain them. The culmination of his work is essentially a questioning. It is up to the reader to carry out that other task which is reading. He is part of the process (what would a book be without a reader?) There is no object without a subject.' Claude Simon, 'Le Poids des mots', *Le Figaro littéraire*, 1559, (3 avril 1976), 13.
9. 'As first reader, the writer treats his own work as he does someone else's. His activity will reflect itself as in a mirror.' Michel Butor, *Répertoire III* (Paris, 1968), p. 17.
10. Claude Simon, *Le Vent* (Paris, 1957), p. 175.
11. 'And then I was there again, dragged along in spite of myself, as if by the drowned man [. . .], pulled along myself as well behind him, placed within the perspective of that time span which stretched out like a grey wall with neither beginning nor end, decrepit, with its old torn posters whose shreds flapped with the

wind, their washed out lettering, their fragments of texts which also had neither beginning nor end, disjointed, side by side, contradicting each other [.]' Ibid., p. 149.
12. Barrenechea, *Borges the Labyrinth Maker*, p. 150.
13. Roland Barthes, *Le Degré zéro de l'écriture suivi de Nouveaux essais critiques* (Paris, 1972), p. 145.
14. 'It is for example after *La Bataille de Pharsale* that he elaborated his theory of generators. As for me (and I also said this at Cerisy), I am in total agreement with the diagram by which he shows the constant overlapping, the constant and mutual engendering of theory by practice and of practice by theory, with the one difference that I would replace the latter word with *reflection*.' Claude Simon, 'Un homme traversé par le travail', *La Nouvelle critique*, 105 (juin–juillet 1977), 33.

PART ONE: FRAME

1 WHAT IS FRAME?

1. 'voice behind voice, empty intervals pounding the voice, voice resembling voices in the accents of their traces, tabula rasa and cylinder, wheel and infinity of volume flattened out, out of the frame, of all the frame-sequences, fantasy frames, frontally framed for the screen of some unknown cinema.' Sollers, *Paradis*.
2. The concept is becoming increasingly important in the fields of linguistics, psychology, and computer science. See, for example, *Frame Conceptions and Text Understanding*, edited by Dieter Metzing (New York, 1980).
3. Erving Goffman, *Frame Analysis* (Harmondsworth, 1974), pp. 10–11.
4. Iouri Lotman, *La Structure du texte artistique*, traduit du russe par Anne Bernard Kreise, Eve Malleret et Joelle Yong, sous la direction d'Henri Meschonnic (Paris, 1973), p. 299.
5. 'that is why the spectator could see the spectators on the stage, but did not notice them'. Ibid.
6. Ibid., p. 302.
7. Quoted by Robbe-Grillet at the 1971 Cerisy Colloquium. See *Nouveau roman: hier, aujourd'hui*, 2 vols (Paris, 1972), II, 280. Boris Uspensky makes a similar observation: 'Here we might refer to G. K. Chesterton's remark that a landscape without a frame means almost nothing, but that it only requires the addition of some border (a frame, a window, an arch) to be perceived as a representation. In order to perceive the work of art as a sign system, it is necessary (although not always sufficient) to designate its borders: it is precisely these borders which create the representation. In many languages the meaning of the word "represent" is etymologically related to the meaning of the word "limit".' *A Poetics of Composition* (London, 1973), p. 140.

8. Leon Battista Alberti, *On Painting and On Sculpture*, edited with translations, introduction and notes by Cecil Grayson (London, 1972), p. 83.
9. Uspensky, *A Poetics of Composition*, p. 143.
10. Ibid.
11. Ibid., p. 145.
12. Ibid., p. 156.
13. See Lotman, *La Structure du texte artistique*, p. 303, and Uspensky, *A Poetics of Composition*, p. 146.
14. Uspensky, *A Poetics of Composition*, p. 146.
15. It is interesting to note the different reactions of the 'real' editors of *Adolphe* to the 'external frame' of that novel. Thus, for example, Gustave Rudler, editing the 1919 Manchester University Press edition, chose to place the title after the 'Avis de l'éditeur' implying that the latter does not constitute an integral part of Constant's novel. An even more drastic step was taken by the editor of the 1936 Librairie Grund (Paris) edition of the novel which contains Adolphe's narrative only, the 'Avis de l'éditeur', 'Lettre à l'éditeur' and 'Réponse' being inexplicably suppressed.
16. Stanley Fish, 'How Ordinary is Ordinary Language?' *New Literary History*, v (1973), 52, quoted by David Lodge in *The Modes of Modern Writing* (London, 1976), p. 161.
17. Jonathan Culler, *Structuralist Poetics* (London, 1975), p. 161.
18. B. S. Johnson, *Travelling People* (Letchworth, 1963), p. 11.
19. 'The force of this use of the imperfect tense lies in expressing the link between the outside and the inside, in placing on the same level, by employing the same tense, the exterior and the interior, reality as it unfolds in the world of objects.' Albert Thibaudet, *Gustave Flaubert* (Paris, 1935), pp. 246-7.
20. Uspensky, *A Poetics of Composition*, pp. 159-60.
21. Martin Battersby has compiled an impressive list of examples which illustrate the wide array of 'trompe l'oeil' works of art in *Trompe l'Oeil: Thy Eye Deceived* (London, 1974).
22. Uspensky, *A Poetics of Composition*, p. 139.
23. 'The novel genre has never known that "formidable erosion of contours" of which Nietzsche speaks.' Gide, *Les Faux-Monnayeurs*.
24. Jorge-Luis Borges, *A Universal History of Infamy*, translated by Norman Thomas di Giovanni (Harmondsworth, 1975), p. 119.
25. 'that distance between the place of reading and the one which the narrative leads us to.' Michel Butor, *Essais sur le roman* (Paris, 1972), p. 50. Similarly, in Julio Cortázar's *Hopscotch*, the reader is referred to as a 'travelling companion' who accompanies the author on a journey of discovery and exploration.
26. Leonardo da Vinci, *Treatise on Painting*, translated and annotated by A. Philip McMahon (New Jersey, 1956), pp. 20-1.
27. 'every object merges at its shaded edges with its neighbour.' Emile Bernard, *Souvenirs sur Paul Cézanne* (Paris, 1912), p. 34.
28. 'the character then becomes like a microcosm which lives indepen-

dently, setting its own existence against that of the world.' Liliane Brion-Guerry, *Cézanne et l'expression de l'espace* (Paris, 1966), p. 181.
29. 'The deliberate ambiguity of the contour suggests mobility: the object does not fit squarely within a restrictive boundary, it either falls short or overspills it depending on whether the play of light produces contraction or expansion, and this alternation becomes a kind of breathing which stirs the air into movement.' Ibid., p. 238.
30. 'And certainly the aim of those descriptions is to make one see and they succeed. Most of the time it was a case of erecting a décor, of defining the frame of the action, of presenting the physical appearance of its protagonists.' Alain Robbe-Grillet, *Pour un nouveau roman* (Paris, 1963), p. 125.
31. 'it was only a frame, which in any case conveyed the same meaning as the painting which it was going to contain.' Ibid., p. 126.
32. 'Placing his easel or camera somewhere within the space he evokes, the novelist will encounter the same problems of framing, composition and perspective as does a painter.' Michel Butor, *Essais sur le roman* (Paris, 1972), p. 53.
33. Maurice Merleau-Ponty, *Themes from the Lectures at the Collège de France, 1952–60*, translated by John O'Neill (Evanston, 1970), p. 4.
34. 'In *La Bataille de Pharsale*, I referred to the criticism formulated by Elie Faure when he talks about the German painters of the Renaissance whom he reproaches precisely for this absence of values, in other words granting as much attention to the drawing of a blade of grass, a pebble or a halberd as to that of a body in movement or of the figures of Faith or Hope . . . And indeed this painting is radically opposed to the Italian invention of chiaroscuro (Rembrandt also . . .) where all the light (and attention) are concentrated on one or a few characters surrounded by large patches of shadow [. . .] On the contrary, in this mode of German painting (and Breughel – I'm thinking of 'The Carrying of the Cross' or 'The Road to Damascus' where one must search hard for a minuscule Christ or Saint Paul, lost in the midst of a crowd of other characters and an immense landscape), the focus is spread equally over the entire surface of the canvas: no longer are we presented with man at the centre of the universe but man forming part of.' Claude Simon, 'Un homme traverse par le travail', interview in *La Nouvelle critique*, 105 (juin–juillet 1977), 32.

Dubuffet similarly affirms that the focus of his work has been those areas of representational and topographical space which culture has hitherto neglected or treated as anonymous background: 'Ces travaux font surtout apparaître des êtres (on pourrait dire aussi bien des objets, ou des figures) là où la culture n'en voit que fonds indifférenciés. Ils tendent même à suggérer que ces fonds prétendument indifférenciés sont innombrablement peuplés de figures – ou du moins de mouvements (s'agissant, indifféremment mêlés, aussi bien de phénomènes provoquant la pensée que de projections de celle-ci provoquant l'apparition pour elle de phénomènes) qui sont tout aussi susceptibles d'être regardés comme êtres

(ou objets, ou figures) que ceux dont la culture propose son restreint registre.'
[Above all these works evoke beings (one could also say objects, or figures) in places where traditional culture only sees undifferentiated background. They even tend to suggest that this background which is supposedly undifferentiated is peopled with innumerable figures – or at least movements (consisting of a haphazard mixture of thought-provoking phenomena as projections of the latter eliciting the appearance of phenomena) which one can just as easily see as beings (or objects, or figures) as those which are recorded within the limited scope of official culture.] *L'Homme du commun à l'ouvrage* (Paris, 1973), p. 445.

35. Patrick Heron, 'The Shape of Colour' in *Concerning Contemporary Art*, edited by Bernard Smith (Oxford, 1975), p. 172.
36. Claude Simon, interview with Claud Duverlie, in *Sub-Stance*, 8 (March 1974), 9.

2 THE FRAMEWORK OF *LA ROUTE DES FLANDRES*

1. 'the twisting road, the road on which you can feel the stones with your feet, the road which turns back, that's the road of art. Word encounters word, word feels word, as cheek touches cheek. Words break up, and instead of a distinct whole – a word pronounced automatically, thrown out like a bar of chocolate in a vending-machine – a word-sound, an articulatory word-movement is born.' Chklovski.
2. 'This narrative which makes no distinctions, does not distinguish, as it were, within itself. It is not really situated. It has not one focal point, but several, and seems to combine at least three different discourses: one which takes place during the exodus, one which dates from captivity, a third which occurs after the war. Hence the reader's disorientation; we fail to reconstruct the story, not only because we are offered more interpretations of facts than facts themselves, but also because there is no fixed point around which these different perspectives can be ordered.' Bernard Pingaud, 'Sur *La Route des Flandres*', *Les Temps Modernes*, 178 (February 1961) 1030.
3. Uspensky, *A Poetics of Composition*, pp. 151–5.
4. Pingaud, 'Sur *La Route des Flandres*', 1027.
5. The term was coined by Dominique Lanceraux in 'Modalités de la narration dans *La Route des Flandres*', *Poétique*, 14 (1973).
6. 'He was holding a letter in his hand, he raised his eyes looked at me then again the letter then me again, behind him I could see passing to and fro the red mahogany ochre patches of the horses which were led to the trough, the mud was so deep that one sank into it up to the ankles but I remember that during the night it had suddenly turned freezing [.]' *La Route des Flandres*, p. 9.
7. ' "Yeah!" said Blum (we were now lying in the dark that is locked together piled up to the extent of not being able to move an arm

or leg without meeting or rather without asking the permission of another arm or leg [.]' Ibid., p. 20.
8. 'And that must have been where I saw it for the first time, a little before or after the place where we stopped to drink, discovering it, staring at it through that sort of half-sleep, that sort of brown mud in which I was steeped so to speak and perhaps because we had to make a detour to avoid it, and more imagining it than seeing it: in other words (like everything else which lined the edge of the road: lorries, cars, suitcases, corpses) something unusual, unreal, hybrid in the sense that what had been a horse (that is to say what one knew, what one could recognize, identify as having been a horse) was now no more than a vague heap of limbs, of hoofs of hide and matted hairs, three quarters covered with mud – Georges wondering without exactly wondering [.]' Ibid., pp. 26–7.
9. 'he was not asleep, was standing perfectly still and not in a barn now, not the heavy and dusty smell of dried hay, of summer past, but that impalpable nostalgic and persistent fragrance of time itself, of years gone by and he floating in the darkness, listening to the silence, the night, the peacefulness, the imperceptible breathing of a woman beside him and after a while he made out the second rectangle drawn by the wardrobe mirror reflecting the dark light of the window [.]' Ibid., pp. 42–3.
10. 'a little dumbfounded, impatient, as if in a living-room someone had suddenly spoken to him without having been introduced or interrupted in mid-sentence [.]' Ibid., p. 18.
11. 'doubtless thinking that one inevitably always finds everywhere and in all circumstances – in the salons or at war – stupid people and with no education, and that done – in other words remembered – forgetting the interrupter, effacing him no longer seeing him even before looking away [.]' Ibid., pp. 18–19.
12. 'And I felt as though I were there, seeing all that the green shades' Ibid., p. 19.
13. 'he saw it spin round below him as though it were placed on a turntable'. Ibid.
14. Lanceraux, 'Modalités de la narration dans *La Route des Flandres*', *Poétique*, 14 (1973) 241.
15. 'the mouth also grey' . . . 'that colourless, spongy and uniformly grey substance'. *La Route des Flandres*, p. 40.
16. 'as though her skin was itself the source of light' . . . 'like a spot on a blind eye'. Ibid., pp. 39, 41.
17. 'summarily moulded in soft clay two thighs a stomach two breasts the round column of the neck and in the depth of the folds like at the centre of those primitive statues with animal names, out of natural history – mussel octopus pulp vulva – making one think of those marine and carnivorous organisms which are blind bereft of lips and eyelashes [.]' Ibid., pp. 41–2.
18. 'as if she were made of a substance resembling that of sponges, but with an invisible grain, dilating and contracting, like those flowers, those marine things half vegetable half animal, those madrepores [.]' Ibid., p. 236.

19. 'but that totally different story which is the singular adventure of the narrator endlessly searching, discovering the world by groping his way in and through writing'. Simon, *Orion aveugle* (Geneva, 1970), p. 15.
20. Stephen Heath, *The Nouveau Roman* (London, 1972), p. 154.
21. Karen L. Gould, *Claude Simon's Mythic Muse* (Columbia, 1979), pp. 46–50.
22. 'and Georges (unless it was still Blum, interrupting himself, clowning around, unless he (Georges) was not in the process of conversing under the cold saxon rain with a little sickly Jew – or the shadow of a little Jew, and who was soon going to be no more than a corpse – yet one more – of a little Jew – but with himself, that is his double, all alone under the grey rain, amidst the tracks, the coal wagons, or perhaps years later, still alone (although he was now lying beside a woman's warm flesh), still alone together with his double, or with Blum, or with no-one): 'Now we're there: History [.].' *La Route des Flandres*, p. 187.
23. 'Hic liber – the huge and emphatic H in the form of two brackets set back to back and linked together by a wavy line, the ends of the brackets rolling up in a spiral like the motifs on those railings gnawed with rust which still guard park entrances [.]' Ibid., p. 83.
24. 'the knot and joint where the human part ends with the horse part is certainly admirable the eye distinguishes the delicateness of the woman's white complexion from the clearness of the horse's bright coat of a clear bay but one then confuses them when trying to determine the Outlines [.]' Ibid., pp. 55–6.
25. 'that kind of fringe which runs to the left and to the right of our vision.' . . . 'in the form of blobs, vague contours'. Ibid., p. 250.
26. 'the contours changing in a continuous fashion, in other words that kind of simultaneous destruction and reconstruction of line and volume (the protrusions gradually fading out while other features seem to emerge, stand out, then fade away and disappear in their turn) as the angle of vision shifts [.]' Ibid., p. 29.
27. 'and no doubt because of my drunken state, impossible to be visually aware of anything other than that the mirror and what was reflected in it onto which my gaze clung so to speak as a drunkard clings to a lamp-post as if it were the only fixed point in a hazy universe [.]' Ibid., p. 27.
28. 'this time I could see thanks to the mirror in the doorway the bottom of the woman's skirt her two calves and her two feet shod with slippers everything leaning back as if she were falling backwards [.]' Ibid., p. 207.
29. 'she not yet having crossed the threshold'. Ibid., p. 86.
30. 'her silhouette outlined for a moment in dark so long as she was in the half-light of the barn, then, as soon as the threshold was crossed, appearing to vanish [.]' Ibid., p. 39.
31. 'as if they had penetrated [. . .] a kind of organic, visceral space.' . . . 'that kind of womb-like warmth so to speak at the heart of which she stood'. Ibid., p. 38–9.

32. 'the orifice of that matrix the primeval crucible which he seemed to be seeing in the entrails of the world' . . . 'multiplying swarming spreading over the surface of the earth'. Ibid., p. 42.
33. 'she seems to be waiting for an act of precision and of nudity if not quite surgical as is suggested by the idea of something which pierces, penetrates, tears open the narrow flesh with a rustling sound, at least almost medical [.]' Ibid., p. 192.
34. Karen Gould, *Claude Simon's Mythic Muse*, pp. 46–50.
35. Plato, *Dialogues*, translated by B. Jowett (Oxford, 1924) 5 vols, III 449.
36. Ibid., III 470.
37. The phrase is borrowed from Ann Jefferson's perceptive analysis of Robbe-Grillet's *Les Gommes* in *The Nouveau Roman and the Poetics of Fiction* (Cambridge, 1980), pp. 18–30.
38. 'what had I searched for in her hoped pursued even on her body in her body words sounds as mad as he was with his illusory pieces of blackened paper scrawls words which our lips pronounced to abuse ourselves with living a life of sounds with no more reality no more substance than that curtain on which we thought we could see the embroidered peacock move palpitate breathe [.]' *La Route des Flandres*, pp. 274–5.
39. 'the disappearance of all ideas of all concepts.' Ibid., p. 299.
40. 'It was not to his father that he wanted to speak. It wasn't to the woman lying invisibly next to him, perhaps it wasn't even to Blum that he was now explaining in whispers in the blackness [.]' Ibid., p. 100.
41. 'But had I really seen it or thought I'd seen it or merely imagined it afterwards or still dreamt it, perhaps I was sleeping had never stopped sleeping with my eyes wide open'. Ibid., p. 314.
42. 'the sporadic canon fire striking the deserted orchards with a deafening monumental and hollow sound like a door banging blown by the wind in an empty house [.]' Ibid.
43. 'birds of the forest' . . . 'they sing, they enchant nature, and no-one must see them.' Honoré de Balzac, *La Comédie humaine* (Paris, 1952), 11 Vols, IV 630.
44. 'When this cohesion of souls is missing, the poet becomes like an angel trying to sing a celestial hymn in the midst of the guffaws of hell.' Ibid., IV 538.
45. 'Yesterday evening I was walking alone [. . .] I was drawn away from my thoughts by the warbling of a thrush perched on the highest branch of a silver birch. At that very moment, this magic sound conjured up for me my father's estate; I forgot the catastrophes I had just witnessed and, suddenly transported into the past, I saw again that countryside where I so often heard the thrush whistle.' René de Chateaubriand, *Oeuvres Completes* (Paris 1904), Kraus reprint 1975, 18 vols, XIII 125.
46. 'I would wonder what the time was; I could hear the whistle of trains which, more or less far off, like the song of a bird in a forest spanning the distance, conjures up for me the stretch of deserted

countryside where the traveller hastens towards the next station.' Marcel Proust, *A la recherche du temps perdu*, 3 vols (Paris, 1954), I 3.
47. 'the riders' wandering is paralleled by that of the reader, those who are lost on the Flanders road imitate those who risk going astray in *La Route des Flandres*, victims both of a confused feeling of having already seen or read what they encounter.' Stuart Sykes, *Les Romans de Claude Simon* (Paris, 1979), p. 64.
48. Although Nerval's narrator is not called 'Gérard' I have, purely for the sake of brevity, followed Proust's example in referring to him by this name without, however, wishing to impute any strict biographical identification with the author.
49. Introduction to Lucius Apuleius, *The Golden Ass*, translated by Robert Graves (Harmondsworth, 1950), p. 12.
50. 'Material man yearned for the bouquet of roses which was to regenerate him in the hands of the beautiful Isis; the eternally youthful and pure goddess appeared to us in the night and made us feel ashamed of our wasted days.' Gérard de Nerval, *Oeuvres*, 2 vols (Paris, 1974), I 242.
51. 'it is an image I am pursuing, nothing more'. Ibid., I 243.
52. 'to love a nun in the form of an actress'. Ibid., I 247.
53. 'by a modulated quiver the trembling voice of ancestors'. Ibid., I 245.
54. 'fresh-blown flower of the night in the pale light of the moon, pink and fair phantom drifting over the green grass half bathed in white vapours.' Ibid., I 246–7. For a discussion of the literary topos in which moonlight, the borrowed light of the sun, is treated as a metaphor of the transfusion of literary heritage, see above, pp. 76–7.
55. For a detailed exposition of the use of colour in Proust's novel, see A. H. Pasco, *The Colour-keys to A la recherche du temps perdu* (Geneva, 1976), especially chapter III, 'Pink and "the necessary inspirer" '.
56. See above pp. 82–3.
57. 'I was going to discover the odour, the taste of this unknown pink fruit'. Proust, *A la recherche du temps perdu*, I 934.
58. 'Flushed with the morning's reflections, her face was more pink than the sky.' Ibid., I 655.
59. 'that beautiful girl whom I could still see, as the train gathered speed, it was like a part of a life which was other than the one I knew, separated from it by a border-line and where the sensations aroused by objects were no longer the same, and which for me to leave now would have been a kind of death.' Ibid., I 657.
60. 'as if the whole of this endless nocturnal ride had no reason, no goal other than the final discovery of that diaphanous flesh in the middle of the night [.]' *La Route des Flandres*, p. 41.
61. 'I stood in the middle of the road in the sylvan peace where I could hear the cuckoos and from time to time the swift invisible and lethargic leap of a fish out of the unchanging mirror of water [.]' Ibid., p. 164.

62. 'no more than a tale of chopped necks in short since according to tradition the family's interpretation or flattering legend, it was in order to avoid the guillotine that the other one had done it [.]' Ibid., p. 90.
63. 'as one passes from one side of a mirror to another'. Ibid., p. 259.
64. 'I put my hand on her right in the middle it was like down faint bird feathers a bird in the hand but also a bush English proverb [.]' Ibid., p. 275.
65. 'as if we had for a moment been emptied completely as if our whole life had with the sound of a cataract rushed forward and out of us wrenching itself extirpating itself out of us out of me of my solitude [.]' Ibid., p. 265.
66. 'again imprisoned, beating furiously against the walls the narrow and impassable limits.' Ibid.
67. 'I was no longer a man but an animal a dog more than a man a beast if I could only get there, know Apuleius's ass [.]' Ibid., p. 92.
68. See Stephen Heath, *The Nouveau Roman*, pp. 176-7.
69. 'the red patch shining dimly in the half-light'. *La Route des Flandres*, p. 251.
70. 'the grey dawn the grass was also covered with dew which I drank drinking her there completely making her enter me completely [. . .] squeezing drinking her stomach the bowls of her breasts escaping under my fingers like water a pink crystalline drop trembling on a blade bending in that light and fluttering breeze which precedes sunrise reflecting containing in its transparency the sky flushed with dawn [.]' Ibid., p. 260.
71. 'crossroads where several roads intersect' Claude Simon, *Orion aveugle*, p. 12.
72. 'And if, rather than [. . .] rapidly negotiating these crossroads having already decided which route to follow, one stops and examines what appears in their light or in the perspectives opened up, unexpected networks of resonance and echos are revealed.' Ibid.
73. 'mussel octopus pulp vulva' . . . 'the same houri the same panting hiccoughing palfrey' . . . 'Liessies, like jubilee jubilate fête Hénin nayin' Hirson hedgehog hirsute'. *La Route des Flandres*, pp. 53, 296, 309.
74. 'mounted' . . . 'to straddle' . . . 'the sorrel-woman' . . . 'discussing rides (animal and human)' . . . 'who had straddled, mounted his wife just as if she were a mare'. Ibid., pp. 185, 20, 283.
75. The passage is quoted above. See note 26.
76. 'that diagrammatic representation of the progress of the different units obviously taking into account neither accidents on the ground nor unforeseen obstacles emerging during combat, the real itinerary taking the form of broken lines zigzagging and sometimes recrossing in a scribble of confusion [.]' *La Route des Flandres*, p. 299.
77. 'He arrives after this sleepless night, and what he then sees, disconnected, so to speak, from reality by the sleepless night and by this

return to a place which for him is more like a past existing at least as much in his heart as on a map, is so closely intermingled with the memories he continues to evoke, that we are constantly obliged to turn back to earlier pages to ascertain where we are now, if it is the present or the past recalled.' Marcel Proust, *Contre Sainte-Beuve* (Paris, 1971), p. 238.

3 THE FRAMEWORK OF *LE PALACE*, *HISTOIRE*, AND *LES GÉORGIQUES*

1. Dominique Lanceraux, 'Modalités de la narration dans *Le Palace* de Claude Simon', *Littérature*, 16 (décembre 1974), 6.
2. 'Then he saw himself, that is years later, and he this residue of himself, or rather this trace, this stain (this excrement in a way) left behind him: pathetic figure that can be seen moving, ridiculous and presumptuous, over there, far off, as if seen through the wrong end of a spyglass, waving, eternally repeating at the bequest of memory [. . .] repeating indefinitely the same slice of life, importunate, obnoxious, imposing himself interfering by force – being able then to see himself with a kind of astonishment slightly annoyed, incredulous, thinking: "That: me? That . . .?" Looking at the microscopic double and appalled by himself: it was almost fifteen years later [.]' *Le Palace*, p. 20.
3. 'The Italian, the student, the scriptor: three narrative voices (rôles, instances) which are superimposed, crisscross, imprinting their movement on the text: one outlining the conditions of audience and organises his own 'hearing'; the student 'reading' in the narrative of the rifle-man what he will remember having imagined about the episode; and one, finally, carrying out the writing.' Lanceraux, 'Modalités de la narration dans *Le Palace* de Claude Simon', 10.
4. John Sturrock, introduction to *Le Palace* (London, 1972), p. xxv.
5. 'But why is he recounting all this?' *Le Palace*, pp. 58, 76.
6. *Le Palace* represents a development from *Le Sacre du Printemps*. The two timespans concerning Bernard and his step-father in the earlier novel are reformulated into the two time spans dealing with the protagonist's two visits to Barcelona in *Le Palace*.
7. Lanceraux, 'Modalités de la narration dans *Le Palace* de Claude Simon', 14; Sturrock, introduction to *Le Palace*, p. xxiv. The critic admits to having earlier thought it was the student who commits suicide.
8. '(the American, the Italian and the student – rather these three parts, these three fragments of himself which were an American, a rifle-man and a young feather-brain [.]' *Le Palace*, p. 157.
9. 'the central enigma of *Histoire* [. . .], the narrative which will not allow itself to be told, always blurred, evaded, censured. The reader imagines, constructs, and destroys that thing which one does not

want to or cannot name.' Anthony Pugh, 'Invitation à une lecture polyvalente' in *Claude Simon: analyse, théorie* (Paris, 1975), p. 392.
10. 'small floury cakes I wondered where she found them . . .' *Histoire*, p. 287.
11. Jakobson's term 'shifter' or 'embrayeur' refers to words such as 'je', 'tu', 'maintenant', 'ici', 'demain' whose reference depends on the context in which they are uttered. As Emile Benveniste says: ' "je" ne peut être identifié que par l'instance du discours qui le contient et par là seulement' [' "I" can only be identified by the instance of discourse which contains it and only by that.'], *Eléments de linguistique générale* (Paris, 1963), p. 252. The reader or listener therefore needs to be aware of the context in which the word is 'framed' in order to know who or what it is referring to. This dependence on frame explains why 'shifters' are so prominent in the vast majority of 'nouveaux romans' (above all in those written by Robbe-Grillet) which focus on frame play. In Simon's 'oeuvre' too the apparent certainty expressed by a word like 'maintenant' often thinly veils a fundamental ambiguity of reference.
12. It is possible to apply a more radical reading of this passage by interpreting the 'je' in this instance as the voice of Charles himself and not the narrator who has momentarily taken the place of his uncle. In this case the 'dédoublement' would be complete. The same 'signifiant', 'je', would be referring, at different moments in the text, to two different 'signifiés'. An opposite example can be found in Buñuel's film 'Cet obscur objet du désir' where the same character is alternately played by two different actresses. Here it is the 'signifié' which remains constant while two different 'signifiants' (the two actresses) are employed. However, Carlos Saura's 'Elisa vida mía' provides a better parallel with the narrative frame play in *Histoire*. Here a disjunctive effect is produced by the fact that this film is narrated by Elisa's father who is writing her autobiography. Thus although the film is narrated by Elisa (it is she who is speaking), the voice that we hear (the voice which is speaking) is her father's. The overlap in the narrative structure brought about by the father assuming Elisa's identity is similar to the one caused in *Histoire* by the narrator's momentary adoption of his uncle's identity.
13. 'each picture overlapping the preceding one or rather seeming to derive from it engendered by it in some way detaching itself from it as if they were all embedded in each other like nests of tables [.] *Histoire*, p. 287.
14. 'and a little earlier (eight or nine o'clock in the morning perhaps, in Saigon)'
'and perhaps one o'clock in the morning in Eberfield'
'and about midday at the end of the morning in Tamatave'
'and two o'clock in the afternoon (Singapore)'
'and three o'clock in the afternoon (Jura)'
'and three o'clock in the afternoon (Singapore)'
'and five o'clock in the afternoon (Helvetia)'

'and eleven o'clock in the morning in Zanzibar'
'and five o'clock in the afternoon, (Herault)'
Histoire, pp. 255, 256, 259, 260, 261, 262.
15. 'and no hour no time a thousand years before or after and before what and after what and not water but a yellow muddy stretch which runs slides along in a monotonous lapping [.]' *Histoire*, p. 262.
16. C.-G. Burström, "Dimensions du temps chez Claude Simon" in *Entretiens* (1972), 141.
17. 'the same looks, the same hard-wearing, impenetrable, interchangeable and ageless faces'. *Le Palace*, p. 44.
18. 'not by means of simple migrations but of a series of internal mutations, of molecular shifts.' Ibid., p. 12.
19. 'as if he were trying to drag out, to reject from himself that violence, that thing which has installed itself in him, uses him [. . .] (like in those games where the loser picks a card, a cursed or evil figure which he has to pass on at all cost to someone else before it condemns him for good) possessing him, consuming him [.]' Ibid., pp. 77–8.
20. 'thinking of both of them in the dark with that pale shadow over them like a uniform coat of grey paint which confused them with the sheets, as if the bed the sheets the bodies were made uniformly out of the same inanimate semi-nude substance stripped or rather devoid of everything in this double headed solitude – apparently intact – in reality decomposing very fast as if under the grey and polished marble an invisible and voracious swarm was relentlessly at work [.]' *Histoire*, p. 359.
21. 'the blurred trace left by the face in the course of one of its many changes of position restoring a sense of depth to the event, suggesting (on the basis of the one snapshot and overlaid on both sides, forming a kind of quadrangle, a parallelepiped stretching out to infinity) the double sequence of moments past and future, the double series, within the same frame and the same décor, of positions respectively occupied by different characters before and after [.]' Ibid., p. 269.
22. 'Sans doute pouvait-il voir cela: c'est-à-dire comme sur ces photos des méthodes d'éducation physique, comme si cet obturateur n'avait pas cessé d'ouvrir et de se refermer pendant tout ce temps' [No doubt he could see that: that is like on those photos illustrating methods of physical education, as if the shutters had not stopped opening and closing throughout this time [.]] *Les Géorgiques*, p. 295. Although Muybridge is not directly mentioned, one can see that his photographs would have the same fascination for Simon as they do for Francis Bacon.
23. 'then nothing more except for the vineyards the cypress hedges the plantations of apricot trees and the hills here and there the roof of a country house or of a cellar protruding from a clump of pine trees plane trees and eucalyptus trees and reaching the top of the hill I saw it: barely darker than the sky perfectly still from here immaterial

like a horizontal strip of paint carefully brushed over the acid green of the vines [.]' *Histoire,* p. 299.
24. 'among the paintings hanging on the wall there was a landscape with pines and between the branches one could see embedded flashes of sky made of a greasy bluish paste like fragments of enamel [.]' Ibid.
25. 'like a horizontal brush-stroke of painting carefully applied'. Ibid.
26. 'But it is only on writing *Histoire* that I began to be more clearly aware of the power and internal dynamism of writing and to let myself be guided more by what the writing was saying – or discovering – than by what I wanted it to say – or "re-cover". 'Réponses de Claude Simon à quelques questions écrites de Ludovic Janvier' in *Entretiens,* 17.
27. 'In the parts of the pond where the water reflected the dark foliage of the laurels where one could see others had accumulated in the green-black bottom brown viscous rotting the most recent russet still sepia stuck together in packets thin films of time of dead summer invisible in the half of the tray which was filled with the sky the bursting clouds but beyond the jagged outline of the crest of the ivy bush we could discern our reflections some unclearly as if we had passed in front of the lens at great speed Are you going to the hairdresser's?' *Histoire,* p. 380.
28. 'the foliage waving again: looking carefully one could see each minuscule drop of dried blood was linked to another by still more microscopic droplets sometimes a thin red line: like a silk thread on which one would have tied knots [.]' Ibid., p. 381.
29. This ironical reference to visual precision is matched, in *Le Palace,* by the student's pursuit of certainty and accuracy as he attempts to reconstitute the past. The futility of his efforts is shown up by the Italian's more fatalistic attitude. Thus, for example, the student interrupts the Italian's narration of the assassination in order to clarify a detail: 'une meuble sur lequel il y avait, dit-il, des choses que venaient prendre les garçons – "Une desserte", dit l'étudiant, et lui: "Si. Sans doute. Parce que je crois bien qu'en haut il y avait des fruits; un de ces trucs comme une pomme de pin. Je n'ai pas eu le temps de bien voir" [a piece of furniture on which there were, he said, things which the waiter came to clear away – "A dessert", said the student, and he: "Yes. No doubt. Because I'm sure there was some fruit on top; one of those things like a pineapple. I didn't have time to see properly".] *Le Palace,* p. 62. Similarly, in *Histoire* a musical analogy underlines the illusion in the notion of exactitude: 'de même que le son tiré par l'archet de la corde d'un violon n'est jamais d'une fréquence fixe mais une hésitation autour de cette notion abstraite et sans réalité qu'est la note exacte'.
[just as the sound drawn by the bow of a violin is never held at a fixed frequency but a hesitation around that abstract and unreal notion of the exact note [.]] *Histoire,* p. 356.
30. 'blood stains scattered on the cross embroidered among the small dark leaves which were also pointed and rolled up at the intersec-

tion of the bands forming a sort of crown around the red heart [.]' Ibid., p. 15.

31. The question of narratorial status is clearly of prime importance since although the first person pronoun is never employed in the novel (except in direct speech and in L. S. M.'s letters) one is constantly aware of a controlling hand (or voice) organising the text. Occasional interventions such as 'Ici il est peut-être nécessaire d'ouvrir une parenthèse' make the narrator particularly conspicuous. However, the ambiguity surrounding the narrative discourse arises from the degree to which one can identify the narrator with the twentieth century descendant of L. S. M., some of whose childhood and war-time experiences are described in intimate detail. The answer seems to be that the two are simultaneously identical and different. Even without prior knowledge of earlier works like *Histoire* and *La Route des Flandres*, one can interpret the descendant (referred to as 'le garçon' and 'un cavalier') as a fictional projection of Simon himself. In this respect, therefore, the narrator and the character are one. However, it would be wrong to neglect a crucial factor distinguishing the two identities. Rather like the distinction between Marcel the narrator and the protagonist whose life is unravelled in the course of *A la recherche du temps perdu*, the gap separating the narrator from the protagonist is so wide in *Les Géorgiques* that at one point in the text the narrator refers to *La Route des Flandres* in a detached manner as though it were written only by the protagonist and not by himself as well: 'il rapporte dans un roman les circonstances et la façon dont les choses se sont déroulées entretemps . . .' [he records in a novel the circumstances and the way in which these things developed in the meantime . . .] *Les Géorgiques*, p. 52. The author thus succeeds in 'fictionalising' his past life (the parts which are described in the text), placing it on the same level as the accounts of the lives of Orwell and L. S. M., which have also been 'fictionalised' by the text; and thus establishes the same distance between the narrator and himself (that is, the configuration of his past experiences) as exists between the narrator and O. or L. S. M. Claude Simon has pointedly warned against confusing the two identities. When asked by an interviewer whether the character in the novel was Simon himself, the author replied: 'Si l'on veut. Mais avec le statut de personnage qui implique une certaine distanciation: ce n'est pas le "narrateur", je crois qu'il faut bien le préciser . . .' [If you like. But with the status of a character implying a certain distancing: it is not the narrator, I think one has to stress . . .] 'Claude Simon ouvre *Les Géorgiques*', *Le Monde* (4 septembre 1981), 11.

32. The countless private and official documents, belonging to Lacombe Saint-Michel (1753–1812) the author's illustrious ancestor who had waged several military campaigns under the 'Ancien Régime', had voted for the death of Louis XVI, was promoted to brigadier-general of the Imperial army, was appointed ambassador in Naples and governor of Barcelona, were fortuitously discovered in the course

of renovating part of Simon's house in Salses at the time of his writing *Leçon de choses*.
33. 'It seems that the artist, following a personal value system, has tried, in the proposed scene, to clearly differentiate the diverse elements according to their growing importance in his mind as is shown by the particular style in which he has treated them, that is, firstly: inanimate objects [. . .]; secondly: flesh, bodies with muscles [. . .]; finally thirdly: the heads of the two characters [.]' *Les Géorgiques*, p. 14.
34. 'It is obvious that one's reading of such a drawing is only possible in terms of a code of writing agreed in advance by both parties, the artist and the spectator. Thus, just as in descriptive geometry it is agreed that two lines which cross signify – and not represent – the existence of a plane, the space enclosed by the walls is merely suggested by a few lines indicating the contours of the dihedron which they form between them or with the ceiling, or again the tiled floor which was drawn in a rigorously calculated perspective.' Ibid., p. 13.
35. 'rectangles of paper covered with little marks out of which (like those microscopic Japanese flowers which, when dipped in water, swell out, unfurl their hidden corolla) the exacting earth, the hills [. . .], the slow drift of the clouds, the dew, the storms, the frost began again to materialise in the unchanging rotation of the unchanging seasons.' Ibid., p. 462.
36. The title 'Les Géorgiques' is another abbreviated sign which can open out into a stream of associations. Through onomastic embedding it contains an oblique reference to *George* Orwell and *Georges*, the name of the protagonist, withheld in this novel but used in *La Route des Flandres*. The connections between Virgil's poem and Simon's novel also hinge on the catabatic myth of Orpheus which is recounted at the end of the *Georgics*. For a discussion of the different manifestations of this myth in *Les Géorgiques*, see my essay, 'The Orpheus myth in *Les Géorgiques*', in *Claude Simon: New Directions*, edited by Alastair Duncan (Edinburgh, 1985), pp. 89–99.
37. 'as in those kaleidoscopes where one can see the small fragmented pictures of an athlete caught in the broken postures of a race on foot, the only difference being that the cylinder would turn in reverse, so that he seemed to be so to speak advancing backwards [.]' *Les Géorgiques*, p. 360.
38. 'a kind of milkiness, a placenta, flashing on and off in the oblique and pyramidal beam of light'. Ibid., p. 212.
39. 'the hidden side of things'. Ibid., p. 215.
40. 'two scenes, two paintings, two episodes which immediately followed one another on the screen were only separated by the brief appearance of a notice where brief announcements sparkled such as: "And the next day", or: "fifteen years later", or again: "A few years earlier . . ."' Ibid., p. 215.
41. 'a time span which is prone to lightning shifts of compression, ellipsis or flashback.' Ibid., p. 215.

42. 'Manifestly he writes (or rather speaks) for the benefit of a certain public, a public whose leanings and opinions he knows, and whose reactions he can predict.'
It was Merleau-Ponty who first drew the distinction between Claude Simon 'parlant' and 'écrivant': 'celui qui parle est celui qui a des opinions, des jugements, etc. celui qui écrit est celui qui sent et vit. [. . .] Le travail ne consiste pas seulement, d'ailleurs, à 'convertir en mots' le vécu; il s'agit de faire parler ce qui est senti' [the one who speaks is the one who has opinions judgements, etc. the one who writes is the one who feels and lives. [. . .] Moreover, the work consists not only in converting lived experience into words; it is a matter of allowing what is felt to speak for itself], 'Cinq notes pour Claude Simon' in *Entretiens*, 45. These observations serve not only as a criticism of Orwell's conception of writing but also of the efforts of L. S. M. and Batti who strive 'pathetically' in their correspondence to 'convertir en mots' (p. 461), to inventory the infinite items of the natural world.

PART TWO: INTERTEXTUALITY

1 WHAT IS INTERTEXTUALITY?

1. 'Most probably if one were to sift carefully through all the publications which immediately preceded the *Fleurs du Mal*, one would find not only all of the words used by Baudelaire, which goes without saying, but also all of his syntagms [.]'. Tzvetan Todorov, *Symbolisme et interprétation* (Paris, 1978), p. 61.
2. 'instruments which are already signifying or meanings which are already expressed'. Maurice Merleau–Ponty, *Signes* (Paris, 1960), p. 113.
3. More modest assessments of individual myths in literature can be found in William Stanford's *The Ulysses Myth* (Oxford, 1963), G. Karl Galinsky's *The Herakles Theme* (Oxford, 1972), and Raymond Trousson's *Le Thème de Prométhée dans la littérature européenne*, 2 vols (Geneva, 1964).
4. 'What one tends to consider on a given specific point as a link between text and external world is nothing other than, on a given specific point, a link based on convention and even complicity between the text and all the dominant texts of a given era [. . .] What one calls the world is in fact only the idea of it held by the dominant ideology through the mass of officially active texts in a given society. The status of what lies outside the text is then that of a provisional fantasm corresponding to an intertextual relation controlled by the dominant ideology.' Jean Ricardou, *Alain Robbe-Grillet: analyse, théorie*, 2 vols (Paris, 1976), I 43–4.
5. 'We will call "intertextuality" that textual interaction which is produced inside one text. For the knowing subject intertextuality is a

concept which will indicate the way in which a text reads history and becomes part of it.' Julia Kristeva, 'Problèmes de la structuration du texte' in *Théorie d'ensemble* (Paris, 1968), p. 311.
6. See Stephen Ullmann, *Language and Style* (Oxford, 1964), p. 180–1.
7. 'So the appearance of original style carries its own context with it, the cliché is tied to the macro-context where it stood out for the first time; it works like a quotation, an allusion to a particular social level, to particular cultural manifestations.' Michael Riffaterre, *Essais de stylistique structurale* (Paris, 1971), p. 170.
8. Michael Riffaterre, 'Intertextual Scrambling', *Romanic Review*, LXVIII, 3, (May 1977], 197–206.
9.   'When the low and heavy sky weighs down like a lid
On the moaning spirit racked by unending spleen'
– Baudelaire
10. Jonathan Culler, 'Presupposition and Intertextuality', *MLN*, XCI, (1976), 1390.
11. Ibid., 1383.
12. Jean Ricardou, ' "Claude Simon", textuellement', in *Claude Simon: analyse, théorie* (Paris, 1975), 11.
13. 'invisible murmur of insects droning all around'. Alain Robbe-Grillet, *Topologie d'une cité fantôme*, pp. 136–8.
14. 'Old outdated novels are read which take place in the heart of unreal Africa, full of incomprehensible dramas in the clammy heat and the shrill sound of crickets.' Ibid.
15. 'The voyeur's bicycle has been stolen. It's an old bicycle abandoned in the sheep pen (it was always seen there) and it's been called that ever since a horrible story was invented about it.' Ibid.
16. 'Then there is as usual a vertiginous staircase and a corridor, with a trail of blood running under the door of a locked room.' Ibid.
17. 'We are part of a complex of evolving cultures within which all sorts of illusions and blunders are made. To rid ourselves of them we must bring references out into the open and put them to the test. To work on quotations is to give prominence to the fact that one is never sole author of a text, that culture is a tissue; self-quotation is one way of considering oneself as another. All this undermines the walls set up by our society between author and reader, singular and plural. It is an awakening and a liberation.' 'Dialogue avec Michel Butor' in André Helbo, *Michel Butor: vers une littérature du signe* (Paris, 1975), p. 12.
18. Bruce Morrissette, *Intextextual Assemblage in Robbe-Grillet from Topology to The Golden Triangle* (Fredericton, 1979), pp. 79–80.
19. See Harold Ogden White, *Plagiarism and Imitation during the English Renaissance* (New York, 1965). The critic dates the first use of the term 'plagiarist' meaning 'literary thief' around 1600.
20. Jorge-Luis Borges, *Labyrinths*, ed. Donald A. Yates and James E. Irby (Harmondsworth, 1970). All further references are to this edition.
21. I am very grateful to Professor K. S. Reid of the University of Newcastle-upon-Tyne for pointing out to me that the labyrinth seems to be modelled on Herodotus's description of the Ethiopian

labyrinth situated beside Lake Moeris (*History*, II 147). The similarities between the two structures are evident: both are made of stone and both possess a network of subterranean chambers. Ronald Christ follows up the De Quincey reference in the postscript and discovers an allusion to Coleridge's description of a nonexistent painting by Piranesi (Ronald Christ, *The Narrow Act: Borges's Art of Allusion* (New York, 1969), p. 201). Thus, a superimposition of different sources and models reiterates the general plural structure of *The Immortal*. Furthermore, the reference to garamants, augyls, and troglodytes can also be traced back to Pliny (*Natural History*, V 43) and Herodotus (IV 182-3). The geographical setting of Borges's tale, the choice of Ethiopia as the locus for the Immortal City, leads back, through Pliny, to Homer. Pliny (V 43) mentions the opening passage in the *Odyssey* (I 23) where the poet recounts that the sun-god is attending a feast in Ethiopia, a remote land divided in two sections. The motif of 'dédoublement' recurs throughout Borges's story: the nightmarish City is an inversion of the original; the senseless structure of the palace is reflected in the maze of subterranean corridors below it; Cartaphilus and Rufus are two halves of one identity. But, after all, aren't 'Ulysses' and 'Odysseus' two names representing two sides of the same person?

22. Ronald Christ, *The Narrow Act*, p. 212.
23. See also Ronald Christ, ibid., for an onomastic breakdown of the name 'Cordovero'.
24. Thomas De Quincey, *Collected Writings*, edited by David Masson, 14 vols (London, 1896), X 455.
25. K. K. Ruthven, *Critical Assumptions* (Cambridge, 1979), p. 112.
26. This is an allusion to the trick played by Odysseus on the cyclops by calling himself 'Nobody' (*Odyssey*, IX 363ff.).
27. 'the rich men who drink the black water of the Aisepos'. Borges, *Obras completas 1923-1972* (Buenos Aires, 1974), p. 240. Two points arise from this quotation. Firstly, it is interesting that Borges should substitute 'varones' (men) for 'troyanos' (trojans). Moreover, as Professor Reid has indicated to me, in *The Immortal* Borges uses, in preference to either of these two words, the term 'teucros' which derives from the Latin word for trojans, 'teucri', and which is used extensively in the *Aeneid*, another example of Borges deliberately choosing to relate to Homer via the chain of writers who have rewritten his work. Secondly, 'the black waters of the Aisepos' are reflected in Pliny's description of the Nile, which runs

> underground below deserts for the space of twenty days' journey until it reaches Ethiopia where it leaps out in a fountain and is called the Black Spring; the stretch of the river running through the middle of Ethiopia is called 'Astapus', which in the native language means 'water issuing from the shades below'. (*Natural History*, V 52).

One of the many ways in which the African world and the Greek

world mirror one another. Doesn't Rufus momentarily confuse 'the atrocious village of the barbarians' with his own 'native city' (p. 140)?
28. The same amphibological play of meaning is possible in the Spanish word 'fuente'.
29. De Quincey, *Collected Writings*, p. 9. See also Pliny, *Natural History*, V 51.
30. See Christine Brooke-Rose, *A Grammar of Metaphor* (London, 1965), p. 264, and Weldon Thornton, *Allusions in Ulysses* (Chapel Hill, 1968), p. 3.
31. Jacques Nathan, *Citations, références et allusions de Marcel Proust dans A la recherche du temps perdu* (Paris, 1969), p. 12.
32. Margaret Mein, *A Foretaste of Proust* (Westmead, 1974), p. 11.
33. 'between two impressions, between two ideas, a very fine harmony exists which others do not perceive.' Proust, *Contre Saint-Beuve* (Paris, 1971), p. 304.
34. 'But if in the second painting or second book he notices something which was not in the first, but which is in a way between the two, in a kind of ideal painting, consisting of a spiritual substance which he can see take shape beyond the painting, he will have received his nourishment and can start again to exist and to be happy.' Ibid.
35. 'it makes books cut into each other and leads them to inscribe themselves beyond their limits in a universal text.' Philippe Sollers, 'Niveaux sémantiques d'un texte moderne' in *Théorie d'ensemble*, p. 323.
36. 'truly aesthetic impressions' . . . 'less pronounced, yet discernible, and basically analagous.' *A la recherche du temps perdu*, III 920.
37. All references are to Marcel Proust, *A la recherche du temps perdu*, 3 vols (Paris, 1954).
38. Jean Ricardou, *Nouveaux problèmes du roman* (Paris, 1978), pp. 89–138.
39. For a translation of this passage, see Part One, Chapter 2 note 45.
40. 'Between the sea and the land lie stretches of pelagian fields, indeterminate borders between two elements: the meadowlark flies above there with the sea lark; the plough and the boat a stone's throw from each other, furrow earth and water. The navigator and the shepherd borrow from each other's language: the sailor says THE WAVES [ARE FLEECED WITH] FOAM, the shepherd says FLOCKS [FLEETS] OF SHEEP.' René de Chateaubriand, *Mémoires d'outre-tombe*, 2 vols (Paris, 1951), I 41–2.
41. 'from under her freckles, that of Mlle Vinteuil's cheeks.' Proust, *A la recherche du temps*, I 113.
42. 'Despite the silent immobility of the hawthorns, that intermittent smell was like a murmur of their intense life with which the altar vibrated like a rustic hedge visited by lively antennae which one was reminded of on seeing certain almost russet stamen which seemed to have kept the springtime virulence, the irritating power of insects today metamorphosed into flowers.' Ibid., I 113–4.
43. 'They announced to me the immense expanse where wheat unfurls,

where the fleecy clouds gather above, and the sight of a single poppy hoisting its red flame at the end of its rope to be lashed by the wind, above its greasy black buoy, made my heart beat, as does the traveller's when he sees on the flat land a beached boat being repaired by a caulker, and cries out before he has even seen it: "The Sea!" ' Ibid., I 138–9.

44. 'A reddish blonde little girl [. . .] raising her face flecked with pink.' Ibid., I 140.
45. 'black coated over with ash'. Ibid., I 66.
46. Mein, *A Foretaste of Proust*, p. 6.
47. 'that unknown and so sweet name of "Champi" '. Proust, *A la recherche du temps perdu*, I 42.
48. 'The time scale of literary works is not the defined time scale of writing, but the indefinite time of reading and memory. The meaning of books is before them and not behind them, it is in us: a book is not a complete meaning, a revelation which we are to experience, it is a repository of forms waiting for their meaning, it is 'the imminence of a revelation which does not come about" and which each of us must produce.' Gérard Genette, *Figures* (Paris, 1966), p. 132.
49. 'However, there is a precise choice: most of the texts belong to a space overshadowed by our culture and which is, on the whole, materialist [. . .] The common denominator of all these authors is their having been refused by the Christian system: thus Bruno, Spinoza, Artaud [. . .] It is a homage to a certain "underworld" of our thought.' Philippe Sollers, 'Ecriture et révolution' in *Théorie d'ensemble*, p. 76.
50. Foreword by Sir Arthur Quiller-Couch in *Parodies and Imitations: Old and New*, edited by J. A. Stanley Adam and Bernard C. White (London, 1912), p. vi.
51. Laurent Jenny, 'La Stratégie de la forme', *Poétique*, 27 (1976), 281.
52. Stuart Gilbert, *James Joyce's Ulysses* (Harmondsworth, 1963), p. 255.
53. Ibid., p. 268.
54. Ibid., p. 255. See also Frank Budgen, *James Joyce and the Making of Ulysses* (London, 1972), pp. 221–9; and Joyce's own explanation of the episode in a letter to Budgen reproduced in Richard Ellmann, *James Joyce* (London, 1976), pp. 489–90.
55. 'Moreover, there is in *La Prise de Constantinople* what I call antipastiches. Historians' texts are indeed inserted but they are transformed by the text which receives them, both on the level of style as on the level of the events themselves through a kind of assimilation.' Jean Ricardou, *Nouveau roman: hier, aujourd'hui*, 2 vols (Paris, 1972), II 281.
56. 'Restitution of the old text, invention of the new text are two correlated activities. The more I restore, the more am I forced to invent (and encouraged in this venture); the more I invent, the more am I capable of restoring.

'Current literature does not therefore merit being called parody. In fact the old model could not be consulted, covered as it is by its

innumerable imitations, it has not come off the shelf. Shadows of the shadows of shadows.' Michel Butor, 'Critique et invention' in *Répertoire III* (Paris, 1968), 13.
57. Georges Charbonnier, *Entretiens avec Michel Butor* (Paris, 1967), p. 144.
58. 'FRANÇOISE VAN ROSSUM-GUYON: And in using these texts, do you transform them?
CLAUDE SIMON: Of course and Rauschenberg too in using reproductions or chromos or scarves, transforms them.'
Nouveau roman: hier, aujourd'hui, II 113–4.

2 LA BATAILLE DE PHARSALE AND ITS FRAGMENTS

1. 'Oh! the sun . . . What tortoise shadow' . . . 'Which quivers, flies and does not fly!' . . . 'Achilles immobile with great strides!' Paul Valéry, quoted in *La Bataille de Pharsale*.
2. 'the gap between being and knowing which is developed by consciousness of consciousness.' Paul Valéry, *Oeuvres*, 2 vols (Paris, 1957), p. 1506.
3. 'Yellow then black the space of a blink and then yellow again'. *La Bataille de Pharsale*, p. 9.
4. Jean Ricardou, *Pour une théorie du nouveau roman* (Paris, 1971), pp. 124–7.
5. This is not to suggest that the 'pure' form of the image, 'soleil noir', is simultaneous, though it is less obviously successive than Simon's version. 'Pharsale' and 'Orion' would be more analogous forms of simultaneity, since the opposition is contained, in both cases, in one word. But here again it is only through reading these words in the context of the novel that this opposition is produced.
6. Claude Simon, interview with Claud Duverlie, *Sub-Stance*, 8, (March 1974), 9.
7. Stephen Heath defines the compositional concept of 'screen' by alluding to Leonardo da Vinci for whom the canvas was a pane of glass which stood upright between the painter (and observer) and the scene or object being painted: 'The pane is at once a frame, the frame of a window, and a screen, the area of projection on which what is seen can be traced and fixed; from the Quattrocento on, the 'pane' delimits and holds a view, the painter's canvas a screen situated between eye and object, point of interception of the light rays'. 'Narrative Space', *Screen*, 17, 3 (Autumn 1976), 80–1. Traditionally, novelists have attempted to obviate the notion of 'screen' in their works by giving the impression that the writing opens directly onto the field of reference. Consequently, it is only with novels whose narrative screen is fragmented into a mosaic of different parts that the reader is conscious of an 'area of projection' separate from the fictional 'world' evoked by the narrative.
8. 'Stagnant waters. Living death. *I perfectly understand that you have*

decided to do nothing naturally it is purely and simply a question of laziness on your part mortally sad *but after all though you can't yet be aware of it* I didn't yet know *since it is something which one has to learn and apparently you have made the firm resolution to do nothing* dead wood dead leaf *but perhaps you are right after all all knowledge only ever leads to more knowledge and words to other words* spiritual death death penalty [.]' *La Bataille de Pharsale*, p. 18.

9. Claude Simon has referred to these textual points of intersection as 'noeuds de signification', a phrase which he borrowed from Jacques Lacan. See 'La fiction mot à mot' in *Nouveau roman: hier, aujourd'hui*, 2 vols (Paris, 1972), II 73.

10. 'wings opened out in the shape of a crossbow' . . . 'Soul of the Just flying off' . . . 'the wings evoking images of birds, feathers, feathered arrows'. *La Bataille de Pharsale*, p. 257.

11. 'the eye does not see but rather remembers not the fateful procession (or series, or enumeration) of parts – hair, shoulders, breasts, hips etc . . . – in their monotonous order, but a combination, a shady and dazzling confusion of light and lines where the exploded, fragmented elements regroup according to the teeming and rigorous disorder of memory [.]' Claude Simon, *Histoire* (Paris, 1967), p. 273. Note the recurrence of the light/shade paradox: '*ombreux* [. . .] enchevêtrement de *lumières*'.

12. 'One must picture the whole system as a mobile endlessly changing around a few rare fixed points, for example the intersection of the line OO' and the route taken by the bird in its flight or again that of the itineraries of the two trips, or again the name PHARSALE appearing both on a Latin school textbook and on a sign on a roadside on the way to Thessaly [.]' *La Bataille de Pharsale*, p. 186.

13. 'now there are no more pigeons [. . .] there was no-one anymore in the field either [. . .] the outside tables of the café are deserted [. . .] the white cat was no longer perched [. . .] a cloud is reflected again [. . .] all the blue painted tables placed in rows outside the café on the narrow pavement were now surrounded by men [. . .] was there really a football pitch how could there have been [. . .] I can remember [. . .] A couple came to sit outside the café [. . .] The couple is in no way unusual [.]' Ibid., pp. 95–8.

14. 'the broad stitches of the net curtain behind the window-pane more visible in the dark grey part than in the strip filled with the light blue.' Ibid., p. 11.

15. 'In the *shaded* parts the hills were tinged with *blue*' (p. 94)
'a lorry half loaded with *pink* blocks [. . .] covered over with a layer of *greyish* dust' (p. 95)
'the wet asphalt has dried it is a dull *grey*' (p. 95)
'the outside of the café is deserted the waiter wearing a *blue* apron' (p. 95)
'a *grey* ass' (p. 96)
'low cloud stretches out becoming tinged with *pink*' (p. 96)
'I saw one of the three hens with their *pink* emaciated necks but not the two others' (p. 96)

'the reflected sky is now very dark the cloud appears all the more striking' (p. 97)
'all the *blue* painted tables' (p. 97)
La Bataille de Pharsale
   The use of colour names here is analogous to the way in which films can create a sense of expectation by alternating different sequences of images each with its own colour combination. See Iouri Lotman, *La Structure du texte artistique* (Paris, 1973), pp. 387–8.

16. The phrase is borrowed from Jean Ricardou, *Le Nouveau roman* (Paris, 1973), p. 127.
17. '[the tables] were now surrounded by seated men I noticed.' *La Bataille de Pharsale*, p. 97.
18. 'There was no newsvendor'. Ibid.
19. 'the couple are in no way remarkable'. Ibid., p. 98.
20. *Cesar*: 'recalling that arrival.'
    Conversation: 'She said [. . .] He said'
    Warrior: 'He turned [. . .] and we mute'
    Machine: 'A chain [. . .] proceeds'
    La Bataille de Pharsale, pp. 122, 128, 135, 147.
21. 'massacre as well as love is a pretext for glorifying form whose calm splendour appears only to those who have penetrated the indifference of nature towards massacre and love.' Ibid., p. 119.
22. 'light which brightens the spectacle of the earth it was the fragment of another world of an unknown planet a view of [.]' Ibid., p. 170.
23. 'everything for the German artist is on the same level in nature detail always masks the whole their universe is not continuous but consists of juxtaposed fragments [.]' Ibid., p. 174.
24. 'one of my arms placed under her shoulders' . . . 'now she surrounds his shoulders with her arms'. Ibid., p. 121.
25. 'now he falls'
    'now he lies on the ground'
    'now she can see him'
    'now I could hear them'
    'now he rushes forward'
    'now the short piece'
    'now she puts her arms around his shoulders'
    'now two little girls'
    'now she is just shouting' Ibid., pp. 118–121.
26. 'perhaps time is a notion which, like that of space, has no place here'. Ibid., p. 106.
27. 'Now she is just shouting but I don't hear her shouting almost all of them have their mouths open no doubt they are shouting too some with pain others in order to rouse themselves to fight the hubbub is so loud that one can no longer hear anything [.]' Ibid., p. 122.
28. 'and neither am I a stranger, a spectator looking on [. . .] but now at the very centre of this maelstrom [. . .] revolving endlessly around the solemn gilt frames and me at the centre [.]' Ibid., pp. 116–17.

29. 'carried immobile on this bench so that I could see words a string of words stretching out inscribed on the kilometres of time of air I mean like those advertisements or those newsflashes where the text unfolds in trembling gold letters on those luminous screens each letter appearing in succession [.]' Ibid., p. 163–4.
30. 'the glass pane the blocked rectangle bursting suddenly fragmenting the space the air itself noisily shattering in splinters of shade of light of streaked shafts dotted black and yellow rushing inside the compartment escaping at great speed then the woman took up her position again and once more I could only see the immobile black and white square [.]' Ibid., p. 157.
31. 'continuing to travel across the vast land plunging still further penetrating'. Ibid., p. 162.
32. 'when he plunges into her again letting out a noise'. Ibid., p. 176.
33. 'who defines the baroque as *movement into space* unfortunately the word *into* is untranslatable having only weak French equivalents like "au dedans de" or "a l'intérieur de" [.]' Ibid., p. 160.
34. 'blind Orion walking towards the light of the rising sun.'
35. 'the rails dividing noisily separating bifurcating coming together diverging again doubling up again multiplying spreading out over a large area [.]' *La Bataille de Pharsale*, p. 164.
36. 'Let O then be the position occupied by the eye of the observer (O) and from where an invisible line OO' links up with the object which is being stared at [.]' Ibid., p. 181.
37. 'to imagine the spectacle which he himself may offer to an external gazer whether it is that of the female observer hidden behind the reflection of the window-pane or that of some other person who could be observing him, either at this time or subsequently, O being therefore only a mere point included within some other cone of vision sweeping the square [. . .] with neither more nor less existence than a trace [.] Ibid., p. 185.
38. A 'mise en abyme' description of the optical effect induced by the variegated pattern of a woman's dress carries an implicit reference to the oscillatory effect of reading the text itself: 'Me demandant ce qui provoquait cette impression de relief à la fin je me rendis compte qu'un troisième fil, gris celui-là, jouait dans le tissu les losanges étant de trois couleurs noirs, blancs et gris de sorte que leur combinaison dessinait comme certains carrelages de petits cubes en perspective accolés les uns aux autres et qui selon la façon dont on les lisait horizontalement verticalement ou en oblique semblaient tour à tour saillir ou s'enfoncer à ,'intérieur d'un espace à trois dimensions cela jusqu'au vertige [.]' [Wondering what it was that conveyed that sense of depth finally I realised that a third thread, grey this time, was woven in the material the diamond pattern consisting of three colours black, white and grey so that their combination created the same effect as that of the tiling of small cubes drawn in perspective placed side by side and which depending on whether they were read horizontally vertically or obliquely appeared by turns to be standing out from or plunging into a

three dimensional space ad infinitum [.]' Ibid., pp. 160–1. The perspective in question is that of the 'Necker cube' discussed by Gestalt psychologists and phenomenologists. Perception of this reversible figure oscillates between two possible interpretations, a choice between two 'frames', and is thereby revealed to be an active process which selects and organises the flux of visual data.

39. 'The three pictures side by side in their order of reading (that is, from left to right: firstly Hercules nonchalantly leaning against the wall next to the telephone, secondly voluptuous interlocutor with the flower, thirdly close-up of strained mask) composing, perhaps without the artist being aware of it, a kind of triptych where one could pass from the first to the third picture by a half-circle turn (a folding-over) the exact centre being occupied by the blood-red mouth of the woman who is immediately framed on the right and on the left by the wall telephone whose position has been inverted between the first and third pictures [.]' *La Bataille de Pharsale*, pp. 69–70.

40. 'one must consider the line OF in its FO direction: let then another observer (or female observer) O. standing at F, that is in the room which corresponds to the window on the fifth floor, and observing the observer (who has turned from subject into object also – the letter O therefore can still, in this situation, continue to designate him) [.]' Ibid., p. 184.

41. In 'De Claude Simon à Proust: un exemple d'intertextualité', *Les Lettres Nouvelles*, 4(1972) . 119, Françoise Van Rossum-Guyon cites the original page references of the Proust quotations in Simon's novel. She has, however, omitted to point out the final two groups of quotations. They are as follows:
La Bataille de Pharsale (pp. 204–5)
'reprit son premier [. . .] besoin de', *A la recherche*, III, 772.
'toujours [. . .] chez eux', ibid., III, 776.
'ce régent [. . .] il l'est de', ibid., III 779.
'parents [. . .] homme qu'ils', ibid., III, 780.
'encre [. . .] telles que', ibid., III, 790.
  La Bataille de Pharsale (p. 206)
'tous ces grands valets [. . .] répétait que', *A la recherche*, III, 794.
'plus obscure [. . .] consolant pour', ibid., III, 801.
'projecteurs [. . .] aéroplanes', ibid., III 801.
'tandis que [. . .] probablement', ibid., III, 808.
'le 43 [. . .] fumée ici', ibid., III, 206.

42. 'Saying that jealousy is like . . . like . . . Remembering the place: roughly in the first third of the book at the top of a right-hand page.' *La Bataille de Pharsale*, p. 20.

43. 'like a kind of multicoloured creature, a centipede'. Ibid., p. 54.

44. 'His jealousy, like an octopus which throws out one tentacle then a second then a third, attached itself firmly to that moment of five o'clock in the evening, then to another again!' Proust, *A la recherche du temps perdu*, I 283.

The theme of jealousy has a further point of intertextual reference in the description of Lucas Cranach's painting 'La Jalousie' (p. 228).

45. 'From the pavement I could see the window of Albertine's room, that window which before was always black in the evening, when she didn't live in the house, which the electric light inside, cut up by the blades of the shutters, streaked from top to bottom with parallel lines of gold. This book of magic spells was so clear for me and it depicted clear-cut pictures in my calm mind [.]' Proust, *A la recherche du temps perdu*, III 330.

46. 'Everything was deserted and black in this district [. . .] Amidst the darkness of all the windows where the lights had long been extinguished in the street, he saw only one which overflowed – between the shutters which squeezed out the mysterious golden pulp – with the light filling the bedroom [.]' Ibid., I 272–3.

47. 'the whole of Proust's novel is governed by an impulse to go beyond the immediate'. Olga Bernal, *Alain Robbe-Grillet: le roman de l'absence* (Paris, 1964), p. 28.

48. 'Below the moving hair, the very slim waist is cut vertically down the back, by the narrow metallic fastener of the dress.' Alain Robbe-Grillet, *La Jalousie* (Paris, 1957), p. 135.

49. 'They reveal bit by bit their incomprehensible, delicate and feminine anatomy with connections which are also delicate and complicated. Their joints, once oiled and rubbed softly, are now jammed and rusty. They reach up to the sky in an emphatic and endless protestation, vaguely ridiculous, like old fallen whores, emaciated limbs: a few rods, the odd rotten shaft, a seat where no driver will ever sit and which no longer serves other than as a perch for some thin hens whose necks are plucked, bright pink.' *La Bataille de Pharsale*, p. 153.

50. For a discussion of Proust's use of 'reciprocal metaphor', see Stephen Ullmann, *Language and Style* (Oxford, 1964), p. 191.

51. 'a bumpy, rocky heap' . . . 'shoulder of the stony hill'. *La Bataille de Pharsale*, pp. 212, 220. This particular reciprocal metaphor seems to mirror Cézanne's remark, expressed in admiration of Poussin: 'Je voudrais, comme dans 'le Triomphe de Flore', marier des courbes de femmes à des épaules de collines'.

['I would like, as in "Le Triomphe de Flore", to marry the curves of women with the shoulders of hills.'] Quoted in Lilianne Brion-Guerry, *Cézanne et l'expression de l'espace* (Paris, 1966), p. 259. An interesting detail of correspondence, to be set within the wider framework of the compositional perspective shared by Simon and Cézanne.

52. 'He looks at the square, the fountain, the statues. He then looks at the people sitting around him outside the café. Finally he lowers his head and looks at the top of the pedestal table at which he is seated. On the table there is his glass at the bottom of which an ice cube finishes melting in the dregs of a yellowish brown liquid.' *La Bataille de Pharsale*, p. 193.

53. 'And in the squares the divinities of public fountains holding a

water spray have heard say he asked me as we parted that my aunt Oriane would divorce Personally I
A vertical gradation of blue glaciers and the towers of the Trocadéro which seemed so close to the turquoise steps [.]' Proust, *A la recherche du temps perdu*, p. 90.

54. 'On the pedestal table there is his glass at the bottom of which an ice-cube finishes melting in the dregs of an orange-brown liquid.' *La Bataille de Pharsale*, p. 193.
55. 'Inside the overturned V formed by the legs one can see: [. . .] a man's hand still gripping the handle of a dagger (the forearm, the hand and the dagger which prolongs it cut across the over-turned V more or less horizontally, like the cross stroke of an A positioned a little lower and slightly askew. The hand holding the dagger [.]' Ibid., pp. 194–5.
56. 'Placed on the table next to a second glass, near the edge of the picture, a man's hand is visible only as far as a jacket sleeve, interrupted immediately by the white vertical margin.' Alain Robbe-Grillet, *La Jalousie*, p. 108.
57. See Part One, Chapter 3 note 11.
58. 'Franck rises from his armchair, with a sudden jump, and places on the low table the glass which he has just finished in one gulp. There is no more trace of the ice cube at the bottom. Franck has advanced forward, stiffly, up to the corridor door. He halts there. His head and bust turn towards A . . ., still sitting.

    'Sorry again for being such a bad mechanic". ' Robbe-Grillet, *La Jalousie*, p. 108.
59. 'At the bottom of the glass which he has put down on the table on leaving, a small piece of ice finishes melting, rounded on one side, displaying a sharp edge on the other'. Ibid., p. 109.
60. 'and even other elements of nature which had not previously existed there made you believe, on stepping off the train, that you had just arrived on holiday in the middle of the countryside'. Proust, *A la recherche du temps perdu*, III 736.
61. 'a double substance for the making of which the artist had wanted to mix bronze with crystal exclusively'. Ibid.
62. 'an expanse of sea, but a vertical gradation of blue glaciers'. Ibid., III 762.
63. 'The silhouetted trees were reflected clearly and purely on that blue-gold snow with the same delicate touch which they reveal in some Japanese paintings or in some of Raphael's backgrounds'. Ibid., III 736.
64. 'the large shadows of the trees conveyed a sense of depth to the water which was normally dark green but which at times [. . .] I saw to be a harsh light blue, verging on violet, seemingly divided up and in a Japanese style'. Ibid., I 169.
65. 'sky blue' . . . 'vast sea' . . . 'celestial flower-bed' . . . 'fathomless depth' with 'infinity' . . . Ibid., I 166–7, III 762, I 170.
66. 'filled by the river where they are in their turn enclosed, both 'container' with transparent sides like hardened water, and

'content' submerged in a larger container of liquid, flowing crystal [. . .] a perpetual alliteration between the water lacking solidity which one's hands could not hold, and the glass lacking fluidity which the palate could not enjoy'. Ibid., I 1680.

67. Stephen Ullmann, *The Image in the Modern French Novel* (London, 1960), p. 229; Gérard Genette, *Figures* III (Paris, 1972), p. 148.
68. See above, pp. 82–4.
69. 'a reading which acts, which writes'. Jean Ricardou, 'Esquisse d'une théorie des générateurs' in *Positions et oppositions sur le roman contemporain* (Paris, 1971), p. 148.
70. *Picasso on Art*, edited by Dore Ashton (London, 1972), p. 51.
71. *Interviews with Francis Bacon*, edited by David Sylvester (London, 1975), p. 37.
72. ' "Greene's novels" he said to me one day, "have often made me want to re-write them." ' Bruce Morrissette, *Intertextual Assemblage in Robbe-Grillet from Topology to the Golden Triangle*, p. 117.
73. 'while she was now no doubt completely absorbed in this greenish world represented by the drawing on the glossy dust jacket [.]' *La Bataille de Pharsale*, p. 172.
74. Nicole Bothorel, Francine Dugast, Jean Thoraval, *Les Nouveaux romanciers* (Paris, 1976), p. 96.
75. 'It is clear that *La Bataille de Pharsale* is not inspired by other texts but re-reads and re-writes them re-distributes them within its own space, one discovers the junctures, the substrata which are both formal and ideological making them serve its own text.' Françoise Van Rossum-Guyon, 'Ut pictura poesis', *Degrés*, 3 (1973), k 12.
76. 'not death which is the punishment reserved for everyone but after your fateful destiny the awareness of your death he was struck so violently in the mouth with [.]' *La Bataille de Pharsale*, p. 67.
77. 'He was struck so violently in the mouth with a dagger that the tip emerged through the nape of the neck.' (Lucan)
78. 'Then I saw him bending over me [. . .] I could have counted the nails each of the four holes for the studs things which are suddenly frozen and of which one keeps a precise mental record: thus before the referee blows his whistle the one wearing pink shorts lying flat on his back [. . .] and the other above him in the air flying figure roughly in the same position [. . .] like a horse rearing its legs having already left the ground the shining dagger which he holds in his hand pointed at the throat [.]' *La Bataille de Pharsale*, pp. 60–1.
79. Note the mirror repetition of Proust's words, the 'images précises' of Marcel's illusory 'grimoire magique' at Albertine's window. See above, pp. 104–5.
80. 'model little tart who deceived him with everybody that Charles so naive with women and that woman who in order to take off her pants only needed [.]' *La Bataille de Pharsale*, p. 20.
81. 'In a moment the warrior is going to receive a blow with a two-edged sword which will enter through his open mouth'. *La Bataille de Pharsale*, p. 200.
82. 'SIMON: So when Ricardou speaks, as he did the other day and

Notes and References 279

quite rightly, about conflict between the referential and scriptural dimensions, I wonder if one could not say that in the composition of the "referential dimension" there already exists, to a great extent, a "scriptural dimension": the old and the new . . .
PUGH: I thought that the Picasso print reproduced in *Orion aveugle*, and which seems to be described in *La Bataille de Pharsale*, had the same symbolic meaning which I attributed . . .
SIMON: You see how the 'referential' space there again consists of a text: a drawing [.]' *Claude Simon: analyse, théorie* (Paris, 1975), p. 423.

PART THREE: MATERIALITY

1 THE MATERIALITY OF FICTION

1. 'Literature therefore only interests me *profoundly* in so far as it involves the mind in certain transformations, – those in which the exciting properties of language play a vital part.' Paul Valéry, *Au sujet du 'Cimetière Marin'*.
2. Serge Doubrovsky went so far as to call Simon the Balzac of the 'nouveau roman' on account of the same 'goût de la description concrète pour le menu détail' displayed by the two novelists. 'Notes sur la genèse d'une écriture' in *Entretiens*, edited by M. Séguier, 31 (1972), 62.
3. 'The founder of the school, Alain Robbe-Grillet, modifies our vision by granting more importance to objects than to human beings [. . .] we are thus faced with a process: all "psychological" considerations are rejected, and a human story is evoked, quite arbitrarily solely by means of the *objects* which surround it and define it [.]' R.-M. Albérès, *Bilan littéraire du XXe siècle* (Paris, 1971), p. 117.
4. Vivian Mercier, *The New Novel: from Queneau to Pinget* (New York, 1971), p. 267.
5. 'An image untied in this way can and will be most of the time clearly-defined and concrete, detailed and realistic, like cinematic images whose chief characteristic is that they cannot be qualified by abstract ideas.' Olga Bernal, *Alain Robbe-Grillet: le roman de l'absence* (Paris, 1964), p. 174.
6. 'an internal film which is continually running inside us'. Ibid., p. 176.
7. 'the cleansing power of vision'. See Stephen Heath, *The Nouveau Roman* (London, 1972), pp. 116–17.
8. 'The concern for precision which is sometimes manically constricting (those non-visual concepts of 'right' and 'left', those enumerations, those measurements, those geometrical markers) does not manage to prevent the world from being a mobile entity even in its most material aspects and in the heart of its apparent

immobility. It is no longer a matter here of passing time, since paradoxically gestures are on the contrary only presented as frozen in an instant. Matter itself is both present and imagined, foreign to man and endlessly being invented in his mind. All the interest of the descriptive pages – in other words the place of man in these pages – does not lie in the object described but in the very movement of description.' Alain Robbe-Grillet, *Pour un nouveau roman* (Paris, 1963), p. 127.

9. 'Properties of a few figures, whether geometrical or not'.
10. 'The metro entrance opens *on to* the pavement *parallel to* the road, *next to* the cafeteria *on the corner of* the avenue [.]' *Les Corps conducteurs*, p. 160.
11. 'we must, when the author tells us that the young man enters the room, comply and accept to go in there with him.' Michel Butor, *Essais sur le roman* (Paris, 1972), p. 25.
12. 'a badly placed spectator in the theatre' . . . 'there is nothing at the end of these gestures, behind these words, nothing *happens* to him.' Maurice Merleau-Ponty, *La Phénoménologie de la perception* (Paris, 1945), p. 459.
13. 'But nothing doing! Where then is the story? All I can see is black and white.' Ibid., pp. 459–60. One is made aware of the same gulf between language and eidetic reproduction in Conrad's *Heart of Darkness* when Marlow suddenly interrupts his tale to address his silent listeners including the anonymous narrator: 'He [Kurtz] was just a word for me. I did not see the man in the name anymore than you do. Do you see him? Do you see the story? Do you see anything?' The question might equally be put to the reader.
14. 'the representational illusion gives rise to a clearly connected effect: the deception of the eye produced by a certain kind of painting, the deception of the reader by a certain kind of literary work. To give the reader the impression of being in direct contact with objects and actions is also to make him forget that he is in contact with a text. Fascinated by the hallucination of actions and objects, the reader is no longer aware that he is turning the pages of a book [.]' Jean Ricardou, *Nouveaux problèmes du roman* (Paris, 1978), p. 186.
15. See Wylie Sypher, *Loss of the Self in Modern Literature and Art* (New York, 1962), pp. 79–86.
16. Merleau-Ponty, *La Phénoménologie de la perception*, pp. 320–4.
17. 'The most transcendental discovery of our era is that of nuclear physics with regard to the constitution of matter. Matter is discontinuous and any meaningful experience in modern painting can and must only have as its starting-point the one idea which is as concrete as it is significant: *the discontinuity of matter*.' Salvador Dali, *Les Cocus du vieil art moderne* (Paris, 1956), p. 95.
18. Michael Spencer, *Michel Butor* (New York, 1974), p. 26.
19. Julio Cortázar, *Hopscotch*, translated from the Spanish by Gregory Rabassa (London, 1967), p. 397.
20. 'the signified must always be sacrificed to the requirements of

form'. 'Réponses de Claude Simon à quelques questions écrites de Ludovic Janvier', in *Entretiens*, p. 26.
21. 'The poor quality of the picture, the ink from the newspaper's print works itself of poor quality, thick and grey, accentuating the sticky, sweaty and humid aspect of the scene.' *Les Corps conducteurs*, p. 149.
22. 'Very often my work brings to mind a formula expression currently employed in Euclidean geometry: namely, "let us consider such and such a figure (triangle, circle, square, etc.) and let us find out what its properties are".

Well, it seems to me that my work is exactly that: it takes a "figure" (any one: for example the opening section ("générique") – the description of the dilapidated room – in *Leçon de choses* and it examines all of its "properties", that is what other images and forms this initial figure has the ability, through language, to evoke, to bring to the fore, to assemble.' 'Le Poids des mots', interview with Monique Joguet in *Le Figaro littéraire*, 1559 (3 avril 1976), 14.
23. 'My approach is like that of a machine which abolishes the names of things, tears down the partitions which the mind sets up between different objects, between the different systems of objects, between the different registers of facts and things and the different levels of thought [.]' Jean Dubuffet, *L'Homme du commun à l'ouvrage* (Paris, 1973), p. 248.
24. 'The taste of a madeleine (that is the quality of a certain sensation – inseparable, one is bound to say, from the taste of the word *madeleine*, its substance, its soft, soaked morphology, (ma . . . eleine) into which the hard tooth of the d sinks), transports Proust, across time and space, from one place to another.' Claude Simon, 'La Fiction mot-à-mot' in *Nouveau roman: hier, aujourd'hui*, 2 vols (Paris, 1972), II 80.
25. 'seven or eight different figures'. Marcel Proust, *A la recherche du temps perdu*, 3 vols (Paris, 1954), II 13. See also Roland Barthes, 'Proust et les noms' in *Le Degré zéro de l'écriture suivi de Nouveaux essais critiques* (Paris, 1972), p. 126.
26. 'this red dress the colour of English sweets [. . .] because "Corinne" made one think of "coral" [.]' *La Route des Flandres*, pp. 234–5.
27. F. R. Palmer, *Semantics* (Cambridge, 1976), p. 78.
28. 'From the speaker's point of view an isotopy constitutes a grid for reading which makes the surface of the text homogeneous since it allows ambiguities to be lifted.' A. J. Greimas, *Sémiotique: dictionnaire raisonné de la théorie du langage* (Paris, 1979), p. 199. See Greimas's introduction to *Essais de sémiotique poétique* (Paris, 1972), and François Rastier's 'Systématique des isotopies' in the same book.
29. Jonathan Culler, *Structuralist Poetics* (London, 1975), p. 95.
30. The other examples of isotopies which the critics cite are taken from jokes and poems. Here again Culler is justified in expressing his doubts about the validity of their argument. The brevity of language, the elliptical connotations, and the simultaneity of effect on the reader and listener all point to a subjective response. *Structuralist Poetics*, p. 91.

31. Ibid.
32. Of course, this is not to deny that interpretations are always possible and sometimes valid even in a novel like *Les Corps conducteurs*.
33. 'But only a bit of saliva emerges which he spits out, remaining there exhausted, unable to move, incapable even of cutting the shiny thread which hangs from his lips linking them with the bottom of the toilet pan.' *Les Corps conducteurs*, p. 112.
34. 'intestinal, cardboard convolutions.' . . . 'like cardboard or celluloid'. Ibid., p. 74.
35. The similarities between the sick man and the toy rabbit also hinge on the idea of convulsion. The physical progression of both is fitful ('par saccades'), and the rabbit keels over when the boy pulls too sharply on the string. The novel ends with the man collapsing onto the floor of his hotel room and staring at the 'trame' (weft) of the carpet.
36. 'all elementary isotopies or elementary isotopic networks established between two sememes belonging to two distinct fields'. François Rastier, 'Systématique des isotopies', p. 88. The need to distinguish between two different categories, or registers, of isotopies is confirmed by the fact that whereas with Rastier the term refers to the units formed by metaphorical association, with Michel Le Guern it refers to the original context from which the constituent elements are displaced: 'La métaphore [. . .] apparaît immédiatement comme étrangère à l'isotopie du texte où elle est insérée'. [Metaphor [. . .] immediately appears as foreign to the isotopy of the text in which it is inserted.'] Le Guern, *Sémantique de la métaphore et de la métonymie* (Paris, 1973), p. 16.
37. 'With poets, objects rise up, shed their old names and take on an extra meaning with their new name. The poet uses images and tropes in order to make comparisons; for example, he calls fire a red flower, or he applies a new epithet to an old word, or else he says like Baudelaire that the corpse's legs were lifted in the air like those of a harlot. In this way the poet creates a semantic shift; we thus feel the novelty, the placing of an object within a new context. The new word is put on to the object like a new piece of clothing. The sign is taken off.' Victor Chklovksi, 'La Construction de la nouvelle et du roman' in *Théorie de la Littérature*, translated by Tzvetan Todorov (Paris, 1966), p. 184. Chklovski's 'fait littéraire' may also be described as a 'fait artistique' since Dubuffet, among other painters, has made comparable remarks about the contextual displacements brought about in his work: 'Je dois dire que j'éprouve une sorte de plaisir à mêler ainsi des faits qui n'appartiennent pas aux mêmes registres, il me semble que cela occasionne toutes manières de *transports* et de polarisations à la faveur de quoi les objets se trouvent éclairés par des lumières inhabituelles susceptibles d'en révéler des sens inconnus'. [I must say that I take a kind of pleasure in mixing in this way facts which do not belong in the same register, it seems to me that this induces all sorts of shifts and polarities thanks to which objects are cast in an unusual light

which is capable of revealing new meanings in them.] Dubuffet, *Prospectus et tous écrits suivants*, 2 vols (Paris, 1967), II 74–5. See also Max Ernst, *Au-delà de la peinture* (Paris, 1937), p. 30.
38. 'I see a black sun whence the moonbeams shine a little too contrived fluctuat nec mergitur it's normal for teachers to be intrigued by language and not us it's logical that physicists are engrossed with matter and we by movement matter wants movement movement wants language language wants us [.]' Philippe Sollers, *H* (Paris, 1973), p. 71.

2 CURRENTS OF DESCRIPTION IN *LES CORPS CONDUCTEURS*

1. 'And even one syllable common to two different names was sufficient for my memory – as for an electrician who makes do with the least conducting body – to re-establish contact between Albertine and my heart' Proust, *La Fugitive*.
2. Claud Duverlie, 'Sur deux oeuvres récentes de Claude Simon', *Die Neuren Sprache*, 9 (September 1972), 547.
3. 'the generative scene of copulation'. Jean-Claude Raillon, 'Eléments d'une physique littérale', *Degrès*, 1, 4, (octobre 1973) g4.
4. 'a fiction where sexuality "does not go", a novel, in short, of the "severed leg" '. Jean Ricardou, *Nouveaux problèmes du roman* (Paris, 1978), p. 240.
5. Duverlie, 'Sur deux oeuvres récentes de Claude Simon', 546.
6. '*Orion aveugle* is the result of a request made by Skira. I inserted these stimuli in order to show how the text had worked since the title of the collection is "The Paths of Creation". But they must not be taken into account in the final text. If *Les Corps conducteurs* had to be accompanied by these extratextual visual stimuli, then it would be a failure in my opinion.' Claude Simon in *Nouveau roman: hier, aujourd'hui*, 2 vols (Paris, 1972), II, 108.
7. 'a pure novel of discoherence finally achieved, perfect example of acute modernity.' Jean Ricardou, ' "Claude Simon", textuellement' in *Claude Simon: analyse, theórie* (Paris, 1975), 19.
8. 'Le Dispositif osiriaque' first appeared as an article in *Etudes Littéraires*, 9, 1 (avril 1976).
9. 'the effect of two contradictory processes: on the one hand, fragmentation, on the other, articulation'. Ricardou, ' "Claude Simon", textuellement', 17.
10. A notable example of a novel based on this principle is, of course, Sterne's *Tristram Shandy*.
11. 'as if they had been borrowed from one of those teams of dancers' . . . 'or again [. . .] from one of those advertisements [.]' *Les Corps conducteurs*, p. 7.
12. 'The male nurse (or the young intern) holds a severed leg under his arm like a parcel.' Ibid.

13. In *Noveaux problèmes du roman*, Ricardou lists a number of common denominators between the two sequences (p. 207).
14. 'On one of the walls of the consulting room there hangs a drawing with a glass cover representing a row of young jocular medical students armed with several surgical instruments and advancing behind a bearded leader towards an operating table on which lies a young naked woman laughing heartily.' *Les Corps conducteurs*, p. 10.
15. 'In *Les Corps conducteurs*, as often happens with Simon, the different sectors which lead to a metonymic intersection also belong to very different spatial units: say, for the sake of brevity, a walk through a North American city and a conference in a South American city, only it is not impossible to see the invalid's walk in the city as a dominant sector on which the book opens and closes and on which the other sectors manage quite successfully to hinge.' Ricardou, ' "Claude Simon", textuellement', 18.
16. 'brings similar signifieds into play' . . . 'brings similar signifiers into play'. Ibid., 16.
17. The first use of the term 'métaphore structurelle' can be found in Ricardou's *Problèmes du noveau roman* (Paris, 1967), p. 48, with reference to *La Route des Flandres*. Unlike traditional metaphor which discards its vehicle once it has been used to evoke the tenor, structural metaphor is a form of association whereby the vehicle bridges the gap between two distinct narrative segments. For instance, the vehicle in the metaphor 'cuisse sectionnée' referring to the mannequin legs in the shop window is reiterated in the 'jambe coupée' held by the intern in the cartoon a few lines later. Similarly, the association can also be between two descriptions within the same segment, as in the reference to the leaves, 'cartonneuses et maladives', of the thin trees lining the pavement in sequence A which not only links up with the previous scene with the doctor (through 'maladives') but also leads on to the description which follows of a delivery man off-loading cardboards boxes ('cartons') from his lorry.
18. 'as if they had been borrowed from one of those battalions of dancers.' *Les Corps Conducteurs*, p. 7.
19. 'encounter of two sequences'. Ricardou, ' "Claude Simon", textuellement', 15.
20. 'The bowl is lowered and he can then see the whole face. Her gaze still fixed on him, she says No softly. No, it's not possible. On the bathroom wall the rectangle of sunlight turns slowly from orange to yellow. Cutting across the chest in a horizontal line level with her armpits the towel only reveals the top end of the opening in the shape of a cello case protected by a sheet of plexiglass behind which one can distinguish large blue and red tubes whose branches divide and crisscross.' *Les Corps conducteurs*, p. 161.
21. 'a series of referentially coherent fictional elements'. Ricardou, *Nouveaux problèmes du roman*, p. 198.
22. Ibid., p. 231.

23. One may draw an analogy between the definition of synecdoche and the concept of 'hyponymy' in semantics where a 'superordinate' or 'upper term' encompasses, by way of a hierarchical classification or 'arborescence', several 'hyponyms' or 'lower terms'. According to F. R. Palmer, 'hyponymy involves the logical relationship of entailment'. *Semantics* (Cambridge, 1976), p. 78.
24. 'Similarly one can read ad libitum, in the figure as complement (for instance, 'crown' for *monarch*), a metonym or a synecdoche, depending on whether one considers, for example, the crown as simply connected with the monarch or as forming part of him, by virtue of the implicit axiom: no monarch without a crown. One can see therefore that just about every metonym can be converted into a synecdoche by having recourse to the global unit, and every synecdoche into a metonym by having recourse to the relations between constituent parts.' Gérard Genette, *Figures III* (Paris, 1972), p. 27.
25. 'The porter, who has now returned near the drum one of whose panels he holds in one hand, his helmet held in the other against his chest, observes the difficult progress of the lady over the vast red carpet. At the other end of the line the clear and cheerful voice of the child repeats Hello? Hello? Above the plateau of the clouds one can see the moon in the empty sky, like a white, not quite round pastille. Between the rabbit lying on its side and the child's hand the loose string snakes along the pavement in gentle curves. The Serpent is an equatorial constellation whose outline is drawn by beautiful stars spread out over a wide expanse of sky. Emerging suddenly from the clouds, the snow-capped outline of a mountain rises up below the plane, incredibly thin and pointed with its breathtaking slopes of ice glistening in the sun, almost vertical, inviolate, and its spine of jagged rocks. It undulates and twists like the dorsal fin of a conger or a murena emerging for a moment, shining, in the swirl of foam. The clouds whipped violently break up, fray into greyish threads clinging to the gleaming mountainsides, the crenellated rocks resembling the vertebra of some monster, some furious and gigantic saurian with a mythical titan's name, of a mining company or of a constellation (Aconcagua, Anaconda, Andromeda) convulsed, crushing under its belly of earth, its millions of tons, the greenish repellent mire of invisible marshes and forests, all below, under the stifling lid of the clouds.' *Les Corps conducteurs*, pp. 29–30.
26. 'The doctor tells him to lower his trousers.' Ibid., p. 8.
27. 'The cruciform shadow of the plane moves [.]' Ibid., p. 15.
28. 'Despite paying attention, he does not manage to grasp [.]' Ibid., p. 33.
29. 'In the milky light which enters through the window [.]' Ibid., p. 56.
30. Some of the omissions from the list are the description of the 'vieux roi' peeping through the curtains at a couple making love which is based on a Picasso drawing, and a description of a

painting that depicts dancing girls on stage (p. 65); both of which, like the description of Poussin's 'Orion aveugle marchant vers le soleil levant', remain unframed by the narrative. There are also two 'mini-sequences' which float independently of the rest of the novel: the description of the conversation with the professor (pp. 114–17), a variant of the scene at the doctor's in sequence B (including a number of correspondences, such as 'figurine'/'sculpture'); and the description of a predatory bird roaming the mountain-tops before perching on a rock to rip open with its beak the putrid carcass of its prey.

31. See above, note 12.
32. 'The plate represents a man's torso'. *Les Corps conducteurs*, p. 9.
33. 'A bald-headed figure, with a long beard, the bust clad in a breastplate which makes way for, from the waist downwards, a short skirt, stands on a beach.' Ibid., p. 14.
34. The first instance of block IV is on page 19: 'Le serpent est lové sur un tronc ou ne subsiste plus que quelques plaques d'écorce et dont l'aubier mis à nu apparaît, d'un blanc jaunâtre comme un os'. [The snake is coiled around a tree-trunk where only a few strips of bark remain and the bared sapwood appears yellowy white like a bone]
35. 'Amid the sparkle of the stars in different sizes outlining the constellations, the centaurs, the peacocks with feathers covered with eyes, the goats with dragon tails, the wolves and eagles, the giant's silhouette stands out in black [.]' Ibid., p. 112.
36. 'The Orion constellation is one of the most beautiful in the equatorial zone.' Ibid., p. 57.
37. For both Ricardou and Raillon, the 'théorie matérialiste du récit' is based on the Marxist concept of a 'logique de la contradiction'.
38. 'Un homme traversé par le travail', *La Nouvelle critique*, 105, (juin–juillet 1977), 33.
39. 'structural metaphor' can either be 'actual (a break carried out necessarily by the writing)' or 'potential (a break carried out eventually by the act of reading).'
40. See above, note 13.
41. 'structural' if 'one focuses on the organisation of the sequences', 'transitory' if 'one focuses on the passage from one sequence to another', 'disjunctive' if 'one focuses on the break from one sequence to another'.
42. 'in so far as the process of break involves at least a comparison, resemblances abound in a work of fiction which is as fragmented as this. Any text which is subjected to analogical segmentation is prone to uniformity.' Ricardou, *Nouveaux problèmes du roman*, p. 218.
43. 'Similitude only provokes a break in texts where assemblage is obtained by the dominance of a process which is antithetical to it. So, here, the operations of unification (juncture, prolongation, continuation, segmentation) clearly all tend to reunite referential elements according to the categories of space and time. In short,

unification is here brought about on the basis of the preponderance of a dimensional bias.' Ibid., p. 219. Ricardou defines the four types of articulation in the following way: 'augmentation' is the development of the narrative within an unbroken fragment; 'continuation' is the return, after a 'coupure', to a preceding fragment; 'prolongation' is the return, after a 'rupture', to a preceding sequence; 'jonction' is the merger of two separate sequences into one.

44. 'elements on the basis of their common features'. Ibid.
45. 'To break a spatio-temporal referential unit, whether by means of linear ruptures obtained by immediate correspondence (direct ordinal metaphors), or by means of cuts obtained by comparison (comparisons, alternatives, and expressive metaphors) or by means of translinear breaks obtained by deferred correspondence (potential ordinal metaphors), is to bring together, always on the basis of their common features, two distinct spatio-temporal segments;' Ibid. See tableaux IX and X for a list of the different types of correspondences.
46. 'On the level of articulation, the segment (fragment, sequence, global sequence) owes its existence to the fact that the totality of the elements which it puts together can be subsumed under a title, or, if one prefers, an *arthreme*. So too, a correspondence (immediate, deferred, axial, radiant) owes its existence to the fact that the totality of elements which it puts together can be subsumed under a title or, if one prefers, a taxeme.' Ibid., p. 223.
47. ('legs [. . .] are ochred') . . . ('leaves [. . .] green turning ochre and sickly') . . . ('The flesh is of an ochred pink').
48. 'Of course classo-articulatory control is not consistently effective. With articulation, it is direct (it relies on an immediate semantic affinity). With assimilation, it is either indirect (having recourse to remote meanings) or deferred (passing through the intermediary of puns). With incorporation, it is delayed: evolving from a montage based on several occurrences. However, it also happens that it is strengthened by "over control" effects: an element is controlled in several different ways by a given dominant taxo-arthreme. Thus "section", at the present stage of the analysis, clearly belongs to the taxeme of cutting and is doubly linked to it in that its phonetico-semantic analysis "sec/scions" brings out the verb "scier" [to saw]. So too, "bataillon" belongs to the taxeme of cutting in that it is a section and it is doubly linked to it in that its phonetico-semantic analysis "bas/taillons" brings out the verb "tailler" [to cut]. Moreover, to the extent that it registers the idea of multitude, it stems from the taxeme of proliferation. It is therefore by several routes that the taxo-arthreme of cancer begins to take control.' Ibid., p. 228–9.
49. 'It is now clear that, on the one hand, classification contradicts articulation on a primary level by separating some of its articles for the benefit of the association of one taxeme with another, and on the other hand, articulation contradicts classification in return

by integrating taxemes on a secondary level through the articulation of a taxo-arthreme'. Ibid., p. 224.
50. 'It is now clear that, on the one hand, articulation contradicts classification on a primary level by separating some of its elements for the benefit of the grouping of an arthreme and, on the other hand, classification contradicts in its turn articulation by assembling arthremes on a secondary level through the classification of an arthro-taxeme.' Ibid., p. 229.
51. 'Whilst classificatory dislocation in *Les Corps conducteurs* is intense, it nevertheless remains governed by a dominant chain of associations: it is in fact this domination which defines the text's ultimate dependence, however disputed, on the dimensional plane.' Ibid., p. 230.
52. 'The sign is lifted' – Chklovski.
53. 'making one think of some apparatus'. *Les Corps conducteurs*, p. 7.
54. 'bright pink' ... 'erect' ... 'standing joyfully on its hindlegs, barking, hanging out its red tongue'. Ibid., pp. 8, 7.
55. Jean-Claude Raillon, 'La Loi de Conduction' in *Claude Simon: analyse, théorie*, p. 279.
56. 'The artist has placed a yellow reflection on the little dome formed by the green pocket in order to obtain a shiny effect.' *Les Corps conducteurs*, p. 10.
57. 'The doctor asks him if it resembles a pinch, a pressure or a burning sensation.' Ibid.
58. Ricardou, *Nouveaux problèmes du roman*, p. 213. As Ricardou says, an amphibology functions in the opposite way to repetition because it is a word which has two meanings. However, it differs from a pun in that the two meanings are not expressed simultaneously. For a few examples, see *Roland Barthes par Roland Barthes* (Paris, 1975), pp. 76–7.
59. 'At the points where his fingers press there is a brick red growth with soft contours, like a bag. Roughly at its centre there is a light green pocket, clinging to its side [.]' *Les Corps conducteurs*, p. 9.
60. 'From the cavity with the guitar-shaped opening the doctor pulls out the coloured organs (or when they are too big, pieces of organs) one by one. These are made of a light substance, like cardboard or celluloid. They are fitted together in an ingenious system of lugs which allows them to be separated – or to be replaced – merely by pulling or pressing. The doctor arranges them carefully on a shelf, the top of which is covered by a white towel, placed next to the examining table.' Ibid., p. 74.
61. 'making one think of some light artificial limb.' Ibid., p. 7.
62. 'Leaning her elbow against the clock face, a marchioness in a metal dress, and a tight corset, bends her head graciously, a vague smile on her lips, towards a young man wearing a three-cornered hat and who is sitting at her feet, plucking a mandoline. Although the hands of the clock are still, it is as if one can hear a silent din, like the avalanche of an invisible glacier: something greyish, ethereal and yet formidably heavy which advanced relentlessly,

an avalanche in slow motion, scraping the floor, the walls; it has been moving for billions of years, patient and insidious.' Ibid., p. 88.
63. 'The boxer's face is only a bloody and formless stain where against a dark red background the painter has dabbed a few touches of vermillion. Head hanging down, mute, locked inside his bell of silence which is pounded by the applause and boos of the public invisible in the darkness surrounding the ring, he appears to concentrate all his strength and willpower into the push of his arms in order to extract himself from the greyish matter where he is now buried almost up to his elbows.' Ibid., p. 106.
64. 'as if he were penetrating one of those old photographs'. Ibid., p. 86.
65. Compare with the description of the boxers in *Le Vent*: 'exactement comme ces boxeurs en carton que les camelots vendent dans la rue, passant sans transition du mouvement à l'immobilité' [just like the cardboard boxers sold by street pedlars, switching abruptly from movement to immobility]. *Le Vent*, p. 86.
66. 'breaking up into clusters of bubbles' . . . 'more or less large pieces'. *Les Corps conducteurs*, p. 91.
67. The soldiers in the forest are later said to carry 'carabines' (p. 206). A further textual link between the conquistadores description and the medical cartoon can be discerned in the fact that the first instance of the former alternates with a description of the delivery of cardboard boxes, 'cartons', to a shop in sequence A. See note 14 above.
68. 'columns of little soldiers wearing camouflage were advancing through a miniature jungle [.]' *Les Corps conducteurs*, p. 155.
69. 'So the general has boarded all the soldiers on to it, leaving the other two vessels at anchor with a group of sailors. As the soldiers begin with much effort to overcome the force of the current they notice a considerable number of canoes full of armed Indians other than those who can be seen in several troops on land, and who seem to be making war-like gestures and to want to defend the mouth of the river by shouts and those postures which fear induces in people who would like to ward off danger by dint of threats [. . .] Jumping out of their landing boats the heavily armoured soldiers run in the water which splashes up in the air.' Ibid., p. 40.
70. 'The number 35 followed by the word CENTAVOS is engraved in the sky tinted no doubt by the twilight'. Ibid., p. 41.
71. The phrase, deriving from Proust's 'éternel imparfait', is borrowed from an article by Roger Huss on the special use of tense in Flaubert's novels: 'Some anomalous uses of the imperfect and the status of action in Flaubert', *French Studies*, XXI, 2 (April 1977), 141.
72. 'Although it has certainly moved forward since a minute ago, nothing has apparently changed in the scenery which surrounds the column of armed men [.]' *Les Corps conducteurs*, p. 107.
73. 'a bright yellow spot, fluttering incoherently, rising, falling, gliding

74. 'As the leader of the column approaches the butterfly again flies up, flutters about indecisively for a moment, like a drunkard, then disappears to the right out of the rectangle of the photograph.' Ibid., p. 109.
75. This is an echo of the Graham Greene pastiche in *La Bataille de Pharsale*.
76. See above, p. 4.
77. 'The abdominal wall has been cut out from the diaphragm to a point level with the pubis, as if a lid had been taken off. The opening created takes more or less the form of a guitar case.' *Les Corps conducteurs*, p. 9.
78. 'Underneath and on the same scale there is a diagram of the same eye cut open revealing the rounded cornea, the front chamber, the pupil, the iris, the vitreous body, the retina and the optic nerve. The cornea and the sclera which surrounds the globe are coloured lavender blue, the front chamber behind the bulging part of the cornea is flesh coloured. The iris is orange red, the crystalline lens is streaked with fine blue lines, like a flattened onion cut in two. The vitreous body is a bluish grey, the retina and the optic nerve are Nile green.' Ibid., p. 154.
79. 'Above a column there is a frame in the upper part of which one can see a grey spot vaguely in the shape of a kidney or a bean and the convex top of which is cut in little crenellations. On the right the word BRAIN is printed. An arrow, pointing downwards, begins from a red spot, at the centre of the lump, and ends at a circle where an enlarged section of the pituitary gland is represented. From there a second curving arrow leads the eye to a kind of horned animal occupying the bottom of the picture, its beak turned to the right. Following the trace of the curved arrow one can read: THE ACTION OF THE GONADS. In the potbellied part of the horned animal there is a small, slightly oblique oval shape from which emerges a thin coil which after following a winding trajectory finally redescends down the central beak of the horned animal.' Ibid., pp. 164–5.
80. 'Well after the doctor has withdrawn his hands the impress of his fingers persists, or rather of a foreign body, enormous, still digging in like a corner. Acute inflammation of the liver, or hepatitis, arises from infectious causes (virus, spirochetes) or chemical ones (phosphorus, alcohol, etc.). A few localised inflammations (amoeba) can lead to abscess of the liver.' Ibid., p. 47.
81. 'The two naked bodies lying on the rumpled bed have in the light now resumed their flesh colour: ochred, pinkish or milky depending on the extent to which the different parts were normally exposed to sun and air. Like those painted wooden statues of saints which are used in processions, swaying on the shoulders of the bearers, and where a small glass window, fitted on to the chest, a limb, reveals some fragment of bone inside, the

skin, on the front of the chest, has been cut open and pulled back from the breasts – the pectoral muscles – to a little above the pubes. On the guitar shaped opening which is slightly squeezed in the middle at waist height, has been placed a moulded plexiglass lid, reproducing the outline of the bodies, the hollow between the man's abdominal muscles, the rounded bulge of the woman's stomach below the fold of the navel. Through the transparent wall one can see the internal organs [.]' Ibid., p. 67–8.

Stephen Bann defines this as 'reciprocal transference' and refers to the same passage in the novel in 'Robert Pinget: The End of a Modern Way', *Twentieth Century Studies*, 6 (December 1971), 19: 'What happens in this passage, and in many others throughout the book, is a kind of *reciprocal transference* between the highly charged sexual description and the highly coloured working model of the body. The continuity of *Les Corps conducteurs* is, therefore, an index of the common intensity of descriptive language, even though what is described arises from different levels of sense. The tendency of the different levels to interpenetrate while remaining conceptually distinct is a measure of their conductivity'.

82. The corresponding phrases are 'l'ouverture ménagée affecte à peu près la forme de la caisse d'une guitare, légèrement étranglée à la hauteur de la taille' [the opening created takes the shape of a guitar case, slightly squeezed at waist height.] (p. 9) and 'un fin tuyau qui se divise à une fourche dont les branches . . .' [a thin pipe which divides at a fork one of whose branches . . .] (p. 10).

83. 'glass window [. . .] which allows one to see' . . . 'Through the transparent wall one can see'. *Les Corps conducteurs*, pp. 67–8.

84. 'The torn rags reveal burnt, sallow skin under which each tendon, muscle and skeletal bone stands out like in those sketches for anatomical plates. From the back one can therefore see: A: the levator proper. B: the shoulder blade stripped of its muscles, except for the Depressor proper. C: the Depressor proper [.]' *Les Corps conducteurs*, p. 183–4. This instance of descriptive confusion is complemented later on by a similar passage enumerating the anatomical items as seen from behind.

85. 'The page is divided into three vertical columns. The accumulation of crammed lettering gives them a greyish hue. The coloured photograph of the boa is placed at the top of the left-hand column. The article on Serpico begins on the preceding page [.]' Ibid., pp. 22–3.

86. 'Above the plane and occupying the centre of the window there is a vertical board, a little taller than the plywood air hostess, on which hangs a reproduction of a map showing the American continent [. . .] All markings come to an end a little short of the coast-line at the same time as the green band which borders it fades out, making way for the yellowish hue of the parchment on which are painted clumps of palm-trees, trees with dense foliage, red parrots, monkeys, winged dragons, blue or brown birds, swamps [.]' Ibid., pp. 217–18.

87. 'Two groups of stars closely bunched depicting two triangles of more or less equal size where one can discern the outline of a face, were interpreted by some ancient peoples as showing the successive positions adopted by a woman's head when in a spasm she throws it back, arching, abandoning the glans which she squeezed between her lips, her hand nevertheless still gripping the tensed penis.' Ibid., pp. 57–8.
88. 'The different stars indicate only roughly the position of the bodies and limbs. Berenice's strand of hair is formed by about twenty stars, of 4 to 6 magnitude.' Ibid., p. 57.
89. 'the meaning of this pantomime is not clear.' *Les Corps conducteurs*, p. 216.

   The same emphasis on the ambiguity of symbolic meaning can be found in *La Bataille de Pharsale*: the statues in front of the parliament building in Belgrade, 'La signification de cette allégorie est obscure' [The meaning of this allegory is obscure.] (p. 241); and Heusey's comment, 'Clair pour qui ne cherche pas à l'approfondir' [Clear for those who do not seek to delve deeper into it.] (p. 91), on a paradoxical statement in Caesar's *Civil War*.
90. 'Only two or three men from the column look up. The Aras have sociable habits: they fly in groups of ten. The military Ara or Ara macao is, with the cockatoo, the largest of parrots [. . .] Their plumage is a beautiful bright red. Their wings are yellow and blue. What a feast of colour it is when the Aras, their wings unfolded, fly up into the rays of the sun! [. . .] the few soldiers who had let themselves be distracted lower their heads again and continue their march.' *Les Corps conducteurs*, p. 174.
91. It appears earlier in the name of another breed of butterfly, 'Hopféria *Militaris*' (p. 149).
92. 'Somewhere the laughing bird, still the same one it seems, continues to make his cry heard from further and further away. With all their willpower summoned in the effort to move their legs, the exhausted marchers no longer even flinch when occasionally a snake or some creature bolts across their path, pay no more attention, except if they are large enough to constitute a possible prey, to the animals which populate the forest. Often amidst the dazzling patches of colour which dance before their eyes invaded with pus or troubled by lack of sleep, they are no longer capable of distinguishing between giant butterflies and certain birds. Both possess incredible colours, and are of incredible sizes [. . .] Others, scarcely fatter, have a slate blue breast, an olive stomach, hazel wings, a long steel grey bifid tail. Aerial acrobats, they are continually performing swerves, dives and fixed point flights [. . .] Like the crested Cockatoo, they appear to derive from the bizarre imagination of a painter. On seeing them, as on seeing the monstrous vegetation or the giant snakes, some of the marchers believe in their state of exhaustion that they are prey to hallucinations and are delirious out loud.' *Les Corps conducteurs*, pp. 212–13.

Notes and References   293

93. Stephen Heath, *The Nouveau Roman* (London, 1972), p. 111.
94. 'One can enumerate about two hundred species in each hectare: side by side trees which are as different as the hevea, the palm tree, the walnut tree, the mango tree, the banana tree, the calabash tree [. . .] Suddenly one gives up listing since it has now become meaningless [.]' *Les Corps conducteurs*, p. 131.
95. John Lyons, *Introduction to Theoretical Linguistics* (Cambridge, 1968), p. 409.
96. For a discussion of the 'semiotic triangle' see F. R. Palmer, *Semantics*, p. 26.
97. 'He advances both slowly enough to allow a few of the images in this series [. . .] enough time to register accurately on his retina, and fast enough [. . .] for them only to appear [. . .] in a vague haze of unidentified forms – or perhaps recognised but forgotten at the moment of perception, the concepts (passage, shoes, greenery) interposing between the gaze and the objects, substituting the latter with a series of prefabricated and hollow images.' *Les Corps conducteurs*, p. 76.
98. 'Seen this way, from close up, contours of the flowers, of the leaves, the veins, obeying the pattern of thread, stand out in tiers'. *Les Corps conducteurs*, p. 226.
99. A similar image can be found in *L'Herbe*: 'la trame même du tissu lui apparaissant maintenant, nette, comme un second dessin, en léger relief celui-là, sous les fleurs imprimées [the very texture of the material now appearing to him, clearly, like a second pattern, slightly in relief, under the printed flowers.] *L'Herbe*, p. 246.

    However, in this novel the 'trame' is the invisible temporal thread which attaches life to death, Louise to Sabine: 'l'immuable et irréversible cheminement vers la mort qui constitue la trame même de toute tragédie, de toute vie' [the immutable and irreversible march towards death which constitutes the very framework of all tragedies, of all life] *L'Herbe*, p. 23.
100. 'if God the Father had created things by naming them, it is by relieving them of their name or by giving them another, that Elstir recreated them. Names which designate things always correspond to an idea deriving from one's intellect, which is foreign to our true impressions, and which forces us to eliminate from them everything which does not relate to that notion.' Marcel Proust, *A la recherche du temps perdu*, 3 vols (Paris, 1954), I 835.
101. Ibid., III 538. See note 1.

PART FOUR: SELF-REFLEXIVITY

1 THE LANGUAGE OF MIRRORS

1. 'I want to show him a new abyss within'. (Pascal)
2. Erving Goffman, *Frame Analysis* (Harmondsworth, 1974), p. 404.

3. The term 'mise en abyme' was first coined by André Gide in his *Journal* of 1889–1939. It derives from the language of heraldry but, as Bruce Morrissette has pointed out, the analogy with heraldry is inapposite since the grounds for the inclusion of an escutcheon within an escutcheon are provided only by marriage, thus precluding the possibility of mirror repetition. (Bruce Morrissette, 'Un Héritage d'André Gide: la duplication intérieure', *Comparative Literature Studies*, VIII, 2 (1971) In *L'Herbe* it is the fact that the infinitely duplicated picture on the box of sweets continues beyond the bounds of perception which causes anguish in the observer: 'l'image de la jeune femme alanguie et du même petit chien frisé au noeud bleu se répétait, indéfiniment reproduite sur le couvercle de la même boîte en réduction que la jeune femme tenait dans sa main (en réalité, c'est-à-dire de façon visible, deux fois seulement, la troisième boîte de berlingots étant déjà si petite que la jeune femme n'y est plus qu'une simple tache sur le vert de l'herbe, et le petit chien un point, mais l'idée de cette répétition sans fin et dont la perception échappe aux sens, à la vue, précipitant l'esprit dans une sorte de vertigineuse angoisse)' [the picture of the languid young woman and of the small curly-haired dog with the blue bow was repeated, indefinitely reproduced on the lid of the same tin in miniature which the young woman held in her hand (in fact, in other words as far as the eye could see, twice only, the third tin of toffees being already so small that the young woman is no more than a mere spot on the green grass, and the little dog just a dot, but the idea of this endless repetition and the perception of which eludes the senses, sight, throwing one into a kind of vertiginous anguish)]. *L'Herbe*, pp. 184–5.
4. Aldous Huxley, *Point Counter Point* (Harmondsworth, 1975), pp. 298–9. Similarly, Thomas de Quincey, in one of the earliest descriptions of 'mise en abyme', views the process as a 'descent': 'There are cases occasionally occurring in the English Drama and the Spanish where a play is exhibited within a play. To go no further, every person remembers the remarkable instance of this in *Hamlet*. Sometimes the same thing takes place in painting. We see a chamber, suppose, exhibited by the artist, on the walls of which (as a customary piece of furniture) hangs a picture. And, as this picture again might represent a room furnished with pictures, in the mere logical possibility of the case we might imagine this descent into a life below going on *ad infinitum*'. (*The Collected Writings*, edited by David Masson, 14 vols (Edinburgh, 1889–1890), X 344.)
5. Ann Jefferson, *The Nouveau Roman and the Poetics of Fiction* (Cambridge, 1980), p. 196.
6. Lucien Dällenbach, *Le Récit spéculaire* (Paris, 1977), p. 18.
7. Ibid., p. 79.
8. The play reveals the ambiguous sexual identity of Théodore, the object of d'Albert's and Rosette's love, who acts the part of Rosalind: 'c'était en quelque sorte une autre pièce dans la pièce, un

drame invisible et inconnu aux autres spectateurs que nous jouions pour nous seuls, et qui, sous des paroles symboliques, résumait notre vie complète et exprimait nos plus cachés désirs' [it was in a sense another play within the play, an invisible drama unknown to the other spectators and which we played for ourselves alone and which, through symbolic language, summed up our lives completely and expressed our most hidden desires]. Gautier, *Mademoiselle de Maupin* (Paris, 1966), p. 276.

9. Emma realises during the performance that her idyllic dream 'était un mensonge imaginé pour le désepoir de tout désir. Elle connaissait à présent la petitesse des passions que l'art exagérait'. [was a lie conceived out of the despair of all desire. She knew now the smallness of passion which art exaggerated.] But she immediately brushes away this truth about herself reflected in the opera: 'S'efforçant donc d'en détourner sa pensée, Emma voulait ne plus voir dans cette reproduction de ses douleurs qu'une fantaisie plastique à amuser les yeux' [Forcing herself then to turn her mind away from it, Emma wanted to see in this representation of her sufferings nothing more than an aesthetic fantasy which was pleasing to the eye]. *Madame Bovary*: Flaubert, *Oeuvres Complètes* (Paris, 1964), 2 vols, I 650.

10. See Jean Ricardou's analysis in *Problèmes du nouveau roman* (Paris, 1967), pp. 173–6.

11. '[. . .] le Vitrail de Caïn, ce signe majeur qui a organisé toute ma vie dans notre année, Bleston' [the stained-glass window of Cain, that major sign which organised my whole life in this our year, Bleston]. Butor, *L'Emploi du temps* (Paris, 1957), p. 433.

12. *The Complete Psychological Works of Sigmund Freud*, 24 vols, translated by James Strachey (London, 1953–1974), IV 338.

13. Cleanth Brooks in *William Faulkner: the Yoknapatawpha County* (New Haven and London, 1963) identifies Shreve in Faulkner's *Absalom, Absalom!* as a 'surrogate for the reader': 'The reader wants to know the secret, but he does not want (or ought not to want) to know too quickly. Shreve, who is in some sense the perfect audience, yearns to know the secret, but only at the proper time when the revelation can come with full significance' (p. 323). Yet to some extent both Shreve and Quentin, like Blum and Georges in *La Route des Flandres*, can be called reader figures since all four characters are 'creating between them, out of the rag-tag and bob-ends of old tales and talking, people who perhaps had never existed at all anywhere'.

14. 'in its literal form as a signifying organisation.' Dällenbach, *Le Récit spéculaire*, p. 123.

15. See Jean Ricardou's analysis in *Pour une théorie du nouveau roman* (Paris, 1971), pp. 124–7.

16. Dällenbach, *Le Récit spéculaire* p. 127.

17. Interview with Charles Haroche in *L'Humanité* (26 octobre 1981), p. 15.

18. Dällenbach, *Le Récit spéculaire*, p. 135. Sir Thomas Browne's state-

ment, 'The man without a Navel yet lives in me', alluding to Adam, the point of human origin, provides a vivid 'métaphore d'origine'. (Quoted by Borges in *Other Inquisitions 1937–1952*, translated by Ruth L. C. Simms (Austin, 1964), p. 22.)
19. 'that which all at once finalises it, founds it, unifies it and fixes its *a priori* conditions of possibility.' Ibid.
20. Samuel Beckett, *Watt* (London, 1953), p. 127.
21. 'an infinite sphere whose centre is everywhere and whose circumference nowhere'. Pascal, *Oeuvres complètes*, preface d'Henri Gouhier (Paris, 1963) p. 526.
22. Jorge-Luis Borges, *The Aleph and Other Stories 1939–1969*, edited and translated by Norman Thomas di Giovanni (London, 1973), p. 21.
23. 'I want him to see a new abyss within, I want to depict for him not only the visible universe, but the vastness which one can conceive of nature englobed by this atom. I wish him to see it in an infinity of universes, each with its firmament, its planets, its earth, in the same proportion as the visible world in this earth of animals, and finally of mites, in which he will find what the former have given, and finding again in the others the same thing endlessly and tirelessly, and to lose himself in these marvels which are as astonishing in their smallness as the others are in their immensity.' Pascal, *Pensées*, XV.
24. 'Cette réflexion est une des caractéristiques fondamentales de l'art contemporain: roman du roman, théâtre du théâtre, cinéma du cinéma . . .; elle l'apparente étroitement à celui de certaines époques antérieures, l'art baroque en particulier; dans les deux cas ce repli interrogatif sur soi est une réponse à un changement de l'image du monde' [This reflection is one of the main features of contemporary art: self-reflecting novels, theatre and cinema . . .; it links it closely with the art of certain earlier periods, the baroque in particular; in both cases this self-questioning gaze corresponds to a change in the view of the world]. Michel Butor, *Répertoire III* (Paris, 1968), p. 18. Among the most notable allusions to the baroque in Simon's work are the sub-title of *Le Vent* in which the novel is described as a 'retable baroque', and the definition of the baroque as 'movement into' quoted in *La Bataille de Pharsale* with reference to the paintings of Poussin.
25. 'the collaboration required of a spectator who is invited to be, to some extent, an actor, and who is introduced into the movement of a work which appears to evolve as he discovers it.' Jean Rousset, *La Littérature de l'Âge Baroque en France* (Paris, 1954), p. 232.
26. 'the eternal silence of these infinite spaces frightens me'. Pascal.
27. The subliminal empathy between María and Castel is not equally balanced. María certainly shows a telepathic capacity to read Castel's mind as when during one of their meetings in the Recoleta park, María responds to a remark which Castel only makes internally. Castel's telepathy is much more likely to be erroneous, as in the example of the disputed smile on María's lips in the same scene.
28. In his excellent introduction to the Harrap edition of *El Túnel*, Peter

Standish points out the significance of Allende's name which in Spanish means 'beyond'. *El Túnel* (London, 1980) p. xxiii.
29. See Ernesto Sábato, *Uno y el universo* (Barcelona, 1981) pp. 99–100. The erosion of temporal divisions is echoed, as we have already seen, in María's 'nocturnal' letter to Castel.
30. See above Part One, Chapter 2 note 59.

2 *TRIPTYQUE*: TOPOGRAPHY OR TOPOLOGY?

1. Sylvère Lotringer, 'Cryptique' in *Claude Simon: analyse, théorie* (Paris, 1975), pp. 313–33; and François Jost, 'Claude Simon: topographies de la description et du texte', *Critique*, xxx, 330, (novembre 1975), 1031–40.
2. 'migration of similar semes'. Lotringer, 'Cryptique', p. 325.
3. 'more subtle pleasures'. Jost, 'Claude Simon: topographies de la description et du texte', 1040.
4. 'the molecular units by definition postulate and always end up by imposing a process of unification on to the molar level'. Lotringer, 'Cryptique', p. 321.
5. Kurt Koffka, *Principles of Gestalt Psychology* (New York, 1935), p. 25.
6. 'There is on the other hand no 'mise en abyme' of the wedding sequence other than the one contained in the poster itself [. . .] It is in fact the absence of a mirror-image which makes the wedding sequence the pivot of the novel.' Lotringer, 'Cryptique', p. 321.
7. ' "central" panel, on which the two other panels seem to pivot and on which they overlap'. Ibid., p. 320.
8. 'Each numbered segment connects with the next one through an associative transition. However, some words could have pointed the narrative into other directions than the one which it in fact takes. Thus it is above all the global topography of the text which one must try to understand in order to explain the choice of a particular orientation.' Jost, 'Claude Simon: topographies de la description et du texte', p. 1038.
9. 'The stems of the umbels are covered over with a faint white down which, in the backlight, surrounds them with a luminous halo. On the thin peduncles opening out like the ribs of an umbrella and which support the disc of flowers, the downy hairs stretch out, rejoin and intermingle, forming a kind of snowy mist.' *Triptyque*, p. 9.
10. 'a silvery dust haze created by the shaft of light' . . . 'the silvery haze of the rain in the beam of a car's headlights' Ibid., pp. 116, 115.
11. 'You're a bit cracked!' Ibid., p. 107.
12. 'The wet sawdust is the same colour as the hazel arms and the girl's hair.' Ibid., p. 23.
13. 'like those musical pieces performed pianissimo in circuses, led by the distracted stick of the conductor who is half turned towards the

ring, serving as a sonorous and facetious backdrop to the flawed acrobatics of the clowns which are punctuated by the wild bursts of laughter from the invisible public [.]' Ibid., p. 61.
14. 'on the limbs and different parts of the skinned carcass one can see like on an anatomical plate the muscles laid out, swollen like spindles which intersect, interweave and run in parallel or overlap one another.' Ibid., p. 84.
15. 'Following a classical technique, with the aid of a Venice red which fades to a shade of pink on the salient features, the artist has first moulded the body in monochrome, carefully detailing the anatomy like on those plates of old treatises on painting, moulding the muscles into a swollen shape like spindles or straps which interlace, cross and overlap one another.' Ibid., p. 81.
16. 'pearly reflections' . . . 'flesh coloured or pearly'. Ibid., pp. 84–5, 82.
17. 'bleeding' . . . 'blood red preparation'. Ibid., pp. 85, 84.
18. 'no doubt the woman [. . .] has bumped before taking out the ribbon [. . .] for the latter, the lampshade and the bulb sway slightly'. Ibid., p. 85.
19. 'only bulb which was probably knocked by some ladder or someone leaving, sways above the bed [.]' Ibid., p. 82.
20. 'the shadows' . . . 'stretch out and retract'. Ibid., pp. 85, 81.
21. Simon in *Claude Simon: analyse, théorie*, p. 425: 'Mais au départ, j'avais en tête deux séries (celle de la campagne et celle de la banlieue industrielle).

Là-dessus, à l'automne 1971, a eu lieu à Paris la grande retrospective de Francis Bacon dont non seulement la peinture m'a fortement impressionné, mais dont certaines oeuvres avaient pour titre *Triptyque*, titre et principe que j'ai trouvés en eux-mêmes tellement excitants que j'ai décidé d'adjoindre à mes deux premières séries une troisième, celle de la station balnéaire, inspirée d'ailleurs elle-même par des toiles de Bacon'. [But initially, I had in mind two sequences (the one set in the countryside and the one in the industrial suburb).

On that subject, in the autumn of 1971, the large retrospective exhibition of Francis Bacon was held in Paris. Not only was I profoundly impressed by the paintings but some works were entitled 'Triptych', a title and principle which I found so exciting in themselves that I decided to add to my first two sequences a third, the one set in the holiday resort, itself inspired by Bacon's paintings.]
22. David Sylvester, *Interviews with Francis Bacon* (London, 1975), p. 78. Bacon describes the images in his paintings as 'organic form that relates to the human image but is a complete distortion of it', p. 8.
23. Ibid., p. 22.
24. The opening lines of the novel present a clear visual emphasis of the underlying pattern of textual overlap: 'L'encrage des différentes couleurs [de la carte postale] ne coïncide pas exactement avec les contours de chacun des objets, de sorte que le vert cru des palmiers

déborde sur le bleu du ciel, le mauve d'une écharpe ou d'une ombrelle morde sur l'ocre du sol ou le cobalt de la mer' [The inking of the different colours of the postcard does not exactly coincide with the contours of each object, so that the harsh green of the palm-trees spills on to the blue of the sky, the mauve of a scarf or an umbrella overlaps on to the ochre of the ground or the cobalt of the sea]. *Triptyque*, p. 7.
25. 'the centre of the ring' . . . 'studded with nails' . . . 'his arm half way down'. Ibid., p. 108.
26. 'There are now three shadows on the ring: the two divergent shadows of the clown and that of the man in tails lit up by only one projector which casts strong shadows on his face. Shadowing the spoken dialogue, the three flat and telscoped silhouettes move on the pale coloured carpet in a distorted fan of movement. The clown shouts I asked you for a hammer but I'm now asking you if you're not cracked!', p. 108–9.
27. 'screwing his gloved index finger against his temple and turning it several times whilst rolling his eyes [.]' Ibid., p. 109.
28. Lucien Dällenbach sees this as an example of 'mise en abyme de l'énonciation'. The clown, 'champion du calembour [pun]', is an 'auto-portrait travesti [mock self-portrait]' of the author. *Le Récit spéculaire* (Paris, 1977), p. 199.
29. 'The doors lock by means of a rudimentary latch, a simple piece of wood which pivots around a screw and turns to wedge in a striking plate consisting of a large nail bent by a hammer and rusting.' *Triptyque*, p. 160.
30. 'a terreplein planted with four old walnut trees'. Ibid., p. 8.
31. 'A long travelling shot follows the two boys running; and behind them the background of foliage glides from left to right.' Ibid., p. 148.
32. Jean Ricardou, *Le Nouveau roman* (Paris, 1973), pp. 124–30.
33. 'From the barn one can see the steeple. From the foot of the waterfall one can also see the steeple but not the barn. From the top of the waterfall one can see both the steeple and the roof of the barn.' *Triptyque*, p. 9.
34. 'No doubt the camera has been hoisted, either on a steeple, or on one of those scaffoldings consisting of metal girders which tower above a mine shaft overlooking the conurbation but in any case following the long thoroughfare since this is viewed from above, dimly lit at long intervals by the street lamps.' Ibid., p. 126.
35. 'whilst the movement of the camera carrying on the two bodies recede into the distance, as if sucked back and shrinking, drawing in with them the circus ring, the trainer with the boots and dyed hair . . .' Ibid., p. 90.
36. 'Inside the frame there are pinned up both sides of a parish bulletin the first of which is decorated at the top by a cross surrounded by rays, a timetable of services written in round-hand alternating in downstrokes and upstrokes, and a printed picture, summarily

coloured, showing young boys wearing berets on which is pinned a small metal cross [.]' Ibid., p. 91.
37. John Sturrock, *The French New Novel* (London, 1969), p. 54: 'the dying Aunt Marie, who can teach the next generation a lesson without even returning to consciousness, has passed on to her niece Louise, the narrator, a box of odds and ends, which the girl spends a long time trying to interpret; this interpretation is an intuitive one, for she is finally able to deduce from the attentive study of a photograph that the lesson of the dying aunt's life has been one of renunciation'. This interpretative approach to the function of 'mise en abyme' is similar to C. E. Magny's who saw the latter as reflecting 'quelques-unes des thèmes majeurs du livre'. See Dällenbach, *Le Récit spéculaire*, p. 34.
38. 'each depicting only one of the three settings, they cannot englobe the fiction in its entirety'. Dällenbach, *Le Récit speculaire*, p. 196.
39. 'On the level of macro-structure, *Triptyque* is solely concerned with creating a pattern of counterpoint between three sequences each of which exerts control over the other two by containing them in the form of a representation.' Ibid., p. 195.
40. The term 'capture' is coined by Ricardou in *Nouveaux problèmes du roman* (Paris, 1978), p. 235; and in *Le Nouveau roman*, pp. 112–17: 'Les événements en question de la première séquence sont captés par la suivante sous forme d'un de ses aspects mineurs: une représentation' [The events in question from the first sequence are encapsulated by the next one by means of one of its minor aspects: a representation].
41. 'The first of the two bands stands out against a night blue background where the globes of street lamps are strung out like a pearl necklace and in their light one glimpses vaguely a row of palm-trees and some pompous architectural constructions . . .' *Triptyque*, p. 64.
42. 'On one of the bands one can read the word SHORTLY and on the other the announcement THIS WEEK which stands out against a night blue background where the globes of street lamps are strung out like a pearl necklace and in their light one glimpses a row of palm-trees and some pompous architecture.' Ibid., p. 94.
43. 'still beautiful with a look of anguish' . . . 'mournful gesture'. Ibid., pp. 64–5.
44. 'A structure comparable to Klein's bottle where the interior manages to englobe its exterior; topographical paradoxes by which, as we know, all claims to hierarchy are wiped out.' Jean Ricardou, 'Un Tour d'écrou textuel', *Magazine Littéraire*, 74, (mars 1973), 33. See also Dällenbach, *Le Récit spéculaire*, p. 192, who draws a similar analogy between Robbe-Grillet's *Projet pour une révolution à New York* and the topologically paradoxical figures of modern mathematics.
45. It is Stuart Sykes who has baptised this as the 'Nice' sequence, 'Ternary form in three novels by Claude Simon', *Symposium*, XXXII, 1, (Spring 1978), 36.
46. Dällenbach's definition of 'mise en abyme' is 'toute enclave entre-

tenant une relation de similitude avec l'oeuvre qui la contient' [any enclave bearing a relation of similitude with the work which contains it] *Le Récit spéculaire*, p. 18.
47. 'an inconceivable space'. Ibid., p. 207.
48. 'It is difficult to work out the disposition of the setting'. *Triptyque*, p. 62.
49. Ricardou, *Nouveaux problèmes du roman*, p. 237.
50. 'the too vast space of the studio whose limits (the dirty walls, the roof above the gangways) disappear in the hollow dark where the sound of hammering, of grinding, and of a clamour of voices can be heard echoing back.' *Triptyque*, p. 131.
51. 'A sense of vacuity, of anonymity and of desolation emerges from the whole as if the protagonists were only there in transit, inside a provisional and artificial frame in which they have no say at all, set up the previous day by some stage-hands ready to dismantle it and isolated by the projectors like a minuscule and ephemeral island of light in the immensity of the cosmos or, more simply, of a vast hangar of a studio, just as black and just as empty.' Ibid., p. 172.

This 'atelier' can also be read as a 'mise en abyme de l'énonciation' with the film director serving as an author figure in the novel. In a film version of *Triptyque* which Claude Simon himself directed for German television he, in fact, played this role.
52. 'In the frame of the skylight, above the couple, one can see the heads of the two laughing boys who are watching the scene.' *Triptyque*, pp. 42–43.
53. 'At the centre of the greyish disc cast by the reflection of the magnifying-glass on to the sheet of paper and placed on the table after having smoothed out the folds, appears a tiny circle on to which the sun's rays reflected off the surface of the lens are directed. In spite of the boy's attention, the hand holding the magnifying-glass trembles slightly causing the focus of light which the boy struggles to maintain in the same place to make correspondingly tiny shifts on the paper. After a while, the paper begins to redden, then, while a faint smoke begins to rise, a hole is formed, with blackened edges gradually expanding.' Ibid., pp. 39–40.
54. 'A reddish-brown mark flashing in the sun appears in one of the fragments. Shaken by the breeze the criss-crossing branches are stirred by gentle movement, lifting and descending, masking and revealing in turn the hair, face, shoulders and arms of a little girl standing behind a bush. The very white, milky skin seems to attract all the light or rather, like in those over-exposed films, to glisten faintly, as if it was itself a source of light. The face haloed by the orange flame is sprinkled with freckles.' Ibid., pp. 118–19.
55. 'until, as if to confirm the impression of catastrophe, a blinding, white spot appears, the reddened circumference of which grows rapidly, devouring indiscriminately the two enlaced bodies, the tools and the walls of the barn, the lights coming back on again

then, the screen empty now, dull and uniformly greyish.' Ibid., pp. 194–5.
56. Stephen Heath, *The Nouveau Roman* (London, 1972), p. 239. Similarly, in Faulkner's *Absalom, Absalom!* the illiterate Aunt Rosa 'swoops down' at a letter she cannot read, 'blazing down at it as if she knew she would have only a second to read it in, only a second for it to remain intact in after her eyes would touch it, before it took fire and so would not be perused but consumed, leaving her sitting there with a black crumbling carbon ash in her hand' (Harmondsworth, 1971), pp. 251–2.
57. 'After a while one notices however that the man's arm which holds the woman's back to the wall slightly moves to and fro.' *Triptyque*, p. 19.
58. 'The butterfly finally goes to settle on an umbel'. Ibid., p. 18 The butterfly is often used as an image of fictional metamorphosis in Simon's work. In *Triptyque*, there is a reference to a butterfly at the first instance, the moment of generation, of each of the three narrative sequences. In *Les Corps conducteurs*, as I pointed out earlier, the ability of the butterfly to break out of the photograph reflects the structure of frame transgression underlying the whole novel. This metaphorical treatment of the allusions to butterflies follows in the tradition already established by Proust and Faulkner. In Elstir's painting, the 'grâce lilliputienne' of the white sails which resemble 'des papillons endormis' against the blue mirror of the sea reflects the novel's governing principle of poetic metamorphosis (II, 431). In *Absalom, Absalom!*, the reference to butterflies serves as an explicit metaphor of the changing phases of the self: 'she would not grow from one metamorphosis – dissolution or adultery – to the next carrying along with her all the old accumulated rubbish-years we call memory, the recognisable *I*, but changing from phase to phase as the butterfly changes once the cocoon is cleared, carrying nothing of what was into what is, leaving nothing of what is behind but eliding complete and intact and unresisting into the next avatar' (p. 161). A perfect example, that is, of a dynamic pattern repeatedly alluded to in Simon's work: namely, that of change which is brought about 'sans transition'.
59. 'After a while, either out of indecision, or because the door is locked on the other side, the hand releases the door-handle and drops alongside the body.' *Triptyque*, p. 23.
60. 'A ladybird with a red shell strewn with black dots symmetrically arranged progresses slowly on the round disc, of unequal surface, formed by the cluster of the umbel's white flowers [. . .] Suddenly it raises its wing-cases, revealing its fine black and transparent wings which it unfolds, then flies off.' Ibid., p. 22.
61. See Part Four, Chapter 2 note 9.
62. 'Reaching this point in the narrative which, besides, closes a chapter, the woman interrupts her reading.' *Triptyque*, p. 126.
63. 'The bell announcing the imminent start of the session has been

silent for a few moments when the din of the two cars apparently chasing each other penetrates from outside . . .' Ibid., pp. 131–2.
64. 'The woods which cover the sides of the valley are bordered with copses of hazel-trees and hornbeams. Their skirt meanders the length of the sloping fields, outlining bands, bays and capes one of which almost reaches the rear of the barn.' Ibid., p. 11.
65. 'From where the barn is one can hear distinctly the powerful and continuous sound of the waterfall echoed by the cliffs of grey rock appearing here and there between the thick foliage on the steep slopes of the valley which at times they crown and are crowned themselves by clumps of shrubbery whose roots are buried in their interstices and whose sickly trunks are twisted against the sky where clouds calmly drift past, their sinuous or jagged contours ceaselessly altering, depicting bulges, bays and capes which swell out, fall in and break up.' Ibid., pp. 11–12.
66. 'Their meandering contours have been calculated so that none of them, considered in isolation, presents the whole picture of a character, an animal, or even a face. Apart from very rare exceptions [. . .] their overall effect offers the whole varied range of greens [. . .] and they form an archipelago of small islands indented with bays and gulfs, bristling with capes, against the red background of the carpet.' Ibid., p. 224.
67. 'The broad and intermingling forms of the oval leaves callously brush against the pained faces of the woman with diamond-laden fingers, of the young bride, the string of pearls created by the luminous globes stretching out along the gulf and the dark blind alley where the two silhouettes, also dark, whose contour is surrounded by a halo cast by the light coming from the road, act out in slow motion a kind of pantomime in which the two bodies now come together, become confused, now part.' Ibid., p. 104.
68. An earlier reference to the confusion of overlapping and darkening leaves as a metaphor of frame transgression can be found in *Histoire*: 'les petites feuilles ovales de l'acacia sont apparues détachées d'un vert cru puis de moins en moins éclairées se brouillant dans une confusion hachée [. . .] elles se perdaient s'enfonçaient disparaissaient dans l'obscurité convergeant vers ce point imaginaire à l'infini où tout se rejoint se confond s'anéantise [.]' [the small oval leaves of the acacia have appeared detached from a harsh green then increasingly darker blurring in a confusion of fragments [. . .] they disappeared plunged lost in the darkness converging on that imaginary point at infinity where everything meets fuses vanishes [.]] *Histoire*, pp. 358–9.
69. 'small pools of light which illuminate the reddish purple facades and then fade out. Broad zones of darkness lie between the street-lamps.' *Triptyque*, p. 114.
70. This description of the film posters, and its delineation of textual osmosis, can be compared with the description of the poster in *Les Corps conducteurs* which, as I showed earlier, highlights the supplementary action performed by the sign in evoking a referent.

In *Triptyque*, as these lines indicate, the semiotic pattern is further complicated by the fact that a description is also affected by interferences stemming from other referential contexts.
71. 'A commentary [. . .] accompanies the slow movement, against the black background, of an uninterrupted string of lights depicting the shapes of gulfs, peninsulas, capes, and piers which drift from right to left. On the beach of darkness, nothing, on either side of the luminous festoons, allows one to distinguish the sea from the land [.]' *Triptyque*, p. 138.
72. 'plunging its myriad bays into the land' . . . 'a fixed boundary, an absolute demarcation, between land and ocean'. Marcel Proust, *A la recherche du temps perdu*, 3 vols (Paris, 1954), II 836.
73. 'It is a book to be used as a Persian carpet. Or again like a talisman, a crystal ball.' Letter of 15 May, 1973 and published in *Critique*, XXXVII, 414, (novembre 1981), 1149–50.

3 FRAME CONFLICT IN *LEÇON DE CHOSES*

1. 'What a great delight it is to drown one's gaze in the immensity of the sky and sea! Solitude, silence, incomparable chastity of the azure! a small sail trembling on the horizon, and which by its smallness and its isolation imitates my irremediable existence, monotonous melody of the swell, all these things think through me or I think through them (for in the vastness of reverie, the *self* is quickly lost!); they think, I say, but musically and picturesquely, without quibbles, without syllogisms, without deductions.' Baudelaire, 'Le *Confiteor* de l'artiste'.
2. 'The description (the composition) can be continued (or completed) more or less indefinitely depending on the amount of detail rendered in its execution, the repercussion of the metaphors put forward, the addition of other objects which are either entirely visible or fragmented by use, time, a shock (or again because only part of them appears within the frame of the painting), not to mention the different hypotheses suggested by the scene.' *Leçon de choses*, pp. 10–11.
3. 'Claude Simon ouvre *les Géorgiques*', *Le Monde*, (4 septembre 1981), p. 13.
4. 'fluffy greyish paper'. *Leçon de choses*, p. 54.
5. The battle of Reichschoffen was fought on 6 August 1870 during the Franco-Prussian War. The defeated French army was led by MacMahon. The reference to the battle in the chapter heading certainly draws attention to Simon's despondent vision of the cyclical recurrence of war. The modern soldiers in sequence B are thus foreshadowed by their military precursors in the battle of Reichschoffen which took place in the same region of France. But there is also a more specific determining factor behind this solitary yet prominent allusion to Reichschoffen in *Leçon de choses*. On 1

March 1882 the '7e Exposition des Artistes Indépendants' opened at 251 rue Saint-Honoré, Paris in the 'Salons du Panorama de la bataille de Reichschoffen'. Claude Monet, who was at that period working in Etretat, contributed some of his paintings, including some seascapes, alongside works by Gauguin, Morisot, Pissarro, Renoir, Sisley and others. Simon's novel thus seizes on the arbitrary connection between the battle and the paintings. In reality, the latter were 'framed' by the former only in so far as the exhibition was housed in the rooms bearing the name of the battle. In *Leçon de choses*, this inconsequential fact becomes the keystone of the thematic fusion between the experience of war and the perception and aesthetic of Impressionist creation. Above all, this empirical datum is absorbed and invested with new meanings in the creative elaboration of the text.

6. 'grey-green, grained paper serving as frame'. *Leçon de choses*, p. 179.
7. 'in a greenish, purplish harmony a rocky coastline which plunges into the sea'. Ibid., p. 179–80.
8. 'A streak of a darker green runs in the margin at each corner of which it depicts an ornamental motif consisting of three loops (a large one framed by two small ones) like spearhead petals.' Ibid., p. 179.
9. 'It is on the basis of what it does not say (cf. 'Thus, it has not been said . . .' 'It has not been mentioned . . .') that the novel will develop. The bare structure simple presentation of the material to be developed ('generators') – organisation of this material (exploded narrative) is no longer a sufficient explanatory model.' François Jost, 'Les Aventures du lecteur', *Poétique*, 29, (février 1977), p. 78.
10. 'When she sees the incandescent tip of the cigar close to her in the darkness she is as if startled, recoils, like someone misled by some optical illusion and suddenly knocking against an object which was foreseen but the distance had been badly judged like with those boats far off in the sea and suddenly (because one has stopped following them with one's eyes and though one knows that their immobility is only apparent) very near. The fishing-boat is now beneath them and skirting the foot of the cliff. [. . .] Far ahead the brightly coloured dress of the little girl runs along the road at the top of the cliff which dips at an incline, preceding the two parasols which oscillate in opposite directions like flowers. On the cliff there are no poppies. She hears his voice. He comes away from the gate and approaches her, black in the blackness, preceded by the red spot of the cigar which seems to be suspended in the night.' *Leçon de choses*, pp. 51–2.
11. 'To the left of the wood, the ground rises in a slope on the hillside sparsely planted with fruit trees, like an orchard which has been abandoned or badly maintained, the ground covered with long grass constellated with spots (umbels, poppies?) of white and red. Three women doubtless with fragile complexions which they protect from the sun with parasols walk down the slope of the orchard.' Ibid., p. 16.

12. 'in order to direct the barrel of the gun on the culvert where are piled and jumbled up . . .'. Ibid., p. 21.
13. 'Large poppies are depicted on the paper (papaver?)' Ibid., p. 33.
14. 'She follows with her eyes the busy flight of a hornet. At ground level there are small yellow flowers. There are, here too, some scabiouses. [. . .] From her position (leaning only on one elbow), the young woman sees the tall umbels swaying gently beneath the chain of billowing clouds which almost merge with the sky. The hornet goes from one to another settling only for a moment. It flies several times to and fro over the space which separates them, crossing or overtaking the small sailing-boat which hastens within the frame of the slightly bending stems. His velvety and stocky body is orange brown, streaked with black. The cow does not appear in the painting. [. . .] The loader reads slowly the title of the reproduction pinned on the wall amidst the giant poppies: ON THE CLIFF.' *Leçon de choses*, pp. 91–3.
15. 'The sun-rays begin to decline. They now strike at a different angle the four stakes which stick out of the grass in the field, framing the inflated mass where one can now recognise the bloated belly, white and pink, of a cow lying on its back and frozen in complete immobility.' Ibid., p. 22.
16. 'as if some giant hand had lifted it and put it down again'. Ibid., p. 92.
17. 'as if it had been taken and turned over as it was, all in one piece, like a toy'. Ibid., p. 22.
18. 'Impressionist art, whose verbal shimmerings are comparable to the style of painting of the same name'. André Rousseaux, 'L'Impressionisme de Claude Simon' in *Littérature du vingtième siècle* (Paris, 1961), p. 176. .
19. Maria Elisabeth Kronegger, *Literary Impressionism* (New Haven, 1973), p. 76.
20. 'writing is not painting, the evocative power of the pictorial representation of a body is completely different from that of the written description of a body, painting is surface, simultaneity, writing is linearity, duration, etc.' Claude Simon, 'Réponses de Claude Simon à quelques questions écrites de Ludovic Janvier', *Entretiens* (1972), p. 26.
21. The narrator in Borges's *El Aleph* notes the same dichotomy between vision and writing: 'What my eyes beheld was simultaneous, but what I shall now write will be successive, because language is successive' (*The Aleph and Other Stories*, edited and translated by Norman Thomas di Giovanni (London, 1973), p. 20.
22. 'Like the painter, and in spite of the fact that he only has at his disposal, instead of a surface, a time span, the writer is none the less able to "abstract from different series" elements which he assembles in a kind of mechanical process or system which are not, of course, optical but scriptural.' Claude Simon, 'La Fiction mot à mot' in *Nouveau roman: hier, aujourd'hui*, 2 vols (Paris, 1972), II 86.
23. The cliff-face in *Leçon de choses* bears a marked resemblance to the

Etretat cliffs favoured by the Impressionists. In fact, at one point the description reiterates an image previously formulated by Maupassant who refers to the cliffs in short stories like 'Adieu' and 'La Roche aux guillemots' in the collection 'Contes du jour et de la nuit' and in his novel *Une Vie*: 'une falaise [. . .] qui plonge dans la mer en dessinant une arche de forme ogivale comme un arc-boutant, ou comme si elle avançait une jambe' [A cliff [. . .] which plunges into the sea displaying a gothic arch like a flying buttress, or as if it were putting one leg forward]. *Leçon de choses*, p. 99. Maupassant's enthusiasm for Monet, expressed in 'La Vie d'un Paysagiste', did not stem from a profound understanding of the Impressionist conception of art, as Monet himself remarks in a letter: 'Il [*Maupassant*] prétend aimer beaucoup cela, mais je ne suis pas convaincu qu'il y comprenne grand-chose'. [He claims to like that a lot, but I am not convinced that he understands a great deal about it.] Quoted by D. Wildenstein, *Claude Monet, biographie et catalogue raisonné*, 3 vols (Lausanne-Paris, 1974–79), II (1882–1886), lettre 604, p. 42.

Though born in a different era and profoundly influenced by twentieth-century art and history, Claude Simon has more in common with Impressionism than do Maupassant and Zola who often enthused about Impressionist painters and their work in novels which were written in a language that was on the whole transparent and linear, and consequently far from impressionist. Simon's writing, on the other hand, may well be singled out as a supreme example of 'literary impressionism' which, as Clive Scott has persuasively argued, is 'the attempt to make language the act of perception rather than analysis of the act, to make language experiential activity rather than a description of activity' ('Symbolism, Decadence and Impressionism' in *Modernism (1890–1930)*, edited by Malcolm Bradbury and James McFarlane (Harmondsworth, 1976), p. 222.)

24. Hence the irony in the name of the arts magazine from which the reproduction has been extracted: 'L'ILLUSTRATION'.
25. 'The viridescent waves, the violet rocks, the foam, the low sky, are indifferently represented by means of little brushstrokes in the shape of commas or minuscule crescents.' *Leçon de choses*, p. 15.
26. 'two thin crescents like horizontal brackets [.]' Ibid., p. 32.
27. 'like broad brushstrokes on a watercolour background where their contours dissolve [.]' Ibid.
28. 'The waves are represented by means of lines in the shape of broad circumflex accents which are flattened out and they resemble rows of low tents in a military camp' Ibid., p. 75.
29. 'Two brackets lying flat, like two cupules, each underlining a point, represent the breasts. Lapping beneath the mermaid there are three short rows of circumflex accents aligned like tents in a military camp or like waves in choppy water.' Ibid., p. 156.
30. 'From afar, in the overall dazzling view one can make out shapes with blurred contours whilst thousands of specks seem to flutter

like those shimmering tempests of down hovering in the air in a hen house after a cockerel fight, rising, turning, and descending again in a swaying movement.' Ibid., p. 15.
31. 'He blows several times between his clenched teeth in order to dislodge the downy fluff.' Ibid., p..19.
32. 'A thick cloud of dust shoots up from under the débris, at first at ground level, then rises turning, taking the feathers of the two hens which swirl round like sparks.' Ibid., p. 44.
33. 'An impalpable dust, yellowish white, stagnates permanently in the place, imponderable, hanging in the air.' Ibid., p. 27.
34. 'endowed with both immobility and movement'. Ibid., p. 89.
35. 'those imponderable characters represented on frescoes or ceilings, floating in the air [.]' Ibid., p. 161.
36. 'From close up one can distinguish the substance of each of the brushstrokes directed from right to left, thick at the start, then widening, sliding as it rises like a tail.' Ibid., p. 15.
37. 'the two boats [. . .] seem to bathe in the same thickness of grey-blue, pearly transparent paste which the painter appears to have spread over the entire surface of the painting [.]' Ibid., p. 92.
38. 'undulate beneath them as if they floated weightlessly in a pinkish water.' Ibid., p. 34.
39. 'The wind blows out almost horizontally the ends of her ribbon which are now stuck together and run through with swift ripples.' Ibid., p. 44.
40. 'He gets up again and says Boudin what a name hell some of 'em you wonder where they dig 'em up hell apart from that I wouldn't mind a piece myself. The gunner turns his head to one side, looks at him uncomprehendingly, and says a piece of what? Of puddin' hey sausage, says the loader.' Ibid., p. 93.
41. 'like those insects whose thorax is linked to the abdomen only by a corselet which is as thin as a thread.' Ibid., p. 88.
42. 'Leaning on the rail, one of them shakes them in the water, gathered in rolls, and they undulate like fat brown snakes.' Ibid., p. 94.
43. 'The wavy line of the hills rows of trees and hedges is silhouetted against a puce-coloured sky where only a few stars shine.' Ibid.
44. 'One can only make out under the layer of dust the fold of flesh.' Ibid., p. 34.
45. 'Finally, the heavy stretched spiral, both rough and shiny on one side, furry on the other, falls on the grass.' Ibid., p. 36.
46. 'she separates the segments with both thumbs'. Ibid., p. 36.
47. 'a fishing village, where some brown nets were drying in the wind, along the cliff and some cabins [.]' *Madame Bovary*: Gustave Flaubert, Oeuvres Complètes, 2 vols (Paris, 1964), I 641.
48. Ibid., p. 628.
49. Ibid., p. 630.
50. 'The evening shadows were falling: the horizontal sun passing between the branches dazzled her eyes. Here and there, all round her, in the leaves or on the ground, spots of light trembled as if some hummingbirds had scattered their feathers as they flew by.

There was silence everywhere: something sweet seemed to emerge from the trees; she could feel her heart, which had started to pound again, and the blood circulate in her body like a stream of milk. Then she heard in the distance, beyond the wood, on the other hills, a vague and prolonged cry. A voice which lingered, and she listened to it in silence, mingling like music with the last vibrations of her strained nerves. Rodolphe, cigar in mouth, was mending one of the two broken reins with his knife.' Ibid., p. 629.
51. 'Her heart is pounding in her chest' . . . 'he looks at the stream of milky flesh'. *Leçon de choses*, pp. 53, 101.
52. 'The iodized wind plays with the long green veil which is wrapped round her boater and blows it against her face'. Ibid., p. 52.
53. 'the sailing-boat with the leaning masts?' Ibid., p. 76.
54. 'On the calm sea, represented by means of thin parallel lines, barely undulating, one can see two clear triangular sails, one in the distance, and in the foreground, a boat viewed frontally (or from behind, the bad print or the half-light preventing one from distinguishing) from each side of which long oars protrude, one almost horizontal, the other slightly pointing upwards. Fringes of luminous diamond droplets hang from the ends of the oars from where they fall back into the sea. On the convex hull of the boat one can distinguish some lines which follow the curve of the edge and stand out in the golden reflection of the sun against the black paint.' Ibid., pp. 99–100.
55. J. Ricardou, *Pour une théorie du nouveau roman* (Paris, 1971), p. 123.
56. 'Through her veil, which fell obliquely from her man's hat on to her hips, one could make out her face in a bluish transparency, as if she were swimming under waves of azure.' *Madame Bovary*: Flaubert, *Oeuvres Complètes*, p. 628. The opening phrase in this sentence is echoed in Simon's novel: A travers les fils soyeux on peut voir briller ses yeux' [Through the silky threads one can see her eyes shine]. *Leçon de choses*, p. 80; 'A travers le voile transparent contre lequel elle lutte (ou avec lequel elle joue) son visage lisse resemble à une délicate porcelaine aux traits estompés par un brouillard couleur d'herbe' [Through the transparent veil with which she struggles (or plays) her smooth face resembles a delicate piece of porcelain whose features are blurred by a mist the colour of grass]. *Leçon de choses*, p. 96.
57. 'like those jack-in-the-boxes which suddenly spring out of a box.' *Madame Bovary*: Flaubert, *Oeuvres Complètes*, p. 630.
58. 'Oval and swollen with spokes, it began with three circular pads.' Ibid., p. 575.
59. 'assailed by a multitude of hypotheses, it bobbed up in their midst like an empty barrel which has drifted out to sea and which floats on the waves.' Ibid., p. 637.
60. 'The women discuss amongst themselves which path they will take on the way back wondering whether to go by the farm or by the cliff'. *Leçon de Choses*, p. 31.
61. Jost, 'Claude Simon: topographies de la description et du texte',

p. 84, mistakenly identifies the lovers' 'rendez-vous' as 'le côté de la falaise' when in fact the couple meet at a 'barrière' on the outskirts of a wood (modelled, perhaps, on the gate one can see in the Renoir painting).

62. 'The hair, the folds of the sheet, the edge of the bed cast black blurred shadows, like broad brushstrokes on a watercolour background where their contours dissolve.' *Leçon de choses*, p. 32.

63. 'The word CLARO is stencilled obliquely and in black ink on the slat which forms the base of the box, streaked with thin veins like strands of hair.' Ibid., p. 33.

64. Jost, 'Claude Simon: topographies de la description et du texte', p. 84.

65. 'While he chews, his hand puts the bread down then takes hold of a small saltcellar and sprinkles some salt over the remainder of the egg. The yellow forms a perfect disc, slightly viridescent at the edge. It crumbles at each bite, leaving an irregular surface, as the teeth cut sharply into the white elastic ring which surrounds it.' *Leçon de choses*, p. 73.

66. 'Without ceasing to explore with his tongue the moist mouth which is once again pressed against his own, the man squeezes the warm and bloated ball of breast. He clenches and relaxes his hand or else brushes the palm of his hand against the elastic nipple. He stands back. She buries her head again in his shoulders. While still caressing her, he looks at the stream of milky flesh with imprecise contours in the darkness marked with a dark moon by the broad areola. He leans forward suddenly and devours it with his mouth.' Ibid., p. 101.

67. 'The orchard, the bridge rising spikily, as well as the road merge in the darkness. However the latter's route can still be made out by means of the white spots (newspapers, clothes?) which can be distinguished in the twilight, scattered along the roadside. This time the dull muffled crash of the collapse of the wall shakes the whole house. It is again followed for a few moments by the sound of a few stones or bricks falling, then there is silence. The crash of the blocks has stopped resounding. For a moment there is complete silence until the voice of the young builder makes itself heard, calling for help, inside the house at first, then outside.' Ibid., p. 114.

68. Simon has commented that he only became aware of this polysemic association in his novel in the course of writing it; it was not part of a premeditated plan: 'arrivé presqu'à la fin de la rédaction de mon brouillon, je me suis rendu compte, en feuilletant je ne sais pour quelle raison le *Littré*, qu'en fait je n'avais fait que développer toutes les connotations du mot 'chute': chute de plâtras, chute d'un pas de falaise, d'une corniche, d'un obus (point de . . .), chute de cheval, chute du jour, chute (probable) d'un point fortifié, chute d'une femme, chute des reins etc.' [on reaching near the end of my rough draft, I realised, leafing through the *Littré* for some reason which I have forgotten, that in fact I had merely developed all the connotations of the word 'fall': fall of rubble, fall of a cliff-face, of

a cornice, of a shell (point of . . .), fall from a horse, nightfall, (probable) fall from a fortified point, downfall of a woman, the small of the back [chute des reins] etc.] 'Un homme traversé par le travail', *La Nouvelle critique*, 105 (juin-juillet 1977), 36.

69. 'The young builder taps the shell of a hardboiled egg against a corner of the top brick on a pile which he has set up by way of a table. His movements are accompanied by the quiet sound of crushed limestone.' *Leçon de choses*, p. 135.

70. 'as if the totality of the images attracted to and penetrating the shiny surface were rushing, so to speak, headlong, crushing against one another in the tight kernel, both beginning and end.' Ibid., pp. 136-7.

71. 'He tries to turn her over on her side. The trestle of the scaffolding creaks with their every movement.' Ibid., p. 137.

72. 'Sobs stifle her. He taps her shoulder awkwardly, raises the thin cigar held between two fingers to his mouth, decides against it and takes it away from his lips without lighting it [. . .] She says you promised me you promised me you'd be careful. He says now now. She lets her skirt fall. She holds in her hand the piece of wet, sticky cloth rolled up into a ball. She makes as if to throw it then changes her mind [. . .] One can only hear the soft sound of sobs escaping from the loader's throat, like the cries of a mouse or a squealing rat. The gunner continues to breathe in slowly the smoke of his cigar, with each inhalation the faint light glows and dims extracting from the shadows his face which melts again in the darkness. Suddenly, without being heralded by any noise or visible movement, the swift hiss of a rocket fired from behind or inside the small wood rips through the silence. The silky sound of the rumpled air intensifies and quickly diminishes while the trail of sparks twists up into the black sky. Having arrived way up at the end of its course, the rocket head bursts, scattering a shower of firebrands around it.' Ibid., p. 169.

73. 'The description (composition) can be continued (or completed) more or less indefinitely . . .'. Ibid., p. 10.

74. 'box of the last batch of hatched eggs from which the escaped chicks scatter across the tiled floor'. Ibid., p. 87.

75. 'His pelvis advances and recoils simultaneously with his vertical movement, in the manner of a horseman riding loose-limbed on his saddle in order to move with the rhythm of a horse at gallop.' Ibid., p. 155.

76. 'On the left, the balustrade ends and one can see in the background the sides of a rectangle viewed from above and behind, a pond no doubt in the park which extends beyond.' Ibid., p. 161.

77. 'I have a taste for and a knowledge of the earth'. Eugène Fromentin, *Dominique* (Paris, 1966), p. 335.

78. 'And then in this contrast between the movement of the waves of boats which pass and houses which remain, between the adventurous life and a static one, there was an intimate analogy which must have struck him more than any other person.' Ibid., p. 43.

79. 'All things could be seen easily in it, if not exactly as they had always been seen, at least as one was now accustomed to seeing them.' Proust, *A la recherche du temps perdu*, 3 vols (Paris, 1954), II 326.
80. 'Once one could truly recognise objects when it was Fromentin who painted them and one no longer recognised them when it was Renoir.' Ibid.
81. Simon comments amusingly on this reciprocal relationship between art and fashion by recalling the oscillating public attitude towards Impressionist painting: 'Éloignez-vous, éloignez-vous et vous verrez que ça représente quelque chose!' people exclaimed when the Impressionists first exhibited their work; but more recently, with the vogue for abstraction and opacity in art, critics have exhorted the public to do the opposite: 'Rapprochez-vous, rapprochez-vous tout près, et alors vous verrez que ça ne représente rien!' ['Stand back, stand back and you will see that it represents something!'
'Come closer, come closer and you will see that it does not represent anything!'] 'Un homme traversé par le travail', p. 35.
82. 'a moral lesson, a "wise lesson": tranquillity is one of the few states of happiness possible.' Roland Barthes, *Le Degré zéro de l'écriture suivi de Nouveaux essais critiques* (Paris, 1972), p. 157.
83. 'I followed very late, with less merit, less courage, but with as much joy, the example which that brave soul had given me almost at the start of his life. He had begun in the peace of untroubled emotions and I have ended there.' Fromentin, *Dominique*, p. 333.
84. 'all these things think through me or I think through them (for in the vastness of rêverie, the *self* is quickly lost!)' Charles Baudelaire, *Oeuvres Complètes*, 2 vols (Paris, 1975), I 278.
85. 'that good prose of agriculture.' Fromentin, *Dominique*, p. 335.
86. 'One had to look carefully at it in order to comprehend where the sea ended, or where the sky began, so vague was the limit, so much did both share the same uncertain pallor, the same stormy palpitation and the same infinite. I cannot tell you at what point this spectacle of vastness repeated twice over, and consequently doubly extended, as high as it was deep, became extraordinary, seen from the platform of the light-house, and with what common emotion it gripped us.' Ibid., pp. 200–1.
87. 'Suddenly, in the depths of the horizon where the sky is now no longer separate from the sea, there sparkles on the left the brief glow of a light-house' . . . 'the instant, the exact second separating day from night.' *Leçon de choses*, p. 171.
88. 'white and black patches whose contours are sinuous and overlap'. Ibid., p. 164.
89. 'The black voices of the little frogs become deafening [. . .] Everything is black. Above her she can no longer see anything other than his shapeless, black face. The black odour of the cigar is stronger than that of the humid fields.' Ibid., p. 100.
90. See note 63.

91. 'inside the dark flesh the long stiffened organ is still taut releasing long spurts of black sperm.' *Leçon de choses*, p. 163. A different version of this motif can be found in *Les Géorgiques* where the narrator describes the black, fragmented trail of soldiers strung out across the limitless expanse of snow whose colour is 'la blancheur du papier'.
92. 'some signal emanating from remote stars and planets.' *Leçon de choses*, p. 171.
93. This reading would seem to be supported by the fact that the roll of names called out at the end of the novel includes 'Sylvie', 'Gilberte' and 'Odette'. See my earlier discussion of the common, elusive ideal pursued by the narrators of the works of Simon, Proust and Nerval, pp. 37–46 above.

CONCLUSION

1. 'a faithful copy of reality' . . . 'a concrete object'. R.-M., Albérès, *Le Roman d'aujourd'hui 1960–1970* (Paris, 1970), p. 240.
2. '1. from the imperfections of our faculties of perception; 2. from the imperfections of our memory; 3. from the choice, voluntary or not of some of its features at the expense of others which are rejected or passed over in silence; 4. from the very nature of writing which unfolds in a duration, is therefore obliged to say successively what is, most often, perceived simultaneously (hence the obligation again to select a certain order, which is itself fatally arbitrary and subjective); 5. from the formal needs and constraints of writing (syntax, composition, rhythm, sounds); 6. from the dynamics of the latter (we are at least as much led by our language as we lead it) . . .' 'Réponses de Claude Simon à quelques questions écrites de Ludovic Janvier' in *Entretiens*, edited by M. Séguier (1972), p. 23.
3. Jean Ricardou, *Nouveaux problèmes du roman* (Paris, 1978), p. 13.
4. 'Now, if you were to ask me to specify what more exactly distinguishes our modernity, I would hazard to suggest perhaps that, all in all, it seems to me to be dominated by two main features (each on reflection deriving from the other) which are, on the one hand, fragmentation, the explosion of forms: on the other, the abandonment of 'trompe l'oeil', of 'make-believe', in favour of the disclosure of the medium or, if you prefer, of the 'material', I mean the painting offering itself as painting, the novel announcing and denouncing itself as text and *fiction in process*.' Interview with Charles Haroche in *L'Humanité* (26 octobre 1981), 15.

Bibliography

THE NOVELS OF CLAUDE SIMON

Le Tricheur (Paris, 1946).
La Corde raide (Paris, 1947).
Gulliver (Paris, 1952).
Le Sacre du printemps (Paris, 1954).
Le Vent (Paris, 1957).
L'Herbe (Paris, 1958).
La Route des Flandres (Paris, 1960).
Le Palace (Paris, 1962).
Histoire (Paris, 1967).
La Bataille de Pharsale (Paris, 1969).
Les Corps conducteurs (Paris, 1971).
Triptyque (Paris, 1973).
Leçon de choses (Paris, 1975).
Les Géorgiques (Paris, 1981).
L'Invitation (Paris, 1988).

SECONDARY MATERIAL

Albérès, R.-M., *Le Roman d'aujourd'hui 1960–1970* (Paris, 1970).
Albérès, R.-M., *Bilan littéraire du XXe siècle* (Paris, 1971)
Alberti, Leon Battista, *On Painting and on Sculpture*, edited with translations, introduction and notes by Cecil Grayson (London, 1972)
Apuleius, Lucius, *The Golden Ass*, translated by Robert Graves (Harmondsworth, 1950)
Ashton, Dore (ed.), *Picasso on Art* (London, 1972)
Astier, Pierre, *La Crise du roman français et le nouveau réalisme* (Paris, 1971)

Bann, Stephen, 'Robert Pinget: The End of a Modern Way', *Twentieth Century Studies*, 6 (December 1971)
Barrenechea, Ana María, *Borges the Labyrinth Maker*, edited and translated by Robert Lima (New York, 1965).
Barthes, Roland, *S/Z* (Paris, 1970).
―――――, *Le Degré zéro de l'écriture suivi de Nouveaux essais critiques* (Paris, 1972).
―――――, *Le Grain de la voix* (Paris, 1981).
Battersby, Martin, *Trompe l'Oeil: The Eye Deceived* (London, 1974).
Beckett, Samuel, *Watt* (London, 1953).
Benveniste, Emile, *Eléments de linguistique générale* (Paris, 1963).
Bernal, Olga, *Alain Robbe-Grillet: le roman de l'absence* (Paris, 1964).
Bernard, Emile, *Souvenirs sur Paul Cézanne* (Paris, 1912).
Borges, Jorge-Luis, *Other Inquisitions 1937–1952*, translated by Ruth L. C. Simms (Austin, 1964).
―――――, *The Aleph and Other Stories 1939–1969*, edited and translated by Norman Thomas di Giovanni (London, 1973).
―――――, *Obras Completas, 1923–1972* (Buenos Aires, 1974).
―――――, *A Universal History of Infamy*, translated by Norman Thomas di Giovanni (Harmondsworth, 1975).
―――――, *Labyrinths*, edited by Donald A. Yates and James E. Irby, (Harmondsworth, 1976).
Bothorel, Nicole, Dugast, Francine, and Thoraval, Jean, *Les Nouveaux romanciers* (Paris, 1976).
Bradbury, Malcolm, and McFarlane, James (eds), *Modernism (1890–1930)* (Harmondsworth, 1976).
Brion-Guerry, Liliane, *Cézanne et l'expression de l'espace* (Paris, 1966).
Brooke-Rose, Christine, *A Grammar of Metaphor* (London, 1965).
Bjurström, C-G., 'Dimensions du temps chez Claude Simon' in *Entretiens* (1972).
Butor, Michel, *Répertoire III* (Paris, 1968).
―――――, *Essais sur le roman* (Paris, 1972).
Charbonnier, Georges, *Entretiens avec Michel Butor* (Paris, 1967).
Chateaubriand, René de, *Oeuvres complètes*, 18 vols, (Paris, 1904), Kraus Reprint, 1975.
Chklovski, Victor, *Sur la théorie de la prose* (Lausanne, 1973).
Christ, Ronald, *The Narrow Act: Borges's Art of Allusion* (New York, 1969).
Cortázar, Julio, *Hopscotch*, translated by Gregory Rabassa (London, 1967).
Culler, Jonathan, *Structuralist Poetics* (London, 1975).

Culler, Jonathan, 'Presupposition and Intertextuality', *Modern Language Notes*, XCI (1976), 1380-96.
Dali, Salvador, *Les Cocus du vieil art moderne* (Paris, 1956).
Dällenbach, Lucien, 'Intertexte et autotexte', *Poétique*, 27 (1976), 282-96.
————, *Le Récit spéculaire* (Paris, 1977).
Da Vinci, Leonardo, *Treatise on Painting*, translated and annotated by A. Philip McMahon (New Jersey, 1956).
Deguy, Michel, 'Claude Simon et la représentation', *Critique*, 187 (December 1962), 1009-32.
De Quincey, Thomas, *Collected Writings*, edited by David Masson, 14 vols (London, 1896).
Dubuffet, Jean, *Prospectus et tous écrits suivants*, 2 vols (Paris, 1967).
————, *L'Homme du commun à l'ouvrage* (Paris, 1973).
Duncan, Alastair (ed.), *Claude Simon: New Directions* (Edinburgh, 1985).
Duverlie, Claud, 'Sur deux oeuvres rêcentes de Claude Simon', *Die Neuren Sprache*, 9 (September 1972), 543-9.
Ernst, Max, *Au-delà de la peinture* (Paris, 1937).
Faulkner, William, *Absalom, Absalom!* (Harmondsworth, 1971).
Flaubert, Gustave, *Oeuvres Complètes*, 2 vols (Paris, 1964).
Fletcher, John, *Claude Simon and Fiction Now* (London, 1975).
Fromentin, Eugène, *Dominique* (Paris, 1966).
Genette, Gérard, *Figures* (Paris, 1966).
————, *Figures II* (Paris, 1969).
————, *Figures III* (Paris, 1972).
Gide, André, *Journal des Faux-Monnayeurs* (Paris, 1927).
Gilbert, Stuart, *James Joyce's Ulysses* (Harmondsworth, 1963).
Goffman, Erving, *Frame Analysis* (Harmondsworth, 1974).
Gould, Karen L., *Claude Simon's Mythic Muse* (Columbia, 1979).
Greimas, A. J., et al., *Essais de sémiotique poétique* (Paris, 1972).
Haroche, Charles, *Les Langages du Roman* (Paris, 1976).
Heath, Stephen, *The Nouveau Roman* (London, 1972).
————, 'Narrative Space', *Screen*, 17, 3 (Autumn 1976), 68-112.
Helbo, André, *Michel Butor: vers une littérature du signe* (Paris, 1975).
Huss, Roger, 'Some Anomalous Uses of the Imperfect and the Status of Action in Flaubert', *French Studies*, XXI, 2 (April 1977).
Huxley, Aldous, *Point Counter Point* (Harmondsworth, 1975).
Jakobson, Roman, *Essais de linguistique générale* (Paris, 1963).
Jefferson, Ann, *The Nouveau Roman and the Poetics of Fiction* (Cambridge, 1980).

Jenny, Laurent, 'La Stratégie de la forme', *Poétique*, 27 (1976), 257–81.
Johnson, B. S., *Travelling People* (Letchworth, 1963).
Jost, François, 'Claude Simon: topographies de la description et du texte', *Critique*, xxx, 330 (novembre 1975), 1031–40.
——————, 'Les Aventures du lecteur', *Poétique*, 29 (février 1977), 77–89.
Koffka, Kurt, *Principles of Gestalt Psychology* (New York, 1935).
Kristeva, Julia, 'Problèmes de la structuration du texte' in Tel Quel, *Théorie d'ensemble* (Paris, 1968).
Kronegger, Maria Elisabeth, *Literary Impressionism* (New Haven, 1973).
Lanceraux, Dominique, 'Modalités de la narration dans *La Route des Flandres*', *Poétique*, 14, (1973), 235–49.
——————, 'Modalités de la narration dans *Le Palace* de Claude Simon', *Littérature*, 16 (décembre 1974), pp. 3–18.
Le Guern, Michel, *Sémantique de la métaphore et de la métonymie* (Paris, 1973).
Lodge, David, *The Modes of Modern Writing* (London, 1976).
Lotman, Iouri, *La Structure du texte artistique* (Paris, 1973).
Loubere, J. A., *The Novels of Claude Simon* (London, 1975).
Lyons, John, *Introduction to Theoretical Linguistics* (Cambridge, 1968).
Mansuy, M. (ed.), *Positions et oppositions sur le roman contemporain* (Paris, 1971).
Mein, Margaret, *A Foretaste of Proust* (Westmead, 1974).
Mercier, Vivian, *The New Novel: from Queneau to Pinget* (New York, 1971).
Merleau-Ponty, Maurice, *La Phénoménologie de la perception* (Paris, 1945).
——————, *Signes* (Paris, 1960)
——————, *Themes from the Lectures at the Collège de France, 1952–1960*, translated by John O'Neill (Evanston, 1970).
Milly, Jean, *Les Pastiches de Proust* (Paris, 1970).
Morrissette, Bruce, *Les Romans de Robbe-Grillet* (Paris, 1963).
——————, 'Un Héritage d'André Gide: la duplication intérieure', *Comparative Literature Studies*, viii, 2 (1971), 125–42.
——————, *Intertextual Assemblage in Robbe-Grillet from Topology to The Golden Triangle* (Fredericton, 1979).
Mortier, Roland, 'Discontinu et rupture dans *La Bataille de Pharsale*', *Degrés*, i, 2 (April 1973).

Nathan, Jacques, *Citations, références et allusions de Marcel Proust dans A la recherche du temps perdu* (Paris, 1969).
Nerval, Gérard de, *Oeuvres*, 2 vols (Paris, 1974).
Nouveau roman: hier, aujourd'hui, colloque de Cerisy dirigé par Jean Ricardou et Françoise Van Rossum-Guyon, 2 vols (Paris, 1972).
Palmer, F. R., *Semantics* (Cambridge, 1976).
Pasco, A. H., *The Colour-keys to A la recherche du temps perdu* (Geneva, 1976).
Pingaud, Bernard, 'Sur *La Route des Flandres*', *Les Temps Modernes*, 178 (février 1961), 1026–37.
Plato, *Dialogues*, translated by B. Jowett (Oxford, 1924), 5 vols (London and Cambridge, Mass., 1938).
Pliny the elder, *Natural History*, with an English translation by H. Rackham, 10 vols (London, 1938–63).
Proust, Marcel, *A la recherche du temps perdu*, 3 vols (Paris, 1954).
—————, *Contre Sainte-Beuve* (Paris, 1971).
Pugh, Anthony, 'Claude Simon: the Narrator and his Double', *Twentieth Century Studies*, 6 (December 1971), 30–9.
—————, 'Invitation à une lecture polyvalente,' in *Claude Simon: analyse, théorie* (Paris, 1975).
—————'Du *Tricheur* à *Triptyque*, et inversement', *Etudes Littéraires*, 9, 1, (avril 1976), 137–160.
Raillon, Jean-Claude, 'Eléménts d'une physique littérale', *Degrés*, I, 4 (octobre 1973), g1–g29.
—————, 'Propositions d'une théorie de fiction', *Etudes Littéraires*, 9, 1 (avril 1976), 81–123.
Ricardou, Jean, *Problèmes du nouveau roman* (Paris, 1967).
—————, 'Esquisse d'une théorie des générateurs' in M. Mansuy (ed.), *Positions et Oppositions sur le roman contemporain* (Paris, 1971).
—————, *Pour une théorie du nouveau roman* (Paris, 1971).
—————, *Nouveau roman: hier, aujourd'hui*, colloque de Cerisy dirigé par Jean Ricardou et Françoise Van Rossum-Guyon, 2 vols (Paris, 1972).
—————, 'Penser la littérature aujourd'hui', *Sud*, 8 (3e trimestre 1972), 32–46.
—————, *Le Nouveau roman* (Paris, 1973).
—————, Interview with Jean Thibaudeau, *La Nouvelle Critique*, 60 (janvier 1973), 66–7.
—————, 'Un Tour d'écrou textuel', *Magazine Littéraire*, 74 (mars 1973), 32–3.

———, *Claude Simon: analyse, théorie*, colloque de Cerisy dirigé par Jean Ricardou (Paris, 1975).
———, *Robbe-Grillet: analyse, théorie*, colloque de Cerisy dirigé par Jean Ricardou, 2 vols (Paris, 1976).
———'Le Dispositif osiriaque', *Etudes Littéraires*, 9, 1 (avril 1976), 9–79.
———, *Nouveaux problèmes du roman* (Paris, 1978).
Riffaterre, Michael, *Essais de stylistique structurale* (Paris, 1971).
———, 'Intertextual Scrambling', *Romanic Review*, LXVIII, 3 (May 1977), 197–206.
Robbe-Grillet, Alain, *La Jalousie* (Paris, 1957).
———, *Pour un nouveau roman* (Paris, 1963).
Robbe-Grillet: analyse, théorie, colloque de Cerisy dirigé par Jean Ricardou, 2 vols (Paris, 1976).
Rousseaux, André, 'L'Impressionisme de Claude Simon' in *Littérature du vingtieme siècle*, 17 (Paris, 1961), 173–9.
Rousset, Jean, *La Littérature de l'Age Baroque en France* (Paris, 1954).
Ruthven, K. K., *Critical Assumptions* (Cambridge, 1979).
Sábato, Ernesto, *El Túnel*, edited by Peter Standish (London, 1980).
Séguier, Marcel (ed.), *Entretiens*, 31 (2ème trimestre, 1972).
Simon, Claude, *Orion aveugle* (Genève, 1970).
———, *Le Palace*, edited by John Sturrock (London, 1972).
Claude Simon: analyse, théorie, colloque de Cerisy dirigé par Jean Ricardou (Paris, 1975).
———, interview with Bettina L. Knapp, *Kentucky Romance Quarterly*, 2 (1970), 179–90.
———, interview with Ludovic Janvier, *Entretiens*, 31 (2ème trimestre, 1972).
———, interview with Claud Duverlie, *Sub-Stance*, 8 (March 1974), 3–20.
———, 'Le Poids des Mots', interview with Monique Joguet broadcast on France Culture, extracts of which appeared in *Le Figaro littéraire*, 1559 (3 avril 1976), 13–14.
———, 'Un homme traversé par le travail', interview with Alain Poirson and Jean-Paul Goux in *La Nouvelle critique*, 105 (juin–juillet 1977), 32–44.
———, 'The Crossing of the Image', interview with Claud Duverlie in *Diacritics*, VII, 4 (Winter 1977), 47–58.
———, 'Claude Simon ouvre *Les Géorgiques*', interview with Jacqueline Piatier in *Le Monde* (4 septembre 1981), 11 and 13.

Simon, Claude, interview with Charles Haroche in *L'Humanité* (26 octobre 1981), 15.
———, *La Chevelure de Bérénice* (Paris, 1984).
———, *Discours de Stockholm* (Paris, 1986).
Smith, Bernard (ed.), *Concerning Contemporary Art* (Oxford, 1975).
Sollers, Philippe, *H* (Paris, 1973).
———, *Paradis* (Paris, 1981).
———, 'Niveaux sémantiques d'un texte moderne' in *Théorie d'Ensemble* (Paris, 1968).
———, 'Ecriture et révolution in Tel Quel, *Théorie d'Ensemble* (Paris, 1968).
Spencer, Michael, *Michel Butor* (New York, 1974).
Sturrock, John, *The French New Novel* (London, 1969).
Sykes, Stuart, 'Claude Simon: Visions of Life in Microscope', *Modern Languages Review*, LXXI (1976), 42–50.
———, 'Ternary form in three novels by Claude Simon', *Symposium*, XXXII, 1 (Spring 1978), 25–40.
———, 'Mise en Abyme in the Novels of Claude Simon', *Forum for Modern Language Studies*, IX 4 (October 1973), 333–45.
———, *Les Romans de Claude Simon* (Paris, 1979).
Sylvester, David, *Interviews with Francis Bacon* (London, 1975).
Sypher, Wylie, *Loss of the Self in Modern Literature and Art* (New York, 1962).
Tel Quel, *Théorie d'ensemble* (Paris, 1968).
Thibaudet, Albert, *Gustave Flaubert* (Paris, 1935).
Thornton, Weldon, *Allusions in Ulysses* (Chapel Hill, 1968).
Todorov, Tzvetan, *Littérature et signification* (Paris, 1967).
———, *Poétique de la prose* (Paris, 1971).
———, *Poétique* (Paris, 1973).
———, (ed.), *Théorie de la Littérature* (Paris, 1966).
———, *Symbolisme et interprétation* (Paris, 1978).
Ullmann, Stephen, *The Image in the Modern French Novel* (London, 1960).
———, *Language and Style* (Oxford, 1964).
Uspensky, Boris, *A Poetics of Composition: the Structure of the Artistic Text and Typology of a Compositional Form*, translated by Valentina Zavarin and Susan Wittig (Berkeley, Los Angeles and London, 1973).
Valery, Paul, *Oeuvres*, 2 vols (Paris, 1957).
Van Rossum-Guyon, Françoise, 'De Claude Simon à Proust: un exemple d'intertextualité', *Les Lettres Nouvelles*, 4 (1972), 107–33.

———, Françoise, 'Ut pictura poesis', *Degrés*, I, 3 (juillet 1973), k1–k15.
Weisgerber, Jean, 'The Use of Quotations in Recent Literature', *Comparative Literature*, XXII, 1 (Winter 1970), 36–45.
Zolkiewski, Stefan, 'Poétique de la composition', *Semiotica*, v, 3 (1972), 205–24.

Index

Albérès, R.-M., 121
Alberti, Leon Battista, 5, 16
Apuleius, Lucius, *The Golden Ass*,
  10, 34, 39, 40, 43, 103, 180,
  209

Bacon, Francis, 112, 198, 199, 262
Balzac, Honoré de, *Illusions
  perdues*, 37, 38
Bann, Stephen, 291
Barrenechea, Ana María, 250
Barth, John, *Lost in the Funhouse*, xi
Barthes, Roland, xiii, 242, 247, 281
Battersby, Martin, 252
Baudelaire, Charles, 70, 81, 187,
  217, 242
Beckett, Samuel, *Watt*, 183, 184
Benveniste, Emile, 261
Bernal, Olga, 122, 276
Bernard, Emile, 16
binary textual pattern, 93–5, 194–7
Bjurström, C.-G., 53
black sun, 89–90, 187, 190
Borges, Jorge-Luis, xiii, 71, 78, 184,
  224, 296
  El Aleph, 183, 306
  El Inmortal, 74–9, 85, 268
Boudin, Eugène, 223, 225, 228, 229
Brasillach, Robert, *Les Sept
  couleurs*, 10
Brion-Guerry, Liliane, 16–17, 276
Brooke-Rose, Christine, 269
Brooks, Cleanth, 295
Browning, Robert, *The Ring and the
  Book*, 16
Budgen, Frank, 270
Buñuel, Luis, *Cet obscur objet du
  désir*, 261

Butor, Michel, xiv, 18, 73, 87, 88,
  124, 126, 296
  L'Emploi du temps, 69, 180
  6,810,000 litres d'eau par seconde,
  72

Caesar, Julius, 103, 117
Cézanne, Paul, 16, 19, 276
  Nature morte avec amour en plâtre,
  13
Chateaubriand, René de, 37–8
  Voyage en Amérique, 72
  Mémoires d'outre-tombe, 81–3
  passim, 85, 111
Chklovski, Victor, 22, 39, 132, 154
Christ, Ronald, 76, 268
Christie, Agatha, *Murder of Roger
  Ackroyd*, 63
Conrad, Joseph, *Heart of Darkness*,
  280
Constant, Benjamin, *Adolphe*, 252
Cortázar, Julio, *Hopscotch*, 126, 252
Courbet, Gustave, 112
Cranach, Lucas, *La Jalousie*, 276
Culler, Jonathan, 10, 70–1, 130,
  281

Da Vinci, Leonardo, 16
Dali, Salvador, 112, 126
Dällenbach, Lucien, 179, 181, 182,
  202, 213, 299, 300–1
David, Louis, *Serment du jeu de
  Paume*, 58
De Quincey, Thomas, 76, 79, 294
De Rougemont, Denis, 69
Delacroix, Eugène, 112
Della Francesca, Piero, 92, 96, 115,
  116

Index

Delvaux, Paul, *La Fenêtre*, 13, 198
Derrida, Jacques, 178
description blocks, 140–3, 145–7, 155–71
Don Quixote, 72, 86
Doubrovsky, Serge, 279
Dubuffet, Jean, 19, 128, 198, 216, 253, 282
Duverlie, Claud, 134, 135

El Greco, 112
Eliot, T. S., 72
  The Wasteland, 74
Ellmann, Richard, 270
Ernst, Max, 112, 283
Escher, M. C., 19, 191
Evans, Michael, 265

Faulkner, William, 10
  The Sound and the Fury, 129
  Absalom, Absalom!, 295, 302
Faure, Elie, 96, 97, 103
Fielding, Henry, *Joseph Andrews*, 72
  Shamela, 86
Fish, Stanley, 9
Flaubert, Gustave, 11
  Salammbô, 72
  Bouvard et Pécuchet, 72
  Madame Bovary, 180, 224, 225, 230–3, 295, 309
frame, 3–21, 207–16, 217–24, 234–40
  frame trangression, 11–17, 101, 116, 162, 197, 198, 215
Freud, Sigmund, 180
Fromentin, Eugène, *Dominique*, 85, 240–4

Galinsky, Karl, 266
Gautier, Théophile, *La Cafetière*, 13
  Mademoiselle de Maupin, 180, 295
Genette, Gérard, 85, 111, 141
Gide, André, xiii, 6, 294
Gilbert, Stuart, 87
Goffman, Erving, 3–4, 177, 178, 181
Graves, Robert, 40
Gray, Thomas, *Pindaric Odes*, 74
Greene, Graham, 72, 113, 114

Greimas, A. J., 129–30, 281

Hamlet, 10
Heath, Stephen, 171, 172, 209, 271
Heron, Patrick, 19
Homer, *Iliad*, 67, 74
  The Odyssey, 74, 77
Huss, Roger, 289
Huxley, Aldous, 178, 181

intertextuality, 37–46, 67–88, 101–18, 224–34
inversion, 110, 204, 268

Jacques le Fataliste, 72
Jakobson, Roman, 261
James, Henry, 17
Jefferson, Ann, 257
Jenny, Laurent, 86
Johnson, B. S., 126
  Travelling People, 10
Jost, François, 192–4, 195
Joyce, James, 72, 87
  Ulysses, 172

Kafka, Franz, 5
  The Metamorphosis, 11, 18
Koffka, Kurt, 297
Kristeva, Julia, 70
Kronegger, Maria, 224

Lacan, Jacques, 272
Lancereaux, Dominique, 27, 48–9, 254
Le Guern, Michel, 282
Lessing, G. H., 224
Livy, 117
Lotman, Iouri, 3, 4, 6, 8, 47, 273
Lotringer, Sylvère, 191–4
Lucan, *Pharsalia*, 89, 103, 114, 117

Macrobius, 74
Magny, C. E., 300
Magritte, René, 9
  L'Eloge de la dialectique, 13
Maughan, Somerset, 68
Maupassant, Guy, 307
Mein, Margaret, 80, 84
Mercier, Vivian, 122

Index

Merleau-Ponty, Maurice, 18, 68, 125, 266
Metzing, Dieter, 251
Millet, Jean, 112
mises en abyme, 10, 60–2, 113, 177–84, 186, 187, 194, 198–210, 211, 237–8, 240, 294
Monet, Claude, 219, 220, 222, 225, 228, 230, 307
Morrissette, Bruce, 74, 113, 294
Muybridge, Edward, 55, 262

Nerval, Gérard de, *Sylvie*, 39–42 passim, 44, 46, 70, 81, 187, 209
Novalis, Friedrich, 134

Ollier, Claude, 87
  Enigma, 72
  La Mise en scène, 72
Orwell, George, *Homage to Catalonia*, 60–4 passim, 243

Palmer, F. R., 285, 293
Pascal, Blaise, 177, 183, 184
Pasco, A. H., 258
Picasso, Pablo, 112, 117, 285
Pingaud, Bernard, 22, 23
Plato, *Timaeus*, 3, 35
Pliny, 77, 268
Plutarch, 92, 114, 117
Poe, Edgar Allan, *The Fall of the House of Usher*, 180
Pope, Alexander, 72
  Iliad, 74
Pound, Ezra, 72
Poussin, Nicolas, 96, 100
preterition, 220–4
Proust, Marcel, *A la recherche du temps perdu*, 38, 39, 40–1, 43, 44, 60, 70, 71, 79–85, 97, 103–7, 110–11, 112, 116, 128–9, 174, 182, 187, 189, 209, 213, 215, 241–2, 243, 264, 278, 302
  Contre Sainte-Beuve, 46, 80
Pugh, Anthony, 49, 50, 117

Quiller Couch, Arthur, 86

Raillon, Jean-Claude, 134, 155, 286
Rastier, François, 129–32 passim, 281, 282
Rauschenberg, Robert, 88
reciprocal metaphor, 107, 276, 291
Reid, Kenneth, 267, 268
Renoir, Auguste, 219, 220, 223, 241–2
Ricardou, Jean, 81, 82, 87, 90, 112, 125, 131, 134, 135, 136–40, 147, 148–54, 156, 157, 162, 166, 181, 210, 248, 273, 284, 286, 288, 295, 300
  La Prise de Constantinople, 69, 182
Richardson, Samuel, *Pamela*, 86
Riffaterre, Michael, 70
Robbe-Grillet, Alain, xiii, 17–8, 87, 99, 121–3 passim, 181, 184, 185
  La Belle captive, 135
  Les Gommes, 69
  Instantanés, 73
  La Jalousie, 72, 103, 104, 107–10, 111–13 passim
  Projet pour une révolution à New York, 73
  Topologie d'une cité fantôme, 72
rose, as symbol of creative inspiration, 40–1, 209
Rousseaux, André, 224
Rousset, Jean, 184
Ruthven, K. K., 77

Sábato, Ernesto, *El Túnel*, 185–90, 297
Sand, George, *François le champi*, 84–5
Saura, Carlos, *Elisa vida mía*, 261
Scott, Clive, 307
Seneca, 67
shifters, 11, 98
Simon, Claude, xiii–xv, 19, 20, 56, 88, 91, 117, 127, 135, 182, 224, 247–8, 249, 298, 301, 310, 312
  La Bataille de Pharsale, 89–118, 154, 182, 282
  Les Corps conducteurs, 123–34, 127, 128, 130–1, 134–74, 198, 302, 303

Simon Claude – *continued*
  Les Géorgiques, 58–64, 248, 264, 313
  L'Herbe, 202, 293, 294
  Histoire, 52–8, 92–3, 248
  Leçon de choses, 217–45, 265, 304, 306
  Orion aveugle, 29, 135
  Le Palace, 47–51, 248, 260, 263
  La Route des Flandres, 22–46, 98, 129, 209, 224, 248, 264, 295
  Le Sacre du printemps, 260
  Triptyque, 154, 191–216, 298–9, 302, 304
  La Vent, xiv, 20, 296
Sollers, Philippe, 80
  H, 132
  Hombres, 74, 86
  Paradis, 3
Standish, Peter, 297
Stanford, William, 266
Sterne, Laurence, *Tristram Shandy*, 72, 182, 283
Sturrock, John, 49, 202, 300
Sykes, Stuart, 39, 300
Sypher, Wylie, 280

Thibaudet, Albert, 10
Thornton, Weldon, 269
Todorov, Tzvetan, xii, 68
triptych structure, 102–10
Trousson, Raymond, 266

Ucello, Paolo, 96
  The Virgin and Infant, 12
Ullmann, Stephen, 111, 276
Uspensky, Boris, 3, 6, 7, 8, 11, 12, 18, 23, 25, 47, 251

Valéry, Paul, 89–90, 92, 121, 182, 224
Van Rossum-Guyon, Françoise, 88, 114, 275
Velázquez, Diego, 112
Verdi, Giuseppe, 113
Vergil, 59, 67, 74, 77
  Aeneid, 268

Walpole, Horace, *The House of Otranto*, 12
White, Harold Ogden, 267
Wildenstein, D., 307

GPSR Compliance
The European Union's (EU) General Product Safety Regulation (GPSR) is a set of rules that requires consumer products to be safe and our obligations to ensure this.

If you have any concerns about our products, you can contact us on

ProductSafety@springernature.com

In case Publisher is established outside the EU, the EU authorized representative is:

Springer Nature Customer Service Center GmbH
Europaplatz 3
69115 Heidelberg, Germany

www.ingramcontent.com/pod-product-compliance
Lightning Source LLC
Chambersburg PA
CBHW031539230426
43749CB00025B/411